RETRIEVING THE
American Past

A CUSTOMIZED U.S. HISTORY READER

Pearson Custom Publishing

New York   Boston   San Francisco

London   Toronto   Sydney   Tokyo   Singapore   Madrid

Mexico City   Munich   Paris   Cape Town   Hong Kong   Montreal

Senior Vice President, Editorial and Marketing: Patrick F. Boles
Senior Sponsoring Editor: Natalie Danner
Development Editors: Katherine R. Gehan and Mary Kate Paris
Editorial Assistant: Jill Johnson
Marketing Manager: Nathan Wilbur
Operations Manager: Eric M. Kenney
Database Product Manager: Jennifer Berry
Rights Manager: Katie Huha
Art Director and Cover Designer: Renée Sartell

Cover Art: Courtesy of Library of Congress and the Chicago History Museum.

Please visit our websites at *www.pearsoncustom.com* and *www.customhistory.com*.

Attention bookstores: For permission to return any unsold stock, contact us at *pe-uscustomreturns@pearson.com*.

**Pearson
Custom Publishing**
is a division of

www.pearsonhighered.com

ISBN 10: 0-558-27915-5
ISBN 13: 978-0-558-27915-8

CONTRIBUTORS

Senior Editor
Saul Cornell

Managing Editor
David Staley

Copy Editor
Ann Heiss

Assistant Managing Editor
Meredith Clark-Wiltz

Contributing Editors

Tyler Anbinder
Kenneth J. Andrien
Jean Harvey Baker
Michael Les Benedict
Mansel Blackford
Paul C. Bowers
Rowland Brucken
John D. Buenker
John C. Burnham
Joan E. Cashin
William R. Childs
Albert J. Churella
Steven Conn
Saul Cornell
Nick Cullather
Jeanette Davis
Merton L. Dillon
Daniel Feller
Charles Coleman Finlay
Emily Greenwald
Mark Grimsley
Bernard N. Grindel
Peter L. Hahn
James Hansen
Susan M. Hartmann
Mary Ann Heiss
Earl J. Hess
Michael J. Hogan
R. Douglas Hurt

Bruce Karhoff
Michael Kazin
Terence Kehoe
K. Austin Kerr
Frank Lambert
Valerie Mendoza
James McCaffrey
Allan R. Millett
Pamela J. Mills
Daniel Nelson
Margaret E. Newell
Josef Ostyn
Carla Gardina Pestana
Patrick D. Reagan
Randolph A. Roth
Hal K. Rothman
John A. M. Rothney
Leila J. Rupp
Richard D. Shiels
David Sicilia
C. Edward Skeen
Amy L. S. Staples
David L. Stebenne
David Steigerwald
Marshall F. Stevenson, Jr.
Warren R. Van Tine
Christopher Waldrep
J. Samuel Walker

Your *Retrieving the American Past* purchase includes access to online resources designed to complement your readings. This Companion Website is located at the following URL:

http://www.pearsoncustom.com/dbrtap/rtap/student

When prompted, enter the User Name: **rtapstudent** and Password: **rtaplearn**

(*Note:* The User Name and Password are case-sensitive, so be sure to use upper and lower case characters exactly as shown above.)

Once logged in, you will have access to the following resources:

- *Link Library.* A collection of vetted web links, organized by key terms and historical figures, which offer you background and context for many of the selections you'll be reading.

- *Documents.* Access (via links) to the full text of historical documents, which can furnish a backdrop to events that might have preceded, or followed, their drafting.

- *The Writing Process.* Advice that can aid you during the writing process. Included are guidelines and suggestions for each phase of writing, from start to finish.

- *Plagiarism.* Suggestions to help you maintain academic honesty, with illustrative examples.

- *Style Guide.* A brief guide to help you follow either MLA or Chicago Manual styles in citing your sources. The Modern Language Association style is widely used for papers in English composition, literature, and foreign languages. History, the fine arts, and some fields in the humanities (but not literature) use traditional footnotes or endnotes, which should conform to standards set by *The Chicago Manual of Style.*

We invite you to explore!

Contents

Marriage in Colonial America

Colonial American Political Culture: Deference or Democracy?

England's New World Experiments, 1607–1732

England's New World Experiments

1607–1732

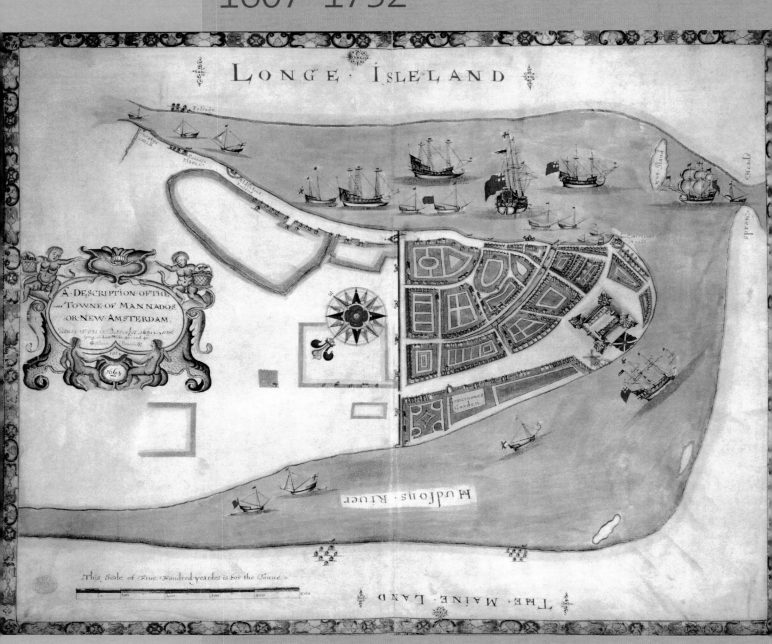

SEVENTEENTH-CENTURY NEW YORK
This map of New York City was presented to James, Duke of York (the future James II), shortly after the English captured New Amsterdam from the Dutch in 1644.

Why were fortifications and warships included so prominently in this image of the city?

Profit and Piety: Competing Visions for English Settlement

In the spring of 1644, John Winthrop, governor of Massachusetts Bay, learned that Native Americans had overrun the scattered tobacco plantations of Virginia, killing as many as five hundred colonists. Winthrop never thought much of the Chesapeake settlements. He regarded the people who had migrated to that part of America as grossly materialistic, and because Virginia had recently expelled several Puritan ministers, Winthrop decided the hostilities were God's way of punishing the tobacco planters for their worldliness. "It was observable," he related, "that this massacre came upon them soon after they had driven out the godly ministers we had sent to them." When Virginians appealed to Massachusetts for military supplies, they received a cool reception. "We were weakly provided ourselves," Winthrop explained, "and so could not afford them any help of that kind."

In 1675, the tables turned. Native Americans declared all-out war against the New Englanders, and soon reports of the destruction of Puritan communities

3

KEY EVENTS

1607   First English settlers arrive at Jamestown

1608–1609   Scrooby congregation (Pilgrims) leaves England for Holland

1609–1611   "Starving time" in Virginia threatens survival of the colonists

1619   Virginia assembly, called House of Burgesses, meets for the first time

1620   Pilgrims sign the Mayflower Compact

1622   Surprise Indian attack devastates Virginia

1624   Dutch investors create permanent settlements along Hudson River ■ James I, king of England, dissolves Virginia Company

1625   Charles I ascends English throne

1634   Colony of Maryland is founded

1636   Puritan settlers found Hartford and other Connecticut Valley towns

1638   Anne Hutchinson exiled to Rhode Island ■ Theophilus Eaton and John Davenport lead settlers to New Haven Colony

1639   Connecticut towns accept Fundamental Orders

1644   Second major Indian attack in Virginia

1649   Charles I executed during English Civil War

1663   Rhode Island obtains royal charter ■ Proprietors receive charter for Carolina

1664   English soldiers conquer New Netherland

1677   New Hampshire becomes a royal colony

1681   William Penn granted patent for his "Holy Experiment"

1702   East and West Jersey unite to form single colony

1732   James Oglethorpe receives charter for Georgia

were circulating in Virginia. "The Indians in New England have burned Considerable Villages," wrote one leading tobacco planter, "and have made them [the New Englanders] desert more than one hundred and fifty miles of those places they had formerly seated."

Sir William Berkeley, Virginia's royal governor, was not displeased by news of New England's adversity. He and his friends held the Puritans in contempt. Indeed, the New Englanders reminded them of the religious fanatics who had provoked civil war in England and who in 1649 had executed Charles I. During this particular crisis, Berkeley noted that he might have shown more pity for the beleaguered New Englanders "had they deserved it of the King." The governor, sounding like a Puritan himself, described the warring Indians as the "Instruments" with which God intended "to destroy the King's Enemies." For good measure, Virginia outlawed the export of foodstuffs to their embattled northern neighbors.

Such extraordinary disunity in the colonies—not to mention lack of compassion—comes as a surprise to anyone searching for the roots of modern nationalism in this early period. English colonization in the seventeenth century did not spring from a desire to build a centralized empire in the New World similar to that of Spain or France. Instead, the English crown awarded colonial charters to a wide variety of entrepreneurs, religious idealists, and aristocratic adventurers who established separate and profoundly different colonies. Not only did New Englanders have little in common with the earliest Virginians and Carolinians, but they were often divided among themselves.

Migration itself helps to explain this striking competition and diversity. At different times, different colonies appealed to different sorts of people. Men and women moved to the New World for various reasons, and as economic, political, and religious conditions changed on both sides of the Atlantic during the course of the seventeenth century, so too did patterns of English migration.

Breaking Away: Decisions to Move to America

English colonists crossed the Atlantic for many reasons. Some wanted to institute a purer form of worship, more closely based on their interpretation of Scripture. Others dreamed of owning land and improving their social position. A few came to the New World to escape bad marriages, jail terms, or the dreary prospect of lifelong poverty. Since most seventeenth-century migrants, especially those who transferred to the Chesapeake colonies, left almost no records of their previous lives in England, it is futile to try to isolate a single cause or explanation for their decision to leave home.

In the absence of detailed personal information, historians usually have assumed that poverty, or the fear of soon falling into poverty, drove people across the Atlantic. No doubt economic considerations figured heavily in the final decision. But so too did religion, and it was not uncommon for the poor of early modern England to be among those demanding the most radical ecclesiastical reform. As a recent historian of seventeenth-century migration concluded, "Individuals left for a variety of motives, some idealistic, others practical, some simple, others complex, many perhaps contradictory and imperfectly understood by the migrants themselves."

Whatever their reasons for crossing the ocean, English migrants to America in this period left a nation wracked by recurrent, often violent political and religious controversy. During the 1620s, autocratic Stuart monarchs—James I (r. 1603–1625) and his son Charles I (r. 1625–1649)—who succeeded Queen Elizabeth on the English throne fought constantly with the elected members of Parliament. At stake were rival notions of constitutional and representative government.

Regardless of the exact timing of departure, English settlers brought with them ideas and assumptions that helped them make sense of their everyday experiences in an unfamiliar environment. Their values were tested and sometimes transformed in the New World, but they were seldom destroyed. Settlement involved a complex process of adjustment. The colonists developed different subcultures in America, and in each it is possible to trace the interaction between the settlers' values and the physical elements, such as the climate, crops, and soil, of their new surroundings. The Chesapeake, the New England colonies, the Middle Colonies, and the Southern Colonies formed distinct regional identities that have survived to the present day.

WHY did the Chesapeake colonies not prosper during the earliest years of settlement?

The Colonies to 1740

The Chesapeake: Dreams of Wealth

After the Roanoke debacle in 1590, English interest in American settlement declined, and only a few aging visionaries such as Richard Hakluyt kept alive the dream of colonies in the New World. These advocates argued that the North American mainland contained resources of incalculable value. An innovative group, they insisted, might reap great profits and at the same time supply England with raw materials that it would otherwise be forced to purchase from European rivals: Holland, France, and Spain.

Moreover, any enterprise that annoyed Catholic Spain or revealed its weakness in America seemed a desirable end in itself to patriotic English Protestants.

QUICK CHECK

Why did some people continue to advocate colonies in the New World?

Anti-Catholicism and hatred of Spain became an integral part of English national identity during this period, and unless one appreciates just how deeply those sentiments ran in the popular mind, one cannot fully understand why ordinary people who had no direct financial stake in the New World so generously supported English efforts to colonize America. Soon after James I ascended to the throne (1603), adventurers were given an opportunity to put their theories into practice in the colonies of Virginia and Maryland, an area known as the Chesapeake, or somewhat later, as the Tobacco Coast.

Entrepreneurs in Virginia

joint-stock company
Business enterprise that enabled investors to pool money for commercial trading activity and funding for sustaining colonies.

During Elizabeth's reign, the major obstacle to successful colonization of the New World had been raising money. No single person, no matter how rich or well connected, could underwrite the vast expenses a New World settlement required. The solution to this financial problem was the **joint-stock company**, a business organization in which scores of people could invest without fear of bankruptcy. A merchant or landowner could purchase a share of stock at a stated price, and at the end of several years the investor could anticipate recovering the initial amount plus a portion of whatever profits the company had made. Joint-stock ventures sprang up like mushrooms. Affluent English citizens, and even some of more modest fortunes, rushed to invest in the companies and, as a result, some projects were able to amass large amounts of capital, enough certainly to launch a new colony in Virginia.

On April 10, 1606, James issued the first Virginia charter. The document authorized the London Company to establish plantations in Virginia. The London Company was an ambitious business venture. Its leader, Sir Thomas Smith, was reputedly London's wealthiest merchant. Smith and his partners gained possession of the territory lying between present-day North Carolina and the Hudson River. These were generous but vague boundaries, to be sure, but the Virginia Company—as the London Company soon called itself—set out immediately to find the treasures Hakluyt had promised.

In December 1606, the *Susan Constant*, the *Godspeed*, and the *Discovery* sailed for America. The ships carried 104 men and boys who had been

CHESAPEAKE COLONIES, 1640 The many deep rivers flowing into the Chesapeake Bay provided English planters with a convenient transportation system, linking them directly to European markets.

Why did Virginia's tobacco planters regard the colony's many rivers as essential to their economic prospects?

6

instructed to establish a fortified outpost some hundred miles up a large naviga-ble river. The natural beauty and economic potential of the region was apparent to everyone. A voyager on the expedition reported seeing "faire meaddowes and goodly tall trees, with such fresh waters running through the woods, as almost ravished [us] at first sight."

The leaders of the colony selected—without consulting resident Native Americans—what the Europeans considered a promising location more than thirty miles from the mouth of the James River. A marshy peninsula jutting out into the river became the site for one of America's most unsuccessful villages, Jamestown. Modern historians have criticized the choice, for the low-lying ground proved to be a disease-ridden death trap; even the drinking water was contami-nated with salt. But Jamestown seemed the ideal place to build a fort, since sur-prise attack by Spaniards or Native Americans rather than sickness appeared the more serious threat in the early months of settlement.

However, avarice soon became an issue. Virginia's adventurers had traveled to the New World in search of the sort of instant wealth they imagined the Spaniards to have found in Mexico and Peru. Published tales of rubies and diamonds lying on the beach probably inflamed their expectations. Even when it must have been apparent that such expectations were unfounded, the first settlers often behaved in Virginia as if they fully expected to become rich. Instead of cooperating for the common good—guarding or farming, for example—individuals pursued per-sonal interests. They searched for gold when they might have helped plant corn. No one was willing to take orders, and those who were supposed to govern the colony looked after their private welfare while disease, war, and starvation ravaged the settlement.

QUICK CHECK

Why did Jamestown come so close to failing in its early years?

Threat of Anarchy

Virginia might have failed had it not been for Captain John Smith. Before coming to Jamestown, he had traveled throughout Europe and fought with the Hungarian army against the Turks—and, if Smith is to be believed, he was saved from certain death by various beautiful women. Because of his reputation for boasting, histori-ans have discounted Smith's account of life in early Virginia. Recent scholarship, however, has affirmed the truthfulness of his curious story.

In Virginia, Smith brought order out of anarchy. While members of the coun-cil in Jamestown debated petty politics, he traded with the local Indians for food, mapped the Chesapeake Bay, and may even have been rescued from execution by a young Indian girl, Pocahontas. In the fall of 1608, he seized control of the ruling council and instituted a tough military discipline. Under Smith, no one enjoyed special privilege. Individuals whom he forced to work came to hate him. But he managed to keep them alive, no small achievement in such a deadly environment.

Scene from John Smith's Memoirs

Leaders of the Virginia Company in London recognized the need to reform the entire enterprise. After all, they had spent considerable sums and had received nothing in return. In 1609, the company directors obtained a new charter from the king, which completely reorganized the Virginia government. Henceforth all commercial and political decisions affecting the colonists rested with the com-pany, a fact that had not been made sufficiently clear in the 1606 charter. Moreover, in an effort to raise scarce capital, the original partners opened the joint-stock company to the general public. For a little more than £12—approximately one year's wages for an unskilled English laborer—a person or group of persons

POWHATAN CEREMONIAL CLOAK In 1608, Powhatan, the father of Pocahontas, gave this shell-decorated ceremonial cloak to Captain Christopher Newport. (*Source: Ashmolean Museum, Oxford, England, U.K.*)

What role do you think such objects played in Native American diplomacy?

could purchase a stake in Virginia. It was anticipated that in 1616 the profits from the colony would be distributed among the shareholders. The company sponsored a publicity campaign; pamphlets and sermons extolled the colony's potential and exhorted patriotic English citizens to invest in the enterprise.

The burst of energy came to nothing. Bad luck and poor planning plagued the Virginia Company. A vessel carrying additional settlers and supplies went aground in Bermuda, and while this misadventure did little to help the people at Jamestown, it provided Shakespeare with the idea for *The Tempest*.

Between 1609 and 1611, the remaining Virginia settlers lacked capable leadership, and perhaps as a result, they lacked food. The terrible winter of 1609–1610 was termed the "starving time." A few desperate colonists were driven to cannibalism, an ironic situation since early explorers had assumed that only Native Americans would eat human flesh. In England, Smith heard that one colonist had killed his wife, powdered [salted] her, and "had eaten part of her before it was known; for which he was executed." The captain, who possessed a droll sense of humor, observed, "Now, whether she was better roasted, broiled, or carbonadoed [sliced], I know not, but such a dish as powdered wife I never heard of." Other people simply lost the will to live.

John Smith, "The Starving Time"

The presence of so many Native Americans was an additional threat to Virginia's survival. The first colonists found themselves living—or attempting to live—in territory controlled by what was probably the most powerful Indian confederation east of the Mississippi River. Under the leadership of their *werowance*, Powhatan, these Indians had by 1608 created a loose association of some thirty tribes, and when Captain John Smith arrived to lead several hundred adventurers, the Powhatans (named for their king) numbered some 14,000 people, of whom 3200 were warriors. These people hoped initially to enlist the Europeans as allies against native enemies.

Powhatan to John Smith (ca. 1609)

When it became clear that the two groups, holding such different notions about labor and property and about the exploitation of the natural environment, could not coexist in peace, the Powhatans tried to drive the invaders out of

Virginia, once in 1622 and again in 1644. The failure of the second campaign ended in the complete destruction of the Powhatan empire.

In June 1610, the settlers who had survived despite starvation and conflicts with the Indians actually abandoned Virginia. Through a stroke of luck, however, a new governor arrived from England just as they commenced their voyage down the James River. The governor and the deputy governors who succeeded him, Sir Thomas Gates and Sir Thomas Dale, ruled by martial law. The new colonists, many of them male and female servants employed by the company, were marched to work by the beat of the drum. Such methods saved the colony but could not make it flourish. In 1616, company shareholders received no profits. Their only reward was the right to a piece of unsurveyed land located three thousand miles from London.

QUICK CHECK ✓

Why did the first Virginia settlers not cooperate for the common good?

Tobacco Saves Virginia

The economic solution to Virginia's problems grew in the vacant lots of Jamestown. Only Indians bothered to cultivate tobacco until John Rolfe, a settler who achieved notoriety by marrying Pocahontas, realized this local weed might be a valuable export. Rolfe experimented with the crop, eventually growing in Virginia a milder variety that had been developed in the West Indies and was more appealing to European smokers.

Virginians suddenly possessed a means to make money. Tobacco proved relatively easy to grow, and settlers who had avoided work now threw themselves into its production with single-minded diligence. In 1617, one observer found that Jamestown's "streets and all other spare places [are] planted with tobacco… the Colony dispersed all about planting tobacco." Although King James I originally considered smoking immoral and unhealthy, he changed his mind when the duties he collected on tobacco imports began to mount.

The Virginia Company sponsored another ambitious effort to transform the colony into a profitable enterprise. In 1618, Sir Edwin Sandys (pronounced Sands) led a faction of stockholders that began to pump life into the dying organization by instituting a series of sweeping reforms and eventually ousting Sir Thomas Smith and his friends. Sandys wanted private investors to develop their own estates in Virginia. Before 1618, there had been little incentive to do so, but by relaxing Dale's martial law and promising an elective representative assembly called the **House of Burgesses**, Sandys thought he could make the colony more attractive to wealthy speculators.

Even more important was Sandys's method for distributing land. Colonists who covered their own

James I, "A Counterblaste to Tobacco"

House of Burgesses
An elective representative assembly in colonial Virginia. It was the first example of representative government in the English colonies.

MARKETING TOBACCO This tobacco label advertises Virginia's most valuable export.

What might an ordinary English person looking at this advertisement imagine race relations were like in Virginia?

transportation cost to America were guaranteed a **headright**, a 50-acre lot for which they paid only a small annual rent. Adventurers were granted additional headrights for each servant they brought to the colony. This procedure allowed prosperous planters to build up huge estates while they also acquired dependent laborers. This land system persisted long after the company's collapse. So too did the notion that the wealth of a few justified the exploitation of many others.

Sandys had only just begun. He also urged the settlers to diversify their economy. Tobacco alone, he argued, was not a sufficient base. He envisioned colonists busily producing iron and tar, silk and glass, sugar and cotton. There was no end to his suggestions. He scoured Europe for skilled artisans and exotic plant cuttings. To finance such a huge project, Sandys relied on a lottery, a game of chance that promised a continuous flow of capital into the company's treasury. The final element in the grand scheme was people. Sandys sent new English settlers by the thousand to Jamestown, ordinary men and women swept up by the same hopes that had carried the colonists of 1607 to the New World.

QUICK CHECK ✓

In what sense did tobacco save the Chesapeake colonies?

headright
System of land distribution through which settlers were granted a 50-acre plot of land from the colonial government for each servant or dependent they transported to the New World. The system encouraged the recruitment of a large servile labor force.

indentured servants
Individuals who contracted to serve a master for a set number of years in exchange for the cost of boat transport to America. Indentured servitude was the dominant form of labor in the Chesapeake colonies before the rise of African slavery.

Wessell Webling, His Indenture (1622)

Time of Reckoning

Between 1619 and 1622, colonists arrived in Virginia in record number. Company records reveal that during this short period, 3570 individuals were sent to the colony. People seldom moved to Virginia in families. Although the first women arrived in Jamestown in 1608, most emigrants were single males in their teens or early twenties who came to the New World as **indentured servants**. In exchange for transportation across the Atlantic, they agreed to serve a master for a stated number of years. The length of service depended in part on the age of the servant. The younger the servant, the longer he or she served. In return, the master promised to give the laborers proper care and, at the conclusion of their contracts, to provide them with tools and clothes according to "the custom of the country."

Powerful Virginians corrupted the system. Poor servants wanted to establish independent tobacco farms. As they discovered, however, headrights were awarded not to the newly freed servant, but to the great planter who had borne the cost of the servant's transportation to the New World and paid for food and clothing during the indenture. And even though indentured servants were promised land at the moment of freedom, they were most often cheated, becoming members of a growing, disaffected landless class in seventeenth-century Virginia.

Whenever possible, planters in Virginia purchased able-bodied workers, in other words, persons (preferably male) capable of performing hard agricultural labor. This preference dramatically skewed the colony's sex ratio. In the early decades, men outnumbered women by as much as six to one. Such gender imbalance meant that even if a male servant lived to the end of his indenture—an unlikely prospect—he could not realistically expect to start a family of his own. Moreover, despite apparent legal safeguards, masters could treat dependent workers as they pleased; after all, these people were legally considered property. Servants were sold, traded, even gambled away in games of chance. It does not require much imagination to see that a society that tolerated such an exploitative labor system might later embrace slavery.

Most Virginians then did not live long enough to worry about marriage. Death was omnipresent. Indeed, extraordinarily high mortality was a major

LIFE IN THE CHESAPEAKE   Shown here is a reconstruction of a free white planter's house from the late seventeenth-century Chesapeake.

Why would English people have moved to Virginia if the material culture was so primitive by contemporary English standards?

reason the Chesapeake colonies developed so differently from those of New England. On the eve of the 1618 reforms, Virginia's population stood at approximately 700. The Virginia Company sent at least 3000 more people, but by 1622 only 1240 were still alive. "It Consequentilie followes," declared one angry shareholder, "that we had then lost 3000 persons within those 3 yeares." The major killers were contagious diseases. Salt in the water supply also took a toll. And on Good Friday, March 22, 1622, the Powhatan Indians slew 347 Europeans in a well-coordinated surprise attack.

No one knows for certain what effect such a horrendous mortality rate had on the men and women who survived. At the very least, it must have created a sense of impermanence, a desire to escape Virginia with a little money before sickness or violence ended the adventure. The settlers who drank to excess aboard the tavern ships anchored in the James River described the colony "not as a place of Habitacion but only of a short sojourninge."

On both sides of the Atlantic people wondered who should be blamed. The burden of responsibility lay, in large measure, with the Virginia Company. In fact, the Company's scandalous mismanagement embarrassed James I, and in 1624, he dissolved the bankrupt enterprise and transformed Virginia into a royal colony. The crown appointed a governor and a council. No provision was made, however, for continuing the House of Burgesses. This assembly had first convened in 1619. While elections to the Burgesses were hardly democratic, it did provide wealthy planters with a voice in government. Even without the king's authorization, the representatives gathered annually after 1629, and in 1639, Charles recognized the body's existence.

QUICK CHECK
What explains the extraordinary death rate in early Virginia?

Maryland: A Catholic Refuge

By the end of the seventeenth century, Maryland society looked remarkably like that of its Chesapeake neighbor, Virginia. At the time of first settlement in 1634, however, no one would have predicted that Maryland, a colony wholly owned by a Catholic nobleman, would have survived, much less become a flourishing tobacco colony.

The driving force behind the founding of Maryland was Sir George Calvert, later Lord Baltimore. Calvert, a talented and well-educated man, enjoyed the patronage of James I. He was awarded lucrative positions in the government, the most important being the king's secretary of state. In 1625, Calvert shocked almost everyone by publicly declaring his Catholicism; in this fiercely anti-Catholic society, persons who openly supported the Church of Rome were immediately stripped of civil office. Although forced to resign as secretary of state, Calvert retained the crown's favor.

Before resigning, Calvert sponsored a settlement on the coast of Newfoundland, but after visiting the place, the proprietor concluded that no English person, whatever his or her religion, would transfer to a place where the "ayre [is] so intolerably cold." He turned his attention to the Chesapeake, and on June 30, 1632, Charles I granted George Calvert's son, Cecilius, a charter for a colony to be located north of Virginia. The boundaries of the settlement, named Maryland in honor of Charles's queen, were so vaguely defined that they generated legal controversies not fully resolved until the mid-eighteenth century when Charles Mason and Jeremiah Dixon surveyed their famous line between Pennsylvania and Maryland.

The Charter
of Maryland
(1632)

Cecilius, the second Lord Baltimore, wanted to create a sanctuary for England's persecuted Catholics. He also intended to make money. Without Protestant settlers, it seemed unlikely Maryland would prosper, and Cecilius instructed his brother Leonard, the colony's governor, to do nothing that might frighten off hypersensitive Protestants. The governor was ordered to "cause all Acts of the Roman Catholic Religion to be done as privately as may be and… [to] instruct all Roman Catholics to be silent upon all occasions of discourse concerning matters of Religion." On March 25, 1634, the *Ark* and *Dove*, carrying about 150 settlers, landed safely, and within days, the governor purchased from the Yaocomico Indians a village that became St. Mary's City, the capital of Maryland.

The colony's charter was a throwback to an earlier feudal age. It transformed Baltimore into a "palatine lord," a proprietor with almost royal powers. Settlers swore an oath of allegiance not to the king of England but to Lord Baltimore. In England, such practices had long ago passed into obsolescence. As the proprietor, Lord Baltimore owned outright almost 6 million acres; he possessed absolute authority over anyone living in his domain.

On paper, at least, everyone in Maryland was assigned a place in an elaborate social hierarchy. Members of a colonial ruling class, persons who purchased 6000 acres from Baltimore, were called lords of the manor. These landed aristocrats were permitted to establish local courts of law. People holding less acreage enjoyed fewer privileges, particularly in government. Baltimore figured that land sales and rents would adequately finance the entire venture.

Baltimore's feudal system never took root in Chesapeake soil. People simply refused to play the social roles the lord proprietor had assigned. These tensions affected the operation of Maryland's government. Baltimore assumed that his brother, acting as his deputy in America, and a small appointed council of local aristocrats would pass necessary laws and carry out routine administration. When an elected assembly first convened in 1635, Baltimore allowed the delegates to discuss only those acts he had prepared. The members of the assembly bridled at such restrictions, insisting on exercising traditional parliamentary privileges. Neither side gained a clear victory in the assembly, and for almost twenty-five years, legislative squabbling contributed to the widespread political instability that almost destroyed Maryland.

LORD BALTIMORE Cecilius Calvert, the second Lord Baltimore, insisted that Maryland tolerate all Christian religions, including Catholicism, something no other colony was willing to do.

What does the young slave in the background tell us about the labor system in the Chesapeake?

The colony drew both Protestants and Catholics, and the two groups might have lived in harmony had civil war not broken out in England. When Cromwell and the Puritan faction executed Charles, transforming England briefly into a republic, it seemed Baltimore might lose his colony. To head off such an event and to placate Maryland's restless Protestants, in 1649, the proprietor drafted the famous "Act concerning Religion," which extended toleration to all individuals who accepted the divinity of Christ. At a time when European rulers regularly persecuted people for their religious beliefs, Baltimore championed liberty of conscience.

However laudable the act may have been, it did not heal religious divisions in Maryland, and when local Puritans seized the colony's government, they promptly repealed the act. For almost two decades, vigilantes roamed the countryside, and during the "Plundering Time" (1644–1646), one armed group temporarily drove Leonard Calvert out of Maryland. In 1655, civil war flared again.

In this troubled sanctuary, ordinary planters and their workers cultivated tobacco on plantations dispersed along riverfronts. In 1678, Baltimore complained that he could not find fifty houses in a space of thirty miles. Tobacco affected almost every aspect of local culture. "In Virginia and Maryland," one Calvert explained, "Tobacco, as our Staple, is our all, and indeed leaves no room for anything Else." A steady stream of indentured servants supplied the plantations with dependent laborers—until they were replaced by African slaves at the end of the seventeenth century.

Europeans sacrificed much by coming to the Chesapeake. For most of the century, their standard of living was primitive when compared with that of people of the same social class who had remained in England. Two-thirds of the planters, for example, lived in houses of only two rooms and of a type associated with the poorest classes in contemporary English society.

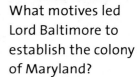

QUICK CHECK ✓

What motives led Lord Baltimore to establish the colony of Maryland?

A "New" England in America

The Pilgrims enjoy almost mythic status in American history. These brave refugees crossed the cold Atlantic in search of religious liberty, signed a democratic compact aboard the *Mayflower*, landed at Plymouth Rock, and gave us our Thanksgiving Day. As with most legends, this one contains only a core of truth.

The Pilgrims were not crusaders who set out to change the world. Rather, they were humble English farmers. Their story began in the early 1600s in Scrooby Manor, a small community located approximately 150 miles north of London. Many people living in this area believed the Church of England retained too many traces of its Catholic origin. Its very rituals compromised God's true believers, and so, in the early years of the reign of James I, the Scrooby congregation formally left the established state church. Like others who followed this logic, they were called Separatists. Since English statute required citizens to attend Anglican services, the Scrooby Separatists moved to Holland in 1608–1609 rather than compromise.

The Netherlands provided the Separatists with a good home—too good. The members of the little church feared they were losing their distinct identity; their children were becoming Dutch. In 1617, therefore, a portion of the original Scrooby congregation vowed to sail to America. Included in this group was William Bradford, a wonderfully literate man who wrote *Of Plymouth Plantation*, one of the first and certainly most poignant accounts of an early American settlement.

Poverty presented the major obstacle to the Pilgrims' plans. They petitioned for a land patent from the Virginia Company of London. At the same time, they looked for someone willing to underwrite the staggering costs of colonization. The negotiations went well, or so it seemed. After stopping in England to take on supplies and laborers, the Pilgrims set off for America in 1620 aboard the *Mayflower*, armed with a patent to settle in Virginia and indebted to a group of English investors who were only marginally interested in religious reform.

Because of an error in navigation, the Pilgrims landed not in Virginia but in New England. The patent for which they had worked so diligently had no validity in the region. In fact, the crown had granted New England to another company. Without a patent, the colonists possessed no authorization to form a civil government, a serious matter since some sailors who were not Pilgrims threatened mutiny. To preserve the struggling community from anarchy, 41 men signed an agreement known as the **Mayflower Compact** to "covenant and combine our selves together into a civil body politick."

Mayflower Compact
Agreement among the Pilgrims aboard the *Mayflower* in 1620 to create a civil government at Plymouth Colony.

Although later praised for its democratic character, the Mayflower Compact could not ward off disease and hunger. During the first months in Plymouth, death claimed approximately half of the 102 people who had initially set out from England. Moreover, debts contracted in England severely burdened the new colony. To their credit, the Pilgrims honored their financial obligations, but it took almost twenty years to satisfy the English investors. Without Bradford, whom they elected as governor, the settlers might have allowed adversity to overwhelm them. Through strength of will and self-sacrifice, however, Bradford persuaded frightened men and women that they could survive in America.

Bradford had a lot of help. Almost anyone who has heard of the Plymouth Colony knows of Squanto, a Patuxt Indian who welcomed the first Pilgrims in excellent English. In 1614 unscrupulous adventurers kidnapped Squanto and sold him in Spain as a slave. Somehow he escaped bondage, making his way to London, where a group of merchants who owned land in Newfoundland taught him to speak English. They apparently hoped that he would deliver moving public testimonials about the desirability of moving to the New World. In any case, Squanto returned to the Plymouth area just before the Pilgrims arrived. Squanto joined Massasoit, a local Native American leader, in teaching the Pilgrims much about hunting and agriculture, a debt that Bradford freely acknowledged. Although evidence for the so-called First Thanksgiving is extremely sketchy, it is certain that without Native American support the Europeans would have starved.

Plymouth Colony

In time, the Pilgrims replicated the humble little farm communities they had once known in England. They formed Separatist congregations to their liking; the population slowly increased, but because Plymouth offered only limited economic prospects, it attracted only a trickle of new settlers. In 1691, the colony was absorbed into its larger and more prosperous neighbor, Massachusetts Bay.

The Puritan Migration to Massachusetts

In the early decades of the seventeenth century, an extraordinary spirit of religious reform burst forth in England, and before it had burned itself out, Puritanism had transformed the face of England and America. Modern historians have difficulty comprehending this powerful spiritual movement. Some consider the Puritans rather neurotic individuals who condemned liquor and sex, dressed in drab clothes, and minded their neighbors' business.

Puritans

Members of reformed Protestant sects in Europe and America who insisted on removing all vestiges of Catholicism from popular religious practice.

The crude caricature is based on a profound misunderstanding of the actual nature of this broad popular movement. The seventeenth-century Puritans were more like today's radical political reformers, men and women committed to far-reaching institutional change, than like naive do-gooders or narrow fundamentalists. To their enemies, of course, the Puritans were irritants, always pointing out civil and ecclesiastical imperfections and urging everyone to try to fulfill the commands of Scripture. A great many people, however, shared their vision, and their values remained a dominant element in American culture at least until the Civil War.

The Puritans were products of the Protestant Reformation. They accepted a Calvinist notion that an omnipotent God predestined some people to salvation and damned others throughout eternity. But instead of waiting passively for Judgment Day, the Puritans examined themselves for signs of grace, for hints that God had in fact placed them among his "elect." A member of this select group, they argued, would try to live according to Scripture, to battle sin and eradicate corruption.

For the Puritans, the logic of everyday life was clear. If the Church of England contained unscriptural elements—clerical garments associated with Catholic ritual, for example—then they must be eliminated. If the pope in Rome was in league with the Antichrist, then Protestant kings had better not form alliances with Catholic states. If God condemned licentiousness and intoxication, then local officials should punish whores and drunks. There was nothing improper about an occasional beer or passionate physical love within marriage, but when sex and drink became ends in themselves, the Puritans thought England's ministers and magistrates should speak out. Persons of this temperament were more combative than the Pilgrims had been. They wanted to purify the Church of England from within, and before the 1630s at least, separatism held little appeal for them.

From the Puritan perspective, the early Stuarts, James I and Charles I, seemed unconcerned about the spiritual state of the nation. James tolerated corruption within his own court; he condoned gross public extravagance. Charles I persecuted Puritan ministers, forcing them either to conform to his theology or lose their licenses to preach. As long as Parliament met, Puritan voters in the various boroughs and countries throughout England elected men sympathetic to their point of view. These outspoken representatives criticized royal policies. Because of their defiance, Charles decided in 1629 to rule England without Parliament and four years later named William Laud, a bishop who represented everything the Puritans detested, archbishop of Canterbury. The last doors of reform slammed shut. The corruption remained.

John Winthrop, the future governor of Massachusetts Bay, was caught up in these events. Little about his background suggested such an auspicious future. He owned a small manor in Suffolk, one that never produced sufficient income to support his growing family. He dabbled in law. But the core of Winthrop's life was his faith in God, a faith so intense his contemporaries immediately identified him as a Puritan. The Lord, he concluded, was displeased with England. Time for reform was running out. In May 1629, he wrote to his wife, "I am verily perswaded God will bringe some heavye Affliction upon this lande, and that speedylye." He was, however, confident that the Lord would "provide a shelter and a hidinge place for us."

John Winthrop, "A Model of Christian Charity" (1630)

QUICK CHECK ✓

Why did the Puritans choose to leave England?

"A City on a Hill"

A fleet bearing Puritan settlers, John Winthrop among them, departed England in March 1630. By the end of the first year, almost two thousand people had arrived in Massachusetts Bay, and before the "**Great Migration**" concluded in the early 1640s, more than sixteen thousand men and women had arrived in the new Puritan colony.

Great Migration

Migration of sixteen thousand Puritan men and women from England to the Massachusetts Bay Colony during the 1630s.

A great deal is known about the background of these particular settlers. A large percentage of them originated in an area northeast of London called East Anglia, a region in which Puritan ideas had taken deep root. London, Kent, and the West Country also contributed to the stream of emigrants. In some instances, entire villages were reestablished across the Atlantic. Many Bay Colonists had worked as farmers in England, but a surprisingly large number came from industrial centers, such as Norwich, where cloth was manufactured for the export trade.

Whatever their backgrounds, they moved to Massachusetts as nuclear families, fathers, mothers, and their dependent children, a form of migration strikingly different from the one that peopled Virginia and Maryland. Moreover, because the settlers had already formed families in England, the colony's sex ratio was more balanced than that found in the Chesapeake colonies. Finally, and perhaps more significantly, once they had arrived in Massachusetts, these men and women survived. Indeed, their life expectancy compares favorably to that of modern Americans. Many factors help explain this phenomenon—clean drinking water and a healthy climate, for example. While the Puritans could not have planned to live longer than did colonists in other parts of the New World, this remarkable accident reduced the emotional shock of long-distance migration.

The first settlers possessed another source of strength and stability. They were bound together by a common sense of purpose. God, they insisted, had formed a special covenant with the people of Massachusetts Bay. On his part, the Lord expected them to live according to Scripture, to reform the church, in other

OLD SHIP MEETINGHOUSE This early Puritan meetinghouse in Hingham, Massachusetts, was called the Old Ship Meetinghouse because its interior design resembled the hull of a ship. The oldest surviving wooden church in the United States, it could accommodate about seven hundred people.

What does the simplicity of decoration in this meetinghouse tell us about Puritan piety?

words, to create an Old Testament "City on a Hill" that would stand as a beacon of righteousness for the rest of the Christian world. If they fulfilled their side of the bargain, the settlers could anticipate peace and prosperity.

Once they settled, the Bay Colonists developed a highly innovative form of church government known as Congregationalism. Under the system, each village church was independent of outside interference. The American Puritans, of course, wanted nothing of bishops. The people were the church, and as a body, they pledged to uphold God's law. In the Salem Church, for example, the members covenanted "with the Lord and with one another and do bind ourselves in the presence of God to walk together in all his ways."

Simply because a person happened to live in a certain community did not mean he or she automatically belonged to the local church. The churches of Massachusetts were voluntary institutions, and in order to join one a man or woman had to provide testimony—a confession of faith—before neighbors who had already been admitted as full members. It was a demanding process. Whatever the personal strains, however, most men and women in early Massachusetts aspired to full membership, which entitled them to the sacraments, and gave some of them responsibility for choosing ministers, disciplining backsliders, and determining difficult questions of theology. Although women and blacks could not vote for ministers, they did become members of the Congregational churches.

The government of Massachusetts was neither a democracy nor a theocracy. The magistrates elected in Massachusetts did not believe they represented the voters, much less the whole populace. They ruled in the name of the electorate, but their responsibility as rulers was to God. In 1638, Winthrop warned against overly democratic forms, since "the best part [of the people] is always the least, and of that best part the wiser is always the lesser." And second, the Congregational ministers possessed no formal political authority in Massachusetts Bay. They could not even hold civil office, and it was not unusual for the voters to ignore the recommendations of a respected minister such as John Cotton.

In New England, the town became the center of public life. In other regions of British America where the county was the focus of local government, people did not experience the same density of social and institutional interaction. In Massachusetts, groups of men and women voluntarily covenanted together to

SEVENTEENTH-CENTURY NEW ENGLAND MANSION

Built in 1668, the house at 54 Turner Street in Salem, Massachusetts, is the oldest surviving seventeenth-century wooden mansion in New England.

How does this mansion represent the transfer of English culture to the New World?

QUICK CHECK

What did the founders of Massachusetts mean when they referred to their colony as a "City on a Hill"?

observe common goals. The community constructed a meetinghouse where religious services and town meetings were held. This powerful sense of shared purpose—something that later Americans have greatly admired—should not obscure the fact that the founders of New England towns also had a keen eye for personal profit. Seventeenth-century records reveal that speculators often made a good deal of money from selling "shares" in village lands. But acquisitiveness never got out of control, and recent studies have shown that entrepreneurial practices rarely disturbed the peace of the Puritan communities. Inhabitants generally received land sufficient to build a house to support a family. Although villagers escaped the kind of feudal dues collected in other parts of America, they were expected to contribute to the minister's salary, pay local and colony taxes, and serve in the militia.

Competing Truths in New England

The European settlers of Massachusetts Bay managed to live in peace—at least with each other. This was a remarkable achievement considering the chronic instability that plagued other colonies at this time. The Bay Colonists disagreed over many issues, sometimes vociferously; whole towns disputed with neighboring villages over common boundaries. But the people inevitably relied on the civil courts to mediate differences. They believed in a rule of law, and in 1648 the colonial legislature, called the General Court, drew up the *Lawes and Liberties*, the first alphabetized code of law printed in English. In clear prose, it explained to ordinary colonists their rights and responsibilities as citizens of the commonwealth. The code engendered public trust in government and discouraged magistrates from the arbitrary exercise of authority.

The Puritans never supported the concept of religious toleration. They transferred to the New World to preserve *their own* freedom of worship; about religious freedom of those deemed heretics, they expressed little concern. The most serious challenges to Puritan orthodoxy in Massachusetts Bay came from two brilliantly charismatic individuals. The first, Roger Williams, arrived in 1631 and immediately attracted a body of loyal followers. Indeed, everyone seemed to have liked Williams as a person.

Williams's *religious ideas*, however, created controversy. He preached extreme separatism. The Bay Colonists, he exclaimed, were impure in the sight of the Lord so long as they remained even nominal members of the Church of England. Moreover, he questioned the validity of the colony's charter, since the king had not first purchased the land from the Indians, a view that threatened the integrity of the entire colonial experiment. Williams also insisted that the civil rulers of Massachusetts had no business punishing settlers for their religious beliefs. It was God's responsibility, not men's, to monitor people's consciences. The Bay magistrates were prepared neither to tolerate heresy nor to accede to Williams's other demands, and in 1636, after attempts to reach a compromise had failed, they banished him from the colony. Williams worked out the logic of his ideas in Providence, a village he founded in what would become Rhode Island.

The magistrates of Massachusetts Bay rightly concluded that the second individual, Anne Hutchinson, posed an even graver threat to the peace of the commonwealth. This extremely intelligent woman, her husband William, and her children followed John Cotton to the New World in 1634. Even contemporaries found her religious ideas, which consisted of a highly personal form of spirituality, usually termed **Antinomianism**, somewhat confusing.

Whatever her thoughts, Hutchinson shared them with other Bostonians, many of them women. Her outspoken views scandalized orthodox leaders of church and state. She suggested that all but two ministers in the colony had lost touch with the "Holy Spirit" and were preaching a doctrine in the Congregational churches that was little better than that of Archbishop Laud. When authorities demanded she explain her unusual opinions, she suggested that she experienced divine inspiration independently of either the Bible or the clergy. In other words, Hutchinson's teachings could not be tested by Scripture, a position that seemed dangerously subjective. Indeed, Hutchinson's theology called the very foundation of Massachusetts Bay into question. Without clear, external standards, one person's truth was as valid as anyone else's, and from Winthrop's perspective, Hutchinson's teachings invited civil and religious anarchy. But her challenge to authority was not simply theological. As a woman, her aggressive speech sparked a deeply misogynist response from the colony's male leaders.

When this woman described Congregational ministers—some of them the leading divines of Boston—as unconverted men, the General Court intervened. For two very tense days in 1637, the ministers and magistrates of Massachusetts Bay cross-examined Hutchinson; in this intense theological debate, she more than held her own. She knew as much about the Bible as did her inquisitors.

Hutchinson defied the ministers and magistrates to demonstrate exactly where she had gone wrong. Just when it appeared Hutchinson had outmaneuvered—indeed, thoroughly embarrassed—her opponents, she let down her guard, declaring forcefully that what she knew of God came "by an immediate revelation.... By the voice of his own spirit to my soul." Here was what her accusers had suspected all along but could not prove. She had confessed in open court that the Spirit can live without the Moral Law. This antinomian statement fulfilled the worst fears of the Bay rulers, and they were relieved to exile Hutchinson and her followers to Rhode Island.

Antinomianism
Religious belief rejecting traditional moral law as unnecessary for Christians who possess saving grace and affirming that an individual could experience divine revelation and salvation without the assistance of formally trained clergy.

QUICK CHECK ✓

In what ways did Roger Williams and Anne Hutchinson pose a threat to the Massachusetts Bay Colony?

Mobility and Division

Massachusetts Bay spawned four new colonies, three of which survived to the American Revolution. New Hampshire became a separate colony in 1677. Its population grew very slowly, and for much of the colonial period, New Hampshire remained economically dependent on Massachusetts, its commercial neighbor to the south.

Far more people were drawn to the fertile lands of the Connecticut River Valley. In 1636, settlers founded the villages of Hartford, Windsor, and Wethersfield. No one forced these men and women to leave Massachusetts, and in their new surroundings, they created a society that looked much like the one they had known in the Bay Colony. Through his writings, Thomas Hooker, Connecticut's most prominent minister, helped all New Englanders define Congregational church polity. Puritans on both sides of the Atlantic read Hooker's beautifully crafted works. In 1639, representatives from the Connecticut towns passed the Fundamental Orders, a blueprint for civil government, and in 1662, Charles II awarded the colony a charter of its own.

In 1638, another group, led by Theophilus Eaton and the Reverend John Davenport, settled New Haven and several adjoining towns along Long Island Sound. These emigrants, many of whom had come from London, lived briefly in Massachusetts Bay but then insisted on forming a Puritan commonwealth of their own, one that established a closer relationship between church and state than the Bay Colonists had allowed. The New Haven colony never prospered, and in 1662, it was absorbed into Connecticut.

Rhode Island experienced a wholly different history. From the beginning, it drew people of a highly independent turn of mind, and according to one Dutch visitor, Rhode Island was "the receptacle of all sorts of riff-raff people.... All the cranks of New-England retire thither." This description, of course, was an exaggeration. Roger Williams founded Providence in 1636; two years later, Anne Hutchinson took her followers to Portsmouth. Other groups settled around Narragansett Bay. Not surprisingly, these men and women appreciated the need for toleration. No one was persecuted in Rhode Island for his or her religious beliefs.

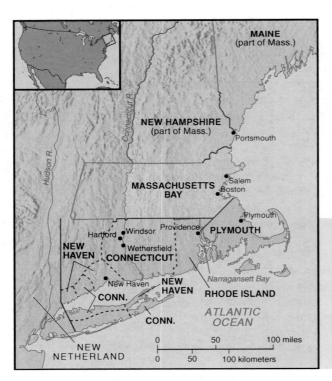

NEW ENGLAND COLONIES, 1650   The early settlers quickly carved up New England. New Haven briefly flourished as a separate colony before being taken over by Connecticut in 1662. Long Island later became part of New York; Plymouth was absorbed by Massachusetts; and in 1677 New Hampshire became a separate colony.

Why do you think Puritan settlers felt compelled to found more than one New England colony?

One might have thought the separate Rhode Island communities would cooperate for the common good. They did not. Villagers fought over land and schemed with outside speculators to divide the tiny colony into even smaller pieces. In 1644, Parliament issued a patent for the "Providence Plantations," and in 1663, the Rhode Islanders obtained a royal charter. These successes did not calm political turmoil. For most of the seventeenth century, colonywide government existed in name only. Despite their constant bickering, however, the settlers of Rhode Island built up a profitable commerce in agricultural goods.

QUICK CHECK ✔

What religious and economic factors led to the settlement of other New England colonies beyond Massachusetts Bay?

Diversity in the Middle Colonies

New York and Pennsylvania were settled for quite different reasons. William Penn, for example, envisioned a Quaker sanctuary; the Duke of York worried chiefly about his own income. Despite the founders' intentions, however, some common characteristics emerged. Both colonies developed a strikingly heterogeneous population, men and women of different ethnic and religious backgrounds. This cultural diversity became a major influence on the economic, political, and ecclesiastical institutions of the Middle Colonies. The raucous, partisan public life of the Middle Colonies foreshadowed later American society.

HOW
did ethnic diversity shape the development of the Middle Colonies?

Anglo-Dutch Rivalry on the Hudson

By the early decades of the seventeenth century, the Dutch had established themselves as Europe's most aggressive traders. Holland—a small, loosely federated nation—possessed the world's largest merchant fleet. Its ships vied for the commerce of Asia, Africa, and America. Dutch rivalry with Spain, a fading though still formidable power, was in large measure responsible for the settlement of New Netherland. While searching for the elusive Northwest Passage in 1609, Henry Hudson, an English explorer employed by a Dutch company, sailed up the river that now bears his name. Further voyages led to the establishment of trading posts in New Netherland, although permanent settlement did not occur until 1624. The area also seemed an excellent base from which to attack Spain's colonies in the New World.

The directors of the Dutch West India Company sponsored two small outposts, Fort Orange (Albany), located well up the Hudson River, and New Amsterdam (New York City) on Manhattan Island. The first Dutch settlers were not actually colonists. Rather, they were salaried employees, and their superiors in Holland expected them to spend most of their time gathering animal furs. They did not receive land for their troubles. Needless to say, this arrangement attracted relatively few Dutch immigrants.

The colony's population may have been small, only 270 in 1628, but it contained an extraordinary ethnic mix. One visitor to New Amsterdam in 1644 maintained he had heard "eighteen different languages" spoken in the city. Even if this report was exaggerated, there is no doubt the Dutch colony drew English,

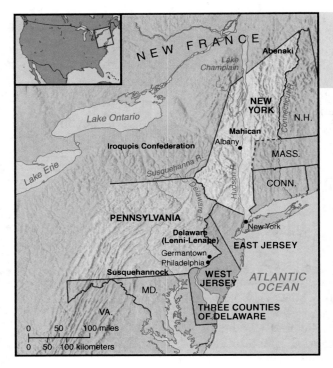

MIDDLE COLONIES, 1685 In the long term, New York and Philadelphia became colonial America's most important commercial ports.

How would you explain this economic success?

Finns, Germans, and Swedes. By the 1640s, a sizable community of free blacks (probably former slaves who had gained their freedom through self-purchase) had developed in New Amsterdam, adding African tongues to the cacophony of languages. The colony's culture was further fragmented by New England Puritans who left Massachusetts and Connecticut to stake out farms on eastern Long Island.

New Netherland lacked capable leadership. The company sent a number of director-generals to oversee judicial and political affairs. Without exception, these men were temperamentally unsuited to govern an American colony. They adopted autocratic procedures, lined their own pockets, and, in one case, blundered into a war that needlessly killed scores of Indians and settlers. The company made no provision for an elected assembly. As much as they were able, the scattered inhabitants living along the Hudson River ignored company directives. They felt no loyalty to the trading company that had treated them so shabbily. Long Island Puritans complained bitterly about the absence of representative institutions. The Dutch system has aptly been described as "unstable pluralism."

In August 1664, the Dutch lost their tenuous hold on New Netherland. The English crown, eager to score an easy victory over a commercial rival, dispatched a fleet of warships to New Amsterdam. The commander of this force, Colonel Richard Nicolls, ordered the colonists to surrender. The last director-general, a colorful character named Peter Stuyvesant (1647–1664), rushed wildly about the city urging the settlers to resist the English. But no one obeyed. Even the Dutch remained deaf to Stuyvesant's appeals. They accepted the Articles of Capitulation, a generous agreement that allowed Dutch nationals to remain in the province and to retain their property.

Charles II had already granted his brother, James, the Duke of York, a charter for the newly captured territory and much else besides. The duke became absolute proprietor over Maine, Martha's Vineyard, Nantucket, Long Island, and the rest of New York all the way to Delaware Bay. The king perhaps wanted to encircle New England's potentially disloyal Puritan population, but whatever his aims may have been, he created a bureaucratic nightmare.

The Duke of York had acquired a thorough aversion to representative government. He had no intention of letting such a participatory system take root in New York. "I cannot *but* suspect," the duke announced, that an assembly "would be of dangerous consequence." The Long Islanders felt betrayed. In part to appease these outspoken critics, Governor Nicolls—one of the few competent administrators to serve in the Middle Colonies—drew up in March 1665 a legal code known as the Duke's Laws. It guaranteed religious toleration and created local governments.

t' Fort nieuw Amsterdam op de Manhatans.

Nieuw Nederlandt.

There was no provision, however, for an elected assembly or, for that matter, for democratic town meetings. The legal code disappointed the Puritan migrants on Long Island, and when the duke's officers attempted to collect taxes, these people protested that they were "inslav'd under an Arbitrary Power."

The Dutch kept silent. For several decades they remained a large unassimilated ethnic group. They continued to speak their own language, worship in their own churches (Dutch Reformed Calvinist), and eye their English neighbors with suspicion. In fact, the colony seemed little different from what it had been under the Dutch West India Company: a loose collection of independent communities ruled by an ineffectual central government.

QUICK CHECK

Why were the Dutch unable to establish a permanent colony in what became New York?

Quakers in America

The founding of Pennsylvania cannot be separated from the history of the Quaker movement. Believers in an extreme form of antinomianism, the **Quakers** saw no need for a learned ministry, since one person's interpretation of Scripture was as valid as anyone else's. This radical religious sect, a product of the social upheaval in England during the Civil War, gained its name from the derogatory term that English authorities sometimes used to describe those who "tremble at the word of the Lord." The name persisted even though the Quakers preferred being called Professors of the Light or, more commonly, Friends.

Quakers practiced humility in their daily lives. They wore simple clothes and employed old-fashioned forms of address that set them apart from their neighbors. Friends refused to honor worldly position and accomplishment or to swear oaths in courts of law. They were also pacifists. According to Quaker belief, all persons were equal in the sight of the Lord, a belief that generally annoyed people of rank and achievement.

Quakers
Members of a radical religious group, formally known as the Society of Friends, who rejected formal theology and stressed each person's "Inner Light," a spiritual guide to righteousness.

Moreover, the Quakers never kept their thoughts to themselves. They preached conversion constantly, spreading the "Truth" throughout England, Ireland, and America. The Friends played important roles in the early history of New Jersey, Rhode Island, and North Carolina, as well as Pennsylvania. In some places, the "publishers of Truth" wore out their welcome. English authorities harassed the Quakers. Thousands were jailed, and in Massachusetts Bay between 1659 and 1661, Puritan magistrates ordered several Friends put to death. Such measures proved counterproductive, for persecution only inspired the persecuted Quakers to redouble their efforts.

QUICK CHECK ✓

What explains Puritan hostility toward the Quakers?

Penn's "Holy Experiment"

William Penn, the founder of Pennsylvania, dedicated his life to the Quaker faith, a commitment that led eventually to the founding of Pennsylvania. He possessed a curiously complex personality. He was an athletic person who threw himself into intellectual pursuits. He was a bold visionary capable of making pragmatic decisions. He came from an aristocratic family and yet spent his entire adult life involved with a religious movement associated with the lower class.

Precisely when Penn's thoughts turned to America is not known. He was briefly involved with the West Jersey proprietorship. This venture may have suggested the possibility of an even larger enterprise. In any case, Penn negotiated in 1681 one of the more impressive land deals in the history of American real estate. Charles II awarded Penn a charter making him the sole proprietor of a vast area

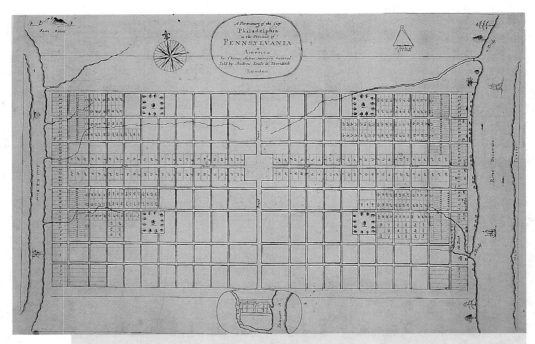

PHILADELPHIA   William Penn's plan for Philadelphia shows the city laid out where the Scool Kill (Schuylkill) and Delaware rivers parallel each other. Four of the five public squares were intended to be parks while the fifth (at center) was designated for public buildings. (*Source: The Library Company of Philadelphia.*)

Do you think Penn chose a good site for his capital city?

called Pennsylvania (literally, "Penn's woods"). The name embarrassed the modest Penn, but he knew better than to look the royal gift horse in the mouth.

Penn lost no time in launching his "Holy Experiment." In 1682, he set forth his ideas in an unusual document known as the Frame of Government. The charter gave Penn the right to create any form of government he desired, and his imagination ran wild. His plan blended traditional notions about the privileges of a landed aristocracy with quite daring concepts of personal liberty. Penn guaranteed that settlers would enjoy among other things liberty of conscience, freedom from persecution, no taxation without representation, and due process of law.

Penn promoted his colony aggressively throughout England, Ireland, and Germany. He had no choice. His only source of revenue was the sale of land and the collection of quitrents. Penn commissioned pamphlets in several languages extolling the quality of Pennsylvania's rich farmland. The response was overwhelming. People poured into Philadelphia and the surrounding area. In 1685 alone, eight thousand immigrants arrived. Most of the settlers were Irish, Welsh, and English Quakers, and they generally moved to America as families. But Penn opened the door to men and women of all nations. He asserted that the people of Pennsylvania "are a collection of divers nations in Europe, as French, Dutch, Germans, Swedes, Danes, Finns, Scotch, Irish, and English."

The settlers were by no means all Quakers. The founder of Germantown, Francis Daniel Pastorius, called the vessel that brought him to the New World a "Noah's Ark" of religions, and within his own household, there were servants who subscribed "to the Roman [Catholic], to the Lutheran, to the Calvinistic, to the Anabaptist, and to the Anglican church, and only one Quaker." Ethnic and religious diversity were crucial in the development of Pennsylvania's public institutions, and its politics took on a quarrelsome quality absent in more homogeneous colonies such as Virginia and Massachusetts.

William Penn, "Model for Government" (1681)

QUICK CHECK ✓

How did the Quaker religion influence the development of Pennsylvania?

Planting the Southern Colonies

In some ways, Carolina society looked much like the one that had developed in Virginia and Maryland. In both areas, white planters forced African slaves to produce staple crops for a world market. But such superficial similarities masked substantial regional differences. In fact, "the South"—certainly the fabled solid South of the early nineteenth century—did not exist during the colonial period. The Carolinas, joined much later by Georgia, stood apart from their northern neighbors. As a historian of colonial Carolina explained, "the southern colonies were never a cohesive section in the same way that New England was. The great diversity of population groups... discouraged southern sectionalism."

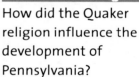

HOW

would you contrast the founding of the Carolinas with the founding of Georgia?

Founding the Carolinas

On March 24, 1663, Charles II granted a group of eight courtiers, styled the Proprietors of Carolina, a charter to the vast territory between Virginia and Florida running west as far as the "South Seas." After a series of initial setbacks, the most energetic proprietor, Anthony Ashley Cooper, later Earl of Shaftesbury, realized that without an infusion of new money Carolina would fail. In 1669, he persuaded Carolinian proprietors to invest their own capital in the colony. Once he received

CHARLESTON This engraving from 1671 of the fortified settlement at Charleston, South Carolina, shows the junction of the Ashley and Cooper rivers. A large number of Charleston's settlers came from the sugar plantations of Barbados.

Why would they have felt it necessary to build such extensive fortifications?

sufficient funds, he dispatched three hundred English colonists to Port Royal under the command of Joseph West. The fleet put in briefly at Barbados to pick up additional recruits, and in March 1670, after being punished by Atlantic gales that destroyed one ship, the expedition arrived at its destination. Only one hundred people were still alive. The unhappy settlers did not remain long at Port Royal, an unappealing, low-lying place badly exposed to Spanish attack. They moved northward, locating eventually along the more secure Ashley River. Later the colony's administrative center, Charles Town (it did not become Charleston until 1783) was established at the junction of the Ashley and Cooper rivers.

Before 1680, almost half the men and women who settled in the Port Royal area came from Barbados. This small Caribbean island, which produced an annual fortune in sugar, depended on slave labor. By the third quarter of the seventeenth century, Barbados had become overpopulated. Wealthy families could not provide their sons and daughters with sufficient land to maintain social status, and as the crisis intensified, Barbadians looked to Carolina for relief.

These migrants, many of whom were quite rich, traveled to Carolina both as individuals and family groups. Some even brought gangs of slaves with them to the American mainland. The Barbadians carved out plantations on the tributaries of the Cooper River and established themselves immediately as the colony's most powerful political faction. "So it was," wrote historian Richard Dunn, "that these Caribbean pioneers helped to create on the North American coast a slave-based plantation society closer in temper to the islands they fled from than to any other mainland English settlement."

Much of the planters' time was taken up with the search for a profitable crop. The early settlers experimented with a number of plants: tobacco, cotton, silk, and grapes. The most successful items turned out to be beef, skins, and naval stores (especially tar used to maintain ocean vessels). By the 1680s, some Carolinians had built up great herds of cattle—seven or eight hundred head in some cases. Traders who dealt with Indians brought back thousands of deerskins from the interior, and they often returned with Indian slaves as well. These commercial resources, together with tar and turpentine, enjoyed a good market. It was not until the

1690s that the planters came to appreciate fully the value of rice, but once they had done so, it quickly became the colony's main staple.

Proprietary Carolina was in a constant political uproar. Factions vied for special privilege. The Barbadian settlers, known locally as the Goose Creek Men, resisted the proprietors' policies at every turn. A large community of French Huguenots located in Craven County distrusted the Barbadians. The proprietors—an ineffectual group following the death of Cooper—appointed a series of utterly incompetent governors who only made things worse. One visitor observed that "the Inhabitants of Carolina should be as free from Oppression as any [people] in the Universe... if their own Differences amongst themselves do not occasion the contrary." By the end of the century, the Commons House of Assembly had assumed the right to initiate legislation. In 1719, the colonists overthrew the last proprietary governor, and in 1729, the king created separate royal governments for North and South Carolina.

QUICK CHECK

How did the Barbadian background of the early settlers shape the economic development of the Carolinas?

Founding of Georgia

The early history of Georgia was strikingly different from that of Britain's other mainland colonies. Its settlement was really an act of aggression against Spain, a country that had as good a claim to this area as did the English. During the eighteenth century, the two nations were often at war, and South Carolinians worried that the Spaniards moving up from bases in Florida would occupy the disputed territory between Florida and the Carolina grant.

The colony owed its existence primarily to James Oglethorpe, a British general and member of Parliament who believed that he could thwart Spanish designs on the area south of Charles Town while at the same time providing a fresh start for London's worthy poor, saving them from debtors' prison. Although Oglethorpe envisioned Georgia as an asylum as well as a garrison, the military aspects of his proposal were especially appealing to the leaders of the British government. In 1732, the king granted Oglethorpe and a board of trustees a charter for a new colony to be located between the Savannah and Altamaha rivers and from "sea to sea." The trustees living in the mother country were given complete control over Georgia politics, a condition the settlers soon found intolerable.

THE CAROLINAS AND GEORGIA Caribbean sugar planters migrated to the Goose Creek area where they eventually mastered rice cultivation. Poor harbors in North Carolina retarded the spread of European settlement in that region.

Why do you think these colonies have no explicit western boundaries?

	ENGLAND'S PRINCIPAL MAINLAND COLONIES				
Name	Original Purpose	Date of Founding	Principal Founder	Major Export	Estimated Population ca. 1700
Virginia	Commercial venture	1607	Captain John Smith	Tobacco	64,560
New Amsterdam (New York)	Commercial venture	1613 (made English colony, 1664)	Peter Stuyvesant, Duke of York	Furs, grain	19,107
Plymouth	Refuge for English Separatists	1620 (absorbed by Massachusetts, 1691)	William Bradford	Grain	Included with Massachusetts
New Hampshire	Commercial venture	1623	John Mason	Wood, naval stores	4,958
Massachusetts	Refuge for English Puritans	1628	John Winthrop	Grain, wood	55,941
Maryland	Refuge for English Catholics	1634	Lord Baltimore (George Calvert)	Tobacco	34,100
Connecticut	Expansion of Massachusetts	1635	Thomas Hooker	Grain	25,970
Rhode Island	Refuge for dissenters from Massachusetts	1636	Roger Williams	Grain	5,894
New Sweden (Delaware)	Commercial venture	1638 (included in Penn grant, 1681; given separate assembly, 1703)	Peter Minuit, William Penn	Grain	2,470
North Carolina	Commercial venture	1663	Anthony Ashley Cooper	Wood, naval stores, tobacco	10,720
South Carolina	Commercial venture	1663	Anthony Ashley Cooper	Naval stores, rice, indigo	5,720
New Jersey	Consolidation of new English territory, Quaker settlement	1664	Sir George Carteret	Grain	14,010
Pennsylvania	Refuge for English Quakers	1681	William Penn	Grain	18,950
Georgia	Discourage Spanish expansion; charity	1733	James Oglethorpe	Rice, wood, naval stores	5,200 (in 1750)

Sources: U.S. Bureau of the Census, *Historical Statistics of the United States: Colonial Times to 1970*, Washington, D.C., 1975; John J. McCusker and Russell R. Menard, *The Economy of British America, 1607–1789*, Chapel Hill, 1985.

During the first years of colonization, Georgia fared no better than had earlier utopian experiments. The poor people of England showed little desire to move to an inclement frontier, and the trustees, in their turn, provided little incentive for emigration. Each colonist received only 50 acres. Another 50 acres could be added for each servant transported to Georgia, but in no case could a settler amass more than 500 acres. Moreover, land could be passed only to an eldest son, and if a planter had no sons at the time of his death, the holding reverted to the trustees. Slavery was prohibited. So too was rum.

Almost as soon as they arrived in Georgia, the settlers complained. The colonists demanded slaves, pointing out to the trustees that unless the new planters possessed an unfree labor force, they could not compete economically with their South Carolina neighbors. The settlers also wanted a voice in local government. In 1738, 121 people living in Savannah petitioned for fundamental reforms in the colony's constitution. Oglethorpe responded angrily, "The idle ones are indeed for Negroes. If the petition is countenanced, the province is ruined." The settlers did not give up. In 1741, they again petitioned Oglethorpe, this time addressing him as "our Perpetual Dictator."

While the colonists grumbled about various restrictions, Oglethorpe tried and failed to capture the Spanish fortress at Saint Augustine (1740). This personal disappointment coupled with the growing popular unrest destroyed his interest in Georgia. The trustees were forced to compromise their principles. In 1738, they eliminated all restrictions on the amount of land a man could own; they allowed women to inherit land. In 1750, they permitted the settlers to import slaves. Soon Georgians could drink rum. In 1751, the trustees returned Georgia to the king, undoubtedly relieved to be free of what had become a hard-drinking, slave-owning plantation society much like that in South Carolina. The king authorized an assembly in 1751, but even with these social and political changes, Georgia attracted very few new settlers.

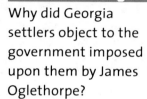

QUICK CHECK

Why did Georgia settlers object to the government imposed upon them by James Oglethorpe?

Conclusion: Living with Diversity

Long after he had returned from his adventures in Virginia, Captain John Smith reflected on the difficulty of establishing colonies in the New World. It was a task for which most people were not temperamentally suited. "It requires," Smith counseled, "all the best parts of art, judgment, courage, honesty, constancy, diligence, and industry, [even] to do neere well." On another occasion, Charles I warned Lord Baltimore that new settlements "commonly have rugged and laborious beginnings."

Over the course of the seventeenth century, women and men had followed leaders such as Baltimore, Smith, Winthrop, Bradford, Penn, and Berkeley to the New World in anticipation of creating a successful new society. Some people were religious visionaries; others were hardheaded businessmen. The results of their efforts, their struggles to survive in an often hostile environment, and their interactions with various Native American groups yielded a spectrum of settlements along the Atlantic coast, ranging from the quasi-feudalism of South Carolina to the Puritan commonwealth of Massachusetts Bay.

The diversity of early English colonization must be emphasized precisely because it is so easy to overlook. Even though the colonists eventually banded together and fought for independence, persistent differences separated New Englanders from Virginians, Pennsylvanians from Carolinians. The interpretive challenge, of course, is to comprehend how European colonists managed over the course of the eighteenth century to overcome fragmentation and to develop the capacity to imagine themselves a nation.

For a list of additional titles related to this chapter's topics, please see www.pearsonamericanhistory.com.

MyHistoryLab

STUDY RESOURCES

KEY TERMS

joint-stock company
House of Burgesses
headright

indentured servants
Mayflower Compact
Puritans

Great Migration
Antinomianism
Quakers

CHAPTER REVIEW

WHY did the Chesapeake colonies not prosper during the earliest years of settlement?

In 1607, the Virginia Company established Jamestown as a profit-making venture. Early settlers relied on tobacco as a profitable cash crop. Sir George Calvert founded Maryland in 1634 as a sanctuary for Catholics. Both colonies depended on the labor of indentured servants, predominately single young men. Disease, oppression, and warfare contributed to social instability.

WHAT role did differences in religion play in the founding of the New England colonies?

Religious persecution drove thousands of Puritans to New England. John Winthrop hoped the settlers would reform English Protestantism and create a "City on a Hill." The Puritans did not welcome dissent. They exiled Roger Williams and Anne Hutchinson to Rhode Island for their religious beliefs. Stable nuclear families and good health helped Puritans to avoid the social turmoil that plagued the Chesapeake colonies.

HOW did ethnic diversity shape the development of the Middle Colonies?

After having conquered the Dutch colony of New Netherland in 1664, the English renamed it New York. Despite the conquest, the Dutch remained an influential minority in the colony, and ethnic rivalries shaped the politics of New York for many decades. In 1681, Charles II granted William Penn, a Quaker, a charter for the establishment of Pennsylvania. Penn's guarantee to respect all Christian settlers' liberty of conscience drew immigrants from all across Northern Europe.

HOW would you contrast the founding of the Carolinas with the founding of Georgia?

Immigrants from Barbados began settling in the Carolinas in the 1670s. Barbadian immigrants to the Carolinas, many of whom were wealthy planters seeking new lands for plantations, brought slavery with them when they moved. Georgia was founded in 1732 as an alternative to debtors' prison for impoverished Englishmen and as a military outpost to guard against the Spanish in Florida.

MAKING CONNECTIONS

1. Would the first Chesapeake colonies have survived if the settlers had not discovered tobacco as a profitable cash crop?

2. Would the historical development of New England have been different if the Puritans had developed a profitable cash crop like tobacco or rice?

3. How did William Penn's leadership style compare to those of John Winthrop and Captain John Smith?

4. How were the European migrants who were attracted to Georgia and the Carolinas different from the migrants from the Chesapeake and Middle Colonies?

PRACTICE QUIZ

1. The _____ financed part of English colonization of the New World.
   a. Catholic company
   b. joint-stock company
   c. Elizabeth company
   d. Settlement company

2. _____ reasons explain why the English settled the Chesapeake colonies.
   a. Religious   b. Economic
   c. Social   d. Peaceful

3. Captain _____ saved the Virginia colony when he took control in 1608.
   a. Cortez   b. Pocahontas
   c. John Smith   d. Powhatan

4. _____ rapidly became the main export product of the early Virginia colony.
   a. Corn   b. Rice
   c. Sugar   d. Tobacco

5. Poor _____ received promises of land by their masters after receiving freedom in the Chesapeake.
   a. Indians   b. African American slaves
   c. women   d. indentured servants

6. The Puritans left England for the New World to _____.
   a. improve their financial earning power
   b. assimilate with Indians
   c. secure religious freedom from persecution
   d. engage in diplomatic negotiations with Indian tribes

7. Which of the following people posed a threat to the Massachusetts Bay colony?
   a. Anne Hutchinson
   b. John Winthrop
   c. James Oglethorpe
   d. Elizabeth I

8. All of the following accurately describe the Quakers *except*
   a. They practiced humility in their daily lives.
   b. Most Quakers lived in the southern colonies of British North America.
   c. They wore simple clothes and used traditional forms of address.
   d. They became pacifists.

9. Which of the following statements *does not* describe New Amsterdam?
   a. It was a large Dutch colony located in Florida.
   b. It began as a fur trading colony.
   c. Salaried employees settled the colony.
   d. The colony exhibited ethnic diversity.

10. Which of the following statements *does not* characterize the colony of Georgia?
   a. It evolved much differently than Britain's other mainland colonies.
   b. It began as an act of aggression against Spain.
   c. James Oglethorpe, a British general, put the colony together.
   d. Large numbers of English elites immediately settled the colony.

QUIZ

Find more practice at www.myhistorylab.com

SAMPLE ESSAY QUESTIONS

1. Contrast the economic, social, and political differences between the New England colonies and the Middle colonies.

2. Trace how the Chesapeake colonies developed over time.

CREDITS

Putting Down Roots:
Opportunity and Oppression in Colonial Society, 1619–1692

Putting Down Roots
Opportunity and Oppression in Colonial Society, 1619–1692

SPOTLIGHT QUESTIONS

WHAT conditions explain the remarkable social stability achieved in early New England?

WHAT factors contributed to political unrest in the Chesapeake region during this period?

HOW did African American slaves preserve an independent cultural identity in the New World?

WHY did England discourage free and open trade in colonial America?

HOW did colonial revolts affect the political culture of Virginia and New England?

THE MASON CHILDREN David, Joanna, and Abigail, *c.* 1670, an early portrait of three children from a wealthy Massachusetts Bay Colony family. (*Source: The Freake-Gibbs Painter, American. The Mason Children: Davis, Joanna and Abigail, 1670. Oil on canvas, 39-1/2" × 42-11/16". The Fine Arts Museum of San Francisco, San Francisco, CA. Gift of Mr. and Mrs. John D. Rockefeller, III.*)

Why do you think these young people dressed as adults rather than as children?

Families in an Atlantic Empire

The Witherspoon family moved from Great Britain to the South Carolina backcountry early in the eighteenth century. Although otherwise indistinguishable from the thousands of other ordinary families that put down roots in English America, the Witherspoons were made historical figures by the candid account of pioneer life produced by their son, Robert, who was only a small child at the time of their arrival.

The Witherspoons' initial reaction to the New World—at least, that of the mother and children—was utter despondence. "My mother

KEY EVENTS

1619 First blacks arrive in Virginia

1660 Charles II is restored to the English throne ∎ First Navigation Act passed by Parliament

1663 Second Navigation (Staple) Act passed

1673 Plantation duty imposed to close loopholes in commercial regulations

1675 King Philip's (Metacomet's) War devastates New England

1676 Bacon's Rebellion threatens Governor ∎ Berkeley's government in Virginia

1684 Charter of the Massachusetts Bay Company revoked

1686 Dominion of New England established

1688 James II driven into exile during Glorious Revolution

1689 Rebellion breaks out in Massachusetts

1692 Salem Village wracked by witch trials

1696 Parliament establishes Board of Trade

1739 Stono Uprising of South Carolina slaves terrifies white planters

and us children were still in expectation that we were coming to an agreeable place," Robert confessed, "but when we arrived and saw nothing but a wilderness and instead of a fine timbered house, nothing but a very mean dirt house, our spirits quite sunk." For many years, the Witherspoons feared they would be killed by Indians, become lost in the woods, or be bitten by snakes.

The Witherspoons managed to survive the early difficult years on the Black River. To be sure, the Carolina backcountry did not look very much like the world they had left behind. The difference, however, apparently did not greatly discourage Robert's father. He had a vision of what the Black River settlement might become. "My father," Robert recounted, "gave us all the comfort he [could] by telling us we would get all these trees cut down and in a short time [there] would be plenty of inhabitants, [and] that we could see from house to house."

Robert Witherspoon's account reminds us just how much the early history of colonial America was an intimate story of families, and not, as some commentators would have us believe, of individuals. Neither the peopling of the Atlantic frontier, the cutting down of the forests, nor the creation of new communities where one could see from "house to house" was a process that involved what we would today recognize as state policy. Men and women made significant decisions about the character of their lives within families. It was within this primary social unit that most colonists earned their livelihoods, educated their children, defined gender, sustained religious tradition, and nursed each other in sickness. In short, the family was the source of their societal and cultural identities.

Early colonial families did not exist in isolation. They were part of larger societies. The character of the first English settlements in the New World varied substantially. During much of the seventeenth century, these initial differences grew stronger as each region responded to different environmental conditions and developed its own traditions. The various local societies in which families like the Witherspoons put down roots reflected several critical elements: supply of labor, abundance of land, unusual demographic patterns, and commercial ties with European markets. In the Chesapeake, for example, an economy based almost entirely on a single staple—tobacco—created an insatiable demand for indentured servants and black slaves. In Massachusetts Bay, the extraordinary longevity of the founders generated a level of social and political stability that Virginians and Marylanders did not attain until the very end of the seventeenth century.

By 1660, it seemed regional differences had undermined the idea of a unified English empire in America. During the reign of Charles II, however, a trend toward cultural convergence began. Although subcultures had evolved in strikingly different directions, countervailing forces such as common language and religion gradually pulled English American settlers together. Parliament took advantage of this trend and began to establish a uniform set of rules for the expanding American empire. The process was slow and uneven, often sparking violent colonial resistance. By the end of the seventeenth century, however, England had made significant progress toward transforming New World provinces into an empire that produced needed raw materials and purchased manufactured goods. If a person was black and enslaved, however, he or she was more apt to experience oppression rather than opportunity in British America.

Social Stability: New England Colonies of the Seventeenth Century

Seventeenth-century New Englanders successfully replicated in America a traditional social order they had known in England. The transfer of a familiar way of life to the New World seemed less difficult for these Puritan migrants than it did for the many English men and women who settled in the Chesapeake colonies. Their contrasting experiences, fundamental to an understanding of the development of both cultures, can be explained, at least in part, by the extraordinary strength and resilience of New England families.

WHAT conditions explain the remarkable social stability achieved in early New England?

Immigrant Families and New Social Order

Early New Englanders believed God ordained the family for human benefit. It was essential to the maintenance of social order, since outside the family, men and women succumbed to carnal temptation. Such people had no one to sustain them or remind them of Scripture. "Without Family care," declared the Reverend Benjamin Wadsworth, "the labour of Magistrates and Ministers for Reformation and Propagating Religion, is likely to be in great measure unsuccessful."

The godly family, at least in theory, was ruled by a patriarch, father to his children, husband to his wife, the source of authority and object of unquestioned obedience. The wife shared responsibility for the raising of children, but in decisions of importance, especially those related to property, she was expected to defer to her spouse.

The New Englanders' concern about the character of the godly family is not surprising. This institution played a central role in shaping their society. In contrast to those who migrated to the colonies of Virginia and Maryland, New Englanders crossed the Atlantic within nuclear families. That is, they moved within established units consisting of a father, mother, and their dependent children rather than as single youths and adults. People who migrated to America within families preserved local English customs more fully than did the youths who traveled to other parts of the continent as single men and women. The comforting presence of immediate family members reduced the shock of adjusting to a strange environment three thousand miles from home. Even in the 1630s, the ratio of men to women in New England was fairly well balanced, about three males for every two females. Persons who had not already married in England before coming to the New World could expect to form nuclear families of their own.

Early New England marriage patterns did not differ substantially from those recorded in seventeenth-century England. The average age for men at first marriage was the mid-twenties. Wives were slightly younger than their husbands, the average age being about 22. There is no evidence that New Englanders favored child brides. Nor, for that matter, were Puritan families unusually large by European standards of the period.

The explanation for the region's impressive growth turned out to be survival rather than fertility. Put simply, people who, under normal conditions, would have died in contemporary Europe lived in New England. Indeed, the life expectancy of seventeenth-century settlers was not very different from our own. Males who survived infancy might have expected to see their seventieth birthday. Twenty percent of the men of the first generation reached the age of eighty. The figures for women were only slightly lower. Why the early settlers lived so long is not entirely clear. No doubt, pure drinking water, a cool climate that retarded the spread of fatal contagious disease, and a dispersed population promoted general good health.

Longer life altered family relations. New England males lived not only to see their own children reach adulthood but also to witness the birth of grandchildren. This may have been one of the first societies in recorded history in which a person could reasonably anticipate knowing his or her grandchildren, a demographic surprise that contributed to social stability. The traditions of particular families and communities literally remained alive in the memories of the colony's oldest citizens.

QUICK CHECK ✓

How did families contribute to social order in seventeenth-century New England?

Puritan Women in New England

New England relied heavily on the work of women. They did not, however, necessarily do the same jobs that men performed. Women usually handled separate tasks, including cooking, washing, clothes making, dairying, and gardening. Their production of food was absolutely essential to the survival of most households. Sometimes wives—and the overwhelming majority of adult seventeenth-century women were married—raised poultry, and by selling surplus birds they achieved some economic independence. When people in one New England community chided a man for allowing his wife to peddle her fowl, he responded, "I meddle not with the geese nor turkeys for they are hers." In fact, during this period women were often described as "deputy husbands," a label that drew attention to their dependence on family patriarchs as well as to their roles as decision makers.

Women also joined churches in greater number than men. Within a few years of founding, many New England congregations contained two female members for every male, a process historians describe as the "feminization of colonial religion." Contemporaries offered different explanations for the gender shift. Cotton Mather, the leading Congregational minister of Massachusetts Bay, argued that God had created "far more *godly Women*" than men. Others thought that the life-threatening experience of childbirth gave women a deeper appreciation of religion.

In political and legal matters, society sharply curtailed the rights of colonial women. According to English common law, a wife exercised no control over property. She could not, for example, sell land, although if her husband decided to dispose of

Prenuptial Agreement (1653)

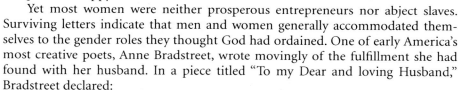

THE NEW ENGLAND PRIMER The primer shown here not only taught Puritan children basic reading and writing skills, but also reinforced religious values.

Why did the schools not leave religious instruction to families and churches?

their holdings, he was free to do so without her permission. Divorce was extremely difficult to obtain in any colony before the American Revolution. Indeed, a person married to a cruel or irresponsible spouse had little recourse but to run away or accept the unhappy situation.

Yet most women were neither prosperous entrepreneurs nor abject slaves. Surviving letters indicate that men and women generally accommodated themselves to the gender roles they thought God had ordained. One of early America's most creative poets, Anne Bradstreet, wrote movingly of the fulfillment she had found with her husband. In a piece titled "To my Dear and loving Husband," Bradstreet declared:

> If ever two were one, then surely we.
> If ever man were lov'd by wife, then thee;
> If ever wife was happy in a man,
> Compare with me ye woman if you can.

Although Puritan couples worried that the affection they felt for a husband or a wife might turn their thoughts away from God's perfect love, this was a danger they were willing to risk.

DOCUMENT

Anne Bradstreet, "Before the Birth of One of Her Children"

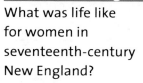

QUICK CHECK ✓

What was life like for women in seventeenth-century New England?

Establishing a New Social Order

During the seventeenth century, New England colonists gradually sorted themselves out into distinct social groupings. Persons who would never have been "natural rulers" in England became provincial gentry in the various northern colonies. It helped, of course, if an individual possessed wealth and education, but these attributes alone could not guarantee a newcomer would be accepted into the local ruling elite, at least not during the early decades of settlement. In Massachusetts and Connecticut, Puritan voters expected their leaders to join Congregational churches and defend orthodox religion.

While most New Englanders accepted a hierarchical view of society, they disagreed over their assigned places. Both Massachusetts Bay and Connecticut passed sumptuary laws—statutes that limited the wearing of fine apparel to the wealthy and prominent—to curb the pretensions of those of lower status. Yet such restraints could not prevent some people from rising and others from falling within the social order.

yeomen
Independent farmers.

Most northern colonists were **yeomen** (independent farmers) who worked their own land. While few became rich in America, even fewer fell hopelessly into debt. Their daily lives, especially for those who settled New England, centered on scattered little communities where they participated in village meetings, church-related matters, and militia training. Possession of land gave agrarian families a sense of independence from external authority. As one man bragged to those who had stayed behind in England, "Here are no hard landlords to rack us with high rents or extorting fines.... Here every man may be master of his own labour and land... and if he have nothing but his hands he may set up his trade, and by industry grow rich."

It was not unusual for northern colonists to work as servants at some point in their lives. This system of labor differed greatly from the pattern of servitude that developed in seventeenth-century Virginia and Maryland. New Englanders seldom recruited servants from the Old World. The forms of agriculture practiced in this region, mixed cereal and dairy farming, made employment of large gangs of dependent workers uneconomic. Rather, New England families placed their adolescent children in nearby homes. These young persons contracted for four or five years and seemed more like apprentices than servants. Servitude was not simply a means by which one group exploited another. It was a form of vocational training program in which the children of the rich as well as the poor participated.

By the end of the seventeenth century, the New England Puritans had developed a compelling story about their own history in the New World. The founders had been extraordinarily godly men and women, and in a heroic effort to establish a purer form of religion, pious families had passed "over the vast ocean into this vast and howling wilderness." Although the children and grandchildren of the first generation sometimes questioned their own ability to please the Lord, they recognized the mission to the New World had been a success: They were "as Prosperous as ever, there is Peace & Plenty, & the Country flourisheth."

QUICK CHECK ✔
What counted more in determining social status in early New England—piety or wealth?

The Challenge of the Chesapeake Environment

WHAT?
factors contributed to political unrest in the Chesapeake region during this period?

An entirely different regional society developed in England's Chesapeake colonies, Virginia and Maryland. This contrast with New England seems puzzling. After all, the two areas were founded at roughly the same time by men and women from the same mother country. In both regions, settlers spoke English, accepted Protestantism, and gave allegiance to one crown. And yet, to cite an obvious example, seventeenth-century Virginia looked nothing like Massachusetts Bay. In an effort to explain the difference, colonial historians have studied environmental conditions, labor systems, and agrarian economies. The most important reason for the distinctiveness of these early southern plantation societies, however, turned out to be the Chesapeake's death rate, a frighteningly high mortality that tore at the very fabric of traditional family life.

Families at Risk

Unlike New England's settlers, the men and women who emigrated to the Chesapeake region did not move in family units. They traveled to the New World as young unmarried servants, youths cut off from the security of traditional kin relations. Although these immigrants came from a cross section of English society, most had been poor to middling farmers. It is now estimated that 70 to 85 percent of the white colonists who went to Virginia and Maryland during the seventeenth century were not free; that is, they owed four or five years' labor in exchange for the cost of passage to America. If the servant was under age 15, he or she had to serve a full seven years. The overwhelming majority of these laborers were males between the ages of 18 and 22. In fact, before 1640, the ratio of males to females stood at 6 to 1. This figure dropped to about $2^1/_2$ to 1 by the end of the century, but the sex ratio in the Chesapeake was never as favorable as it had been in early Massachusetts.

Most immigrants to the Chesapeake region died soon after arriving. It is difficult to ascertain the exact cause of death in most cases, but malaria and other diseases took a frightful toll. Life expectancy for Chesapeake males was about 43, some ten to twenty years less than for men born in New England! For women, life was even shorter. A full 25 percent of all children died in infancy; another 25 percent did not see their twentieth birthdays. The survivors were often weak or ill, unable to perform hard physical labor.

Because of the unbalanced sex ratio, many adult males simply could not find wives. Migration not only cut them off from their English families but also deprived them of an opportunity to form new ones. Without a constant flow of immigrants, the population of Virginia and Maryland would have actually declined.

High mortality compressed the family life cycle into a few short years. One partner in a marriage usually died within seven years. Only one in three Chesapeake marriages survived as long as a decade. Not only did children not meet grandparents—they often did not even know their own parents. Widows and widowers quickly remarried, bringing children by former unions into their new homes, and it was not uncommon for a child to grow up with persons to whom he or she bore no blood relation.

Women were obviously in great demand in the early southern colonies. Some historians have argued that scarcity heightened the woman's bargaining power in the marriage market. If she was an immigrant, she did not have to worry about obtaining parental consent. She was on her own in the New World and free to select whomever she pleased. If a woman lacked beauty or strength, if she were a person of low moral standards, she could still be confident of finding an American husband. Such negotiations may have provided Chesapeake women with a means of improving their social status.

Nevertheless, liberation from some traditional restraints on seventeenth-century women must not be exaggerated. As servants, women were vulnerable to sexual exploitation by their masters. Moreover, in this unhealthy environment, childbearing was extremely dangerous, and women in the Chesapeake usually died twenty years earlier than their New England counterparts.

QUICK CHECK ✓

How did the high mortality rates in the early Chesapeake colonies affect economic and family life?

The Structure of Planter Society

Colonists who managed somehow to survive grew tobacco—as much tobacco as they possibly could. This crop became the Chesapeake staple, and since it was relatively easy to cultivate, anyone with a few acres of cleared land could harvest leaves for export. Cultivation of tobacco did not, however, produce a society roughly equal in wealth and status. To the contrary, tobacco generated inequality. Some planters amassed large fortunes; others barely subsisted. Labor made the difference, for to succeed in this staple economy, one had to control the labor of other men and women. More workers in the fields meant larger harvests, and, of course, larger profits. Since free persons showed no interest in growing another man's tobacco, not even for wages, wealthy planters relied on white laborers who were not free, as well as on slaves. The social structure that developed in the seventeenth-century Chesapeake reflected a wild, often unscrupulous scramble to bring men and women of three races—black, white, and Indian—into various degrees of dependence.

Great planters dominated Chesapeake society. The group was small, only a trifling portion of the population of Virginia and Maryland. During the early decades of the seventeenth century, the composition of Chesapeake gentry was continually in flux. Some gentlemen died before they could establish a secure claim to high social status; others returned to England, thankful to have survived. Not until the 1650s did the family names of those who would become famous eighteenth-century gentry appear in the records. The first gentlemen were not—as genealogists sometimes discover to their dismay—dashing cavaliers who had fought in the English Civil War for King Charles I. Rather, such Chesapeake gentry as the Burwells, Byrds, Carters, and Masons consisted originally of the younger sons of English merchants and artisans.

Freemen formed the largest class in Chesapeake society. Their origins were strikingly different from those of the gentry, or for that matter, from those of New England's yeomen farmers. Chesapeake freemen traveled to the New World as **indentured servants,** signing contracts in which they sold their labor for a set number of years in exchange for passage from Europe. If they had dreamed of becoming great planters, they were gravely disappointed. Most seventeenth-century freemen lived on the edge of poverty. Some freemen, of course, did better in America than they would have in contemporary England, but in both Virginia and Maryland, historians have found a sharp economic division separating the gentry from the rest of white society.

Below the freemen came indentured servants. Membership in this group was not demeaning; after all, servitude was a temporary status. But servitude in the Chesapeake colonies was not the benign institution it was in New England. Great planters purchased servants to grow tobacco. No one seemed overly concerned whether these laborers received decent food and clothes, much less whether they acquired trade skills. Young people, thousands of them, cut off from family ties, sick often to the point of death, unable to obtain normal sexual release, regarded their servitude as a form of slavery. Not surprisingly, the gentry worried that unhappy servants and impoverished freemen, what the planters called the "giddy multitude," would rebel at the slightest provocation, a fear that turned out to be fully justified.

The character of social mobility—and this observation applies only to whites—changed considerably during the seventeenth century. Until the 1680s, it was relatively easy for a newcomer who possessed capital to become a member of the planter elite. No one paid much attention to the reputation or social standing of one's English family.

Sometime after the 1680s, however—the precise date is impossible to establish— a dramatic demographic shift occurred. Although infant mortality remained high, life expectancy rates for those who survived childhood in the Chesapeake improved

indentured servants
Freemen who signed contracts in which they sold their labor for a set number of years in exchange for passage from Europe.

Goltlieb Mittelberger, "The Passage of Indentured Servants"

HENRY DARNALL III AS A CHILD   This painting (*ca.* 1710) by the German émigré painter Justus Engelhardt Kuhn depicts the son of a wealthy planter family in Maryland armed with a bow and arrow.

Why would the painter place the planter's son within an idealized European landscape rather than in a Chesapeake scene?

significantly, and for the first time in the history of Virginia and Maryland, important leadership positions went to men who had actually been born in America. This transition has been described by one political historian as the "emergence of a creole majority," in other words, as the rise of an indigenous ruling elite. Before this time, immigrant leaders had died without heirs or had returned as quickly as possible to England. The members of the new creole class took a greater interest in local government. Their activities helped give the tobacco colonies the kind of political and cultural stability that had eluded earlier generations of planter adventurers.

The key to success in this creole society was ownership of slaves. Those planters who held more blacks could grow more tobacco and thus could acquire fresh capital needed to purchase additional laborers. Over time, the rich not only became richer; they also formed a distinct ruling elite that newcomers found increasingly difficult to enter.

Opportunities for advancement also decreased for freemen in the region. Studies of mid-seventeenth-century Maryland reveal that some servants managed to become moderately prosperous farmers and small officeholders. But as the gentry consolidated its hold on political and economic institutions, ordinary people discovered it was much harder to rise in Chesapeake society. Those men and women with more ambitious dreams headed for Pennsylvania, North Carolina, or western Virginia.

Social institutions that figured importantly in the daily experience of New Englanders were either weak or nonexistent in the Chesapeake colonies. In part, the sluggish development resulted from the continuation of high infant mortality rates. There was little incentive to build elementary schools, for example, if half the children would die before reaching adulthood. The great planters sent their sons to England or Scotland for their education, and even after the founding of the College of William and Mary in Virginia, the gentry continued to patronize English schools. As a result of this practice, higher education in the South languished for much of the colonial period.

Tobacco influenced the spread of other institutions in the region. Planters were scattered along the rivers, often separated from their nearest neighbors by miles of poor roads. Since the major tobacco growers traded directly with English merchants, they had no need for towns.

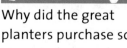

QUICK CHECK

Why did the great planters purchase so many indentured servants during this period?

Race and Freedom in British America

HOW
?

did African American slaves preserve an independent cultural identity in the New World?

Many people who landed in the colonies had no desire to come to the New World. They were Africans taken as slaves to cultivate rice, sugar, and tobacco. As the Native Americans were exterminated and the supply of white indentured servants dried up, European planters demanded ever more African laborers.

Roots of Slavery

A great deal is known about the transfer of African peoples across the Atlantic. During the entire history of this human commerce, between the sixteenth and nineteenth centuries, slave traders carried almost eleven million blacks to the Americas. Most of these men and women were sold in Brazil or in the Caribbean. A relatively small number of Africans reached British North America, and of this group, the majority arrived after 1700. Because slaves performed hard physical labor, planters preferred purchasing young males. In many early slave communities, men outnumbered women by a ratio of two to one.

English colonists did not hesitate to enslave black people or, for that matter, Native Americans. While the institution of slavery had long before died out in the mother country, New World settlers quickly discovered how well this particular labor system operated in the Spanish and Portuguese colonies. The decision to bring African slaves to the colonies, therefore, was based primarily on economic considerations.

English masters, however, seldom justified the practice purely in terms of planter profits. Indeed, they adopted a quite different pattern of rhetoric. English writers associated blacks in Africa with heathen religion, barbarous behavior, sexual promiscuity—in fact, with evil itself. From such a racist perspective, the

VIRGINIAN LUXURIES Undated, unsigned, and hidden on the back of another painting, the two-part painting *Virginian Luxuries* depicts a white man kissing a black woman and whipping a black man.

How did gender figure in the brutality of slavery?

enslavement of Africans seemed unobjectionable. The planters maintained that if black slaves converted to Christianity, shedding their supposedly savage ways, they would benefit from their loss of freedom.

Africans first landed in Virginia in 1619 as a cargo of slaves stolen by a Dutch trader from a Spanish merchant ship in the Caribbean. For the next fifty years, the status of the colony's black people remained unclear. English settlers classified some black laborers as slaves for life, as chattel to be bought and sold at the master's will. But other Africans became servants, presumably for stated periods of time, and it was even possible for a few blacks to purchase their freedom. Several seventeenth-century Africans became successful Virginia planters.

One reason Virginia lawmakers tolerated such confusion was that the black population remained very small. By 1660, fewer than fifteen hundred people of African origin lived in the entire colony (compared to a white population of approximately twenty-six thousand), and it hardly seemed necessary for the legislature to draw up an elaborate slave code to control so few men and women. If the planters could have obtained more black laborers, they certainly would have done so. There is no evidence that the great planters preferred white indentured servants to black slaves. The problem was supply. During this period, slave

The Atlantic Slave Trade

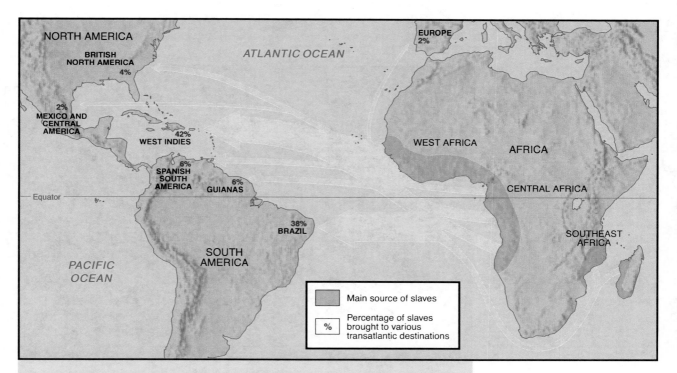

ORIGINS AND DESTINATIONS OF AFRICAN SLAVES, 1619–1760 Although many African slaves were carried to Britain's North American colonies, far more slaves were sold in the Caribbean sugar colonies and Brazil, where because of horrific health conditions, the death rate far exceeded that of the British mainland colonies.

Why do you think that far more African slaves were transported to Brazil and the Caribbean than to British North America?

traders sold their cargoes on Barbados or the other sugar islands of the West Indies, where they fetched higher prices than Virginians could afford. In fact, before 1680, most blacks who reached England's colonies on the North American mainland came from Barbados or through New Netherland rather than directly from Africa.

By the end of the seventeenth century, the legal status of Virginia's black people was no longer in doubt. They were slaves for life, and so were their children after them. This transformation reflected changes in the supply of Africans to British North America. After 1672, the **Royal African Company** was chartered to meet the colonial planters' demands for black laborers. Historian K. G. Davies terms this organization "the strongest and most effective of all European companies formed exclusively for the African trade." Between 1695 and 1709, more than eleven thousand Africans were sold in Virginia alone; many others went to Maryland and the Carolinas. Although American merchants—most of them based in Rhode Island—entered the trade during the eighteenth century, the British continued to supply the bulk of the slaves to the mainland market for the entire colonial period.

The expanding black population apparently frightened white colonists, for as the number of Africans increased, lawmakers drew up ever stricter slave codes. It was during this period that racism, always a latent element in New World societies, was fully revealed. By 1700, slavery was unequivocally based on

Royal African Company
Slaving company created to meet colonial planters' demands for black laborers.

ABOARD A SLAVE SHIP   This watercolor, *Slave Deck of the Albanoz* (1846), by naval officer Lieutenant Godfrey Meynell, shows slaves packed with cargo in the hold of a ship after being taken captive in West Africa.

If African slaves were such a valuable commodity in the New World, why did ship captains crowd so many slaves onto unhealthy vessels?

the color of a person's skin. Blacks fell into this status simply because they were black. A vicious pattern of discrimination had been set in motion. Even conversion to Christianity did not free the African from bondage. The white planter could deal with his black property as he alone saw fit, and one revolting Virginia statute excused masters who killed slaves, on the grounds that no rational person would purposely "destroy his own estate." Black women constantly had to fear sexual violation by a master or his sons. Children born to a slave woman became slaves regardless of the father's race. Unlike the Spanish colonies, where persons of lighter color enjoyed greater privileges in society, the English colonies tolerated no mixing of the races. Mulattoes and pure Africans received the same treatment.

QUICK CHECK ✔

Why did the slave population in British North America remain relatively small for most of the seventeenth century?

Constructing African American Identities

The slave experience varied substantially from colony to colony. The daily life of a black person in South Carolina, for example, was quite different from that of an African American who happened to live in Pennsylvania or Massachusetts Bay. The size and density of the slave population determined in large measure how successfully blacks could maintain a separate cultural identity. In the lowlands of South Carolina during the eighteenth century, 60 percent of the population was black. The men and women were placed on large, isolated rice plantations, and their contact with whites was limited. In these areas blacks developed creole languages, which mixed the basic vocabulary of English with words borrowed from various African tongues. Until the end of the nineteenth century, one creole language, Gullah, was spoken on some of the Sea Islands along the Georgia–South Carolina coast. Slaves on the large rice plantations also were able to establish elaborate and enduring kinship networks that may have helped reduce the more dehumanizing aspects of bondage.

In the New England and Middle Colonies, and even in Virginia, African Americans made up a smaller

SLAVE AUCTIONS This public notice announces a slave auction to be held at the Charles Town wharf (1769).

Why did the planters of South Carolina purchase so many Africans when they might have purchased white indentured servants?

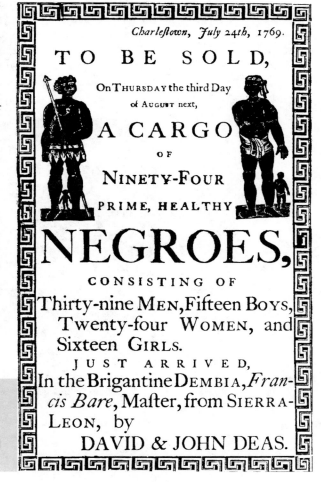

Charleſtown, July 24th, 1769.

TO BE SOLD,

On THURSDAY the third Day of AUGUST next,

A CARGO

OF

NINETY-FOUR

PRIME, HEALTHY

NEGROES,

CONSISTING OF

Thirty-nine MEN, Fifteen BOYS, Twenty-four WOMEN, and Sixteen GIRLS.

JUST ARRIVED,

In the Brigantine DEMBIA, *Francis Bare*, Maſter, from SIERRA-LEON, by

DAVID & JOHN DEAS.

percentage of the population: 40 percent in Virginia, 8 percent in Pennsylvania, and 3 percent in Massachusetts. In such environments, contact between blacks and whites was more frequent than in South Carolina and Georgia. These population patterns had a profound effect on northern and Chesapeake blacks, for while they escaped the physical drudgery of rice cultivation, they found the preservation of an independent African identity difficult. In northern cities, slaves working as domestics and living in the houses of their masters saw other blacks but had little opportunity to develop creole languages or reaffirm a common African past.

James Oglethorpe, The Stono Rebellion (1739)

The process of establishing African American traditions involved an imaginative reshaping of African and European customs into something that was neither African nor European. It was African American. The slaves accepted Christianity, but they did so on their own terms—terms their masters seldom fully understood. Blacks transformed Christianity into an expression of religious feeling in which an African element remained vibrant. In music and folk art, they gave voice to a cultural identity that even the most degrading conditions could not eradicate.

A major turning point in the history of African American people occurred during the early decades of the eighteenth century. At this time, blacks living in England's mainland colonies began to reproduce successfully. The number of live births exceeded deaths, and from that date, the expansion of the African American population owed more to natural increase than to the importation of new slaves. Even though thousands of new Africans arrived each year, the creole population was always much larger than that of the immigrant blacks. This demographic shift did not take place in the Caribbean or South American colonies until a

WEDDING IN THE SLAVE QUARTERS *Old Plantation,* a watercolor by an unknown artist (about 1800), shows that African wedding customs survived plantation slavery.

Can you see other things in this painting that reveal a distinctive African American identity?

much later date. Historians believe that North American blacks enjoyed a healthier climate and better diet than did other New World slaves.

Although mainland blacks lived longer than the blacks of Jamaica or Barbados, they were, after all, still slaves. They protested their debasement in many ways, some in individual acts of violence, others in organized revolt. The most serious slave rebellion of the colonial period was the Stono Uprising, which took place in September 1739. One hundred fifty South Carolina blacks rose up and, seizing guns and ammunition, murdered several white planters. "With Colours displayed, and two Drums beating," they marched toward Spanish Florida, where they had been promised freedom. The local militia soon overtook the rebellious slaves and killed most of them. Although the uprising was short-lived, such incidents helped persuade whites everywhere that their own blacks might secretly be planning bloody revolt.

QUICK CHECK ✔

How did African American slaves preserve cultural practices associated with West African societies?

Blueprint for Empire

Until the middle of the seventeenth century, English political leaders largely ignored the American colonists. Private companies and aristocratic proprietors had created these societies, some for profit, others for religious sanctuary, but in no case did the crown provide financial or military assistance. After the Restoration of Charles II in 1660, Englishmen of various sorts—courtiers, merchants, parliamentarians—concluded that the colonists should be brought more tightly under the control of the mother country. The regulatory policies that evolved during this period formed a framework for an empire that survived with only minor adjustment until 1765.

WHY

did England discourage free and open trade in colonial America?

Response to Economic Competition

By the 1660s the dominant commercial powers of Europe adopted economic principles that later critics would term **mercantilism.** Proponents of this position argued that since trading nations were engaged in a fierce competition for the world's resources—mostly for raw materials transported from dependent colonies—one nation's commercial success translated directly into a loss for its rivals. It seemed logical, therefore, that England would want to protect its own markets from France or Holland by passing mercantilist trade policies discouraging its colonies from trading with other European powers. For seventeenth-century planners free markets made no sense. They argued that trade tightly regulated by the central government represented the only way to increase the nation's wealth at the expense of competitors.

National interest alone, however, did not shape public policy. Instead, the needs of several powerful interest groups led to the rise of English commercial regulation. Each group looked to colonial commerce to solve a different problem. For his part, the king wanted money. For their part, English merchants were eager to exclude Dutch rivals from lucrative American markets and needed government assistance to compete successfully with the Dutch, even in Virginia or

mercantilism
An economic theory that shaped imperial policy throughout the colonial period, mercantilism was built on the assumption that the world's wealth was a fixed supply. In order to increase its wealth, a nation needed to export more goods than it imported. Favorable trade and protective economic policies, as well as new colonial possessions rich in raw materials, were important in achieving this balance.

Why did seventeenth-century English rulers support mercantilism?

Massachusetts Bay. From the perspective of the landed gentry who sat in Parliament, England needed a stronger navy, and that in turn meant expansion of the domestic shipbuilding industry. And almost everyone agreed England should establish a more favorable balance of trade, that is, increase exports, decrease imports, and grow richer at the expense of other European states. None of these ideas was particularly innovative, but taken together they provided a blueprint for England's first empire.

Regulating Colonial Trade

Parliament passed a Navigation Act in 1660. The statute was the most important piece of imperial legislation drafted before the American Revolution. Colonists from New Hampshire to South Carolina paid close attention to the details of this statute, which stated (1) that no ship could trade in the colonies unless it had been constructed in either England or America and carried a crew that was at least 75 percent English (for these purposes, colonists counted as Englishmen), and (2) that certain **enumerated goods** of great value that were not produced in England—tobacco, sugar, cotton, indigo, dyewoods, ginger—could be transported from the colonies only to an English or another colonial port. In 1704, Parliament added rice and molasses to the enumerated list; in 1705, rosins, tars, and turpentines needed for shipbuilding were included.

enumerated goods
Certain essential raw materials produced in the North American colonies, such as tobacco, sugar, and rice, specified in the Navigation Acts, which stipulated that these goods could be shipped only to England or its colonies.

The act of 1660 was masterfully conceived. It encouraged the development of domestic shipbuilding and prohibited European rivals from obtaining enumerated goods anywhere except in England. Since the Americans had to pay import duties in England (for this purpose colonists did not count as Englishmen) on such items as sugar and tobacco, the legislation also provided the crown with another source of income.

In 1663, Parliament passed a second Navigation Act known as the Staple Act, which stated that, with a few noted exceptions, nothing could be imported into America unless it had first been transshipped through England, a process that greatly added to the price ultimately paid by colonial consumers.

Navigation Acts
A series of commercial restrictions passed by Parliament intended to regulate colonial commerce in such a way as to favor England's accumulation of wealth.

The **Navigation Acts**, a series of trade regulations passed by Parliament in the second half of the seventeenth century, attempted to eliminate the Dutch, against whom the English fought three wars in this period (1652–1654, 1664–1667, and 1672–1674), as the intermediaries of American commerce. Just as English merchants were celebrating their victory, however, an unanticipated rival appeared on the scene: New England merchant ships sailed out of Boston, Salem, and Newport to become formidable world competitors in maritime commerce.

During the 1660s, the colonists showed little enthusiasm for the new imperial regulations. Reaction to the Navigation Acts varied from region to region. Virginians bitterly protested them. The collection of English customs on tobacco greatly reduced the colonial planters' profits. Moreover, the exclusion of the Dutch from the trade meant that growers often had to sell their crops at artificially low prices. The Navigation Acts hit the small planters especially hard, for they were least able to absorb increased production costs. Even though the governor of Virginia lobbied on the planters' behalf, the crown turned a deaf ear.

At first, New Englanders simply ignored the commercial regulations. Indeed, one Massachusetts merchant reported in 1664 that Boston entertained "near one hundred sail of ships, this year, of ours and strangers." The strangers, of course, were the Dutch, who had no intention of obeying the Navigation Acts so long as they could reach colonial ports. Some New England merchants found clever ways to circumvent the Navigation Acts. These crafty traders picked up cargoes of enumerated goods such as sugar or tobacco, sailed to another colonial port (thereby technically fulfilling the letter of the law), and then made directly for Holland or France. Along the way they paid no customs.

To plug the loophole, Parliament passed the Navigation Act of 1673. This statute established a plantation duty, a sum of money equal to normal English customs duties to be collected on enumerated products at the various colonial ports. New Englanders could now sail wherever they pleased within the empire, but they could not escape paying customs.

Parliament passed the last major piece of imperial legislation in 1696. Among other things, the statute tightened enforcement procedures, putting pressure specifically on the colonial governors to keep England's competitors out of American ports. The act of 1696 also expanded the American customs service and for the first time set up vice-admiralty courts in the colonies. Established to settle disputes that occurred at sea, vice-admiralty courts required neither juries nor oral cross-examination, both traditional elements of the common law. But they were effective and sometimes even popular for resolving maritime questions quickly enough to send the ships to sea again with little delay. The year 1696 witnessed one other significant change in the imperial system. William III replaced the ineffective Lords of Trade with a body of policy advisers that came to be known as the Board of Trade. This group was expected to monitor colonial affairs closely and to provide government officials with the best available advice on commercial and other problems. For several decades, at least, it energetically carried out its responsibilities.

The members of Parliament believed these reforms would compel the colonists to accept the Navigation Acts, and in large measure they were correct. By 1700, American goods transshipped through the mother country accounted for a quarter of all English exports, an indication the colonists found it profitable to obey the commercial regulations. In fact, during the eighteenth century, smuggling from Europe to America dried up almost completely.

QUICK CHECK

How did the Navigation Acts establish the foundation for a commercial empire?

Colonial Political Revolts

The Navigation Acts created an illusion of unity. English administrators superimposed a system of commercial regulation on a number of different, often unstable American colonies and called it an empire. But these statutes did not remove long-standing differences. Within each society, men and women struggled to bring order out of disorder, to establish stable ruling elites, to diffuse ethnic and racial tensions, and to cope with population pressures that imperial planners only dimly understood. During the final decades of the seventeenth century, these efforts sometimes sparked revolt.

First, the Virginians rebelled, and then a few years later, political violence swept through Maryland, New York, and Massachusetts Bay, England's most populous mainland colonies. Historians once interpreted these events as rehearsals

HOW

did colonial revolts affect the political culture of Virginia and New England?

for the American Revolution, or even for Jacksonian democracy. They perceived the rebels as frontier democrats, rising in protest against an entrenched aristocracy.

Recent research suggests, however, that this view seriously misconstrued the character of these late-seventeenth-century rebellions. The uprisings certainly did not involve confrontations between ordinary people and their rulers. Indeed, the events were not in any modern sense of the word ideological. In each colony, the local gentry split into factions, usually the "outs" versus the "ins," and each side proclaimed its political legitimacy.

Civil War in Virginia: Bacon's Rebellion

After 1660, the Virginia economy suffered a prolonged depression. Returns from tobacco had not been good for some time, and the Navigation Acts reduced profits even further. Indentured servants complained about lack of food and clothing. No wonder that Virginia's governor, Sir William Berkeley, despaired of ever ruling "a People where six parts of seven at least are Poor, Endebted, Discontented and Armed." In 1670, he and the House of Burgesses disfranchised all landless freemen, persons they regarded as troublemakers, but the threat of social violence remained.

Things changed when Nathaniel Bacon arrived in Virginia in 1674. This ambitious young man came from a respectable English family and set himself up immediately as a substantial planter. But he wanted more. Bacon envied the government patronage monopolized by Berkeley's cronies, a group known locally as the Green Spring faction. When Bacon attempted to obtain a license to engage in the fur trade, he was rebuffed. This lucrative commerce was reserved for the governor's friends. If Bacon had been willing to wait, he probably would have been accepted into the ruling clique, but as subsequent events would demonstrate, Bacon was not a man of patience.

Nathaniel Bacon's Declaration (July 30, 1676)

Events beyond Bacon's control thrust him suddenly into the center of Virginia politics. In 1675, Indians reacting to white encroachment attacked several outlying plantations, killing a few colonists, and Virginians expected the governor to send an army to retaliate. Instead, early in 1676, Berkeley called for the construction of a line of defensive forts, a plan that seemed to the settlers both expensive and ineffective. Indeed, the strategy raised embarrassing questions. Was Berkeley protecting his own fur monopoly? Was he planning to reward his friends with contracts to build useless forts?

While people speculated about such matters, Bacon stepped forward. He boldly offered to lead a volunteer army against the Indians at no cost to the hard-pressed Virginia taxpayers. All he demanded was an official commission from Berkeley giving him military command and the right to attack other Indians, not just the hostile Susquehannocks. The governor steadfastly refused. With some justification, Berkeley regarded his upstart rival as a fanatic on the subject of Indians. The governor saw no reason to exterminate peaceful tribes simply to avenge the death of a few white settlers.

Declaration Against Nathaniel Bacon (1676)

What followed would have been comic had not so many people died. Bacon thundered against the governor's treachery; Berkeley labeled Bacon a traitor. Both men appealed to the populace for support. On several occasions, Bacon marched his followers to the frontier, but they either failed to find the enemy or, worse, massacred friendly Indians. At one point, Bacon burned Jamestown to the ground, forcing the governor to flee to the colony's Eastern Shore. Bacon's bumbling lieutenants chased Berkeley across Chesapeake Bay only to be captured themselves. Thereupon, the governor mounted a new campaign.

As **Bacon's Rebellion** dragged on, it became increasingly apparent that Bacon and his gentry supporters had only the vaguest notion of what they were trying to achieve. The members of the planter elite never seemed fully to appreciate that the rank-and-file soldiers, often black slaves and poor white servants, had serious, legitimate grievances against Berkeley's corrupt government and were demanding substantial reforms, not just a share in the governor's fur monopoly.

When Charles II learned of the fighting in Virginia, he dispatched a thousand regular soldiers to Jamestown. By the time they arrived, Berkeley had regained full control over the colony's government. In October 1676, Bacon died after a brief illness, and within a few months, his band of rebel followers had dispersed.

Berkeley, now an old and embittered man, was recalled to England in 1677. His successors, especially Lord Culpeper (1680–1683) and Lord Howard of Effingham (1683–1689), seemed interested primarily in enriching themselves at the expense of the Virginia planters. Their self-serving policies, coupled with the memory of near anarchy, helped heal divisions within the Virginia ruling class. For almost a century, in fact, the local gentry formed a united front against greedy royal appointees.

Bacon's Rebellion
An armed rebellion in Virginia (1675–1676) led by Nathaniel Bacon against the colony's royal governor, Sir William Berkeley. Although some of his followers called for an end of special privilege in government, Bacon was chiefly interested in gaining a larger share of the lucrative Indian trade.

QUICK CHECK ✔
What were the underlying causes of Bacon's Rebellion?

The Glorious Revolution in the Bay Colony

During John Winthrop's lifetime, Massachusetts settlers developed an inflated sense of their independence from the mother country. After 1660, however, it became difficult even to pretend that the Puritan colony was a separate state. Royal officials demanded full compliance with the Navigation Acts. Moreover, the growth of commerce attracted new merchants to the Bay Colony, men who were Anglicans rather than Congregationalists and who maintained close business contacts in London. These persons complained loudly of Puritan intolerance. The Anglican faction was never large, but its presence divided Bay leaders. A few Puritan ministers and magistrates regarded compromise with England as treason, a breaking of the Lord's covenant. Other spokesmen, recognizing the changing political realities within the empire, urged a more moderate course.

In 1675, in the midst of this ongoing political crisis, the Indians dealt the New Englanders a terrible setback. **Metacomet**, a Wampanoag chief the whites called King Philip, declared war against the colonists. The powerful Narragansett Indians, whose lands the settlers had long coveted, joined Metacomet, and in little more than a year of fighting, the Indians destroyed scores of frontier villages, killed hundreds of colonists, and disrupted the entire regional economy. More than one thousand Indians and New Englanders died in the conflict. The war left the people of Massachusetts deeply in debt and more than ever uncertain of their future. As in other parts of colonial America, the defeated Indians were forced off their lands, compelled by events to become either refugees or economically marginal figures in white society.

Metacomet
Wampanoag chief, also known as King Philip, who declared war against the colonies in 1675.

In 1684, the debate over the Bay Colony's relation to the mother country ended abruptly. The Court of Chancery, sitting in London and acting on a petition from the king, annulled the charter of the Massachusetts Bay Company. In one stroke of a pen, the patent that Winthrop had so lovingly carried to America in 1630, the foundation for a "City on a Hill," was gone. The decision forced the most stubborn Puritans to recognize they were part of an empire run by people who did not share their particular religious vision.

James II, a monarch who disliked representative institutions, decided to restructure the government of the entire region in the **Dominion of New England.** In various stages from 1686 to 1689, the Dominion incorporated Massachusetts, Connecticut, Rhode Island, Plymouth, New York, New Jersey, and New Hampshire under a single appointed royal governor. For this demanding position, James selected Sir Edmund Andros (pronounced Andrews), a military veteran of tyrannical temperament. Andros arrived in Boston in 1686, and within a matter of months he had alienated everyone: Puritans, moderates, and even Anglican merchants. Not only did Andros abolish elective assemblies, but he also enforced the Navigation Acts with such rigor that he brought about commercial depression. Andros declared normal town meetings illegal, collected taxes the people never approved, and packed the courts with supporters who detested the local population. Eighteenth-century historian and royal governor Thomas Hutchinson compared Andros unfavorably with the Roman tyrant Nero.

In the fall of 1689, the ruling class of England had deposed James II, an admitted Catholic, and placed his Protestant daughter, Mary, and her husband, William of Orange, on the throne as joint monarchs. As part of the settlement, William and Mary accepted a Bill of Rights, a document stipulating the constitutional rights of all Englishmen. Early in 1689, news of this **Glorious Revolution** reached Boston. Almost immediately, the Bay Colonists overthrew the hated Andros regime. The New England version of the Glorious Revolution (April 18, 1689) was so popular that no one came to the governor's defense. Andros was jailed without a single shot having been fired.

Thanks largely to the tireless lobbying of Increase Mather, who pleaded the colonists' case in London, William abandoned the Dominion of New England, and in 1691, Massachusetts received a new royal charter. This document differed substantially from the company patent of 1629. The freemen no longer selected their governor. The choice now belonged to the king. Membership in the General Court was determined by annual election, and these representatives in turn chose the men who sat in the council or upper house, subject always to the governor's veto. Moreover, the franchise, restricted here as in other colonies to adult males, was determined on the basis of personal property rather than church membership, a change that brought Massachusetts into conformity with general English practice. On the local level, town government remained much as it had been in Winthrop's time.

Dominion of New England
Incorporation of Massachusetts, Connecticut, Rhode Island, Plymouth, New York, New Jersey, and New Hampshire under a single appointed royal governor that lasted from 1686 to 1689.

Glorious Revolution
Overthrow of James II, an admitted Catholic, and acceptance of his Protestant daughter, Mary, and her husband, William of Orange, as joint monarchs who promised to uphold the constitution.

QUICK CHECK ✔

Why did colonists overthrow the Dominion of New England in 1689?

Contagion of Witchcraft

The instability of the Massachusetts government following Andros's arrest—what Reverend Samuel Willard described as "the short Anarchy accompanying our late Revolution"—allowed what under normal political conditions would have been an isolated, though ugly, local incident to expand into a major colonial crisis.

Excessively fearful men and women living in Salem Village, a small, unprosperous farming community, nearly overwhelmed the new rulers of Massachusetts Bay.

Accusations of witchcraft were not uncommon in seventeenth-century New England. Puritans believed that an individual might make a compact with the devil, but during the first decades of settlement, authorities executed only about fifteen alleged witches. Sometimes villagers simply left suspected witches alone. Never before had fears of witchcraft plunged an entire community into panic.

The terror in Salem Village began in late 1691, when several adolescent girls began to behave in strange ways. They cried out for no apparent reason; they twitched on the ground. When concerned neighbors asked what caused their suffering, the girls announced they were victims of witches, seemingly innocent persons who lived in the community. The arrest of several alleged witches did not relieve the girls' "fits," nor did prayer solve the problem. Additional accusations were made, and at least one person confessed, providing a frightening description of the devil as "a thing all over hairy, all the face hairy, and a long nose." In June 1692,

Woodcut of Witch Hangings

WILLIAM AND MARY   William III and Mary II reigned as joint monarchs of England after the Glorious Revolution of 1688. Mary ascended the throne when her father, James II, was deposed. Her husband, William, ruled Holland before accepting the English throne.

Why do you think William III had himself depicted as a soldier in full body armor?

COTTON MATHER   The publication of Cotton Mather's *Memorable Providences, Relating to Witchcrafts and Possessions* (1689) contributed to the hysteria that resulted in the Salem witchcraft trials. Mather is shown here surrounded by some of the forms a demon assumed in the "documented" case of an English family besieged by witches.

Why do you think the educated leaders of New England did not forcefully condemn the witchcraft trials while they were in progress?

spectral evidence

In the Salem witch trials, the court allowed reports of dreams and visions in which the accused appeared as the devil's agent to be introduced as testimony. The accused had no defense against this kind of evidence. When the judges later disallowed this testimony, the executions for witchcraft ended.

QUICK CHECK ✔

Why were so many apparently innocent people convicted of witchcraft in Salem from 1691 to 1692?

a special court convened and began to send men and women to the gallows. By the end of the summer, the court had hanged nineteen people; another was pressed to death. Several more suspects died in jail awaiting trial.

Then suddenly, the storm was over. Led by Increase Mather, a group of prominent Congregational ministers belatedly urged leniency and restraint. Especially troubling to the clergymen was the court's decision to accept **spectral evidence**, that is, reports of dreams and visions in which the accused appeared as the devil's agent. Worried about convicting people on such dubious testimony, Mather declared, "It were better that ten suspected witches should escape, than that one innocent person should be condemned." The colonial government accepted the ministers' advice and convened a new court, which promptly acquitted, pardoned, or released the remaining suspects. After the Salem nightmare, witchcraft ceased to be a capital offense.

No one knows exactly what sparked the terror in Salem Village. The community had a history of religious discord, and during the 1680s, the people split into angry factions over the choice of a minister. Economic tensions played a part as well. Poorer, more traditional farmers accused members of prosperous, commercially oriented families of being witches. The underlying misogyny of the entire culture meant the victims were more often women than men. Terror of attack by Native Americans may also have played a part in this ugly affair. Indians in league with the French in Canada had recently raided nearby communities, killing people related to the families of the bewitched Salem girls, and significantly, during the trials some victims described the Devil as a "tawny man."

Conclusion: Foundations of an Atlantic Empire

"It is no little Blessing of God," Cotton Mather announced proudly in 1700, "that we are part of the *English* nation." A half century earlier, John Winthrop would not have spoken these words, at least not with such enthusiasm. The two men were, of course, products of different political cultures. It was not so much that the character of Massachusetts society had changed. In fact, the Puritan families of 1700 were much like those of the founding generation. Rather, the difference was in England's attitude toward the colonies. Rulers living more than three thousand miles away now made political and economic demands that Mather's contemporaries could not ignore.

The creation of a new imperial system did not, however, erase profound sectional differences. By 1700, for example, the Chesapeake colonies were more, not less, committed to the cultivation of tobacco and slave labor. Although the separate regions were being pulled slowly into England's commercial orbit, they did not have much to do with each other. The elements that sparked a powerful sense of nationalism among colonists dispersed over a huge territory would not be evident for a very long time. It would be a mistake, therefore, to anticipate the coming of the American Revolution.

For a list of additional titles related to this chapter's topics, please see www.pearsonamericanhistory.com. MyHistoryLab

STUDY RESOURCES

KEY TERMS

yeomen

indentured servants

Royal African Company

mercantilism

enumerated goods

Navigation Acts

Bacon's Rebellion

Metacomet

Dominion of New England

Glorious Revolution

spectral evidence

CHAPTER REVIEW

WHAT conditions explain the remarkable social stability achieved in early New England?

Seventeenth-century New Englanders migrated to America in family groups, ensuring that the ratio of men to women remained roughly even, making it easier for young people to find marriage partners and start families. Stable marriage, together with New England's healthy climate, led to rapid population growth. While many New Englanders served as servants early in life, most seventeenth-century colonists were eventually able to acquire property.

WHAT factors contributed to political unrest in the Chesapeake region during this period?

Most immigrants to the early Chesapeake colonies were single young men who traveled as indentured servants. Disease killed many of them shortly after arriving. Men outnumbered women, making it difficult for freemen to find marriage partners. Because of the short life expectancy, marriages did not last long. Economic inequality and family instability contributed to political unrest.

HOW did African American slaves preserve an independent cultural identity in the New World?

In the Chesapeake, slavery did not become the primary source of labor until the 1680s. As slaves were imported into the colonies at a greater rate, African men and women torn from their homes were forced to build a new culture in the New World. Although white colonists, afraid of the growing slave population, passed slave codes restricting the freedom of slaves and black freemen, many slaves still managed to hold onto elements of their African heritage.

WHY did England discourage free and open trade in colonial America?

During the seventeenth century, Parliament passed a number of mercantilist laws declaring that the raw materials and commerce of their colonies would benefit only the mother country, and not a European rival. Parliament passed a series of seventeenth-century commercial regulations, representing England's new blueprint for the empire.

HOW did colonial revolts affect the political culture of Virginia and New England?

During Bacon's Rebellion, landless freemen rose up against the governor and demanded Indian lands. Although the rebellion failed, it unified Virginia's ruling elite. In 1684, James II restructured the Massachusetts Bay government to increase crown authority. New Englanders threw off the Dominion of New England in 1689 and negotiated for government charters that allowed significant local autonomy.

MAKING CONNECTIONS

1. Would New Englanders have enjoyed such social cohesion if they had endured Virginia's high mortality rates?
2. What factors would have drawn ambitious, young English people in the first half of the seventeenth century to the Chesapeake region rather than to New England?
3. Since living with large numbers of unfree Africans frightened whites, why did colonists continue to import so many slaves?
4. Did the mercantilist system best serve the interests of the English or of the American colonists?
5. Why did colonial rebellions of the seventeenth century not lead to demands for political independence?

PRACTICE QUIZ

1. The institution of _____ strongly influenced Puritan society.
   a. Divorce **b.** Love
   c. The family **d.** The military

2. Maryland and _____ comprised the Chesapeake colonies.
   a. New York **b.** Virginia
   c. New England **d.** The Carolinas

3. Most immigrants to the Chesapeake region _____ soon after arrival.
   a. gained lands
   b. rose to political power
   c. died from disease and overwork
   d. enslaved Indians

4. The key to white advancement in Chesapeake society was the ownership of _____ slaves by the late 1600s.
   a. African **b.** Indian
   c. Asian **d.** White

5. Slave traders carried nearly _____ million Africans to the New World.
   a. 31 **b.** 21
   c. 11 **d.** 5

6. The most serious slave rebellion during the colonial period in North America was
   a. Nat Turner's revolt
   b. The Stono Uprising
   c. The Haitian revolt
   d. The Gabriel Prosser Conspiracy

7. One of the most important pieces of English commercial legislation passed in the 1600s was the
   a. Navigation Acts **b.** Stamp Act
   c. Quebec Act **d.** Sugar Act

8. Which of the following *does not* accurately reflect the development of African American identity during the colonial period?
   a. Slave identity varied from colony to colony.
   b. The size and density of the slave community shaped slave identity.
   c. Black slaves were unable to develop creole languages.
   d. Slaves on large plantations developed kinship networks.

9. All of the following statements describe Bacon's Rebellion *except*
   a. Indians attacked Virginia settlements, causing panic among settlers.
   b. Settlers criticized the governor for building forts to stop Indian attacks.
   c. Nathaniel Bacon stepped forward to lead an army against the Indians.
   d. Bacon defeated a large army sent from England to remove him.

10. Historians think that the Salem Witchcraft Trials may have been caused by all of the following reasons *except*
    a. Puritan fears of slave rebellion
    b. Religious discord
    c. Economic tensions
    d. Misogyny

Find more practice at www.myhistorylab.com

SAMPLE ESSAY QUESTIONS

1. Explain how the Puritans fostered social stability in their communities.

2. Why and how did Africans become the slaves in British North America?

Answers to Practice Quiz 1. c 2. b 3. c 4. a 5. c 6. b 7. a 8. c 9. d 10. a

CREDITS

Experience of Empire:
Eighteenth-Century America, 1680–1763

Experience of Empire
Eighteenth-Century America, 1680–1763

BOSTON HARBOR This engraving of a work originally done by William Burgis depicts the port of Boston at mid-century.

Why do you think the artist focused so much attention on ships and wharves?

Constructing an Anglo-American Identity: The Journal of William Byrd

William Byrd II (1674–1744) was a type of British American one would not have encountered during the earliest years of settlement. This successful Tidewater planter was a product of a new, more cosmopolitan environment, and as an adult, Byrd seemed as much at home in London as in his native Virginia. In 1728, at the height of his political influence in Williamsburg, the capital of colonial Virginia, Byrd accepted a commission to help survey a disputed boundary between North Carolina and Virginia. During his

KEY EVENTS

1680 El Popé leads Pueblo revolt against the Spanish in New Mexico

1706 Birth of Benjamin Franklin

1734–1736 First expression of the Great Awakening at Northampton, Massachusetts

1740 George Whitefield electrifies listeners at Boston

1745 Colonial troops capture Louisbourg

1748 American Lutheran ministers ordained in Philadelphia

1754 Albany Congress meets

1755 Braddock is defeated by the French and Indians in western Pennsylvania

1756 Seven Years' War is formally declared

1759 British are victorious at Quebec

1763 Peace of Paris ending French and Indian War is signed

1769 Junípero Serra begins to build missions in California

1821 Mexico declares independence from Spain

long journey into the distant backcountry, Byrd kept a detailed journal, a satiric, often bawdy chronicle of daily events that is now regarded as a classic of early American literature.

On his trip into the wilderness, Byrd met many different people. No sooner had he departed a familiar world of tobacco plantations than he came across a self-styled "Hermit," an Englishman who apparently preferred the freedom of the woods to the constraints of society. "He has no other Habitation but a green Bower or Harbour," Byrd reported, "with a Female Domestick as wild & as dirty as himself."

As the boundary commissioners pushed farther into the backcountry, they encountered highly independent men and women of European descent, small frontier families that Byrd regarded as living no better than savages. He attributed their uncivilized behavior to a diet of too much pork. "The Truth of it is, these People live so much upon Swine's flesh... [that it] makes them... extremely hoggish in their Temper, & many of them seem to Grunt rather than Speak in their ordinary conversation." The wilderness journey also brought Byrd's party of surveyors into regular contact with Native Americans, whom he properly distinguished as Catawba, Tuscarora, Usheree, and Sapponi Indians.

Byrd's journal invites us to view the rapidly developing eighteenth-century backcountry from a fresh perspective. It was not a vast empty territory awaiting the arrival of European settlers. Maps often sustain this erroneous impression, depicting cities and towns, farms and plantations clustered along the Atlantic coast; they suggest a "line of settlement" steadily pushing outward into a huge blank area with no mark of civilization. The people Byrd met on his journey into the backcountry would not have understood such maps. After all, the empty space on the maps was their home. They experienced the frontier as populous zones of many cultures stretching from the English and French settlements in the north all the way to the Spanish borderlands in the far southwest.

The point is not to discount the significance of the older Atlantic settlements. During the eighteenth century, Britain's thirteen mainland colonies underwent a profound transformation. The population in the colonies grew at unprecedented rates. German and Scots-Irish immigrants arrived in huge numbers. So too did African slaves.

Wherever they lived, colonial Americans of this period were less isolated from one another than colonists had been during most of the seventeenth century. Indeed, after 1690, men and women expanded their cultural horizons, becoming part of a larger Anglo-American empire. The change was striking. Colonists whose parents or grandparents had come to the New World to confront a "howling wilderness" now purchased imported European manufactures, read English journals, participated in imperial wars, and sought favors from a growing number of resident royal officials. No one—not even the inhabitants of the distant frontiers—could escape the influence of Britain. The cultural, economic, and political links connecting the colonists to the imperial center in London grew stronger with time.

WILLIAM BYRD II Byrd's *History of the Dividing Line Run in the Year 1728* contains a marvelously satirical account of the culture of poor country farmers in North Carolina.

Do you think Byrd thought of himself as an American or as a British person living in America?

This surprising development raises a difficult question for the modern historian. If the eighteenth-century colonists were so powerfully attracted to Great Britain, then why did they ever declare independence? The answer may well be that as the colonists became more British, they inevitably became more American as well. This was a development of major significance, for it helps to explain the appearance after midcentury of genuine nationalist sentiment. Political, commercial, and military links that brought the colonists into more frequent contact with Great Britain also made them more aware of other colonists. It was within an expanding, prosperous empire that they first began seriously to consider what it meant to be American.

Tensions in the Backcountry

Accurate population data from the colonial period are extremely difficult to find. The first national census did not occur until 1790. Still, various sources surviving from prerevolutionary times indicate that the total white population of Britain's thirteen mainland colonies rose from about 250,000 in 1700 to 2,150,000 in 1770, an annual growth rate of 3 percent.

Few societies in recorded history have expanded so rapidly, and if the growth rate had not dropped substantially during the nineteenth and twentieth centuries, the current population of the United States would stand at well more than one billion people. Natural reproduction was responsible for most of the growth. More families bore children who in turn lived long enough to have children of their own. Because of this sudden expansion, the population of the late colonial period was strikingly young; approximately one-half of the populace at any given time was under age 16.

Not only was the total population increasing at a very rapid rate; it also was becoming more dispersed and heterogeneous. Each year witnessed the arrival of thousands of non-English Europeans. Unlike those seventeenth-century English settlers in search of religious sanctuary or instant wealth, the newcomers generally

WHAT difficulties did Native Americans face in maintaining their cultural independence on the frontier?

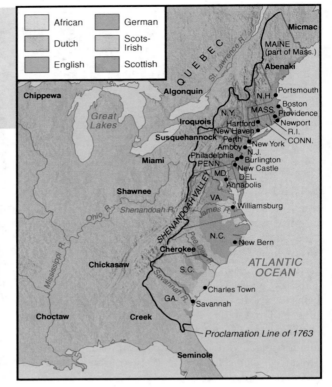

DISTRIBUTION OF EUROPEAN AND AFRICAN IMMIGRANTS IN THE THIRTEEN COLONIES A flood of non-English immigrants swept the British colonies between 1700 and 1775.

What effect did the arrival of non-English immigrants have on American settlement patterns?

backcountry
In the eighteenth century, the edge of settlement extending from western Pennsylvania to Georgia. This region formed the second frontier as settlers moved westward from the Atlantic coast into the nation's interior.

transferred in the hope of obtaining their own land and setting up as independent farmers. These people often traveled to the **backcountry**, a region stretching approximately eight hundred miles from western Pennsylvania to Georgia. Although they planned to follow customs they had known in Europe, they found the challenge of surviving on the British frontier far more demanding than they had anticipated. They plunged into a complex, fluid, often violent society that included large numbers of Native Americans and African Americans as well as other Europeans.

Scots-Irish Flee English Oppression

During the seventeenth century, English rulers thought they could thoroughly dominate Catholic Ireland by transporting thousands of lowland Scottish Presbyterians to the northern region of that war-torn country. These settlers became known as the Scots-Irish. The plan failed. English officials who were members of the Anglican Church discriminated against the Presbyterians. They passed laws that placed the Scots-Irish at a severe disadvantage when they traded in England; they taxed them at exorbitant rates.

After several poor harvests, many of the Scots-Irish elected to emigrate to America, where they hoped to find the freedom and prosperity that had been denied them in Ireland. Often entire Presbyterian congregations followed charismatic ministers to the New World, intent on replicating a distinctive, fiercely independent culture on the frontier. It is estimated that 150,000 Scots-Irish migrated to the colonies before the Revolution.

Most Scots-Irish immigrants landed initially in Philadelphia, but instead of remaining in that city, they carved out farms on Pennsylvania's western frontier. The colony's proprietors welcomed the influx of new settlers, for it seemed they would form an ideal barrier between the Indians and the older, coastal communities. The Penn family soon had second thoughts, however. The Scots-Irish squatted on whatever land looked best, and when colony officials pointed out that large tracts had already been reserved, the immigrants retorted that "it was against the laws of God and nature that so much land should be idle when so many Christians wanted it to labour on and to raise their bread." Wherever they located, the Scots-Irish challenged established authority.

QUICK CHECK ✓

Why did so many Scots-Irish migrate to America during the eighteenth century?

Germans Search for a Better Life

A second large body of non-English settlers, more than 100,000 people, came from the upper Rhine Valley, the German Palatinate. Some of the migrants, especially those who relocated to America around the turn of the century, belonged to small pietistic Protestant sects whose religious views were somewhat similar to those of the Quakers. These Germans moved to the New World primarily in the hope of finding religious toleration. Under the guidance of Francis Daniel Pastorius (1651–1720), a group of Mennonites established in Pennsylvania a prosperous community known as Germantown.

By midcentury, however, the characteristics of the German migration had begun to change. Large numbers of Lutherans transferred to the Middle Colonies. Unlike members of the pietistic sects, these men and women were not in search of religious freedom. Rather, they traveled to the New World looking to better their material lives. The Lutheran Church in Germany initially tried to maintain control over the distant congregations, but even though the migrants themselves fiercely preserved many aspects of traditional German culture, they were eventually forced to accommodate to new social conditions. Henry Melchior Mühlenberg (1711–1787), a tireless leader, helped German Lutherans through a difficult cultural adjustment, and in 1748, Mühlenberg organized a meeting of local pastors and lay delegates that ordained ministers of their own choosing, an act of spiritual independence that has been called "the most important single event in American Lutheran history."

The German migrants—mistakenly called Pennsylvania Dutch because the English confused *deutsch* (meaning "German") with *Dutch* ("a person from Holland")—began reaching Philadelphia in large numbers after 1717, and by 1766, persons of German stock accounted for more than one-third of Pennsylvania's total population. Even their most vocal detractors admitted the Germans were the best farmers in the colony.

After 1730, Germans and Scots-Irish pushed south from western Pennsylvania into the Shenandoah Valley, thousands of them settling in the backcountry of Virginia and the Carolinas. The Germans usually remained wherever they found unclaimed fertile land. By contrast, the Scots-Irish often moved two or three times, acquiring a reputation as a rootless people.

QUICK CHECK ✓

Why did the new German and Scots-Irish immigrants to America move west after they arrived in the colonies?

Wherever the newcomers settled, they often found themselves living beyond the effective authority of the various colonial governments. To be sure, backcountry residents petitioned for assistance during wars against the Indians, but most of the time they preferred to be left alone. These conditions heightened the importance of religious institutions within the small ethnic communities. Although the original stimulus for coming to America may have been a desire for economic independence and prosperity, backcountry families—especially the Scots-Irish—flocked to evangelical Protestant preachers, to Presbyterian, and later Baptist and Methodist ministers who not only fulfilled the settlers' spiritual needs but also gave scattered backcountry communities a pronounced moral character that survived long after the colonial period.

Native Americans Stake Out a Middle Ground

During much of the seventeenth century, various Indian groups who contested the English settlers for control of coastal lands suffered terribly, sometimes from war, but more often from the spread of contagious diseases such as smallpox. The two races found it very difficult to live in close proximity. As one Indian informed the members of the Maryland assembly in 1666, "Your hogs & Cattle injure Us, You come too near Us to live & drive Us from place to place. We can fly no farther; let us know where to live & how to be secured for the future from the Hogs & Cattle."

Against such odds the Indians managed to survive. By the eighteenth century, the site of the most intense and creative contact between the races had shifted to the huge territory between the Appalachian Mountains and the Mississippi River, where several hundred thousand Native Americans made their homes.

Many Indians had only recently migrated to the area. The Delaware, for example, retreated to far western Pennsylvania and the Ohio Valley to escape almost continuous confrontation with advancing European invaders. Other Indians drifted west in less happy circumstances. They were refugees, the remnants of Native American groups who had lost so many people that they could no longer sustain an independent cultural identity. These survivors joined with other Indians to establish new multiethnic communities. Stronger groups of Indians, such as the Creek, Choctaw, Chickasaw, Cherokee, and Shawnee, generally welcomed the refugees. Strangers were formally adopted to take the places of family members killed in battle or overcome by sickness.

middle ground
A geographical area where European and Native American cultures interacted with neither holding a clear upper hand.

The concept of a **middle ground**—a geographical area where two district cultures interacted with neither holding a clear upper hand—helps us more fully to comprehend how eighteenth-century Indians held their own in the backcountry beyond the Appalachian Mountains. The Native Americans never intended to isolate themselves completely from European contact. They relied on white traders, French as well as English, to provide essential metal goods and weapons. The goal of the Indian confederacies was rather to maintain a strong independent voice in these commercial exchanges, whenever possible playing the French against the British, and so long as they had sufficient military strength they compelled everyone who came to negotiate in the "middle ground" to give them proper respect. Native Americans took advantage of rivals when possible; they compromised when necessary. It is best to imagine the Indians' middle ground as an open, dynamic process of creative interaction.

TISHCOHAN AND WAMPUM BELT Tishcohan, chief of the Delaware tribe that lost much of its land in Thomas Penn's Walking Purchase of 1737, is shown here in a 1735 portrait by Gustavus Hesselius. Although treaties and agreements with European settlers were often detrimental to Native Americans, some alliances in the "middle ground" allowed tribes to play off the French against the British. Alliances were often signified by tokens such as certificates, calumets (ceremonial pipes), wampum belts, and medals. (*Source: Gustavus Hesselius, "Tishcohan," Native American Portrait, 1735. Courtesy of The Historical Society of Pennsylvania Collection, Atwater Kent Museum of Philadelphia.*)

Do you think the European artist produced an accurate reproduction of this Native American chief?

However desirable they may have appeared, European goods subtly eroded traditional structures of Native American authority. During the period of earliest encounter with white men, Indian leaders reinforced their own power by controlling the character and flow of commercial exchange. If a trader wanted a rich supply of animal skins, for example, he soon learned that he had better negotiate directly with a chief or tribal elder. But as the number of European traders operating within the "middle ground" expanded, ordinary Indians began to bargain on their own account, obtaining colorful and durable manufactured items without first consulting a Native American leader. Independent commercial dealings of this sort tended further to weaken the Indians' ability to resist organized white aggression. As John Stuart, a superintendent of Indian affairs, explained in 1761, "A modern Indian cannot subsist without Europeans; And would handle a Flint Ax or any other rude utensil used by his ancestors very awkwardly; So that what was only convenience at first is now become Necessity."

The survival of the middle ground depended ultimately on factors over which the Native Americans had little control. Imperial competition between France and

QUICK CHECK ✓

How did Native Americans manipulate the "middle ground" to their advantage?

Great Britain enhanced the Indians' bargaining position, but after the British defeated the French in 1763, the Indians no longer received the same solicitous attention as they had in earlier times. Keeping old allies happy seemed to the British a needless expense. Moreover, contagious disease continued to take a fearful toll. In the southern backcountry between 1685 and 1790, the Indian population dropped an astounding 72 percent. In the Ohio Valley, the numbers suggest similar rates of decline.

Spanish Borderlands of the Eighteenth Century

WHY was the Spanish empire unable to achieve effective control on its northern frontier?

The Spanish empire continued to shape the character of borderlands societies well into the eighteenth century. As anyone who visits the modern American Southwest quickly discovers, Spanish administrators and priests—not to mention ordinary settlers—left a lasting imprint on the cultural landscape of this country.

Until 1821, when Mexico declared independence from Madrid, Spanish authorities struggled to control a vast northern frontier. During the eighteenth century, the Spanish empire in North America included widely dispersed settlements such as San Francisco, San Diego, Santa Fe, San Antonio, and St. Augustine. In these borderland communities, European colonists mixed with peoples of other races and backgrounds, forming multicultural societies.

Conquering the Northern Frontier

In the late sixteenth century Spanish settlers, led by Juan de Oñate, established European communities north of the Rio Grande. The Pueblo Indians resisted the invasion of colonists, soldiers, and missionaries, and in a major rebellion in 1680 led by El Popé, the native peoples drove the whites completely out of New Mexico. Not until 1692 were the Spanish able to reconquer this fiercely contested area. By then, Native American hostility coupled with the settlers' failure to find precious metal had cooled Spain's enthusiasm for the northern frontier.

Concern over French encroachment in the Southeast led Spain to colonize St. Augustine (Florida) in 1565. Although the enterprise never flourished, it claims attention as the first permanent European settlement established in what would become the United States, predating the founding of Jamestown and Plymouth by several decades. Pedro Menéndez de Avilés brought some fifteen hundred soldiers and settlers to St. Augustine, where they constructed an impressive fort, but the colony failed to attract additional Spanish migrants.

QUICK CHECK ✓

Why did the Spanish not more aggressively develop California and the Southwest?

California never figured prominently in Spain's plans for the New World. Early explorers reported finding only impoverished Indians living along the Pacific coast. Adventurers saw no natural resources worth mentioning, and since the area proved extremely difficult to reach from Mexico City—the overland trip could take months—California received little attention. Fear that the Russians might seize the entire region belatedly sparked Spanish activity, however, and after 1769, two indomitable servants of empire, Fra Junípero Serra and Don Gaspar de Portolá, organized permanent missions and *presidios* (forts) at San Diego, Monterey, San Francisco, and Santa Barbara.

SPANISH MISSION Baroque-style eighteenth-century Spanish mission at San Xavier del Bac in present-day Arizona. Spanish missions dotted the frontier of northern New Spain from Florida to California.

What role did religion play in Spain's expansion into the American Southwest?

Peoples of the Spanish Borderlands

In sharp contrast to the English frontier settlements of the eighteenth century, the Spanish outposts in North America grew very slowly. A few Catholic priests and imperial administrators traveled to the northern provinces, but the danger of Indian attack as well as a harsh physical environment discouraged ordinary colonists. The European migrants were overwhelmingly male, most of them soldiers in the pay of the empire. Although some colonists came directly from Spain, most had been born in other Spanish colonies such as Minorca, the Canaries, or New Spain, and because European women rarely appeared on the frontier, Spanish males formed relationships with Indian women, fathering large numbers of mestizos, children of mixed race.

As in other European frontiers of the eighteenth century, encounters with Spanish soldiers, priests, and traders altered Native American cultures. The experience here was quite different from that of the whites and Indians in the British backcountry. The Spanish exploited Native American labor, reducing entire Indian villages to servitude. Many Indians moved to the Spanish towns, and although they lived in close proximity to the Europeans—something rare in British America—they were consigned to the lowest social class, objects of European contempt. However much their material conditions changed, the Indians of the Southwest resisted strenuous efforts to convert them to Catholicism. The Pueblo maintained their own religious forms—often at great personal risk—and they sometimes murdered priests who became too intrusive. Angry Pueblo Indians at Taos reportedly fed the hated Spanish friars corn tortillas containing urine and mouse meat.

The Spanish empire never had the resources necessary to secure the northern frontier fully. The small military posts were intended primarily to discourage other European powers such as France, Great Britain, and Russia from taking possession of territory claimed by Spain. It would be misleading, however, to stress the fragility of Spanish colonization. The urban design and public architecture of many southwestern cities still reflect the vision of the early Spanish settlers, and to a large extent, the old borderlands remain Spanish speaking to this day.

QUICK CHECK ✓

How successful were the Spanish in assimilating the Pueblos to imperial rule?

71

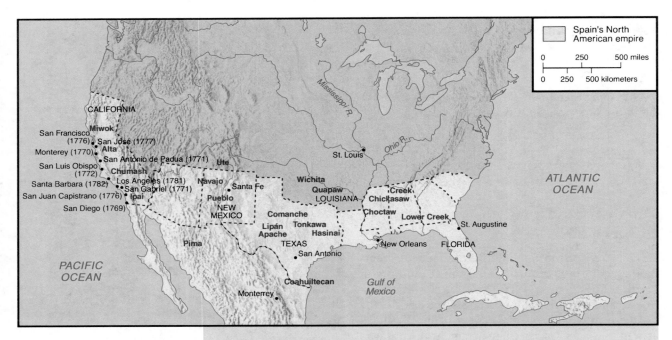

THE SPANISH BORDERLANDS, CA. 1770 In the eighteenth century, Spain's North American empire extended across what is now the southern United States from Florida through Texas and New Mexico to California.

Why was Spanish imperial authority so weak north of Mexico?

The Impact of European Ideas on American Culture

HOW did European ideas affect the character of eighteenth-century American life?

The character of the older, more established British colonies changed almost as rapidly as that of the backcountry. The rapid growth of an urban cosmopolitan culture impressed eighteenth-century commentators, and even though most Americans still lived on scattered farms, they had begun to participate aggressively in an exciting consumer marketplace that expanded their imaginative horizons.

American Enlightenment

Enlightenment
Philosophical and intellectual movement that began in Europe during the eighteenth century. It stressed the application of reason to solve social and scientific problems.

European historians often refer to the eighteenth century as an Age of Reason. During this period, a body of new, often radical, ideas swept through the salons and universities, altering the way that educated Europeans thought about God, nature, and society. This intellectual revolution, called the **Enlightenment**, involved the work of Europe's greatest minds, men such as Newton and Locke, Voltaire and Hume. The writings of these thinkers eventually reached the colonies, where they received a mixed reception. On the whole, the American Enlightenment was rather tame compared to its European counterpart, for while the

72

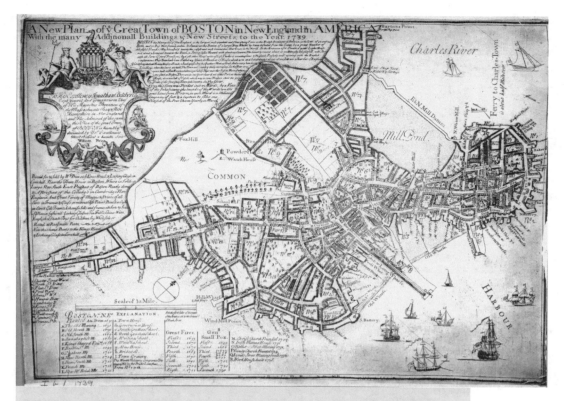

BOSTON   This 1743 map of Boston depicts the port city as an active commercial and cultural center, with many wharves, buildings, churches, and meeting halls.

Why do you think the streets of Boston were not laid out in a straighter, more efficient manner?

colonists welcomed experimental science, they defended the tenets of traditional Christianity.

Enlightenment thinkers shared basic assumptions. Philosophers of the Enlightenment replaced the concept of original sin with a much more optimistic view of human nature. A benevolent God, having set the universe in motion, gave human beings the power of reason to enable them to comprehend the orderly workings of his creation. Everything, even human society, operated according to these mechanical rules. The responsibility of right-thinking men and women, therefore, was to make certain that institutions such as church and state conformed to self-evident natural laws. It was possible to achieve perfection in this world. In fact, human suffering had come about only because people had lost touch with the fundamental insights of reason.

For many Americans, the appeal of the Enlightenment was its focus on a search for useful knowledge, ideas, and inventions that would improve the quality of human life. What mattered was practical experimentation. A speech delivered in 1767 before the members of the American Society in Philadelphia reflected the new utilitarian spirit: "Knowledge is of little Use when confined to mere Speculation," the colonist explained, "But when speculative Truths are

QUICK CHECK ✓

What were the basic intellectual assumptions of the American Enlightenment?

reduced to Practice, when Theories grounded upon Experiments... and the Arts of Living made more easy and comfortable... Knowledge then becomes really useful."

The Enlightenment spawned scores of earnest scientific tinkerers, people who dutifully recorded changes in temperature, the appearance of strange plants and animals, and the details of astronomic phenomena. While these eighteenth-century Americans made few earth-shattering discoveries, they did encourage their countrymen, especially those who attended college, to apply reason to the solution of social and political problems.

Benjamin Franklin

Benjamin Franklin (1706–1790) absorbed the new cosmopolitan culture. European thinkers regarded him as a genuine *philosophe*, a person of reason and science, a role that he self-consciously cultivated when he visited England and France in later life. Franklin had little formal education, but as a young man working in his brother's print shop, he managed to keep up with the latest intellectual currents. In his *Autobiography*, Franklin described the excitement of discovering a new British journal. It was like a breath of fresh air to a boy growing up in Puritan New England. "I met with an odd volume of *The Spectator*," Franklin recounted; "... I had never before seen any of them. I bought it, read it over and over, and was much delighted with it. I thought the writing excellent, and wished if possible to imitate it."

Colonial Products

After he had moved to Philadelphia in 1723, Franklin devoted himself to the pursuit of useful knowledge, ideas that would increase the happiness of his fellow Americans. Franklin never denied the existence of God. Rather, he pushed the Lord aside, making room for the free exercise of human reason. Franklin tinkered, experimented, and reformed. Almost everything he encountered in his daily life aroused his curiosity. His investigation of electricity brought him world fame, but Franklin was never satisfied with his work in this field until it yielded practical application. In 1756, he invented the lightning rod. He also designed a marvelously efficient stove that is still used today. In modern America, Franklin has become exactly what he would have wanted to be, a symbol of material progress through human ingenuity.

Franklin energetically promoted the spread of reason. In Philadelphia, he organized groups that discussed the latest European literature, philosophy, and science. In 1727, for example, he "form'd

BENJAMIN FRANKLIN Benjamin Franklin exemplified the scientific curiosity and search for practical knowledge characteristic of Enlightenment thinkers of the eighteenth century. Franklin's experiments on electricity became world famous and inspired many others to study the effects of the strange force.

What was the relation between the Enlightenment and electricity?

most of my ingenious Acquaintances into a Club for mutual Improvement, which we call'd the Junto." Four years later Franklin took a leading part in the formation of the Library Company, a voluntary association that for the first time allowed people like him to pursue "useful knowledge." The members of these societies communicated with Americans living in other colonies, providing them not only with new information but also with models for their own clubs and associations. Such efforts broadened the intellectual horizons of many colonists, especially those who lived in cities.

QUICK CHECK ✓

What characteristics did Benjamin Franklin possess that made him an Enlightenment figure?

Economic Transformation

The colonial economy kept pace with the stunning growth in population. During the first three-quarters of the eighteenth century, the population increased at least eightfold, and yet even with so many additional people to feed and clothe, the per capita income did not decline. Indeed, with the exception of poor urban dwellers, such as sailors whose employment varied with the season, white Americans did quite well. An abundance of land and the extensive growth of agriculture accounted for their economic success. New farmers were able not only to provide for their families' well-being but also to sell their crops in European and West Indian markets. Each year, more Americans produced more tobacco, wheat, or rice—to cite just the major export crops—and by this means, they maintained a high level of individual prosperity without developing an industrial base.

At midcentury, colonial exports flowed along well-established routes. More than half of American goods produced for export went to Great Britain. The Navigation Acts (a series of commercial restrictions passed by Parliament in the second half of seventeenth century) were still in effect, and "enumerated" items such as tobacco had to be landed first at a British port. Furs were added to the restricted list in 1722. The White Pines Acts passed in 1711, 1722, and 1729 forbade Americans from cutting white pine trees without a license. The purpose of this legislation was to reserve the best trees for the use of the Royal Navy. The Molasses Act of 1733—also called the Sugar Act—placed a heavy duty on molasses imported from foreign ports; the Hat and Felt Act of 1732 and the Iron Act of 1750 attempted to limit the production of colonial goods that competed with British exports.

These statutes might have created tensions between the colonists and the mother country had they been rigorously enforced. Crown officials, however, generally ignored the new laws. New England merchants imported molasses from French Caribbean islands without paying the full customs; ironmasters in the Middle Colonies continued to produce iron. Even without the Navigation Acts, however, a majority of colonial exports would have been sold on the English market. The emerging consumer society in Great Britain was beginning to create a new generation of buyers who possessed enough income to purchase American goods, especially sugar and tobacco. This rising demand was the major market force shaping the colonial economy.

LISTEN

The Connecticut Peddler

consumer revolution
Period between 1740 and 1770 when English exports to the American colonies increased by 360 percent, a result of the Americans' huge demand for manufactured goods.

QUICK CHECK ✓

Why did Americans in the first half of the eighteenth century not complain about the Navigation Acts?

Birth of a Consumer Society

After midcentury, Americans began buying more English goods than their parents or grandparents had done, giving birth to a **consumer revolution**. Between 1740 and 1770, English exports to the American colonies increased by an astounding 360 percent.

In part, this new American market shift reflected a fundamental transformation in the British economy. The pace of the British economy picked up dramatically after 1690. Small factories produced certain goods more efficiently and more cheaply than the colonists could. The availability of these products altered the lives of most Americans, even those with modest incomes. Staffordshire china replaced crude earthenware; imported cloth replaced homespun. Franklin noted in his *Autobiography* how changing consumer habits affected his life. For years, he had eaten his breakfast in an earthenware bowl with a pewter spoon, but one morning it was served "in a china bowl, with a spoon of silver." Franklin observed that "this was the first appearance of plate and china in our house which afterwards in the course of years, as our wealth increased, augmented gradually to several hundred pounds in value." In this manner, British industrialization undercut American handicraft and folk art.

To help Americans purchase manufactured goods, British merchants offered generous credit. Colonists deferred settlement by agreeing to pay interest on their debts. The temptation to acquire English finery blinded many people to hard economic realities. They gambled on the future, hoping bumper farm crops would reduce their dependence on the large merchant houses of London and Glasgow. Obviously, some persons lived within their means, but the aggregate American debt continued to grow. Colonial leaders tried various expedients to remain solvent—issuing paper money, for example—and while these efforts delayed a crisis, the balance-of-payments problem was clearly very serious.

The eighteenth century also saw a substantial increase in intercoastal trade. Southern planters sent tobacco and rice to New England and the Middle Colonies, where these staples were exchanged for meat and wheat as well as goods imported

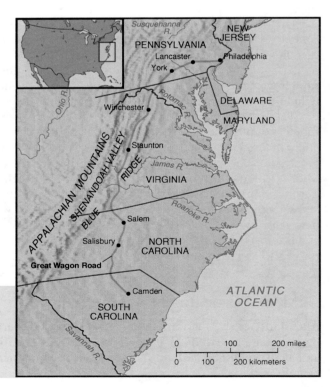

THE GREAT WAGON ROAD   By the mid-eighteenth century, the Great Wagon Road had become a major highway for the settlers in Virginia and the Carolina backcountry.

Why did the Great Wagon Road run roughly north-to-south rather than east-to-west?

from Great Britain. By 1760, approximately 30 percent of the colonists' total tonnage capacity was involved in this extensive "coastwise" commerce. In addition, backcountry farmers in western Pennsylvania and the Shenandoah Valley carried their grain to market along an old Iroquois trail that became known as the Great Wagon Road, a rough, hilly highway that by the time of the Revolution stretched 735 miles along the Blue Ridge Mountains to Camden, South Carolina. Most of their produce was carried in long, gracefully designed Conestoga wagons. These vehicles—sometimes called the "wagons of empire"—had been invented by German immigrants living in the Conestoga River Valley in Lancaster County, Pennsylvania.

The shifting patterns of trade had immense effects on the development of an American culture. First, the flood of British imports eroded local and regional identities. Commerce helped to "Anglicize" American culture by exposing colonial consumers to a common range of British manufactured goods. Deep sectional differences remained, of course, but Americans from New Hampshire to Georgia were increasingly drawn into a sophisticated economic network centered in London. Second, the expanding coastal and overland trade brought colonists of different backgrounds into more frequent contact. Ships that sailed between New England and South Carolina, and between Virginia and Pennsylvania, provided dispersed Americans with a means to exchange ideas and experiences on a more regular basis. Mid-eighteenth–century printers, for example, established several dozen new journals; these were weekly newspapers that carried information not only about the mother country and world commerce but also about events in other colonies.

QUICK CHECK

How did Americans manage to pay for so many new consumer goods?

Religious Revivals in Provincial Societies

A sudden, spontaneous series of Protestant revivals in the mid-seventeenth century, known as the **Great Awakening**, had a profound impact on the lives of ordinary people. This new, highly personal appeal to a "new birth" in Christ caused men and women of all backgrounds to rethink basic assumptions about church and state, institutions and society.

The Great Awakening

Whatever their origins, the seeds of the Great Awakening were generally sown on fertile ground. In the early decades of the century, many Americans—but especially New Englanders—complained that organized religion had lost vitality. They looked back at Winthrop's generation with nostalgia, assuming that common people at that time must have possessed greater piety than did later, more worldly colonists. Congregational ministers seemed obsessed with dull, scholastic matters; they no longer touched the heart. And in the Southern Colonies, there were simply not enough ordained ministers to tend to the religious needs of the population.

The Great Awakening arrived unexpectedly in Northampton, a small farm community in western Massachusetts, sparked by Jonathan Edwards, the local

HOW

did the Great Awakening transform the religious culture of colonial America?

Great Awakening
Widespread evangelical religious revival movement of the mid-1700s. The movement divided congregations and weakened the authority of established churches in the colonies.

Jonathan Edwards, "Sinners in the Hands of an Angry God"

Benjamin Franklin on George Whitefield (1771)

Congregational minister. Edwards accepted the traditional teachings of Calvinism, reminding his parishioners that their eternal fate had been determined by an omnipotent God, there was nothing they could do to save themselves, and they were totally dependent on the Lord's will. He thought his fellow ministers had grown soft. They left men and women with the mistaken impression that sinners might somehow avoid eternal damnation simply by performing good works.

Although Edwards was an outstanding theologian, he did not possess the dynamic personality required to sustain the revival. That responsibility fell to George Whitefield, a young, inspiring preacher from England who toured the colonies from New Hampshire to Georgia. While Whitefield was not an original thinker, he was an extraordinarily effective public speaker. And like his friend Benjamin Franklin, he came to symbolize the powerful cultural forces that were transforming the Atlantic world.

Whitefield's audiences came from all groups of American society: rich and poor, young and old, rural and urban. While Whitefield described himself as a Calvinist, he welcomed all Protestants. He spoke from any pulpit that was available. "Don't tell me you are a Baptist, an Independent, a Presbyterian, a dissenter," he thundered, "tell me you are a Christian, that is all I want."

GEORGE WHITEFIELD The fervor of the Great Awakening was intensified by the eloquence of itinerant preachers such as George Whitefield, the most popular evangelical of the mid-eighteenth century. (*Source: John Wollaston, "George Whitefield," ca. 1770. National Portrait Gallery, London.*)

How did a preacher from England become the most popular minister in colonial America?

Whitefield was a brilliant entrepreneur. Like Franklin, with whom he published many popular volumes, the itinerant minister possessed an almost intuitive sense of how this burgeoning consumer society could be turned to his own advantage, and he embraced the latest merchandising techniques. He appreciated, for example, the power of the press in selling the revival, and he regularly promoted his own work in advertisements placed in British and American newspapers. The crowds flocked to hear Whitefield, while his critics grumbled about the commercialization of religion. One anonymous writer in Massachusetts noted that there was "a very wholesome law of the province to discourage Pedlars in Trade" and it seemed high time "to enact something for the discouragement of Pedlars in Divinity also."

QUICK CHECK ✓

What explains the Reverend George Whitefield's extraordinary popularity among colonial Americans?

Evangelical Religion

Other American-born **itinerant preachers**, who traveled from settlement to settlement throughout the colonies to spread their message, followed Whitefield's example. The most famous was Gilbert Tennent, a Presbyterian of Scots-Irish background who had been educated in the Middle Colonies. His sermon "On the Danger of an Unconverted Ministry," printed in 1741, set off a storm of protest from established ministers who were understandably insulted by assertions that they did not understand true religion. Lesser known revivalists traveled from town to town, colony to colony, challenging local clergymen who seemed hostile to evangelical religion. Men and women who thronged to hear the itinerants were called "New Lights," and during the 1740s and 1750s, many congregations split between defenders of the new emotional preaching and those who regarded the entire movement as dangerous nonsense.

Despite Whitefield's successes, many ministers remained suspicious of the itinerants and their methods. Some complaints may have amounted to little more than sour grapes. One "Old Light" spokesman labeled Tennent "a monster! impudent and noisy." He claimed Tennent told anxious Christians that "they were damned! damned! damned! This charmed them; and, in the most dreadful winter I ever saw, people wallowed in snow, night and day, for the benefit of his beastly brayings; and many ended their days under these fatigues." Charles Chauncy, minister of the prestigious First Church of Boston, raised much more troubling issues. How could the revivalists be certain God had sparked the Great Awakening? Perhaps the itinerants had relied too much on emotion? "Let us esteem those as friends of religion," Chauncy advised, "… who warn us of the danger of enthusiasm, and would put us on our guard, that we may not be led aside by it."

Despite occasional anti-intellectual outbursts, the New Lights founded several important centers of higher learning. They wanted to train young men who would carry on the good works of Edwards, Whitefield, and Tennent. In 1746, New Light Presbyterians established the College of New Jersey, which later became Princeton University. Just before his death, Edwards was appointed its president. The evangelical minister Eleazar Wheelock launched Dartmouth (1769); other revivalists founded Brown (1764) and Rutgers (1766).

The Great Awakening also encouraged men and women who had been taught to remain silent before traditional figures of authority to speak up, to take an active role in their salvation. They could no longer rely on ministers or institutions. The individual alone stood before God. Knowing this, New Lights made religious

itinerant preachers
Traveling revivalist ministers of the Great Awakening movement. These charismatic preachers spread revivalism throughout America.

choices that shattered the old harmony among Protestant sects, and in its place, they introduced a noisy, often bitterly fought competition. As one New Jersey Presbyterian explained, "There are so many particular *sects* and *Parties* among professed Christians... that we know not... in which of these different *paths*, to steer our course for *Heaven*."

Expressive evangelicalism struck a particularly responsive chord among African Americans. Itinerant ministers frequently preached to large sympathetic audiences of slaves. Richard Allen (1760–1831), founder of the African Methodist Episcopal Church, reported he owed his freedom in part to a traveling Methodist minister who persuaded Allen's master of the sinfulness of slavery. Allen himself was converted, as were thousands of other black colonists. According to one historian, evangelical preaching "shared enough with traditional African styles and beliefs such as spirit possession and ecstatic expression... to allow for an interpenetration of African and Christian religious beliefs."

With religious contention came an awareness of a larger community, a union of fellow believers that extended beyond the boundaries of town and colony. In fact, evangelical religion was one of several forces at work during the mid-eighteenth century that brought scattered colonists into contact with one another for the first time. In this sense, the Great Awakening was a "national" event long before a nation actually existed.

People who had been touched by the Great Awakening shared an optimism about the future of America. With God's help, social and political progress was possible, and from this perspective, of course, the New Lights did not sound much different than the mildly rationalist American spokesmen of the Enlightenment. Both groups prepared the way for the development of a revolutionary mentality in colonial America.

QUICK CHECK ✓

What message did evangelical ministers bring to ordinary Americans?

Clash of Political Cultures

WHAT kept the colonial assemblies of the eighteenth century from being fully democratic?

The political history of the eighteenth century illuminates a growing tension within the empire. Americans of all regions repeatedly stated their desire to replicate British political institutions. Parliament, they claimed, provided a model for the American assemblies. Although England never had a formal written constitution, it did develop over the centuries a system of legal checks and balances that, in theory at least, kept the monarch from becoming a tyrant. The colonists claimed that this unwritten constitution preserved their rights and liberties. However, the more the colonists studied British political theory and practice—in other words, the more they attempted to become British—the more aware they became of major differences.

Governing the Colonies: The American Experience

The colonists assumed—perhaps naively—that their own governments were modeled on the balanced constitution of Great Britain. They argued that within their political systems, the governor corresponded to the king and the governor's council to the House of Lords. The colonial assemblies were perceived as American reproductions of the House of Commons and were expected to preserve the interests of the people against those of the monarch and aristocracy. As the colonists discovered, however, general theories about a mixed constitution were even less relevant in America than they were in Britain.

By midcentury a majority of the mainland colonies had royal governors appointed by the crown. Many were career army officers who through luck, charm, or family connection had gained the ear of someone close to the king. These patronage posts did not generate income sufficient to interest the most powerful or talented personalities of the period, but they did draw middle-level bureaucrats who were ambitious, desperate, or both. It is perhaps not surprising that most governors decided simply not to "consider any Thing further than how to sit easy."

Whatever their demerits, royal governors in America possessed enormous powers. In fact, royal governors could do certain things in America that a king could not do in eighteenth-century Britain. Among these were the right to veto legislation and dismiss judges. The governors also served as military commanders in each province.

Political practice in America differed from the British model in another crucial respect. Royal governors were advised by a council, usually a body of about twelve wealthy colonists selected by the Board of Trade in London upon the recommendation of the governor. During the seventeenth century, the council had played an important role in colonial government, but its ability to exercise independent authority declined steadily over the course of the eighteenth century. Its members certainly did not represent a distinct aristocracy within American society.

If royal governors did not look like kings, nor American councils like the House of Lords, colonial assemblies bore little resemblance to the eighteenth-century House of Commons. The major difference was the size of the American franchise. In most colonies, adult white males who owned a small amount of land could vote in colonywide elections. One historian estimates that 95 percent of this group in Massachusetts were eligible to participate in elections. The number in Virginia was about 85 percent. These figures—much higher than those in contemporary England—have led some scholars to view the colonies as "middle-class democracies," societies run by moderately prosperous yeomen farmers who—in politics at least—exercised independent judgment. There were too many of them to bribe, no "rotten" boroughs, and when these people moved west, colonial assemblies usually created new electoral districts.

Colonial governments were not democracies in the modern sense of that term. Possessing the right to vote was one thing, exercising it quite another. Americans participated in elections when major issues were at stake—the formation of banks in mid-eighteenth-century Massachusetts, for example—but most of the time they were content to let members of the rural and urban gentry represent them in the assemblies. To be sure, unlike modern democracies, these colonial politics excluded women and nonwhites from voting. The point to remember, however, is that the power to expel legislative rascals was always present in America, and it was this political reality that kept autocratic gentlemen from straying too far from the will of the people.

QUICK CHECK ✓

What was the structure of royal government in eighteenth-century America?

Colonial Assemblies

Elected members of the colonial assemblies believed that they had a special obligation to preserve colonial liberties. They perceived any attack on the legislature as an assault on the rights of Americans. The elected representatives brooked no criticism, and several colonial printers landed in jail because they criticized actions taken by a lower house.

So aggressive were these bodies in seizing privileges, determining procedures, and controlling money bills that some historians have described the political development of eighteenth-century America as "the rise of the assemblies." No doubt this is exaggerated, but the long series of imperial wars against the French, demanding large public expenditures, transformed the small, amateurish assemblies of the seventeenth century into the more professional, vigilant legislatures of the eighteenth.

This political system seemed designed to generate hostility. There was simply no reason for the colonial legislators to cooperate with appointed royal governors. Alexander Spotswood, Virginia's governor from 1710 to 1722, for example, attempted to institute a bold new land program backed by the crown. He tried persuasion and gifts and, when these failed, chicanery. But the members of the House of Burgesses refused to support a plan that did not suit their own interests. Before leaving office, Spotswood gave up trying to carry out royal policy in America.

Instead, he allied himself with the local Virginia gentry who controlled the House as well as the Council, and because they awarded their new friend with large tracts of land, he became a wealthy man.

A few governors managed briefly to recreate in America the political culture of patronage, the system that eighteenth-century Englishmen took for granted. Most successful in this endeavor was William Shirley, who held office in Massachusetts from 1741 to 1757. The secret to his political successes in America was connection to people who held high office in Great Britain. But Shirley's practices—and those of men like him—clashed with the colonists' perception of politics. They really believed in the purity of the balanced constitution. They insisted on complete separation of executive and legislative authority.

A major source of shared political information was the weekly journal, a new and vigorous institution

COLONIAL NEWSPAPERS Colonial newspapers were an important means of political participation. The masthead of this edition of *The Massachusetts Spy* declares its journalistic objectivity: "A Weekly, Political, and Commercial Paper; open to ALL Parties, but influenced by None." (*Source: North Wind Picture Archives.*)

What did it mean for a journal to claim it was a "Political and Commercial Paper"?

in American life. In New York and Massachusetts especially, weekly journals urged readers to preserve civic virtue, to exercise extreme vigilance against the spread of privileged power.

The rise of the assemblies shaped American culture in other, subtler ways. Over the course of the century, the language of the law became increasingly English in character. The Board of Trade, the Privy Council, and Parliament scrutinized court decisions and legislative actions from all thirteen mainland colonies. As a result, varying local legal practices that had been widespread during the seventeenth century became standardized. Indeed, according to one historian, the colonial legal system by 1750 "was substantially that of the mother country." Not surprisingly, many men who served in colonial assemblies were either lawyers or persons who had received legal training. When Americans from different regions met—as they frequently did in the years before the Revolution—they discovered that they shared a commitment to the preservation of the English common law.

As eighteenth-century political developments drew the colonists closer to the mother country, they also brought Americans a greater awareness of each other. As their horizons widened, they learned they operated within the same general imperial system. Like the revivalists and merchants—people who crossed old boundaries—colonial legislators laid the foundation for a larger cultural identity.

QUICK CHECK ✓

Why were the plans of royal governors so often defeated by colonial assemblies?

Century of Imperial War

The scope and character of warfare in the colonies changed radically during the eighteenth century. The founders of England's mainland colonies had engaged in intense local conflicts with the Indians, such as King Philip's War (1675–1676) in New England. But after 1690, the colonists were increasingly involved in hostilities that originated on the other side of the Atlantic, in rivalries between Great Britain and France over political and commercial ambitions. The external threat to security forced people in different colonies to devise unprecedented measures of military and political cooperation.

WHY

did colonial Americans support Great Britain's wars against France?

The French Threat

On paper, at least, the British colonies enjoyed military superiority over the settlements of New France. Louis XIV, king of France from 1643 to 1715, possessed an impressive army of 100,000 well-armed troops, but he dispatched few of them to the New World. He left the defense of Canada and the Mississippi Valley to the companies engaged in the fur trade. Meeting this challenge seemed almost impossible for the French outposts strung out along the St. Lawrence River and the Great Lakes. In 1754, New France contained only 75,000 inhabitants as compared to 1.2 million people living in Britain's mainland colonies.

For most of the century, the theoretical advantages enjoyed by the English colonists did them little good. While the British settlements possessed a larger

MAP

The Struggle for the Continent

THEYANOGUIN Native Americans often depended on trade goods supplied by the British and sometimes adopted British dress. Here the Mohawk chief Theyanoguin, called King Hendrick by the British, wears a cloak he received from Queen Anne of England during a visit to London in 1710. During the Seven Years' War, Theyanoguin mobilized Mohawk support for the British.

In what ways does Theyanoguin's attire reflect the "consumer revolution" of the eighteenth century?

and more prosperous population, they were divided into separate governments that sometimes seemed more suspicious of each other than of the French. When war came, French officers and Indian allies exploited these jealousies with considerable skill. Moreover, although the population of New France was comparatively small, it was concentrated along the St. Lawrence, so that while the French found it difficult to mount effective offensive operations against the English, they could easily mass the forces needed to defend Montreal and Quebec.

During the early decades of the eighteenth century, English colonists came to believe that the French planned to "encircle" the English settlements, to confine the English to a narrow strip of land along the Atlantic coast. The English noted as early as 1682 that La Salle had claimed for the king of France a territory— Louisiana—that included all the people and resources located on "streams and Rivers" flowing into the Mississippi River. To make good on their claim, the French constructed forts on the Chicago and Illinois rivers. In 1717, they established a military post two hundred miles up the Alabama River, well within striking distance of the Carolina frontier, and in 1718, they settled New Orleans. One New Yorker declared in 1715 that "it is impossible that we and the French can both inhabit this Continent in peace but that one nation must at last give way to the other."

On their part, the French suspected their rivals intended to seize all of North America. Land speculators and frontier traders pushed aggressively into territory claimed by the French and owned by the Native Americans. In 1716, one Frenchman urged his government to hasten the development of Louisiana, since "it is not difficult to guess that their [the British] purpose is to drive us entirely out… of North America."

QUICK CHECK ✓

Why during the eighteenth century did Britain's American colonists come to view the French as a serious threat?

BRITISH ASSAULT AT LOUISBOURG   This mid-eighteenth-century lithograph portrays colonial assault troops, under the command of William Pepperell, establishing a beachhead at Freshwater Cove near Louisbourg. Pepperell's troops went on to capture the French fortress.

In what ways does this lithograph celebrate British nationalism?

King George's War and Its Aftermath

In 1743, after many small frontier engagements, the Americans were dragged into King George's War (1743–1748), known in Europe as the War of the Austrian Succession, in which the colonists scored a magnificent victory over the French. Louisbourg, a gigantic fortress on Cape Breton Island, the easternmost promontory of Canada, guarded the approaches to the Gulf of St. Lawrence and Quebec. It was described as the Gibraltar of the New World. An army of New England troops under the command of William Pepperell captured Louisbourg in June 1745, a feat that demonstrated the British colonists were able to fight and to mount effective joint operations.

The French were not prepared to surrender an inch. But as they recognized, not only were the English colonies growing more populous, but they also possessed a seemingly inexhaustible supply of manufactured goods to trade with the Indians. The French decided in the early 1750s, therefore, to seize the Ohio Valley before the Virginians could do so. They established forts throughout the region, the most formidable being Fort Duquesne, located at the strategic fork in the Ohio River and later renamed Pittsburgh.

Although France and England had not officially declared war, British officials advised the governor of Virginia to "repell force by force." The Virginians needed little encouragement. They were eager to make good their claim to the Ohio Valley,

NORTH AMERICA, 1750   By 1750, the French had established a chain of settlements southward through the heart of the continent from Quebec to New Orleans. The British saw this as a threat to their own seaboard colonies, which were expanding westward.

Why did the British colonists regard France as a more serious threat than Spain?

Albany Plan

Plan of intercolonial cooperation proposed by prominent colonists including Benjamin Franklin at a conference in Albany, New York, in 1754. The plan envisioned the formation of a Grand Council of elected delegates from the colonies that would have powers to tax and provide for the common defense. It was rejected by the colonial and British government but was a prototype for colonial union.

and in 1754, militia companies under the command of a promising young officer, George Washington, constructed Fort Necessity not far from Fort Duquesne. The plan failed. French and Indian troops overran the badly exposed outpost (July 3, 1754). Among other things, the humiliating setback revealed that a single colony could not defeat the French.

Benjamin Franklin, for one, appreciated the need for intercolonial cooperation. When British officials invited representatives from Virginia and Maryland as well as the northern colonies to Albany (June 1754) to discuss relations with the Iroquois, Franklin used the occasion to present a bold blueprint for colonial union. His so-called **Albany Plan** envisioned the formation of a Grand Council, made up of elected delegates from the various colonies, to oversee matters of

THE ALBANY PLAN The first political cartoon to appear in an American newspaper was created by Benjamin Franklin in 1754 to emphasize the importance of the Albany Plan.

What message did this rattlesnake communicate to American colonists?

common defense, western expansion, and Indian affairs. A President General appointed by the king would preside.

First reaction to the Albany Plan was enthusiastic. To take effect, however, it required the support of the separate colonial assemblies as well as Parliament. It received neither. The assemblies were jealous of their fiscal authority, and the English thought the scheme undermined the Crown's power over American affairs.

			A CENTURY OF CONFLICT: MAJOR WARS, 1689–1763				
Dates	**European Name**	**American Name**	**Major Allies**	**Issues**	**Major American Battle**	**Treaty**
1689–1697	War of the League of Augsburg	King William's War	Britain, Holland, Spain, their colonies, and Native American allies against France, its colonies, and Native American allies	Opposition to French bid for control of Europe	New England troops assault Quebec under Sir William Phips (1690)	Treaty of Ryswick (1697)
1702–1713	War of the Spanish Succession	Queen Anne's War	Britain, Holland, their colonies, and Native American allies against France, Spain, their colonies, and Native American allies	Austria and France hold rival claims to Spanish throne	Attack on Deerfield (1704)	Treaty of Utrecht (1713)
1743–1748	War of the Austrian Succession (War of Jenkin's Ear)	King George's War	Britain, its colonies, and Native American allies, and Austria against France, Spain, their Native American allies, and Prussia	Struggle among Britain, Spain, and France for control of New World territory; among France, Prussia, and Austria for control of central Europe	New England forces capture of Louisbourg under William Pepperell (1745)	Treaty of Aix-la-Chapelle (1748)
1756–1763	Seven Years' War	French and Indian War	Britain, its colonies, and Native American allies against France, its colonies, and Native American allies	Struggle among Britain, Spain, and France for worldwide control of colonial markets and raw materials	British and Continental forces capture Quebec under Major General James Wolfe (1759)	Peace of Paris (1763)

In 1755, the Ohio Valley again became the scene of fierce fighting. Even though there was still no formal declaration of war, the British resolved to destroy Fort Duquesne, and to that end, they dispatched units of the regular army to America. In command was Major General Edward Braddock, an obese, humorless veteran who inspired neither fear nor respect. One colonist described Braddock as "very indolent, Slave to his passions, women & wine, as great an Epicure as could be in his eating, tho a brave man."

On July 9, Braddock led a joint force of twenty-five hundred British redcoats and colonists to humiliating defeat. The French and Indians opened fire as Braddock's army waded across the Monongahela River, about eight miles from Fort Duquesne. Along a narrow road already congested with heavy wagons and confused men, Braddock ordered a counterattack, described by one of his officers as "without any form or order but that of a parcell of school boys coming out of s[c]hool." Nearly 70 percent of Braddock's troops were killed or wounded in western Pennsylvania. The general himself died in battle. The French, who suffered only light casualties, remained in firm control of the Ohio Valley.

QUICK CHECK ✓

Why did Benjamin Franklin's Albany Plan receive so little support?

Seven Years' War

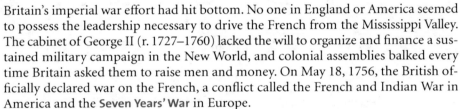

The Seven Years' War

Seven Years' War
Worldwide conflict (1756–1763) that pitted Britain against France for control of North America. With help from the American colonists, the British won the war and eliminated France as a power on the North American continent. Also known in America as the *French and Indian War*.

Britain's imperial war effort had hit bottom. No one in England or America seemed to possess the leadership necessary to drive the French from the Mississippi Valley. The cabinet of George II (r. 1727–1760) lacked the will to organize and finance a sustained military campaign in the New World, and colonial assemblies balked every time Britain asked them to raise men and money. On May 18, 1756, the British officially declared war on the French, a conflict called the French and Indian War in America and the **Seven Years' War** in Europe.

Had it not been for William Pitt, the most powerful minister in George's cabinet, the military stalemate might have continued. This supremely self-confident Englishman believed he was the only person capable of saving the British empire, an opinion he publicly expressed. When he became effective head of the ministry in December 1756, Pitt had an opportunity to demonstrate his talents.

In the past, warfare on the European continent had worked mainly to France's advantage. Pitt saw no point in continuing to concentrate on Europe, and in 1757 he advanced a bold new imperial policy, one based on commercial assumptions. In Pitt's judgment, the critical confrontation would take place in North America, where Britain and France were struggling to control colonial markets and raw materials. Indeed, according to Pitt, America was "where England and Europe are to be fought for." He was determined, therefore, to expel the French from the continent, however great the cost.

To direct the grand campaign, Pitt selected two relatively obscure officers, Jeffrey Amherst and James Wolfe. It was a masterful choice, one that a less self-assured man than Pitt would never have risked. Both officers were young, talented, and ambitious, and on July 26, 1758, forces under their direction captured Louisbourg, the same fortress the colonists had taken a decade earlier!

This victory cut the Canadians' main supply line with France. The small population of New France could no longer meet the military demands placed on it. As the situation became increasingly desperate, the French forts of the Ohio Valley and the Great Lakes began to fall. Duquesne was simply abandoned late in 1758 as

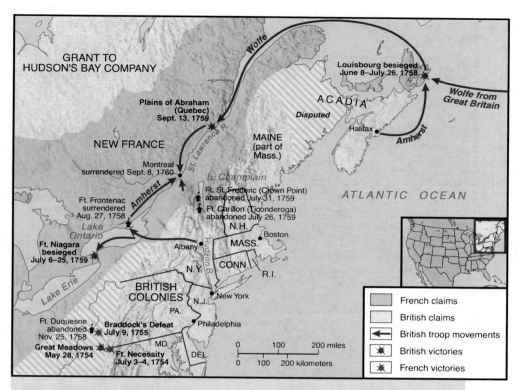

THE SEVEN YEARS' WAR, 1756–1763 Major battle sites. The conflict ended with Britain driving France from mainland North America.

Why did it take so long for Britain to defeat the French forces in North America?

French and Indian troops under the Marquis de Montcalm retreated toward Quebec and Montreal. During the summer of 1759, the French surrendered key forts at Ticonderoga, Crown Point, and Niagara.

The **Peace of Paris of 1763**, signed on February 10, almost fulfilled Pitt's grandiose dreams. Great Britain took possession of an empire that stretched around the globe. Only Guadeloupe and Martinique, the Caribbean sugar islands, were given back to the French. After a centurylong struggle, the French had been driven from the mainland of North America. Even Louisiana passed out of France's control into Spanish hands. The treaty gave Britain title to Canada, Florida, and all the land east of the Mississippi River. Moreover, with the stroke of a diplomat's pen, eighty thousand French-speaking Canadians, most of them Catholics, became the subjects of George III.

The Americans were overjoyed. It was a time of good feelings and national pride. Together, the English and their colonial allies had thwarted the "Gallic peril." Samuel Davies, a Presbyterian who had brought the Great Awakening to Virginia, announced confidently that the long-awaited victory would inaugurate "a new heaven and a new earth."

Peace of Paris of 1763
Treaty ending the French and Indian War, which marked the beginning of Great Britain's expansion of its empire outside of Europe.

QUICK CHECK ✔

How did the Peace of Paris of 1763 transform North American politics?

NORTH AMERICA AFTER 1763 The Peace of Paris of 1763 redrew the map of North America. Great Britain received all the French holdings except for a few islands in the Atlantic and some sugar-producing islands in the Caribbean.

Why do you think that some British leaders favored taking these islands as part of the peace treaty, instead of taking control of Canada?

Perceptions of War

The Seven Years' War made a deep impression on American society. Even though Franklin's Albany Plan had failed, the military struggle had forced the colonists to cooperate on an unprecedented scale. It also drew them into closer contact with Britain. They became aware of being part of a great empire, military and commercial, but in the very process of waging war, they acquired a more intimate sense of an America that lay beyond the plantation and the village. Conflict had carried thousands of young men across colonial boundaries, exposing them to a vast territory full of opportunities for a booming population. Moreover, the war trained a corps of American officers, people like George Washington, who learned from firsthand experience that the British were not invincible.

British officials later accused the Americans of ingratitude. England, they claimed, had sent troops and provided funds to liberate the colonists from the threat of French attack. The Americans, appreciative of the aid from England, cheered on the British but dragged their feet at every stage, refusing to pay the bills. These charges were later incorporated into a general argument justifying parliamentary taxation in America.

The British had a point. The colonists were, in fact, slow in providing the men and materials needed to fight the French. Nevertheless, they did make a significant contribution to the war effort, and it was perfectly reasonable for Americans to regard themselves at the very least as junior partners in the empire.

QUICK CHECK ✓

Why did victory over France not generate greater mutual respect between American colonists and the British?

Conclusion: Rule Britannia?

James Thomson, an Englishman, understood the hold of empire on the popular imagination of the eighteenth century. In 1740, he composed words that British patriots have proudly sung for more than two centuries:

> Rule Britannia, rule the waves,
> Britons never will be slaves.

Colonial Americans—at least, those of British background—joined the chorus. By midcentury they took their political and cultural cues from Great Britain. They fought its wars, purchased its consumer goods, flocked to hear its evangelical preachers, and read its many publications. Without question, the empire provided the colonists with a compelling source of identity.

An editor justified the establishment of New Hampshire's first newspaper in precisely these terms. "By this Means," the publisher observed, "the spirited *Englishman*, the mountainous *Welshman*, the brave *Scotchman*, and *Irishman*, and the loyal *American*, may be firmly united and mutually RESOLVED to guard the glorious Throne of BRITANNIA… as *British Brothers*, in defending the Common Cause." Even new immigrants, the Germans, Scots-Irish, and Africans, who felt no political loyalty to Great Britain and no affinity to English culture, had to assimilate to some degree to the dominant English culture of the colonies.

Americans hailed Britannia. In 1763, they were the victors, the conquerors of the backcountry. In their moment of glory, the colonists assumed that Britain's rulers saw the Americans as "Brothers," as equal partners in the business of empire. Only slowly would they learn the British had a different perception. For them, "American" was a way of saying "not quite English."

For a list of additional titles related to this chapter's topics, please see www.pearsonamericanhistory.com.

MyHistoryLab

STUDY RESOURCES

KEY TERMS

backcountry

middle ground

Enlightenment

consumer revolution

Great Awakening

itinerant preachers

Albany Plan

Seven Years' War

Peace of Paris of 1763

CHAPTER REVIEW

WHAT difficulties did Native Americans face in maintaining their cultural independence on the frontier?

Britain's American colonies experienced extraordinary population and economic growth during the eighteenth century. German and Scots-Irish migrants poured into the backcountry, where they clashed with Native Americans. The Indians successfully played off French and British imperial ambitions in the "middle ground," but disease and encroachment by ordinary European settlers undermined the Indians' ability to resist.

WHY was the Spanish empire unable to achieve effective control on its northern frontier?

During the late 1600s and early 1700s, the Spanish Empire steadily expanded its authority north of Mexico. New Spanish settlements were established in the Southwest and California. Although the Spanish constructed missions and forts, a lack of settlers and troops made it impossible for them to impose effective imperial authority and much of the territory they claimed remained under the control of Indian peoples.

HOW did European ideas affect the character of eighteenth-century American life?

During the Enlightenment, educated Europeans and American colonists, like Benjamin Franklin, brought scientific reason to the study of religion, nature, and society. By mid-century, economic growth sparked a consumer revolution that introduced colonists to an unprecedented array of imported manufactured items. New ideas and new goods helped integrate the American colonies into mainstream British culture.

HOW did the Great Awakening transform the religious culture of colonial America?

The Great Awakening brought a new form of evangelical religion to ordinary colonial Americans. It emphasized personal salvation through a "New Birth" and membership in a large community of believers. Itinerant preachers, such as George Whitefield, drew huge crowds throughout the colonies. Other ministers followed Whitefield, inviting ordinary Americans to question traditional religious authorities.

WHAT kept the colonial assemblies of the eighteenth century from being fully democratic?

Most eighteenth-century colonial governments contained a royal governor, an appointed governor's council, and an elected assembly. Although these representative assemblies did not allow women, blacks, or the poor to vote, they did enfranchise a significant percentage of the white adult male population. Assemblies guarded their privileges and powers, often coming into conflict with royal governors who attempted to expand their authority.

WHY did colonial Americans support Great Britain's wars against France?

France and Great Britain waged constant war in North America. By 1750, Britain's American colonists believed the French in Canada planned to encircle their settlements, cutting them off from the rich lands of the Ohio Valley. The Seven Years' War drove the French from Canada, a stunning victory that generated unprecedented enthusiasm for the British Empire in the colonies.

MAKING CONNECTIONS

1. What factors ultimately served to undermine the "middle ground"?
2. What impact did the Spanish empire have on the culture of the borderlands?
3. What impact did Enlightenment ideas and commercial goods have on American politics?

4. What are the similarities and differences between the impact of the Enlightenment and the Great Awakening on colonial society?

5. Why did colonists place greater political trust in their elected assemblies than in their royally appointed governors?

PRACTICE QUIZ

1. George _____ became a leading evangelist.
   a. Whitefield
   b. Welsh
   c. English
   d. Williams

2. The Spanish leader _____ established settlements in New Mexico.
   a. Christopher Columbus
   b. Hernando Cortez
   c. Francisco Pizarro
   d. Juan de Oñate

3. _____ was a place that Spain feared the Russians would take as a colony in the 1700s.
   a. Mexico
   b. California
   c. Florida
   d. South America

4. The scientist and diplomat _____ received heavy influence from the Enlightenment.
   a. Benjamin Franklin
   b. George Washington
   c. Roger Williams
   d. Nathaniel Bacon

5. The _____ became a religious movement in the colonies during the mid-1700s.
   a. Industrial Revolution
   b. Great Awakening
   c. Little Ice Age
   d. Glorious Revolution

6. Mexico achieved independence from Spain in
   a. 1810
   b. 1776
   c. 1800
   d. 1821

7. Historians refer to the eighteenth century in Europe as an Age of
   a. Treachery
   b. Regression
   c. Reason
   d. Retreat

8. All of the following accurately describe German immigrants to the American colonies *except*
   a. German immigrants failed to preserve aspects of their traditional culture.
   b. Over 100,000 Germans came to the British North American colonies.
   c. Many Germans held religious views similar to American Protestants.
   d. Many German Lutherans lived in the Middle Colonies.

9. The Albany Plan included the following *except*
   a. A President General appointed by the king would preside.
   b. The formation of a Grand Council of all the colonies.
   c. The Grand Council would consist of elected delegates from each colony.
   d. The Grand Council would oversee matters of common defense against Indians and the French.

10. Which of the following was *not* an outcome of the Peace of Paris of 1763?
    a. Great Britain took possession of a global empire.
    b. The British gave back two Caribbean sugar islands to the French.
    c. Britain gained title to California.
    d. The Spanish received French Louisiana.

Find more practice at
www.myhistorylab.com

SAMPLE ESSAY QUESTIONS

1. Explain native people's role in Spanish colonization of California and New Mexico.

2. In what ways did Native Americans manipulate the middle ground to their advantage?

CREDITS

The American Revolution:

From Elite Protest to Popular Revolt, 1763–1783

The American Revolution
From Elite Protest to Popular Revolt, 1763–1783

BOSTON

CHARLES TOWN

WHY did Americans resist parliamentary taxation?

Structure of Colonial Society

WHAT events led to the erosion of the bonds of empire during the 1760s?

Eroding the Bonds of Empire

WHAT events in 1775 and 1776 led to the colonists' decision to declare independence?

Steps Toward Independence

WHY did it take eight years of warfare for the Americans to gain independence?

Fighting for Independence

BUNKER HILL *The Battle of Bunker Hill by Winthrop Chandler, which also shows the burning of Charles Town. (Source: "The Battle of Bunker Hill," c. 1776–77 by Winthrop Chandler. Oil on panel; 34 7/8 × 53 5/8 inches/Gift of Mr. and Mrs. Gardner Ricardson, 1982. 281./Courtesy of the Museum of Fine Arts, Boston. Reproduced with permission. © 2005 Museum of Fine Arts, Boston. All Rights Reserved.)*

How do you think a small, untrained American force was able to achieve this victory?

Moment of Decision: Commitment and Sacrifice

Even as the British army poured into Boston in 1774, demanding complete obedience to king and Parliament, few Americans welcomed the possibility of revolutionary violence. For many colonial families, it would have been easier, certainly safer, to accede to imperial demands for taxes enacted without their representation. But they did not do so.

For the Patten family, the time of reckoning arrived in the spring of 1775. Matthew Patten had been born in Ulster, a Protestant Irishman, and with Scots-Irish friends and relatives, he migrated to New Hampshire, where they founded a settlement of fifty-six families known as Bedford. Matthew farmed the unpromising, rocky soil that he, his wife, Elizabeth, and their children called home. In time, distant decisions about taxes and representation shattered the peace of Bedford, and the Pattens found themselves drawn into a war not of their own making but which, nevertheless, compelled them to sacrifice the security of everyday life for liberty.

On April 20, 1775, accounts of Lexington and Concord reached Bedford. Matthew noted in his diary, "I Received the Melancholy news in the morning that General Gage's troops had fired on our Countrymen at Concord yesterday." His son John marched with neighbors in support of the Massachusetts soldiers. The departure was tense. The entire family helped John prepare. "Our Girls sit up all night baking bread and fitting things for him," Matthew wrote.

KEY EVENTS

1764 Parliament passes Sugar Act to collect American revenue

1765 Stamp Act receives support of House of Commons (March) ■ Stamp Act Congress meets in New York City (October)

1766 Stamp Act repealed the same day that Declaratory Act becomes law (March 18)

1767 Townshend Revenue Acts stir American anger (June–July)

1770 Parliament repeals all Townshend duties except one on tea (March) ■ British troops "massacre" Boston civilians (March)

1772 Samuel Adams forms committee of correspondence

1773 Lord North's government passes Tea Act (May) ■ Bostonians hold Tea Party (December)

1774 Parliament punishes Boston with Coercive Acts (March–June) ■ First Continental Congress convenes (September)

1775 Patriots take stand at Lexington and Concord (April) ■ Second Continental Congress gathers (May) ■ Americans hold their own at Bunker Hill (June)

1776 Congress votes for independence; Declaration of Independence is signed ■ British defeat Washington at Long Island (August) ■ Americans score victory at Trenton (December)

1777 General Burgoyne surrenders at Saratoga (October)

1778 French treaties recognize independence of the United States (February)

1780 British take Charles Town (May)

1781 Washington forces Cornwallis to surrender at Yorktown (October)

1783 Peace treaty signed (September)

The demands of war had only just begun. In late 1775 John volunteered for an American march on British Canada. On the long trek over impossible terrain, the boy died. The father recorded his emotions in the diary. John "was shot through his left arm at Bunker Hill fight and now was lead after suffering much fategue to the place where he now lyes in defending the just Rights of America to whose end he came in the prime of life by means of that wicked Tyrannical Brute (nea worse than Brute) of Great Britain [George III]. He was Twenty four years and 31 days old."

The initial stimulus for rebellion came from the gentry, from the rich and well-born, who resented Parliament's efforts to curtail their rights within the British empire. But as these influential planters, wealthy merchants, and prominent clergymen discovered, the revolutionary movement generated a momentum that they could not control. As relations with Britain deteriorated, particularly after 1765, the traditional leaders of colonial society encouraged the ordinary folk to join the protest—as rioters, as petitioners, and finally, as soldiers. Newspapers, sermons, and pamphlets helped transform what had begun as a squabble among the gentry into a mass movement, and once the people had become involved in shaping the nation's destiny, they could never again be excluded.

Had it not been for ordinary militiamen like John Patten in the various colonies, the British would have easily crushed American resistance. Although some accounts of the Revolution downplay the military side of the story, leaving the impression that a few famous "Founding Fathers" effortlessly carried the nation to independence, a more persuasive explanation must recognize the centrality of armed violence in achieving nationhood.

The American Revolution involved a massive military commitment. If common American soldiers had not been willing to stand up to seasoned British troops, to face the terror of the bayonet charge, independence would have remained a dream of intellectuals. Proportionate to the population, a greater percentage of Americans died in military service during the Revolution than in any war in American history, with the exception of the Civil War.

The concept of liberty so magnificently expressed in revolutionary pamphlets was not, therefore, simply an abstraction, an exclusive concern of political theorists such as Thomas Jefferson and John Adams. It also motivated ordinary folk—the Patten family, for example—to take up weapons and risk death. Those who survived the ordeal were never quite the same, for the very experience of fighting, of assuming responsibility in

98

PATTEN FARMSTEAD The family home of the Patten family in Bedford, New Hampshire.

Why would colonists who lived in modest homes like this one have been willing to support elite merchants and planters in the revolutionary movement?

battle and perhaps even of taking the lives of British officers, gave dramatic new meaning to the idea of social equality.

Structure of Colonial Society

Colonists who were alive during the 1760s did not anticipate the coming of national independence. For many Americans, the period generated optimism. The population continued to grow. Indeed, in 1776, approximately 2.5 million people, black and white, were living in Great Britain's thirteen mainland colonies. The striking ethnic and racial diversity of these men and women amazed European visitors.

The American population on the eve of independence was also extraordinarily young, a fact of great importance in understanding the development of effective political resistance. Nearly 60 percent of the American people were under age 21. At any given time, most people in this society were small children, and many of the young men who fought the British during the Revolution either had not been born or had been infants during the Stamp Act crisis. Any explanation for the coming of independence, therefore, must take into account the continuing political mobilization of so many young people.

Postwar Americans also experienced a high level of prosperity. To be sure, some major port cities went through a difficult period as colonists who had been employed during the Seven Years' War were thrown out of work. Sailors and ship workers were especially vulnerable to layoffs of this sort. In general, however,

WHY did Americans resist parliamentary taxation?

COAT OF ARMS OF GEORGE III In the eighteenth century, the royal coat of arms was evident in the colonies as a representation of the British empire.

What symbols did early Americans adopt to express their national identity?

white Americans did very well. The quality of their material lives was not substantially lower than that of the English. In 1774, the per capita wealth of the Americans—this figure includes blacks as well as whites—was £37.4. This sum exceeds the per capita wealth of many developing countries today. On the eve of revolution, £37.4 would have purchased about 310 bushels of wheat, 1600 pounds of rice, 11 cows, or 6 horses. A typical white family of five—a father, mother, and three dependent children—not only would have been able to afford decent food, clothing, and housing but also would have had money left over with which to purchase consumer goods. Even the poorest colonists seem to have benefited from a rising standard of living, and although they may not have done as well as their wealthier neighbors, they too wanted to preserve gains they had made.

Breakdown of Political Trust

Ultimate responsibility for preserving the empire fell to George III. When he became king of England in 1760, he was only 22 years of age. The new monarch was determined to play an aggressive role in government. This decision caused considerable dismay among England's political leaders. For decades, a powerful, though loosely associated, group of men who called themselves **Whigs** had set policy and controlled patronage. George II had accepted this situation, and so long as the Whigs in Parliament did not meddle with his beloved army, the king had let them rule the nation.

In one stroke, George III destroyed this time-tested arrangement. He selected as his chief minister the Earl of Bute, a Scot whose chief qualification for office appeared to be his friendship with the young king. The Whigs who dominated Parliament were outraged. Bute had no ties with the members of the House of Commons; he owed them no favors.

By 1763 Bute, despairing of public life, left office. His departure, however, neither restored the Whigs to preeminence nor dampened the king's enthusiasm for domestic politics. Everyone agreed George had the right to select whomever

Whigs
In the mid-eighteenth century, the Whigs were a political faction that dominated Parliament. Generally they were opposed to royal influence in government and wanted to increase the authority of Parliament.

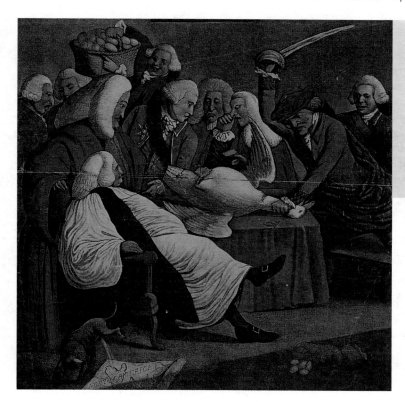

POLITICAL CARTOONS Cartoons became a popular way of criticizing government during this period. Here, King George III watches as the kilted Lord Bute slaughters the goose America. A cabinet member holds a basket of golden eggs at rear. At front left, a dog urinates on a map of British America.

Do you consider the artist of this cartoon to be guilty of treason against the king and Parliament?

he desired for cabinet posts, but until 1770, no one seemed able to please the monarch. Ministers came and went, often for no other reason than George's personal distaste. Because of this chronic instability, subministers (minor bureaucrats who directed routine colonial affairs) did not know what was expected of them. In the absence of clear long-range policy, some ministers made narrowly based decisions; others did nothing. With such turbulence surrounding him, the king showed little interest in the American colonies.

The king, however, does not bear the sole responsibility for England's loss of empire. The members of Parliament who actually drafted the statutes that gradually drove a wedge between the colonies and Britain must share the blame, for they failed to provide innovative answers to the explosive constitutional issues of the day.

The central element in the Anglo-American debate was a concept known as **parliamentary sovereignty**, the doctrine that Parliament enjoyed absolute legislative authority throughout England and its colonies. According to this theory of government, parliamentary decisions superceded any legislation passed by colonial assemblies. The English ruling classes viewed the role of Parliament from a historical perspective that most colonists never shared. They insisted that Parliament was the dominant element within the constitution. Indeed, this elective body protected rights and property from an arbitrary monarch. During the reign of the Stuarts, especially under Charles I (r. 1625–1649), the authority of Parliament had been challenged, and it was not until the Glorious Revolution of 1688 that the English crown formally recognized Parliament's supreme authority in matters such as taxation. Almost no one, including George III, would have dissented from a speech made in 1766 before the House of Commons, in which a representative declared, "The parliament hath, and must have, from the nature

parliamentary sovereignty
Principle that emphasized Parliament's complete legislative authority within the British constitution.

QUICK CHECK ✔

Why were members of the British government adamant in their defense of parliamentary sovereignty?

and essence of the constitution, has had, and ever will have a sovereign supreme power and jurisdiction over every part of the dominions of the state, *to make laws in all cases whatsoever.*"

Such a constitutional position did not leave much room for compromise. Most members of Parliament took a hard line on this issue. The notion of dividing or sharing sovereignty simply made no sense to the English ruling class. As Thomas Hutchinson, royal governor of Massachusetts, explained, no middle ground existed "between the supreme authority of Parliament and the total dependence of the colonies: it is impossible there should be two independent legislatures in one and the same state."

No Taxation Without Representation: The American Perspective

Americans most emphatically did not see it in their "interest" to maintain the "supremacy of Parliament." The crisis in imperial relations forced the colonists first to define and then to defend principles deeply rooted in their own political culture. For more than a century, their ideas about the colonies' role within the British empire had remained a vague, untested bundle of assumptions about personal liberties, property rights, and representative institutions.

By 1763, however, certain fundamental American beliefs had become clear. From Massachusetts to Georgia, colonists aggressively defended the powers of the provincial assemblies. They drew on a rich legislative history of their own. Over the course of the century, the American assemblies had steadily expanded their authority over taxation and expenditure. Since no one in Britain bothered to clip their legislative wings, these provincial bodies assumed a major role in policymaking and routine administration. In other words, by midcentury the assemblies looked like American copies of Parliament. It seemed unreasonable, therefore, for the British suddenly to insist on the supremacy of Parliament, for as the legislators of Massachusetts observed in 1770, "This house has the same inherent rights in this province as the house of commons in Great Britain."

The constitutional debate turned ultimately on the meaning of representation itself. In 1764, a British official informed the colonists that even though they had not elected members to Parliament—indeed, even though they had had no direct contact with the current members—they were nevertheless "virtually" represented by that august body. The members of Parliament, he declared, represented the political interests of everyone who lived in the British empire. It did not really matter whether everyone had cast a vote.

QUICK CHECK ✔

How did Parliament and the American colonists differ in their ideas about representative government?

The colonists ridiculed this notion of virtual representation. The only representatives the Americans recognized as legitimate were those actually chosen by the people for whom they spoke. On this crucial point they would not compromise. As John Adams insisted, a representative assembly should actually mirror its constituents: "It should think, feel, reason, and act like them." Since the members of Parliament could not possibly "think" like Americans, it followed logically they could not represent them. And if they were not genuine representatives, the members of Parliament—pretensions to sovereignty notwithstanding—had no business taxing the American people. Thus, in 1764 the Connecticut Assembly declared in bold letters, "NO LAW CAN BE MADE OR ABROGATED WITHOUT THE CONSENT OF THE PEOPLE BY THEIR REPRESENTATIVES."

Justifying Resistance

The political ideology that had the greatest popular appeal among the colonists contained a strong moral component, one that British rulers and American **Loyalists** (people who sided with the king and Parliament during the Revolution) never fully understood. The origins of this highly religious perspective on civil government are difficult to locate with precision, but certainly, the Great Awakening (a widespread evangelical revival movement of the mid-1700s) created a general awareness of an obligation to conduct public as well as private affairs according to Scripture.

Americans expressed their political beliefs in a language they had borrowed from English writers. The person most frequently cited was John Locke, the influential seventeenth-century philosopher whose *Two Treatises of Government* (first published in 1690) seemed, to colonial readers at least, a brilliant description of what was in fact American political practice. Locke claimed that all people possessed natural and inalienable rights. In order to preserve these God-given rights—the rights of life, liberty, and property, for example—free men (the status of women in Locke's work was less clear) formed contracts. These agreements were the foundation of human society as well as civil government, and they required the consent of the people who were actually governed. There could be no coercion. Locke justified rebellion against arbitrary forms of government that were by their very nature unreasonable. Americans delighted in Locke's ability to unite traditional religious values with a spirited defense of popular government, and they seldom missed a chance to quote from the works of "the Great Mr. Locke."

Revolutionary Americans also endorsed a body of ideas associated with the so-called Commonwealthman tradition. These radical eighteenth-century English writers helped persuade the colonists that *power* was extremely dangerous, a force that would surely destroy liberty unless it was countered by *virtue*. Persons who shared this highly charged moral outlook regarded bad policy as not simply the result of human error. Rather, it was an indication of sin and corruption.

Insistence on public virtue—sacrifice of self-interest to the public good—became the dominant theme of revolutionary political writing. American pamphleteers seldom took a dispassionate, legalistic approach to their analysis of power and liberty. More commonly, they exposed plots hatched by corrupt courtiers, such as the Earl of Bute. None of them—or their readers—had any doubt that Americans were more virtuous than were the people of England.

During the 1760s, however, popular writers were not certain how long the colonists could hold out against arbitrary taxation, standing armies, Anglican bishops—in other words, against a host of external threats designed to crush American liberty. In 1774, for example, the people of Farmington, Connecticut, declared that "the present ministry, being instigated by the devil and led by their wicked and corrupt hearts, have a design to take away our liberties and properties, and to enslave us forever." These Connecticut farmers described Britain's leaders as "pimps and parasites." This highly emotional, conspiratorial rhetoric sometimes shocks modern readers who assume that America's revolutionary leaders were products of the Enlightenment, persons who relied solely on reason to solve social and political problems. Whatever the origins of their ideas may have been, the colonial pamphleteers successfully roused ordinary men and women to resist Britain with force of arms.

Colonial newspapers spread these ideas through a large dispersed population. A majority of adult white males—especially those in the Northern Colonies—were

Loyalists
Throughout the conflict with Great Britain, many colonists sided with the king and Parliament. Also called Tories, these people feared that American liberty might promote social anarchy.

QUICK CHECK ✓

How did American colonists justify their resistance to parliamentary sovereignty?

literate, and it is not surprising that the number of journals published in this country increased dramatically during the revolutionary period. For the first time in American history, persons living in various parts of the continent could closely follow events that occurred in distant American cities. Because of the availability of newspapers, the details of Bostonians' confrontations with British authorities were known throughout the colonies, and these shared political experiences drew Americans more closely together, making it possible—in the words of John Adams—for "Thirteen clocks… to strike together—a perfection of mechanism which no artist had ever before effected."

Eroding the Bonds of Empire

WHAT

events led to the erosion of the bonds of empire during the 1760s?

The Seven Years' War saddled Great Britain with a national debt so huge that more than half the annual national budget went to pay the interest on it. Almost everyone in government assumed that with the cessation of hostilities, the troops would be disbanded, thus saving a lot of money. George III had other plans. He insisted on keeping the largest peacetime army in British history on active duty, supposedly to protect Indians from predatory American frontiersmen.

For their part, colonists doubted the value of this expensive army. Britain did not leave enough troops in America to maintain peace on the frontier effectively. The weakness of the army was dramatically demonstrated during the spring of 1763.

The native peoples of the backcountry—the Seneca, Ottawa, Miami, Creek, and Cherokee—had begun discussing how they might turn back the tide of white settlement. The powerful spiritual leader Neolin, known as the Delaware Prophet and claiming vision from the "Master of Life," helped the Indians articulate their fear and anger. He urged them to restore their cultures to the "original state that they were in before the white people found out their country." If moral regeneration required violence, so be it. Neolin converted Pontiac, an Ottawa warrior, to the cause, and he, in turn, coordinated an uprising among the western Indians who had been French allies and who hated all British people—even those sent to protect them from land-grabbing colonists. The formidable Native American resistance was known as Pontiac's Rebellion. In May, Pontiac attacked Detroit; other Indians harassed the Pennsylvania and Virginia frontiers. At the end of the year, after his followers began deserting, Pontiac sued for peace. During even this brief outbreak, the British army proved unable to defend exposed colonial settlements, and several thousand people lost their lives.

From the perspective of the Native Americans who inhabited the Ohio Valley this was a period of almost unmitigated disaster. In fact, more than any other group, the Indians suffered as a direct result of imperial reorganization. The defeat of the French made it impossible for native peoples to play off one imperial power against European rivals in the middle ground, and the victorious British made it clear that they regarded their former Indian allies as little more than a nuisance. Diplomatic gifts stopped; humiliating restrictions were placed on trade.

Even worse, Pontiac's rising unloosed vicious racism along the colonial frontier, and American colonists often used any excuse to attack local Indians, peaceful or not. Late in 1763 a group of vigilantes known as the Paxton Boys murdered a score of Christian Indians, women and children, living near Lancaster, Pennsylvania. White neighbors treated the killers as heroes, and the atrocity ended only after the Paxton Boys threatened to march on Philadelphia in search of administrators who dared to criticize such cold-blooded crimes. One of the administrators, Benjamin Franklin, observed sadly, "It grieves me to hear that our Frontier People are yet greater Barbarians than the Indians, and continue to murder them in time of Peace."

Whatever happened to the Indians, the colonists fully intended to settle the fertile region west of the Appalachian Mountains. After the British government issued the Proclamation of 1763, which prohibited governors from granting land beyond the headwaters of rivers flowing into the Atlantic, disappointed Americans viewed the army as an obstruction to legitimate economic development, a domestic police force that cost too much money.

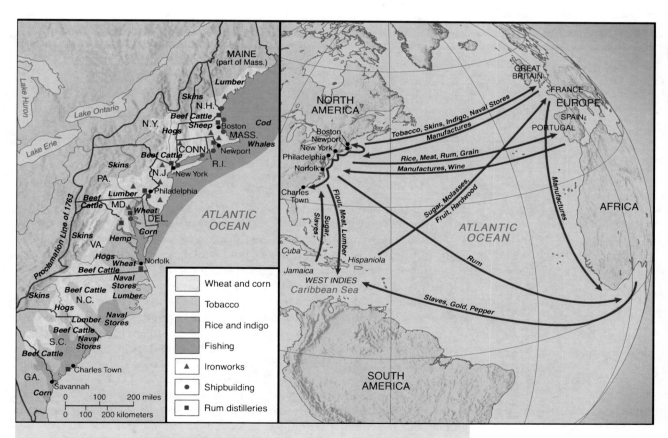

COLONIAL PRODUCTS AND TRADE Although the American colonists produced many agricultural staples that were valuable to Britain, they were dependent on British manufactures such as cloth, metal goods, and ceramics.

Were colonial Americans part of a global economy?

Paying Off the National Debt

The task of reducing England's debt fell to George Grenville, the rigid, somewhat unimaginative chancellor of the exchequer who replaced Bute in 1763 as the king's first minister. After carefully reviewing the state of Britain's finances, Grenville concluded that the colonists would have to contribute to the maintenance of the army. The first bill he steered through Parliament was the Revenue Act of 1764, known as the Sugar Act.

This legislation placed a new burden on the Navigation Acts that had governed the flow of colonial commerce for almost a century. Those acts had forced Americans to trade almost exclusively with Britain. The statutes were not, however, primarily intended as a means to raise money for the British government. The Sugar Act—and the acts that soon followed—redefined the relationship between America and Great Britain. Parliament now expected the colonies to generate revenue. The preamble of the Sugar Act proclaimed explicitly: "It is just and necessary that a revenue be raised… in America for defraying the expenses of defending, protecting, and securing the same."

The Americans immediately protested Grenville's unconstitutional scheme. According to the members of the Rhode Island Assembly, the Sugar Act taxed the colonists in a manner "inconsistent with their rights and privileges as British subjects." James Otis, a fiery orator from Massachusetts, exclaimed the legislation deprived Americans of "the right of assessing their own taxes."

The act generated no violence. In fact, ordinary men and women were only marginally involved in the drafting of formal petitions. The protest was still confined to the members of the colonial assemblies, to the merchants, and to the well-to-do Americans who had personal interests in commerce.

James Otis, The Rights of the British Colonies Asserted and Proved

QUICK CHECK ✓

Why did Parliament think that the colonies should contribute to paying off Britain's national debt?

The Protest Spreads

Stamp Act of 1765
Placed a tax on newspapers and printed matter produced in the colonies, causing a mass political movement among colonists.

Passage of the **Stamp Act of 1765**, which placed a tax on newspapers and printed matter produced in the colonies, transformed a debate among gentlemen into a mass political movement. Colonial agents had presented Grenville with alternative schemes for raising money in America, but Grenville rejected them. The majority of the House of Commons assumed that Parliament possessed the right to tax the colonists, and when the chancellor of the exchequer announced a plan to squeeze £60,000 annually out of the Americans by requiring them to purchase special seals or stamps to validate legal documents, the members responded with enthusiasm. The Stamp Act was scheduled to go into effect on November 1, 1765, and in anticipation of brisk sales, Grenville appointed stamp distributors for every colony.

During discussion in Parliament, several members warned that the act would raise a storm of protest in the colonies. Colonel Isaac Barré, a veteran of the Seven Years' War, reminded his colleagues that the Americans were "sons of liberty" and would not surrender their rights without a fight. But Barré's appeal fell on deaf ears. Throughout the colonies, extra-legal groups known as the "Sons of Liberty" put political and economic pressure on neighbors who wanted to remain neutral in the contest with Great Britain.

Word of the Stamp Act reached America in May, and it was soon clear that Barré had gauged the colonists' response correctly. The most dramatic incident occurred in Virginia's House of Burgesses. Patrick Henry, young and eloquent, whom contemporaries compared in fervor to evangelical preachers, introduced

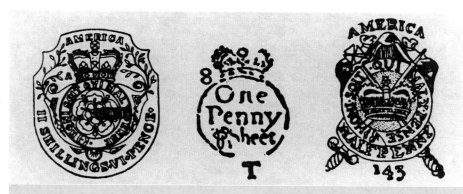

STAMP ACT The Stamp Act placed a tax on documents and printed matter—newspapers, marriage licenses, wills, deeds, even playing cards and dice. The stamps (like those shown here) varied in denomination. A tax stamp affixed to a legal document or bill of sale signified that the required tax had been paid.

Why did these stamps spark violent protest in America?

five resolutions protesting the Stamp Act on the floor of the assembly. He timed his move carefully. It was late in the session; many of the more conservative burgesses had already departed for their plantations. Even then, Henry's resolves declaring that Virginians had the right to tax themselves as they alone saw fit passed by narrow margins. The fifth resolution, stricken almost immediately from the legislative records, announced that any attempt to collect stamp revenues in America was "illegal, unconstitutional, and unjust, and has a manifest tendency to destroy British as well as American liberty."

Henry's five resolutions, known popularly as the Virginia Resolves, might have remained a local matter had it not been for the colonial press. Newspapers throughout America printed Henry's resolutions, but, perhaps because editors did not really know what had happened in Williamsburg, they reported that all five resolutions had received the burgesses' full support. Several journals even carried two resolves that Henry had not dared to introduce. A result of this misunderstanding, of course, was that the Virginians appeared to have taken an extremely radical position on the issue of the supremacy of Parliament, one that other Americans now trumpeted before their own assemblies. No wonder Francis Bernard, royal governor of Massachusetts, called the Virginia Resolves an "alarm bell."

Not to be outdone by Virginia, Massachusetts called a general meeting to protest Grenville's policy. Nine colonies sent representatives to the **Stamp Act Congress** that convened in New York City in October 1765. It was the first intercolonial gathering held since the abortive Albany Congress of 1754. The delegates drafted petitions to the king and Parliament that restated the colonists' belief "that no taxes should be imposed on them, but with their own consent, given personally, or by their representatives." The tone of the meeting was restrained, even conciliatory. The congress studiously avoided any mention of independence or disloyalty to the crown.

Resistance to the Stamp Act soon spread from the assemblies to the streets. By taxing deeds, marriage licenses, and playing cards, the Stamp Act touched the lives of ordinary women and men. Anonymous artisans and seamen, angered by Parliament's apparent insensitivity and fearful that the statute would increase unemployment and poverty, organized mass protests in the major colonial ports.

Benjamin Franklin, Testimony Against the Stamp Act (1766)

Stamp Act Congress

Meeting of colonial delegates in New York City in October 1765 to protest the Stamp Act, a law passed by Parliament to raise revenue in America. The delegates drafted petitions denouncing the Stamp Act and other taxes imposed on Americans without colonial consent.

1765 Stamp Act Protest

By November 1, 1765, stamp distributors in almost every American port had publicly resigned, and without distributors, the hated revenue stamps could not be sold. The courts soon reopened; most newspapers were published. Daily life in the colonies was undisturbed with one exception: The Sons of Liberty, a semi-secret society formed to protest imperial policy, persuaded—some said coerced—colonial merchants to boycott British goods until Parliament repealed the Stamp Act. The merchants showed little enthusiasm for such tactics, but the threat of tar and feathers stimulated cooperation.

The boycott movement was in itself a masterful political innovation. Never before had a resistance movement organized itself so centrally around the market decisions of ordinary consumers. The colonists depended on British imports—cloth, metal goods, and ceramics—and each year they imported more consumer goods than they could possibly afford. In this highly charged moral atmosphere, one in which ordinary people talked constantly of conspiracy and corruption, it is not surprising that Americans of different classes and backgrounds advocated a radical change in buying habits. Private acts suddenly became part of the public sphere. Personal excess threatened to contaminate the entire political community. This logic explains the power of an appeal made in a Boston newspaper: "Save your money and you can save your country." In 1765 the boycott movement had little effect on the sale of British goods in America. By 1773, however, this political weapon had come into its own and seriously reduced the flow of British commerce, especially the trade for tea.

Women Signing an Anti-tea Agreement

The boycotts mobilized colonial women. They were excluded from voting and civil office, but such legal discrimination did not mean that women were not part of the broader political culture. Since wives and mothers spent their days involved with household chores, they assumed special responsibility to reform consumption, to root out luxury, and to promote frugality. Indeed, in this realm they possessed real power; they monitored the ideological commitment of the entire family. Throughout the colonies, women altered styles of dress, made homespun cloth, and shunned imported items on which Parliament had placed a tax.

On March 18, 1766, the House of Commons voted 275 to 167 to rescind the Stamp Act. Lest its retreat on the Stamp Act be interpreted as weakness, the House of Commons passed the Declaratory Act (March 1766), a shrill defense of parliamentary supremacy over the Americans "in all cases whatsoever." The colonists' insistence on no taxation without representation failed to impress British rulers. England's merchants, supposedly America's allies, claimed sole responsibility for the Stamp Act repeal. The colonists had only complicated the task, the merchants lectured, and if the Americans knew what was good for them, they would keep quiet.

The Stamp Act crisis eroded the colonists' respect for imperial officeholders in America. Suddenly, these men—royal governors, customs collectors, military personnel—appeared alien, as if their interests were not those of the people over whom they exercised authority. One person who had been forced to resign the post of stamp distributor for South Carolina noted several years later, "The Stamp Act had introduc'd so much Party Rage, Faction, and Debate that the ancient Harmony, Generosity, and Urbanity for which these People were celebrated is destroyed, and at an End."

QUICK CHECK ✓

Was the repeal of the Stamp Act a victory for the American cause?

Fueling the Crisis

Charles Townshend, the new chancellor of the exchequer, claimed he could solve the American controversy. In January 1767, he surprised everyone by blithely announcing that he knew a way to obtain revenue from the Americans.

DAUGHTERS OF LIBERTY The boycott movement drew many colonial women into popular politics. In this 1774 woodcut, a Daughter of Liberty stands ready to resist British oppression.

Did colonial women play a significant role in revolutionary resistance?

The members of the House of Commons were so pleased with the news that they promptly voted to lower taxes in England, an action that threatened fiscal chaos.

A budgetary crisis forced Townshend to make good on his extraordinary boast. His scheme turned out to be a grab bag of duties on American imports of paper, glass, paint, lead, and tea, which collectively were known as the Townshend Revenue Acts (June–July 1767). He hoped to generate sufficient funds to pay the salaries of royal governors and other imperial officers, thus freeing them from dependence on the colonial assemblies.

The chancellor recognized that without tough instruments of enforcement, his duties would not produce the promised revenues. Therefore, he created an American Board of Customs Commissioners, a body based in Boston and supported by reorganized vice-admiralty courts located in Boston, Philadelphia, and Charles Town. And for good measure, Townshend persuaded Parliament to order the governor of New York to veto all bills passed by that colony's assembly until it supplied resident British troops in accordance with the Quartering Act (May 1765) that required the colonies to house soldiers in barracks, taverns, and vacant buildings and to provide the army with firewood, candles, and beer, among other items. Many Americans regarded this as more taxation without representation, and in New York, at least, colonists refused to pay.

Americans showed no more willingness to pay Townshend's duties than they had to buy Grenville's stamps. In major ports, the Sons of Liberty organized boycotts of British goods. Men and women took oaths before neighbors promising not to purchase certain goods until Parliament repealed unconstitutional taxation.

The Liberty Song

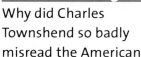

Why did Charles Townshend so badly misread the American situation?

Surge of Force

In October 1768, British rulers made another mistake, one that raised tensions almost to the pitch they had reached during the Stamp Act riots. The issue at the heart of the trouble was the army. In part to save money and in part to intimidate colonial troublemakers, the ministry transferred four thousand regular troops (redcoats) from Nova Scotia and Ireland to Boston. To make relations worse, redcoats—men who were ill treated and underpaid—competed in their spare time for jobs

THE BOSTON MASSACRE   This etching by Paul Revere shows British redcoats firing on ordinary citizens, an event know as the *Boston Massacre*. In subsequent editions, the blood spurting from the dying Americans became more conspicuous.

Was this etching an example of American propaganda?

with local dockworkers and artisans. Work was already in short supply, and the streets crackled with tension.

When colonists questioned why the army had been sent to a peaceful city, pamphleteers responded that it was there to further a conspiracy originally conceived by Bute to oppress Americans, to take away their liberties, to collect illegal revenues. Today such rhetoric may sound excessive, but to Americans who had absorbed the political theories of the Commonwealthmen, a pattern of tyranny seemed obvious.

Colonists had no difficulty interpreting the violence that erupted in Boston on March 5, 1770. In the gathering dusk of that afternoon, young boys and street toughs threw rocks and snowballs at soldiers in a small, isolated patrol outside the offices of the hated customs commissioners in King Street. The details of this incident are obscure, but it appears that as the mob grew and became more threatening, the soldiers panicked. In the confusion, the troops fired, leaving five Americans dead.

Pamphleteers promptly labeled the incident a massacre. The victims of this **Boston Massacre** were seen as martyrs and were memorialized in extravagant terms. In one eulogy, Joseph Warren addressed the dead men's widows and children, dramatically re-creating the gruesome scene in King Street. "Behold thy

Boston Massacre
A violent confrontation between British troops and the ordinary people of Boston on March 5, 1770. Five citizens were killed when the troops fired into the crowd. The incident inflamed anti-British sentiment in Massachusetts.

murdered husband gasping on the ground," Warren cried, "… take heed, ye orphan babes, lest, whilst your streaming eyes are fixed upon the ghastly corpse, your feet slide on the stones bespattered with your father's brains." Apparently, to propagandists like Warren, it mattered little that the five civilians had been bachelors! Paul Revere's engraving of the massacre, appropriately splattered with blood, became an instant best-seller. Confronted with such intense reaction and with the possibility of massive armed resistance, Crown officials wisely moved the army to an island in Boston Harbor.

At this critical moment, the king's new first minister restored a measure of tranquility. Lord North, congenial, well-meaning, but not very talented, became chancellor of the exchequer following Townshend's death in 1767. North was appointed the first minister in 1770, and for the next twelve years—indeed, throughout most of the American crisis—he managed to retain his office. The secret to his success seems to have been an ability to get along with George III and to build an effective majority in Parliament.

One of North's first recommendations to Parliament was the repeal of the Townshend duties. Not only had these ill-conceived duties unnecessarily angered the colonists, but they also hurt English manufacturers. By taxing British exports such as glass and paint, Parliament had only encouraged the Americans to develop their own industries; thus, without much prodding, the House of Commons dropped all the Townshend duties—with the notable exception of tea. The tax on tea was retained not for revenue purposes, North insisted, but as a reminder that England's rulers still subscribed to the principles of the Declaratory Act. They would not compromise the supremacy of Parliament.

Samuel Adams (1722–1803) refused to accept the notion that the repeal of the Townshend duties had secured American liberty. During the early 1770s, while colonial leaders turned to other matters, Adams kept the cause alive with a drumfire of publicity. He reminded the people of Boston that the tax on tea remained in force. He organized public anniversaries commemorating the repeal of the Stamp Act and the Boston Massacre. Adams was a genuine revolutionary, an ideologue filled with a burning sense of indignation at the real and alleged wrongs suffered by his countrymen.

With each new attempt by Parliament to assert its supremacy over the colonists, more and more Bostonians listened to what Adams had to say. He observed ominously that the British intended to use the tea revenue to pay judicial salaries, thus freeing the judges from dependence on the assembly. When in November 1772 Adams suggested the formation of a **committee of correspondence** to communicate grievances to villagers throughout Massachusetts, he received broad support. Americans living in other colonies soon copied his idea. It was a brilliant stroke. Adams developed a structure of political cooperation completely independent of royal government.

IMAGE

Handbill "On the Death of Five Young Men"

DOCUMENT

Boston Gazette Description of the Boston Massacre

committee of correspondence
Vast communication network formed in Massachusetts and other colonies to communicate grievances and provide colonists with evidence of British oppression.

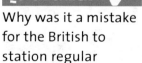

QUICK CHECK ✓

Why was it a mistake for the British to station regular troops in Boston?

The Final Provocation: The Boston Tea Party

In May 1773, Parliament passed the Tea Act, legislation the Americans might have welcomed. After all, it lowered the price for their favorite beverage. Parliament wanted to save one of Britain's largest businesses, the East India Company, from possible bankruptcy. This commercial giant imported Asian tea into England, where it was resold to wholesalers. The tea was also subject to heavy duties. The company tried to pass these charges on to the consumers, but American tea drinkers preferred the cheaper leaves that were smuggled in from Holland.

The Tea Act changed the rules. Parliament not only allowed the company to sell directly to American retailers, thus cutting out intermediaries, but also eliminated the duties paid in England. If all had gone according to plan, the agents of the East India Company in America would have undersold their competitors, including the Dutch smugglers, and with the new profits would have saved the business.

But Parliament's logic was flawed. First, since the tax on tea, collected in American ports, remained in effect, this new act seemed a devious scheme to win popular support for Parliament's right to tax the colonists without representation. Second, the act threatened to undercut powerful colonial merchants who did a good business trading in smuggled Dutch tea. Considering the American reaction, the British government might have been well advised to devise another plan to rescue the ailing company. In Philadelphia, and then at New York City, colonists turned back the tea ships before they could unload.

Hewes, "A Retrospect on the Boston Tea Party"

In Boston, however, the issue was not so easily resolved. Governor Hutchinson, a strong-willed man, would not permit the vessels to return to England. Local patriots would not let them unload. And so, crammed with the East India Company's tea, the ships sat in Boston Harbor waiting for the colonists to make up their minds. On the night of December 16, 1773, they did so in dramatic style. A group of men disguised as Mohawk Indians boarded the ships and pitched 340 chests of tea worth £10,000 over the side. Even at the time, John Adams sensed the event would have far-reaching significance. "This Destruction of the Tea," he scribbled in his diary, "is so bold, so daring, so firm, intrepid, and inflexible, and it must

THE BOSTON TEA PARTY Colonists toss chests of tea overboard while disguised as Mohawk Indians in a historic depiction of the Boston Tea Party of December 16, 1773. At right a bottle of tea leaves preserved from the protest.

Was reconciliation with Britain possible after this event?

CHRONICLE OF COLONIAL-BRITISH TENSION

Legislation	Date	Provisions	Colonial Reaction
Sugar Act	April 5, 1764	Revised duties on sugar, coffee, tea, wine, other imports; expanded jurisdiction of vice-admiralty courts	Several assemblies protest taxation for revenue
Stamp Act	March 22, 1765; repealed March 18, 1766	Printed documents (deeds, newspapers, marriage licenses, etc.) issued only on special stamped paper purchased from stamp distributors	Riots in cities; collectors forced to resign; Stamp Act Congress (October 1765)
Quartering Act	May 1765	Colonists must supply British troops with housing, other items (candles, firewood, etc.)	Protest in assemblies; New York Assembly punished for failure to comply, 1767
Declaratory Act	March 18, 1766	Parliament declares its sovereignty over the colonies "in all cases whatsoever"	Ignored in celebration over repeal of the Stamp Act
Townshend Revenue Acts	June 26, 29, July 2, 1767; all repealed—except duty on tea, March 1770	New duties on glass, lead, paper, paints, tea; customs collections tightened in America	Nonimportation of British goods; assemblies protest; newspapers attack British policy
Tea Act	May 10, 1773	Parliament gives East India Company right to sell tea directly to Americans; some duties on tea reduced	Protests against favoritism shown to monopolistic company; tea destroyed in Boston (December 16, 1773)
Coercive Acts (Intolerable Acts)	March–June 1774	Closes port of Boston; restructures Massachusetts government; restricts town meetings; troops quartered in Boston; British officials accused of crimes sent to England or Canada for trial	Boycott of British goods; First Continental Congress convenes (September 1774)
Prohibitory Act	December 22, 1775	Declares British intention to coerce Americans into submission; embargo on American goods; American ships seized	Drives Continental Congress closer to decision for independence

have so important consequences, and so lasting, that I can't but consider it as an epocha in history."

When news of the **Boston Tea Party** reached London in January 1774, the North ministry was stunned. The people of Boston had treated parliamentary supremacy with utter contempt, and British rulers saw no humor whatsoever in the destruction of private property by subjects of the Crown dressed in costume. To quell such rebelliousness, Parliament passed a series of laws called the **Coercive Acts.** (In America, they were referred to as the Intolerable Acts.) The legislation (1) closed the port of Boston until the city fully compensated the East India Company for the lost tea; (2) restructured the Massachusetts government by transforming the upper house from an elective to an appointed body and restricting the number of legal town meetings to one a year; (3) allowed the royal governor to transfer British officials arrested for offenses committed in the line of duty to England, where there was little likelihood they would be convicted; and (4) authorized the army to quarter troops wherever they were needed, even if this required the compulsory requisition of uninhabited private buildings. George III enthusiastically supported this tough policy; he appointed General Thomas Gage to serve as the colony's new royal governor. Gage apparently won the king's favor by announcing that in America, "Nothing can be done but by forcible means."

Boston Tea Party
Assault on British ships in which American insurgents disguised as Mohawk Indians threw hundreds of chests of tea into Boston Harbor as a means of protesting British taxes and the involvement of the East India Company.

Coercive Acts of 1774
Also known as the *Intolerable Acts,* the four pieces of legislation passed by Parliament in 1774 in response to the Boston Tea Party that were meant to punish the colonies.

1774
Illustration,
List of Crimes
by the
Massachusetts
Governor

The sweeping denial of constitutional liberties confirmed the colonists' worst fears. To men like Samuel Adams, it seemed as if Britain really intended to enslave the American people. Colonial moderates found their position shaken by the vindictiveness of the Coercive Acts. Edmund Burke, one of America's last friends in Parliament, noted sadly on the floor of Commons, that "this is the day, then, that you wish to go to war with all America, in order to conciliate that country to this."

If in 1774 the House of Commons thought it could isolate Boston from the rest of America, it was in for a rude surprise. Colonists living in other parts of the continent recognized immediately that the principles at stake in Boston affected all Americans. Charity suddenly became a profoundly political act. People from Georgia to New Hampshire sent livestock, grain, and money to Boston. Ordinary colonists showed they were prepared to make a personal sacrifice for the cause of America.

The sticking point remained—as it had been in 1765—the sovereignty of Parliament. No one in Britain could think of a way around this constitutional impasse. In 1773, Benjamin Franklin had offered a suggestion. "The Parliament," he observed, "has no right to make any law whatever, binding on the colonies... the king, and not the king, lords, and commons collectively, is their sovereign." But so long as it still seemed possible to coerce the Americans into obedience, Britain's rulers had little incentive to accept such a humiliating compromise.

QUICK CHECK ✓

Did the Coercive Acts represent an overreaction by Parliament to the Boston Tea Party?

Steps Toward Independence

WHAT events in 1775 and 1776 led to the colonists' decision to declare independence?

First Continental Congress
Meeting of delegates from twelve colonies in Philadelphia in September 1774. The Congress denied Parliament's authority to legislate for the colonies, condemned British accusations toward the colonies, created the Continental Association, and endorsed a call to take up arms.

During the summer of 1774, committees of correspondence analyzed the perilous situation in which the colonists found themselves. The committees endorsed a call for a Continental Congress, a gathering of fifty-five elected delegates from twelve colonies (Georgia sent none but agreed to support the action taken). This **First Continental Congress** convened in Philadelphia on September 5. It included some of America's most articulate, respected leaders; among them were John Adams, Samuel Adams, Patrick Henry, Richard Henry Lee, Christopher Gadsden, and George Washington.

Differences of opinion soon surfaced. Delegates from the Middle Colonies—Joseph Galloway of Pennsylvania, for example—wanted to proceed with caution, but Samuel Adams and other more radical members pushed the moderates toward confrontation. Boston's master politician engineered congressional acceptance of the Suffolk Resolves, a bold statement drawn up in Suffolk County, Massachusetts, that encouraged forcible resistance of the Coercive Acts.

After this decision, the tone of the meeting was established. Moderate spokesmen introduced conciliatory measures, which received polite discussion but failed to win a majority vote. Just before returning to their homes (September 1774), the delegates created the "Association," an intercolonial agreement to halt all commerce with Britain until Parliament repealed the Intolerable Acts. This was a brilliant revolutionary decision. The Association authorized a vast network of local committees to enforce nonimportation, a policy by which colonial consumers and shopkeepers promised not to buy goods from Britain. Violators were denounced, shamed, forced either to apologize publicly for their actions or to be shunned by all their patriot neighbors. In many of the communities, the committees *were* the government, distinguishing, in the words of James Madison, "Friends from Foes." George III sneered at these activities. "I am not sorry," he confided, "that the line of conduct seems now chalked out... the New England Governments are in a state of Rebellion, blows must decide whether they are to be subject to this country or independent."

Shots Heard Around the World

The king was correct. Before Congress reconvened, "blows" fell at Lexington and Concord, two small villages in eastern Massachusetts. On the evening of April 18, 1775, General Gage dispatched troops from Boston to seize rebel supplies. Paul Revere, a renowned silversmith and active patriot, warned the colonists that the redcoats were coming. The militia of Lexington, a collection of ill-trained farmers, boys as well as old men, decided to stand on the village green on the following morning, April 19, as the British soldiers passed on the road to Concord. No one planned to fight, but in a moment of confusion, someone fired; the redcoats discharged a volley, and eight Americans lay dead.

Word of the incident spread rapidly, and by the time the British force reached its destination, the countryside swarmed with "minutemen," special companies of Massachusetts militia prepared to respond instantly to military emergencies. The redcoats found nothing of significance in Concord and so returned. The long march back to Boston turned into a rout. Lord Percy, a British officer who brought up reinforcements, remarked more in surprise than bitterness that "whoever looks upon them [the American soldiers] as an irregular mob, will find himself much mistaken." On June 17, colonial militiamen again held their own against seasoned troops at the battle of Bunker Hill. The British finally took the hill, but after this costly "victory" in which he suffered 40 percent casualties, Gage complained that the Americans had displayed "a conduct and spirit against us, they never showed against the French."

QUICK CHECK

Why did the British general Thomas Gage underestimate the Americans' military resolve?

Beginning "The World Over Again"

Members of the **Second Continental Congress** gathered in Philadelphia in May 1775. They faced an awesome responsibility. British government in the mainland colonies had almost ceased to function, and with Americans fighting redcoats, the country desperately needed strong central leadership. Slowly, often reluctantly, Congress took control of the war. The delegates formed a Continental Army and appointed George Washington its commander, in part because he seemed to have greater military experience than anyone else available and in part because he looked like he should be commander in chief. The delegates were also eager to select someone who did not come from Massachusetts, a colony that seemed already to possess too much power in national councils. The members of Congress purchased military supplies and, to pay for them, issued paper money. But while they were assuming the powers of a sovereign government, the congressmen refused to declare independence. They debated and fretted, listened to the appeals of moderates who played on the colonists' remaining loyalty to Britain, and then did nothing.

Convinced that military force could make up for earlier failures of policy, the British government found a way to transform colonial moderates into angry rebels. In December 1775, Parliament passed the Prohibitory Act, declaring war on American commerce. Until the colonists begged for pardon, they could not trade with the rest of the world. The British navy blockaded their ports and seized American ships on the high seas. Lord North also hired German mercenaries to

Second Continental Congress

This meeting took place in Philadelphia in May 1775, in the midst of rapidly unfolding military events. It organized the Continental Army and commissioned George Washington to lead it, then began requisitioning men and supplies for the war effort.

115

LEXINGTON AND CONCORD This 1775 engraving by Amos Doolittle, a Connecticut artist, reconstructs the American attack on the British regulars as they marched from Concord back to Boston. The minutemen fired from cover, killing and wounding many redcoats who expected little armed resistance.

Why did British officers believe that the guerilla tactics adopted by the Americans were a dishonorable way to fight?

put down the rebellion. And in America, Virginia's royal governor Lord Dunmore further undermined the possibility of reconciliation by urging the colony's slaves to take up arms against their masters. Few did so, but the effort to stir up black rebellion infuriated the Virginia gentry.

Thomas Paine (1737–1809) pushed the colonists even closer to forming an independent republic. In England, Paine had tried and failed in a number of jobs, but while still in England, Paine had the good fortune to meet Benjamin Franklin, who presented him with letters of introduction to the leading patriots of Pennsylvania. At the urging of his new American friends, Paine produced *Common Sense* in 1776, an essay that became an instant best-seller. In only three months, it sold more than 120,000 copies. Paine confirmed in forceful prose what the colonists had been thinking but had been unable to state in coherent form. "My motive and object in all my political works," he declared, "... have been to rescue man from tyranny and false systems of government, and enable him to be free."

Common Sense systematically stripped kingship of historical and theological justification. For centuries, the English had maintained the fiction that the monarch could do no wrong. When the government oppressed the people, the royal counselors received the blame. The Crown was above suspicion. To this, Paine cried nonsense. Monarchs ruled by force. George III was simply a "royal brute," who by his arbitrary behavior had surrendered his claim to the colonists' obedience. The pamphlet also

Common Sense
Revolutionary tract written by Thomas Paine in January 1776. It called for independence and the establishment of a republican government in America.

116

PAINE'S *COMMON SENSE*   The message of Thomas Paine's pamphlet *Common Sense* (title page shown) was clear and direct. Paine's powerful argument called for "The Free and Independent States of America." He assured ordinary Americans not only that they could live without a king, but also that they would win the war.

Should Paine be considered a Founding Father in the same way as Washington and Jefferson?

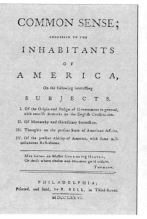

insisted that all power came from the people. Indeed, *Common Sense* was a powerful democratic manifesto.

Paine's greatest contribution to the revolutionary cause was persuading ordinary folk to sever their ties with Great Britain. It was not reasonable, he argued, to regard England as the mother country. "Europe, and not England," he explained, "is the parent country of America. This new world hath been the asylum for the persecuted lovers of civil and religious liberty from *every part* of Europe." No doubt that message made a deep impression on Pennsylvania's German population. The time had come for the colonists to form an independent republic. "We have it in our power," Paine wrote in one of his most moving statements, "to begin the world over again… the birthday of a new world is at hand."

Thomas Jefferson "Rough Draft" of the Declaration of Independence

CONGRESS VOTING INDEPENDENCE   Oil painting by Robert Edge Pine and Edward Savage, 1785. The committee appointed by Congress to draft a declaration on independence included (center, standing) John Adams, Roger Sherman, Robert Livingston, Thomas Jefferson, and (center foreground, seated) Benjamin Franklin. The committee members are shown submitting Jefferson's draft to the speaker.

Why did it take so long to declare independence?

On July 2, 1776, after a long and tedious debate, Congress finally voted for independence. The motion passed: twelve states for, none against (with New York abstaining). Thomas Jefferson, a young Virginia planter who enjoyed a reputation as a graceful writer, drafted a formal declaration that was accepted with alterations two days later. Much of the Declaration of Independence consisted of a list of specific grievances against George III and his government. Like a skilled lawyer, Jefferson presented the evidence for independence. The document did not become famous for those passages. Long after the establishment of the new republic, the Declaration challenged Americans to make good on the principle that "all men are created equal." John Adams nicely expressed the patriots' fervor when he wrote on July 3, "Yesterday the greatest question was decided, which ever was debated in America, and a greater perhaps, never was or will be decided among men."

QUICK CHECK ✔

Why do you think Thomas Paine's *Common Sense* became an instant best-seller?

Fighting for Independence

WHY did it take eight years of warfare for the Americans to gain independence?

Only fools and visionaries expressed optimism about America's prospects of winning independence in 1776. The Americans had taken on a formidable military power. The population of Britain was perhaps four times that of its former colonies. England also possessed a strong manufacturing base, a well-trained regular army supplemented by thousands of hired German troops (Hessians), and a navy that dominated the world's oceans. Many British officers had battlefield experience. They already knew what the Americans would slowly learn: Waging war requires discipline, money, and sacrifice.

The British government entered the conflict fully confident that it could beat the Americans. In 1776, Lord North and his colleagues regarded the war as a police action. They anticipated that a mere show of armed force would intimidate the upstart colonists. As soon as the rebels in Boston had been humbled, the British argued, people living in other colonies would desert the cause for independence. General Gage, for example, told the king that the colonists "will be Lions, whilst we are Lambs,... if we take a resolute part they will undoubtedly prove very weak." Since this advice confirmed George's views, he called Gage "an honest determined man."

As later events demonstrated, of course, Britain had become involved in an impossible military situation. Three separate elements neutralized advantages held by the larger power over its adversary. First, the British had to transport men and supplies across the Atlantic, a logistic challenge of unprecedented complexity. Unreliable lines of communication broke down under the strain of war.

Second, America was too vast to be conquered by conventional military methods. Redcoats might gain control over the major port cities, but as long as the Continental Army remained intact, the rebellion continued. As Washington explained, "the possession of our Towns, while we have an Army in the field, will avail them little... It is our Arms, not defenceless Towns, they have to subdue." Even if England had recruited enough soldiers to occupy the entire country, it would still have lost the war. As one Loyalist instructed the king, "if all America becomes a garrison, she is not worth your attention." Britain could only win by crushing the American will to resist.

And third, British strategists never appreciated the depth of the Americans' commitment to a political ideology. In the wars of eighteenth-century Europe, such beliefs had seldom mattered. European troops before the French Revolution served because they were paid or because the military was a vocation, but most certainly not because they hoped to advance a set of constitutional principles. Americans were different. To be sure, some young men were drawn to the military by bounty money or by the desire to escape unhappy families. A few were drafted. But taking such people into account, one still encounters among the American troops a remarkable commitment to republican ideals. One French officer reported from the United States, "It is incredible that soldiers composed of men of every age, even of children of fifteen, of whites and blacks, almost naked, unpaid, and rather poorly fed, can march so well and withstand fire so steadfastly."

The American Revolution

Building a Professional Army

Washington insisted on organizing a regular well-trained field army. Some advisers urged the commander in chief to wage a guerrilla war, one in which small partisan bands would sap Britain's will to rule Americans. But Washington rejected that course. He recognized that the Continental Army served not only as a fighting force but also as a symbol of the republican cause. Its very existence would sustain American hopes, and so long as the army survived, American agents could plausibly solicit foreign aid. This thinking shaped Washington's wartime strategy; he studiously avoided "general actions" in which the Continental Army might be destroyed. Critics complained about Washington's caution, but as they soon discovered, he understood better than they what independence required.

If the commander in chief was correct about the army, however, he failed to comprehend the political importance of the militia. These scattered, almost amateur, military units seldom altered the outcome of battle, but they did maintain control over large areas of the country not directly affected by the British army. Throughout the war, they compelled men and women who would rather have remained neutral to actively support the American effort.

For the half million African American colonists, most of them slaves, the fight for independence took on special poignancy. After all, they wanted to achieve personal as well as political freedom, and many African Americans supported those who seemed most likely to deliver them from bondage. It is estimated that some five thousand African Americans took up arms to fight against the British. The Continental Army included two all-black units, one from Massachusetts and the other from Rhode Island. In 1778, the legislature of Rhode Island voted to free any slave who volunteered to serve, since, according to the lawmakers, history taught that "the wisest, the freest, and bravest nations… liberated their slaves, and enlisted them as soldiers to fight in defence of their country." In the South, especially in Georgia and South Carolina, more than ten thousand African Americans supported the British, and after the patriots had won the war, these men and women left the United States, relocating to Nova Scotia, Florida, and Jamaica, with some eventually resettling in Africa.

QUICK CHECK

Why did George Washington insist on organizing a regular field army?

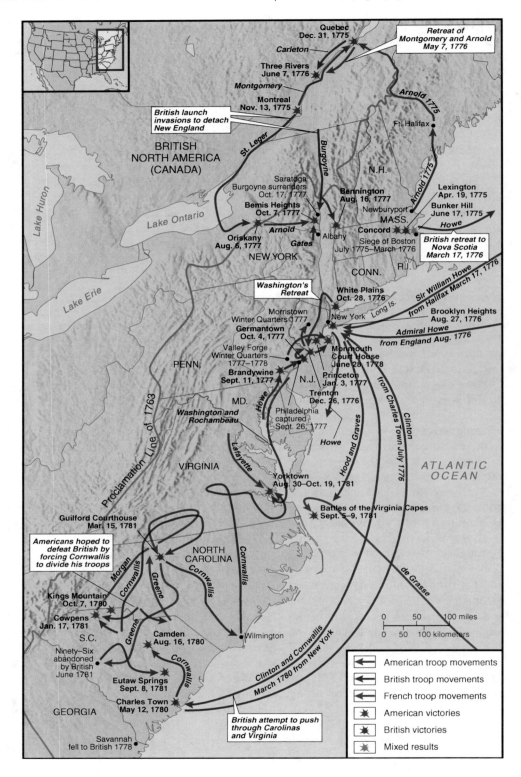

THE AMERICAN REVOLUTION, 1775–1781 Battles were fought in the colonies, on the western frontier, and along the Gulf of Mexico. The major engagements of the first years of the war, from the spontaneous rising at Concord in 1775 to Washington's well-coordinated attack on Trenton in December 1776, were fought in the northern colonies. In the middle theater of war, Burgoyne's attempt in 1777 to cut off New England from the rest of the colonies failed when his army was defeated at Saratoga. Action in the final years of the war, from the battles at Camden, Kings Mountain, Cowpens, and Guilford Courthouse to the final victory at Yorktown, occurred in the southern theater of war.

Why did British military strategists shift the focus of war from New England to the South?

"Times That Try Men's Souls"

After the embarrassing defeats in Massachusetts, the king appointed General Sir William Howe to replace the ill-fated Gage. British rulers now understood that a simple police action would not be sufficient to crush the American rebellion. Parliament authorized sending more than fifty thousand troops to the mainland colonies, and after evacuating Boston—an untenable strategic position—the British forces stormed ashore at Staten Island in New York Harbor on July 3, 1776. From this more central location, Howe believed he could cut the New Englanders off from the rest of America.

When Washington learned the British were planning to occupy New York City, he transferred many of his inexperienced soldiers to Long Island, where they suffered a major defeat (August 27, 1776). In a series of engagements disastrous for the Americans, Howe drove the Continental Army across the Hudson River into New Jersey.

Swift victories in New York and New Jersey persuaded General Howe that few Americans enthusiastically supported independence. He issued a general pardon, therefore, to anyone who would swear allegiance to George III. The results were encouraging. More than three thousand men and women who lived in areas occupied by the British army took the oath. This group included one frightened signer of the Declaration of Independence. Howe perceived that a lasting peace in America would require his troops to treat "our enemies as if they might one day become our friends." A member of Lord North's cabinet grumbled that this was "a sentimental manner of making war." The pardon plan eventually failed not because Howe lacked toughness but because his soldiers and officers treated loyal Americans as inferior, an attitude that did little to promote good relations. In any case, as soon as the redcoats left a pardoned region, the rebel militia retaliated against those who had deserted the patriot cause.

In December 1776, Washington's bedraggled army retreated across the Delaware River into Pennsylvania. American prospects appeared bleaker than at any other time during the war. The Continental Army lacked basic supplies, and many men who had signed up for short-term enlistments prepared to go home. "These are the times that try men's souls," Paine wrote in a pamphlet titled *American Crisis.* "The summer soldier and the sunshine patriot will, in this crisis, shrink from the service of their country, but he that stands it *now* deserves... love and thanks..." Before winter, Washington determined to attempt one last desperate stroke.

Letter from a Revolutionary War Soldier

BRITISH DEFEAT AT THE BATTLE OF PRINCETON   Oil painting by William Mercer, ca. 1786–1790. The painting shows George Washington (left, on horseback) directing cannon fire with his sword.

Did it take courage to fight on an American battlefield?

QUICK CHECK

Why did the first year of war go so badly for the Americans?

Howe played into Washington's hands. The British forces were dispersed in small garrisons across the state of New Jersey, and while the Americans could not possibly have defeated the combined British army, they did possess the capacity—with luck—to capture an exposed post. On the night of December 25, Continental soldiers slipped over the ice-filled Delaware River and at Trenton took nine hundred sleeping Hessian mercenaries by complete surprise.

Victory in a Year of Defeat

In the summer of 1777, General John Burgoyne, a dashing though overbearing officer, descended from Canada with a force of more than seven thousand troops. They intended to clear the Hudson Valley of rebel resistance; join Howe's army, which was to come up to Albany; and thereby cut New England off from the other states. Burgoyne fought in a grand style. Accompanied by a German band, thirty carts filled with the general's liquor and belongings, and two thousand dependents and camp followers, the British set out to thrash the Americans. The campaign was a disaster. Military units, mostly from New England, cut the enemy force apart in the deep woods north of Albany. At the battle of Bennington (August 16), the New Hampshire militia under Brigadier General John Stark overwhelmed a thousand German mercenaries. After this setback, Burgoyne's forces struggled forward, desperately hoping that Howe would rush to their rescue, but when it became clear that their situation at Saratoga was hopeless, the haughty Burgoyne was forced to surrender fifty-eight hundred men to the American General Horatio Gates (October 17).

Soon after Burgoyne left Canada, General Howe unexpectedly decided to move his main army from New York City to Philadelphia. Exactly what he hoped to achieve was not clear, even to Britain's rulers, and of course, when Burgoyne called for assistance, Howe was in Pennsylvania. Howe's campaign began in late July. The British forces sailed to the head of the Chesapeake Bay and then marched north to Philadelphia. Washington's troops obstructed the enemy's progress, first at Brandywine Creek (September 11) and then at Paoli (September 20), but the outnumbered Americans could not stop the British from entering Philadelphia.

Anxious lest these defeats discourage Congress and the American people, Washington attempted one last battle before the onset of winter. In an engagement at Germantown (October 4), the Americans launched a major counterattack on a fog-covered battlefield, but just at the moment when success seemed assured, they broke off the fight. "When every thing gave the most flattering hopes of victory," Washington complained, "the troops began suddenly to retreat." Bad luck, confusion, and incompetence contributed to the failure. A discouraged Continental Army dug in at Valley Forge, twenty miles outside of Philadelphia, where camp diseases took twenty-five hundred American lives. In their misery, few American soldiers realized their situation was not nearly as desperate as it had been in 1776.

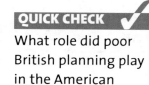

QUICK CHECK

What role did poor British planning play in the American victory at Saratoga?

The French Alliance

Even before the Americans declared their independence, agents of the government of Louis XVI began to explore ways to aid the colonists, not so much because the French monarchy favored the republican cause but because it hoped to embarrass the English. The French deeply resented the defeat they had sustained during the Seven Years' War. During the early months of the Revolution, the French covertly sent tons of essential military supplies to the Americans. The negotiations for these arms involved secret agents and fictitious trading companies, the type of clandestine operation more typical of modern times than of the eighteenth century. But when American representatives, Benjamin Franklin for one, pleaded for official recognition of American independence or for outright military alliance, the French advised patience. The international stakes were too great for the king openly to back a cause that had little chance of success.

The American victory over General Burgoyne at Saratoga, however, convinced the French that the rebels had formidable forces and were serious in their resolve. Franklin soon went to Paris to meet with French officials. In meetings, he hinted that the Americans might accept a British peace initiative. If the French wanted the war to continue, if they really wanted to embarrass their old rival, then they had to do what the English refused: formally recognize the independence of the United States.

The stratagem paid off handsomely. On February 6, 1778, the French presented American representatives with two separate treaties. The first, called the Treaty of Amity and Commerce, established commercial relations between France and the United States. It tacitly accepted the existence of a new, independent republic. The Treaty of Alliance was even more generous, considering America's obvious military and economic weaknesses. In the event that France and England went to war (they did so on June 14, as everyone expected), the French agreed to reject "either Truce or Peace with Great Britain... until the independence of the United States shall have been formally or tacitly assured by the Treaty or Treaties that shall terminate the War." Even more amazing, France surrendered its claim to

123

all territories formerly owned by Great Britain east of the Mississippi River. The Americans pledged they would not sign a separate peace with Britain without first informing their new ally. And in return, France made no claim to Canada, asking only for the right to take possession of certain British islands in the Caribbean. Never had Franklin worked his magic to greater effect.

French intervention instantly transformed British military strategy. What had been a colonial rebellion suddenly became a world conflict. Scarce military resources, especially newer fighting ships, had to be diverted from the American theater to guard the English Channel. In fact, there was talk in London of a possible French invasion. Although the threat of such an assault was not very great until 1779, the British did have cause for concern. The French navy posed a serious challenge to the overextended British fleet. By concentrating their warships in a specific area, the French could hold off or even defeat British squadrons, an advantage that would figure significantly in the American victory at Yorktown.

QUICK CHECK ✓

What role did French support play in the winning of the Revolutionary War?

The Final Campaign

Military strategists calculated that Britain's last chance of winning the war lay in the Southern Colonies, a region largely untouched in the early years of fighting. Intelligence reports reaching London indicated that Georgia and South Carolina contained a sizable body of Loyalists, men who would take up arms for the crown if only they received support and encouragement from the regular army. The southern strategy devised by British leaders in 1779 turned the war into a bitter

BATTLE OF YORKTOWN French assistance on land and sea helped the Americans defeat the British in the American Revolution. In this French print of the battle at Yorktown, French ships block the entrance of Chesapeake Bay, preventing British vessels from resupplying their troops on land. Yorktown, which was unknown to the French artist who made this print, is depicted as a European walled city.

Could the Americans have won at Yorktown without French support?

guerrilla conflict, and during the last months of battle, British officers worried that their search for an easy victory had inadvertently opened a Pandora's box of uncontrollable partisan furies.

The southern campaign opened in the spring of 1780. Savannah had already fallen, and General Henry Clinton, who had replaced Howe after Saratoga, reckoned that if the British could take Charles Town, they would be able to control the entire South. A large fleet carrying nearly eight thousand redcoats reached South Carolina in February. Complacent Americans had allowed the city's fortifications to decay, and in a desperate, last-minute effort to preserve Charles Town, General Benjamin Lincoln's forces dug trenches and reinforced walls, but to no avail. Clinton and his second in command, General Cornwallis, gradually encircled the city, and on May 12, Lincoln surrendered an American army of almost six thousand men.

Despite this victory, partisan warfare had become evident in the British army. Tory raiders showed little interest in serving as regular soldiers in Cornwallis's army. They preferred night riding, indiscriminate plundering or murdering of neighbors against whom they harbored ancient grudges. The British had unleashed a horde of bandits across South Carolina. Men who genuinely supported independence or who had merely fallen victim to Loyalist guerrillas bided their time. They retreated westward, waiting for their enemies to make a mistake. Their chance came on October 7 at Kings Mountain, North Carolina. In the most vicious fighting of the Revolution, the backwoodsmen decimated a force of British regulars and Tory raiders who had strayed too far from base. One witness reported that when a British officer tried to surrender, he was summarily shot down by at least seven American soldiers.

Cornwallis, confused by the enemy's guerilla tactics and poorly supplied, squandered his strength chasing American forces across the Carolinas. Whatever military strategy had compelled him to leave Charles Town had long since been abandoned, and in early 1781, Cornwallis informed Clinton, "Events alone can decide the future Steps." Events, however, did not run in the British favor. Congress sent General Nathanael Greene to the South with a new army. This young Rhode Islander was the most capable general on Washington's staff. Greene joined Daniel Morgan, leader of the famed Virginia Riflemen, and in a series of tactically brilliant engagements, they sapped the strength of Cornwallis's army, first at Cowpens, South Carolina (January 17, 1781), and later at Guilford Courthouse, North Carolina (March 15). Clinton fumed in New York City. In his estimation, the inept Cornwallis had left "two valuable colonies behind him to be overrun and conquered by the very army which he boasts to have completely routed but a week or two before."

Cornwallis pushed north into Virginia, planning apparently to establish a base of operations on the coast. He selected **Yorktown**, a sleepy tobacco market located on a peninsula bounded by the York and James rivers. Washington watched these maneuvers closely. The canny Virginia planter knew this territory intimately, and he sensed that Cornwallis had made a serious blunder. When Washington learned the French fleet could gain temporary dominance in the Chesapeake Bay, he rushed south from New Jersey. With him marched thousands of well-trained French troops under the Comte de Rochambeau. All the pieces fell into place. The French admiral, the Comte de Grasse, cut Cornwallis off from the sea, while Washington and his lieutenants encircled the British on land. On October 19, 1781, Cornwallis surrendered his entire army of six thousand men. When Lord North heard of the defeat at Yorktown, he moaned, "Oh God! It is all over." The British still controlled New York City and

Yorktown
Tobacco market located on a peninsula bounded by the York and James rivers, where Cornwallis surrendered an army to French and American forces, effectively ending the Revolution.

QUICK CHECK ✓

Why did the "southern campaign" not work out as British strategists had anticipated?

Charles Town, but except for a few skirmishes, the fighting ended. The task of securing the independence of the United States was now in the hands of the diplomats. The preliminary agreement signed in Paris on September 3, 1783, not only guaranteed the independence of the United States; it also transferred all the territory east of the Mississippi River, except Spanish Florida, to the new republic. The **Treaty of Paris of 1783** established generous boundaries on the north and south and gave the Americans important fishing rights in the North Atlantic.

Treaty of Paris of 1783 Agreement signed between American delegates and Great Britain that ended the American Revolution and also transferred territory east of the Mississippi River, except for Spanish Florida, to the new republic.

The Loyalist Dilemma

No one knows for certain how many Americans actually supported the Crown during the Revolution. Some Loyalists undoubtedly kept silent and avoided making a public commitment that might have led to banishment or loss of property. But for many persons, neutrality proved impossible. Almost 100,000 men and women permanently left America. While a number of these exiles had served as imperial officeholders—Thomas Hutchinson, for example—in the main, they came from all ranks and backgrounds. A large number of humble farmers, more than 30,000, resettled in Canada. Others relocated to England, the West Indies, or Africa.

The political ideology of the Loyalists was not substantially different from that of their opponents. Like other Americans, they believed that men and women were entitled to life, liberty, and the pursuit of happiness. The Loyalists were also convinced that independence would destroy those values by promoting disorder. By turning their backs on Britain, a source of tradition and stability, the rebels seemed to have encouraged licentiousness, even anarchy in the streets. The Loyalists suspected that Patriot demands for freedom were self-serving, even hypocritical, for as Perserved Smith, a Loyalist from Ashfield, Massachusetts, observed, "Sons of liberty... did not deserve the name, for it was evident all they wanted was liberty from oppression that they might have liberty to oppress!"

The Loyalists were caught in a difficult squeeze. The British never quite trusted them. After all, they were Americans. During the early stages of the war Loyalists organized militia companies and hoped to pacify large areas of the countryside with the support of the regular army. The British generals were unreliable partners, however, for no sooner had they called on loyal Americans to come forward than the redcoats marched away, leaving the Tories exposed to rebel retaliation. And in England, the exiles found themselves treated as second-class citizens. While many of them received monetary compensation for their sacrifice, they were never regarded as the equals of native-born English citizens. Not surprisingly, the Loyalist community in London was gradually transformed into a collection of bitter men and women who felt unwelcome on both sides of the Atlantic.

Although many Loyalists eventually returned to their homes, a sizeable number could not do so. For them, the sense of loss remained a heavy emotional burden. Perhaps the most poignant testimony came from a young mother living in exile in Nova Scotia. "I climbed to the top of Chipman's Hill and watched the sails disappear in the distance," she recounted, "and such a feeling of loneliness came over me that though I had not shed a tear through all the war I sat down on the damp moss with my baby on my lap and cried bitterly."

QUICK CHECK ✓

Why did so many Loyalists decide to leave the United States during the Revolution?

Conclusion: Preserving Independence

The American people had waged war against the most powerful nation in Europe and emerged victorious. The treaty marked the conclusion of a colonial rebellion, but it remained for the men and women who had resisted taxation without representation to work out the full implications of republicanism. What would be the shape of the new government? What powers would be delegated to the people, the states, the federal authorities? How far would the wealthy, well-born leaders of the rebellion be willing to extend political, social, and economic rights?

For many Americans the challenge of nation building appeared even more formidable than waging war against Great Britain. As Philadelphia physician Dr. Benjamin Rush explained, "There is nothing more common than to confound the terms of American Revolution with those of the late American war. The American war is over, but this is far from being the case with the American Revolution. On the contrary, nothing but the first act of the great drama is closed."

For a list of additional titles related to this chapter's topics, please see www.pearsonamericanhistory.com. MyHistoryLab

STUDY RESOURCES

KEY TERMS

Whigs

parliamentary sovereignty

Loyalists

Stamp Act of 1765

Stamp Act Congress

Boston Massacre

committee of correspondence

Boston Tea Party

Coercive Acts of 1774

First Continental Congress

Second Continental Congress

Common Sense

Yorktown

Treaty of Paris of 1783

CHAPTER REVIEW

WHY did Americans resist parliamentary taxation?

During the 1760s British rulers claimed that Parliament could make laws for the colonists "in all cases whatsoever." Americans challenged the concept of "parliamentary sovereignty." Drawing upon the work of John Locke, the English philosopher, they insisted that God had given them certain natural and inalienable rights. By attempting to tax them without representation, Parliament threatened those basic rights.

WHAT events led to the erosion of the bonds of empire during the 1760s?

Wars in America cost British taxpayers a lot of money. Parliament concluded that the colonists should help reduce the rising national debt, but when it passed the Stamp Act (1765), Americans protested. Ordinary colonists boycotted British manufactured goods. Taken aback, Parliament repealed the hated statute, while maintaining in the Declaratory Act (1766) its complete legislative authority over the Americans.

WHAT events in 1775 and 1776 led to the colonists' decision to declare independence?

In 1775, following battles at Lexington and Concord, militiamen from throughout New England descended upon Boston, besieging the British troops encamped there. In response, the Continental Congress formed the Continental Army and appointed George Washington commander. In 1776, Thomas Paine's *Common Sense* convinced ordinary colonists that a republic was a better form of government than monarchy, and Congress declared independence.

WHY did it take eight years of Warfare for the Americans to gain independence?

After a string of American defeats, which exposed weaknesses in military training and recruitment, a victory at Saratoga in 1777 convinced the French to form an alliance with the rebelling colonists. In 1781, supported by French soldiers and warships, Washington forced a British army under General Cornwallis to surrender at Yorktown. The shooting war effectively ended following this surrender, and American diplomats negotiated a favorable peace settlement in 1783.

MAKING CONNECTIONS

1. Were British political leaders or American agitators more to blame for the imperial crisis?
2. With more enlightened leadership, could king and Parliament have preserved Britain's American empire?
3. Did Lexington and Concord make national independence inevitable?
4. Given the logistical problems facing the British, could they have possibly won the Revolutionary War?

PRACTICE QUIZ

1. In 1760 _____ III become King of England.
   a. George
   b. Charles
   c. Louis
   d. John

2. The _____ party dominated the British Parliament during the late 1700s.
   a. Democrat
   b. Republican
   c. Whig
   d. Monarchy

3. The idea of _____ representation in Parliament produced contention between Great Britain and the American colonies during the late 1700s.
   a. French
   b. Virtual
   c. Indian
   d. Religious

4. American _____ sided with the king during the American Revolution.
   a. Patriots
   b. Backwoodsmen
   c. Indentured servants
   d. Loyalists

5. In 1765 the _____ Act generated a firestorm of protest in the American colonies.
   a. Sugar
   b. Tea
   c. Stamp
   d. Townshend

6. The _____ Massacre by British troops united the American colonists in 1770.
   a. Boston
   b. Philadelphia
   c. New York
   d. Baltimore

7. The Boston _____ Party became a symbol of colonial protest to British taxation and importation policies.
   a. Sugar
   b. Tea
   c. Wood
   d. Fur

8. All of the following accurately characterize French assistance to the American colonists during the Revolution *except*
   a. The French officially recognized the U.S. government.
   b. The French provided officers and troops.
   c. The French provided ships.
   d. The French laid claim to Canada if the British lost the war.

9. The Battle of Yorktown is characterized by all of the following *except*
   a. General Cornwallis selected Yorktown as his base of operations.
   b. Washington possessed thousands of well-trained German troops.
   c. A French admiral cut off General Cornwallis from the sea.
   d. Washington encircled the British on land and captured the army.

10. Which of the following was *not* an aspect of the Treaty of Paris?
    a. It guaranteed the independence of the United States.
    b. It transferred Louisiana territory to the U.S.
    c. It transferred all the territory east of the Mississippi River, except Spanish Florida, to the U.S.
    d. It established generous boundaries on the north.

Find more practice at www.myhistorylab.com

SAMPLE ESSAY QUESTIONS

1. Explain the short- and long-term causes of the American Revolution.

2. Summarize how the American colonies militarily defeated Great Britain and achieved independence.

CREDITS

The Republican Experiment, 1783–1788

The Republican Experiment
1783–1788

SPOTLIGHT QUESTIONS

WHAT were the limits of equality in the "republican" society of the new United States?

WHY did many Americans regard the Articles of Confederation as inadequate?

WHY did Constitutional delegates compromise on representation and slavery?

WHAT issues separated Federalists from Antifederalists during debates over ratification?

OUTLINE

Defining Republican Culture

Stumbling Toward a New National Government

"Have We Fought for This?"

Whose Constitution? Struggle for Ratification

TONTINE COFFEE HOUSE
By Francis Guy, 1797. The Tontine is the large building at left, on the corner of Wall and Water Streets in New York City, where merchants and traders met daily to transact business. (*Source: "Tontine Coffee House," by Francis Guy, oil on canvas, c. 1797/Collection of The New-York Historical Society [negative number 6211, accession number 1907.32]*)

Does this picture suggest that Americans in the 1790s were optimistic about the future of the "republican experiment"?

A New Political Morality

In 1788, Lewis Hallam and John Henry petitioned the General Assembly of Pennsylvania to open a theater. Although a 1786 state law banned the performance of stage plays and other "disorderly sports," many Philadelphia leaders favored the request to hold "dramatic representations" in their city. A committee appointed to study the issue concluded that a theater would contribute to "the general refinement of manners and the polish of society." Some supporters even argued that the sooner the United States had a professional theater the sooner the young republic would escape the "foreign yoke" of British culture.

The Quakers of Philadelphia dismissed such claims out of hand. They warned that such "seminaries of lewdness and irreligion" would quickly undermine "the virtue of the people." They pointed out that "no sooner is a playhouse opened than it becomes surrounded with... brothels." Since Pennsylvania was already suffering from a "stagnation of commerce [and] a scarcity of money"—unmistakable signs of God's displeasure—it seemed unwise to risk divine punishment by encouraging new "hot-beds of vice."

Such rhetoric did not sit well with other citizens who interpreted the revolutionary experience from an entirely different perspective. At issue, they insisted, was

133

KEY EVENTS

1776   Second Continental Congress authorizes colonies to create republican government (May) ■ Eight states draft new constitutions; two others already enjoy republican government by virtue of former colonial charters

1777   Congress accepts Articles of Confederation after long debate (November)

1781   States ratify Articles of Confederation following settlement of Virginia's western land claims ■ British army surrenders at Yorktown (October)

1783   Society of the Cincinnati raises a storm of criticism

1785   Land Ordinance for Northwest Territory passed by Congress

1786   Annapolis Convention suggests second meeting to revise the Articles of Confederation (September) ■ Shays's Rebellion frightens American leaders

1787–1788   The federal Constitution is ratified by all states except North Carolina and Rhode Island

1791   Bill of Rights (first ten amendments to the Constitution) ratified by states

not popular morality, but state censorship. If the government silenced the stage, then "the same authority... may, with equal justice, dictate the shape and texture of our dress, or the modes and ceremonies of our worship." Depriving those who wanted to see plays of an opportunity to do so, they argued, "will abridge the natural right of every freeman, to dispose of his time and money, according to his own tastes and dispositions."

Throughout post–Revolutionary America everyday matters such as the opening of a new playhouse provoked passionate public debate. The divisions were symptomatic of a new, uncertain political culture struggling to find the proper balance between public morality and private freedom. During the long fight against Great Britain, Americans had defended individual rights. The problem was that the same people also believed that a republic that compromised its virtue could not long preserve liberty and independence.

In 1776, Thomas Paine had reminded ordinary men and women that "the sun never shined on a cause of greater worth.…'Tis not the concern of a day, a year, or an age; posterity are virtually involved in the contest, and will be more or less affected, even to the end of time, by the proceedings now." During the 1780s Americans understood their responsibility not only to each other, but also to history. They worried, however, that they might not successfully meet the challenge. Individual states seemed intent on looking out for local interests rather than the national welfare. Revolutionary leaders such as George Washington and James Madison concluded that the United States needed a strong central government to protect rights and property. Their creative quest for solutions brought forth a new and enduring constitution.

Defining Republican Culture

WHAT were the limits of equality in the "republican" society of the new United States?

Today, the term *republican* no longer possesses the evocative power it did for most eighteenth-century Americans. For them, it defined not a political party, but rather, an entire political culture. Those Americans who read deeply in ancient and renaissance history knew that most republics had failed, often within a few years, only to be replaced by tyrants who cared not at all what ordinary people thought about the public good. To preserve their republic from such a fate, victorious revolutionaries such as Samuel Adams recast fundamental political values. For them, **republicanism** represented more than a particular form of government. It was a way of life, a core ideology, an uncompromising commitment to maintain liberty and equality, while guarding against the corrupting influences of power and self-interest.

White Americans came out of the Revolution with an almost euphoric sense of the nation's special destiny. This expansive outlook, encountered among so many ordinary men and women, owed much to the spread of Protestant evangelicalism. However skeptical Jefferson and Franklin may have been about revealed religion, the great mass of American people subscribed to an almost utopian vision of the country's future. To this new republic, God had promised progress and prosperity.

In certain quarters, however, the celebration of liberty met with mixed response. Some Americans—often the very men who had resisted British tyranny—worried that the citizens of the new nation were caught up in a wild, destructive scramble for material wealth. Democratic excesses seemed to threaten order, to endanger the rights of property. Surely a republic could not long survive unless its citizens showed greater self-control. For people concerned about the loss of order, the state assemblies appeared to be the greatest source of instability. Popularly elected representatives lacked what men of property defined as real civic virtue, an ability to work for the common good rather than their private interests.

Working out the tensions between order and liberty, between property and equality, generated an outpouring of political genius. At other times in American history, persons of extraordinary talent have been drawn to theology, commerce, or science, but during the 1780s, the country's intellectual leaders—Thomas Jefferson, James Madison, Alexander Hamilton, and John Adams, among others—focused their creative energies on the problem of how republicans ought to govern themselves.

republicanism
Concept that ultimate political authority is vested in the citizens of the nation. The character of republican government was dependent on the civic virtue of its citizens to preserve the nation from corruption and moral decay.

Social and Political Reform

Following the war, Americans aggressively ferreted out and, with republican fervor, denounced any traces of aristocratic pretense. As colonists, they had long resented the claims that certain Englishmen were privileged simply because of noble birth. Even so committed a republican as George Washington had to be reminded that artificial status was contrary to republican principles. In 1783, he and the officers who had served during the Revolution formed the Society of the Cincinnati, a hereditary organization in which membership passed from father to eldest son. The soldiers wanted to maintain old friendships, but anxious republicans throughout America let out a howl of protest, and one South Carolina legislator, Aedanus Burke, warned that the Society intended to create "an hereditary peerage… [which would] undermine the Constitution and destroy civil liberty." After an embarrassed Washington called for appropriate reforms of the Society's bylaws, the Cincinnati crisis receded. The fear of privilege remained, however, and wealthy Americans dropped honorific titles such as "esquire." Lawyers of republican persuasion chided judges who had adopted the English custom of wearing great flowing wigs to court.

The appearance of equality was as important as its actual achievement. In fact, the distribution of wealth in postwar America was more uneven than it had been in the mid-eighteenth century. The sudden accumulation of large fortunes by new families made other Americans particularly sensitive to aristocratic display, for it seemed intolerable that a revolution waged against a monarchy should produce a class of persons legally, or even visibly, distinguished from their fellow citizens.

In an effort to root out the notion of a privileged class, states abolished laws of primogeniture and entail. In colonial times, these laws allowed a landholder either to pass his entire estate to his eldest son or to declare that his property could never be divided, sold, or given away. Jefferson claimed that the repeal of these practices would eradicate "antient [sic] and future aristocracy; a foundation [has been] laid for a government truly republican." Jefferson may have exaggerated the social impact of this reform; however, the symbolism of the law counted as much as real social practice. Republican legislators wanted to cleanse traces of the former feudal order from the statute books.

Republican ferment also encouraged many states to lower property requirements for voting. After the break with Great Britain, such a step seemed logical. As one group of farmers declared, no man can be "free & independent" unless he possesses "a voice… in the choice of the most important Officers in the Legislature." Pennsylvania and Georgia allowed all white male taxpayers to participate in elections. Other states were less democratic, but with the exception of Massachusetts, they reduced property qualifications.

The most important changes in voting patterns were the result of western migration. As Americans moved to the frontier, they received full political representation in their state legislatures, and because new districts tended to be poorer than established coastal settlements, their representatives seemed less cultured, less well trained than those sent by eastern voters. Moreover, western delegates resented traveling so far to attend legislative meetings, and they lobbied successfully to transfer state capitals to more convenient locations. During this period, Georgia moved the seat of its government from Savannah to Augusta, South Carolina from Charles Town to Columbia, North Carolina from New Bern to Raleigh, Virginia from Williamsburg to Richmond, New York from New York City to Albany, and New Hampshire from Portsmouth to Concord.

After gaining independence, Americans also reexamined the relation between church and state. Republican spokespersons such as Thomas Jefferson insisted that rulers had no right to interfere with the free expression of an individual's religious beliefs. As governor of Virginia, he advocated the disestablishment of the Anglican Church, an institution that had received tax monies and other benefits during the colonial period. Jefferson and his allies regarded such special privilege not only as a denial of religious freedom—after all, rival denominations did not receive tax money—but also as a vestige of aristocratic society.

In 1786, Virginia cut the last ties between church and state. Other southern states disestablished the Anglican Church, but in Massachusetts and New Hampshire, Congregational churches continued to enjoy special status. Moreover, while Americans championed toleration, they seldom favored philosophies that radically challenged Christian values.

QUICK CHECK ✓

During the 1780s, why were Americans so sensitive to the dangers of "aristocratic display"?

African Americans in the New Republic

Revolutionary fervor forced Americans to confront the most appalling contradiction to republican principles—slavery. The Quaker leader John Woolman (1720–1772) probably did more than any other white person of the era to remind people of the evils of this institution. A trip he took through the Southern Colonies as a young man forever impressed upon Woolman "the dark gloominess" of slavery. In a sermon, the outspoken humanitarian declared "that Men having Power too often misapplied it; that though we made Slaves of the Negroes, and the Turks made Slaves of the Christians, I believed that Liberty was the natural Right of all Men equally."

During the revolutionary period, abolitionist sentiment spread. Both in private and in public, people began to criticize slavery in other than religious language. No doubt, the double standard of their own political rhetoric embarrassed many white Americans. They hotly demanded liberation from parliamentary enslavement at the same time that they held several hundred thousand blacks in permanent bondage.

By keeping the issue of slavery before the public through writing and petitioning, African Americans powerfully undermined arguments advanced in favor of human bondage. They demanded freedom, reminding white lawmakers that African American men and women had the same natural right to liberty as did other Americans. In 1779, for example, a group of African Americans living in Connecticut pointedly asked the members of the state assembly "whether it is consistent with the present Claims, of the United States, to hold so many Thousands, of the Race of Adam, our Common Father, in perpetual Slavery." In New Hampshire, nineteen persons who called themselves "natives of Africa" reminded local legislators that "private or public tyranny and slavery are alike detestable to minds conscious of the equal dignity of human nature."

Slave Petition to the General Assembly in Connecticut (1779)

The scientific accomplishments of Benjamin Banneker (1731–1806), Maryland's African American astronomer and mathematician, and the international fame of Phillis Wheatley (1753–1784), Boston's celebrated "African muse," made it increasingly difficult for white Americans to maintain credibly that African Americans could not hold their own in a free society. Wheatley's poems went through many editions, and after reading her work, the great French philosopher Voltaire rebuked a friend who had claimed "there never would be Negro poets." As Voltaire discovered, Wheatley "writes excellent verse in English." Banneker, like Wheatley, enjoyed a well-deserved reputation, in his case for contributions as a scientist. After receiving a copy of an almanac that Banneker had published in Philadelphia, Thomas Jefferson concluded "that nature has given to our black brethren, talents equal to those of the other colors of men."

Benjamin Banneker, Letter to Thomas Jefferson (1791)

PHILLIS WHEATLEY   This engraving of Phillis Wheatley appeared in her volume of verse, *Poems on Various Subjects, Religious and Moral* (1773), the first book published by an African American.

How might white readers have responded to Wheatley's work?

In the northern states, there was no real economic justification for slavery, and white laborers, often recent European immigrants, resented having to compete in the workplace against slaves. This economic situation, combined with the acknowledgment of the double standard represented by slavery, contributed to the establishment of antislavery societies. In 1775, Franklin helped organize a group in Philadelphia called the Society for the Relief of Free Negroes, Unlawfully Held. John Jay, Alexander Hamilton, and other prominent New Yorkers founded a Manumission Society in 1785. By 1792, antislavery societies were meeting from Virginia to Massachusetts, and in the northern states at least, these groups, working for the same ends as various Christian evangelicals, put slaveholders on the intellectual defensive for the first time in American history.

In several states north of Virginia, the abolition of slavery took a number of different forms. Even before achieving statehood, Vermont drafted a constitution (1777) that specifically prohibited slavery. In 1780, the Pennsylvania legislature passed a law effecting the gradual emancipation of slaves. Although the Massachusetts assembly refused to address the issue directly, the state courts took up the challenge and liberated the African Americans. A judge ruled slavery unconstitutional in Massachusetts because it conflicted with a clause in the state bill of rights declaring "all men… free and equal." According to one enthusiast, this decision freed "a Grate number of Blacks… who… are held in a state of slavery within the bowels of a free and christian Country." By 1800, slavery was well on the road to extinction in the northern states.

These positive developments did not mean that white people accepted blacks as equals. In fact, in the very states that outlawed slavery, African Americans faced systematic discrimination. Free blacks were generally excluded from voting, juries, and militia duty—they were denied rights and responsibilities usually associated with full citizenship. They rarely enjoyed access to education, and in cities such as Philadelphia and New York, where African Americans went to look for work, they ended up living in segregated wards or neighborhoods. Even in the churches—institutions that had often spoken out against slavery—free African Americans were denied equal standing with white worshippers. Humiliations of this sort persuaded African Americans to form their own churches. In Philadelphia, Richard Allen, a former slave, founded the Bethel Church for Negro Methodists (1793) and later organized the **African Methodist Episcopal Church** (1814), an institution of great cultural as well as religious significance for nineteenth-century American blacks.

African Methodist Episcopal Church
Church founded by former slave Richard Allen during a time when African Americans were denied equal standing with white worshippers.

RICHARD ALLEN Born to slaves, Richard Allen became a zealous evangelical minister. Allen organized the African Methodist Episcopal Church in 1814.

Why did African Americans feel the need to set up their own churches?

Even in the South, where African Americans made up a large percentage of the population, slavery disturbed thoughtful white republicans. Some planters simply freed their slaves, and by 1790, the number of free blacks living in Virginia was 12,766. By 1800, the figure had reached 30,750. There is no question that this trend reflected the uneasiness among white masters. Richard Randolph, one of Virginia's wealthier planters, explained that he freed his slaves "to make restitution, as far as I am able, to an unfortunate race of bond-men, over whom my ancestors have usurped and exercised the most lawless and monstrous tyranny." George Washington also manumitted his slaves. To be sure, most southern slaveholders, especially those living in South Carolina and Georgia, rejected this course of action. Their economic well-being depended on slave labor. Perhaps more significant, however, is the fact that no southern leader during the era of republican experimentation defended slavery as a positive good. Such overtly racist rhetoric did not become part of the public discourse until the nineteenth century.

Despite promising starts in that direction, the southern states did not abolish slavery. The economic incentives to maintain a servile labor force, especially after the invention of the cotton gin in 1793 and the opening up of the Alabama and Mississippi frontier, overwhelmed the initial abolitionist impulse. An opportunity to translate the principles of the American Revolution into social practice had been lost, at least temporarily. Jefferson reported in 1805, "I have long since given up the expectation of any early provision for the extinction of slavery among us." Unlike some contemporary Virginians, the man who wrote the Declaration of Independence condoned slavery on his own plantation, even fathering several children by a woman who, since she was his slave, had little choice in the matter of her pregnancy.

QUICK CHECK ✓

Why did the new republican governments not bring liberty and equality to African Americans living in the United States?

The Challenge of Women's Rights

The revolutionary experience accelerated changes in the way ordinary people viewed the family. At the beginning of the eighteenth century, fathers claimed authority over other members of their families simply on the grounds that they were fathers. As patriarchs, they demanded obedience. Fathers could treat wives and children however they pleased. The English philosopher John Locke (1632–1704) powerfully undermined arguments of this sort. In his popular treatise *Some Thoughts Concerning Education* (1693), Locke insisted that the mind was not formed at birth. The child learned from experience, and if the infant witnessed violent, arbitrary behavior, then the baby would become an abusive adult. As Locke warned parents, "If you punish him [the child] for what he sees you practice yourself, he will not think that Severity to proceed from Kindness in you careful to amend a Fault in him; but will be apt to interpret it, as Peevishness and Arbitrary Imperiousness of a Father." Enlightened eighteenth-century mothers and fathers—especially, fathers—condemned tyranny in the home.

Adams Family Letters (March, April 1776)

It was in this changing intellectual environment that American women began making new demands not only on their husbands but also on republican institutions. Abigail Adams, wife of future President John Adams and one of the generation's most articulate women, instructed her husband, as he set off for the opening of the Continental Congress: "I desire you would Remember the Ladies, and be more generous and favourable to them than your ancestors. Do not put such unlimited power into the hands of the Husbands." John responded in a condescending manner. The "Ladies" would have to wait until the country achieved independence. In 1777, Lucy Knox took an even stronger line with her husband, General Henry Knox. When he was about to return home from the army, she warned him, "I hope you will not consider yourself as commander in chief in your own house—but be convinced... that there is such a thing as equal command."

If Knox accepted Lucy's argument, he did so because she was a good republican wife and mother. In fact, women justified their assertiveness largely on the basis of political ideology. If survival of republics really depended on the virtue of their citizens, they argued, then it was the special responsibility of women as mothers to nurture the right values in their children and as wives to instruct their husbands in proper behavior. Contemporaries claimed that the woman who possessed "virtue and prudence" could easily "mold the taste, the manners, and the conduct of her admirers, according to her pleasure." In fact, "nothing short of a general reformation of manners would take place, were the ladies to use their power in discouraging our licentious manners."

Molly Wallace, Valedictory Address (1792)

Ill-educated women could not possibly fulfill these high expectations. Women required education that was at least comparable to what men received. Scores of female academies were established during this period to meet what many Americans, men as well as women, now regarded as a pressing social need. The schools may have received widespread encouragement precisely because they did not radically alter traditional gender roles. After all, the educated republican woman of the late eighteenth century did not pursue a career; she returned to the home, where she followed a familiar routine as wife and mother. The frustration of not being allowed to develop her talents may explain the bitterness of a graduation oration delivered by an otherwise obscure woman in 1793: "Our high and mighty Lords... have denied us the means of knowledge, and then reproached us for want of it.... They doom'd the sex to servile or frivolous employments, on purpose to degrade their minds, that they themselves might hold unrivall'd, the power and pre-eminence they had usurped."

During this period, women began to petition for divorce on new grounds. One case is particularly instructive concerning changing attitudes toward women and the family. In 1784, John Backus, an undistinguished Massachusetts silversmith, was hauled before a local court and asked why he beat his wife. He responded that "it was Partly owing to his Education for his father treated his

ABIGAIL ADAMS This portrait of Abigail Adams, wife of President John Adams, was painted by Benjamin Blyth, c. 1766.

What did Abigail mean when she asked her husband to "Remember the Ladies"?

mother in the same manner." The difference between Backus's case and his father's was that Backus's wife refused to tolerate such abuse, and she sued successfully for divorce. Studies of divorce patterns in Connecticut and Pennsylvania show that after 1773, women divorced on about the same terms as men.

The war itself presented some women with fresh opportunities. In 1780, Ester DeBerdt Reed founded a large volunteer women's organization in Philadelphia—the first of its kind in the United States—that raised more than $300,000 for Washington's army. Other women ran family farms and businesses while their husbands fought the British. And in 1790, the New Jersey legislature explicitly allowed women who owned property to vote.

Despite these scattered gains, republican society still defined women's roles exclusively in terms of mother, wife, and homemaker. Other pursuits seemed unnatural, even threatening, and it is perhaps not surprising, therefore, that in 1807, New Jersey lawmakers—angry over a close election in which women voters apparently determined the result—repealed female suffrage in the interests of "safety, quiet, and good order and dignity of the state." Even an allegedly progressive thinker such as Jefferson could not imagine allowing women to participate in serious politics. When in 1807 his secretary of the treasury, Albert Gallatin, called attention to the shortage of educated people to serve in government jobs and suggested recruiting women, Jefferson responded sharply: "The appointment of a woman to office is an innovation for which the public is not prepared, nor am I."

QUICK CHECK ✓

What evidence argues that this was a period of significant progress for women in the United States?

The States: Experiments in Republicanism

In May 1776, the Second Continental Congress invited the states to adopt constitutions. The old colonial charters filled with references to king and Parliament were clearly no longer adequate, and within a few years, most states had taken action. Rhode Island and Connecticut already enjoyed republican government by virtue of their unique seventeenth-century charters that allowed the voters to select both governors and legislators. Eleven other states plus Vermont created new political structures, and their deliberations reveal how Americans living in different regions and reacting to different social pressures defined fundamental republican principles.

DOCUMENT

The Virginia Declaration of Rights (June 12, 1776)

Several constitutions were boldly experimental, and some states later rewrote documents that had been drafted in the first flush of independence. These early constitutions were provisional, but they nevertheless provided the framers of the federal Constitution of 1787 with invaluable insights into the strengths and weaknesses of government based on the will of the people.

Despite disagreements over details, Americans who wrote the various state constitutions shared certain political assumptions. First, they insisted on preparing *written* documents. However logical the decision to produce written documents may have seemed to the Americans, it represented a major break with English practice. Political philosophers in the mother country had long boasted of Britain's unwritten constitution, a collection of judicial reports and parliamentary statutes. But this highly vaunted system had not protected the colonists from oppression; hence, after declaring independence, Americans demanded that their state constitutions explicitly define the rights of the people as well as the power of their rulers.

Second, the authors of the state constitutions believed men and women possessed certain **natural rights** over which government exercised no control whatsoever. So that future rulers—potential tyrants—would know the exact limits of authority, these fundamental rights were carefully spelled out. Indeed, the people of Massachusetts rejected the proposed state constitution of 1778 largely because it lacked a full statement of their basic rights. They demanded a guarantee of "rights of conscience, and… security of persons and property, which every member in the State hath a right to expect from the supreme power."

Eight state constitutions contained specific declarations of rights. The length and character of these lists varied, but, in general, they affirmed three fundamental freedoms: religion, speech, and press. They protected citizens from unlawful searches and seizures; they upheld trial by jury.

natural rights
Fundamental rights over which the government could exercise no control. An uncompromising belief in such rights energized the popular demand for a formal bill of rights in 1791.

QUICK CHECK ✓

Following independence, why did the states insist on drafting *written* constitutions?

Stumbling Toward a New National Government

WHY did many Americans regard the Articles of Confederation as inadequate?

When the Second Continental Congress convened in 1775, the delegates found themselves waging war in the name of a country that did not yet exist. As the military crisis deepened, Congress gradually—often reluctantly—assumed greater authority over national affairs, but everyone agreed such narrowly conceived measures were a poor substitute for a legally constituted government. The separate states could not possibly deal with the range of issues that now confronted the American people. Indeed, if independence meant anything in a world of sovereign nations, it implied the creation of a central authority capable of conducting war, borrowing money, regulating trade, and negotiating treaties.

Articles of Confederation

The challenge of creating a viable central government proved more difficult than anyone anticipated. Congress appointed a committee to draw up a plan for confederation. John Dickinson, the lawyer who had written an important revolutionary pamphlet titled *Letters from a Farmer in Pennsylvania*, headed the committee.

Dickinson envisioned the creation of a strong central government, and the report his committee presented on July 12, 1776, shocked delegates who assumed that the constitution would authorize a loose confederation of states. Dickinson's plan placed the western territories, land claimed by the separate states, under congressional control. In addition, Dickinson's committee called for equal state representation in Congress.

Since some states, such as Virginia and Massachusetts, were more populous than others, the plan fueled tensions between large and small states. Also unsettling was Dickinson's recommendation that taxes be paid to Congress on the basis of a state's total population, black as well as white, a formula that angered southerners who did not think slaves should be counted.

Not surprisingly, the draft of the plan—the **Articles of Confederation**—that Congress finally approved in November 1777 bore little resemblance to Dickinson's original plan. The Articles jealously guarded the sovereignty of the states. The delegates who drafted the framework shared a general republican conviction that power—especially power so far removed from the people—was inherently dangerous and that the only way to preserve liberty was to place as many constraints as possible on federal authority.

The result was a government that many people regarded as powerless. The Articles provided for a single legislative body consisting of representatives selected annually by the state legislatures. Each state possessed a single vote in Congress. It could send as many as seven delegates, as few as two, but if they divided evenly on a certain issue, the state lost its vote. There was no independent executive and no veto over legislative decisions. The Articles also denied Congress the power of taxation, a serious oversight in time of war. The national government could obtain funds only by asking the states for contributions, called requisitions, but if a state failed to cooperate—and many did—Congress limped along without financial support. Amendments to this constitution required assent by all thirteen states. The authors of the new system expected the weak national government to handle foreign relations, military matters, Indian affairs, and interstate disputes. They most emphatically did not award Congress ownership of the lands west of the Appalachian Mountains.

The new constitution sent to the states for ratification encountered apathy and hostility. Most Americans were far more interested in local affairs than in the actions of Congress. When a British army marched through a state, creating a need for immediate military aid, people spoke positively about central government, but as soon as the threat had passed, they sang a different tune. During this period, even the slightest encroachment on state sovereignty rankled republicans who feared centralization would inevitably promote corruption.

John Dickinson, from *Letters from a Farmer in Pennsylvania*

Articles of Confederation

Ratified in 1781, this document was the United States' first constitution, providing a framework for national government. The articles sharply limited central authority by denying the national government any taxation or coercive powers.

The Articles of Confederation (1777)

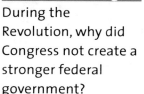

QUICK CHECK ✔

During the Revolution, why did Congress not create a stronger federal government?

Western Land: Key to the First Constitution

The major bone of contention with the Articles, however, was the disposition of the vast, unsurveyed territory west of the Appalachians that everyone hoped the British would soon surrender. Although the region was claimed by the various states, most of it actually belonged to the Native Americans. In a series of land grabs that federal negotiators called treaties, the United States government took the land comprising much of modern Ohio, Indiana, Illinois, and Kentucky. Since the Indians had put their faith in the British during the war, they could do little to resist the humiliating

NORTHWEST TERRITORY The U.S. government auctioned off the land in the Northwest Territory, the region defined by the Ohio River, the Great Lakes, and the Mississippi River. Proceeds from the sale of one section in each township were set aside for the construction of public schools.

During the 1780s, why did so many Americans demand access to the Northwest Territories?

MAP

Western Land Claims Ceded by the States

QUICK CHECK ✓

Why did the question of the western lands cause such conflict between the states under the Articles of Confederation?

treaty agreements at Fort McIntosh (1785), Fort Stanwix (1784), and Fort Finney (1786). As John Dickinson, then serving as the president of the Supreme Executive Council of Pennsylvania, told the Indians, since Great Britain has surrendered "the back country with all the forts... that they [the Indians] must now depend upon us for the preservation." If they dared to resist, "we will instantly turn upon them our armies... and extirpate them from the land where they were born and now live."

Some states, such as Virginia and Georgia, claimed land all the way from the Atlantic Ocean to the elusive "South Seas," in effect extending their boundaries to the Pacific coast by virtue of royal charters. State legislators—their appetites whetted by aggressive land speculators—anticipated generating large revenues through land sales. Connecticut, New York, Pennsylvania, and North Carolina also announced intentions to seize blocks of western land.

Other states were not blessed with vague or ambiguous royal charters. The boundaries of Maryland, Delaware, and New Jersey had been established many years earlier, and it seemed as if people living in these states would be permanently cut off from the anticipated bounty. In protest, these "landless" states stubbornly refused to ratify the Articles of Confederation. Marylanders were particularly vociferous. All the states had made sacrifices for the common good during the Revolution, they complained, and it appeared only fair that all states should profit from the fruits of victory, in this case, from the sale of western lands. Maryland's spokesmen feared that if Congress did not void Virginia's excessive claims to all of the Northwest Territory (the land west of Pennsylvania and north of the Ohio River) as well as to a large area south of the Ohio, beyond the Cumberland Gap, known as Kentucky, then Marylanders would desert their home state in search of cheap Virginia farms, leaving Maryland an underpopulated wasteland.

The states resolved the bitter controversy in 1781 as much by accident as by design. Virginia agreed to cede its holdings north of the Ohio River to the Confederation on condition that Congress nullify the land companies' earlier purchases from the Indians. A practical consideration had softened Virginia's resolve. Republicans such as Jefferson worried about expanding their state beyond the mountains; with poor transportation links, it seemed impossible to govern such a large territory effectively from Richmond. The western settlers might even come to regard Virginia as a colonial power insensitive to their needs. Marylanders who dreamed of making fortunes on the land market grumbled, but when a British army appeared on their border, they prudently accepted the Articles (March 1, 1781). Congress required another three years to work out the details of the Virginia cession. Other landed states followed Virginia's example. These transfers established an important principle, for after 1781, it was agreed that the West belonged not to the separate states but to the United States.

Northwest Ordinance: The Confederation's Major Achievement

Whatever the weaknesses of Congress may have been, it did score one impressive triumph. Congressional action brought order to western settlement, especially in the Northwest Territory, and incorporated frontier Americans into an expanding federal system. In 1781, the prospects for success did not seem promising. For years, colonial authorities had ignored people who migrated far inland, sending neither money nor soldiers to protect them from Indian attack. Tensions between the seaboard colonies and the frontier regions had sometimes flared into violence. Disorders occurred in South Carolina in 1767, in North Carolina in 1769, and in Vermont in 1777. With thousands of men and women, most of them squatters, pouring across the Appalachian Mountains, Congress had to act quickly to avoid the past errors of royal and colonial authorities.

The initial attempt to deal with this explosive problem came in 1784. Jefferson, then serving as a member of Congress, drafted an ordinance that became the basis for later, more enduring legislation. Jefferson recommended carving ten new states out of the western lands located north of the Ohio River and recently ceded to the United States by Virginia. He specified that each new state establish a republican form of government. When the population of a territory equaled that of the smallest state already in the Confederation, the region could apply for full statehood. In the meantime, free white males could participate in local government, a democratic guarantee that frightened some of Jefferson's more conservative colleagues.

The impoverished Congress was eager to sell off the western territory as quickly as possible. After all, the frontier represented a source of income that did not depend on the unreliable generosity of the states. A second ordinance, passed in 1785 and called the Land Ordinance, established an orderly process for laying out new townships and marketing public lands. Public response disappointed Congress. Surveying the lands took far longer than anticipated, and few persons possessed enough hard currency to make even the minimum purchase. Nevertheless, small homesteaders settled wherever they pleased, refusing to pay either government or speculators for the land.

Congress worried about the excess liberty on the frontier. In the 1780s, the West seemed to be filling up with people who by eastern standards were uncultured. Timothy Pickering, a New Englander, declared that "the emigrants to the frontier lands are the least worthy subjects in the United States. They are little less savage than the Indians; and when possessed of the most fertile spots, for want of industry, live miserably." The charge was as old as the frontier itself. Indeed, seventeenth-century Englishmen had said the same things of the earliest Virginians. The lawless image stuck, however, and even a sober observer such as Washington insisted that the West crawled with "banditti." The Ordinance of 1784 placed the government of the territories in the hands of people about whom congressmen and speculators had second thoughts.

These various currents shaped the Ordinance of 1787, one of the final acts passed under the Confederation. The bill, also called the **Northwest Ordinance,** provided a new structure for government of the Northwest Territory. The plan authorized the creation of between three and five territories, each to be ruled by a governor, a secretary, and three judges appointed by Congress. When the population reached five thousand, voters who owned property could elect an assembly, but its decisions were subject to the governor's absolute veto. Once sixty thousand

Northwest Ordinance (July 13, 1787)

Northwest Ordinance
Legislation that formulated plans for governments in America's northwestern territories, defined a procedure for the territories' admission to the Union as states, and prohibited slavery north of the Ohio River.

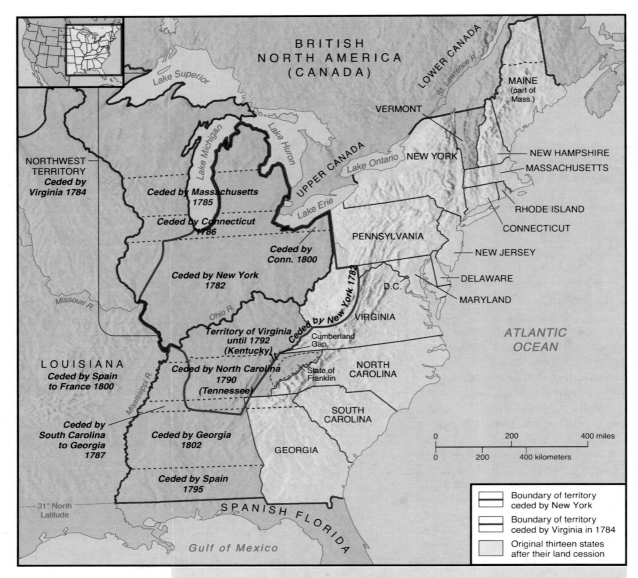

WESTERN LAND CLAIMS CEDED BY THE STATES   After winning the war, the major issue facing the Continental Congress under the Articles of Confederation was mediating conflicting states' claims to rich western land. By 1802, the states had ceded all rights to the federal government.

How was the government of the United States able to resolve conflicts over western lands without resorting to violence?

persons resided in a territory, they could write a constitution and petition for full statehood. While these procedures represented a retreat from Jefferson's original proposal, the Ordinance of 1787 contained several significant features. A bill of rights guaranteed the settlers the right to trial by jury, freedom of religion, and due process of law. In addition, the act outlawed slavery, a prohibition that freed

LAND ORDINANCE OF 1785

Grid pattern of a township
36 sections of 640 acres (1 square mile each)

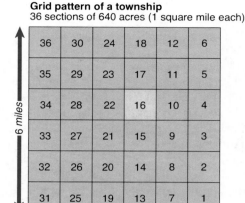

6 miles

36	30	24	18	12	6
35	29	23	17	11	5
34	28	22	16	10	4
33	27	21	15	9	3
32	26	20	14	8	2
31	25	19	13	7	1

6 miles

16 Income of one section reserved for the support of public education

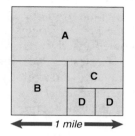

1 mile

A Half-section 320 acres
B Quarter-section 160 acres
C Half-quarter section 80 acres
D Quarter-quarter section 40 acres

the future states of Ohio, Indiana, Illinois, Michigan, and Wisconsin from the curse of human bondage.

By contrast, settlement south of the Ohio River received far less attention from Congress. Long before the end of the war, thousands of Americans streamed through the Cumberland Gap into a part of Virginia known as Kentucky. The most famous of these settlers was Daniel Boone. In 1775, the population of Kentucky was approximately one hundred; by 1784, it had jumped to thirty thousand.

QUICK CHECK ✓

How did the Northwest Ordinance resolve the problem of the western lands?

"Have We Fought for This?"

By 1785, the country seemed to have lost direction. The buoyant optimism that sustained revolutionary patriots had dissolved into pessimism and doubt. Many Americans, especially those who had provided leadership during the Revolution, agreed something had to be done. In 1786, Washington bitterly observed, "What astonishing changes a few years are capable of producing. Have we fought for this? Was it with these expectations that we launched into a sea of trouble, and have bravely struggled through the most threatening dangers?"

WHY did Constitutional delegates compromise on representation and slavery?

The Genius of James Madison

The conviction of people such as Washington that the nation was indeed in a state of crisis reflected tensions within republican thought. To be sure, they supported open elections and the right of individuals to advance their own economic well-being, but when these elements seemed to undermine social and political order, they expressed the fear that perhaps liberty had been carried too far. The situation had changed quite rapidly. As recently as the 1770s, men of republican persuasion had insisted that the greatest threat to the American people was concentration of power in the hands of unscrupulous rulers. With this principle in mind, they transformed state governors into mere figureheads and weakened the Confederation in the name of popular liberties.

By the mid-1780s, persons of property and standing saw the problem in a different light. Recent experience suggested to them that ordinary citizens did not in fact possess sufficient virtue to sustain a republic. The states had been plagued not by executive tyranny but by an excess of democracy, by a failure of the majority to preserve the property rights of the minority, by an unrestrained individualism that promoted anarchy rather than good order.

Many state leaders did not seem particularly concerned about the fiscal health of the national government. Local presses churned out worthless currency, and in some states, assemblies passed laws impeding the collection of debt. In Rhode Island, the situation became absurd. State legislators made it illegal for merchants to reject Rhode Island money even though everyone knew it had no value. No wonder Governor William Livingston of New Jersey declared in 1787, "We do not exhibit the virtue that is necessary to support a republican government."

As Americans tried to interpret these experiences within a republican framework, they were checked by the most widely accepted political wisdom of the age. Baron de Montesquieu (1689–1755), a French political philosopher of immense international reputation and author of *The Spirit of the Laws* (1748), declared flatly that a republican government could not flourish in a large territory. The reasons were clear. If the people lost direct control over their representatives, they would fall prey to tyrants. Large distances allowed rulers to hide their corruption; physical separation presented aristocrats with opportunities to seize power.

In the United States, most learned men treated Montesquieu's theories as self-evident truths. His writings seemed to demonstrate the importance of preserving the sovereignty of the states, for however much these small republics abused the rights of property and ignored minority interests, it was plainly unscientific to maintain that a republic consisting of thirteen states, several million people, and thousands of acres of territory could long survive.

James Madison rejected Montesquieu's argument, and in so doing, he helped Americans to think of republican government in radical new ways. This soft-spoken, rather unprepossessing Virginian was the most brilliant American political thinker of his generation. One French official described Madison as "a man one must study a long time in order to make a fair appraisal." Those who listened carefully to what Madison had to say, however, soon recognized his genius for translating theory into practice.

Madison delved into the writings of a group of Scottish philosophers, the most prominent being David Hume (1711–1776), and from their works he concluded that Americans need not fear a greatly expanded republic. Madison perceived that "inconveniences of popular States contrary to prevailing Theory, are in proportion not to the extent, but to the narrowness of their limits." Indeed, it was in small states such as Rhode Island that legislative majorities tyrannized the propertied minority. In a large territory, Madison explained, "the Society becomes broken into a greater variety of interest, of pursuits, of passions, which check each other, whilst those who may feel a common sentiment have less opportunity of communication and contact."

QUICK CHECK ✓

How did James Madison respond to republican fears that a nation as large as the United States could never be successfully governed as a republic?

Constitutional Reform

A concerted movement to overhaul the Articles of Confederation began in 1786, when Madison and his friends persuaded the Virginia assembly to recommend a convention to explore the creation of a unified system of "commercial regulations." Congress supported the idea. In September, delegates from five states arrived in Annapolis, Maryland, to discuss issues that extended far beyond commerce. The small turnout was disappointing, but the occasion provided strong nationalists with an opportunity to hatch an even bolder plan. The Annapolis delegates advised Congress to hold a second meeting in Philadelphia "to take into consideration the situation of the United States, to devise such further provisions as shall appear to them necessary to render the constitution of the Federal Government adequate to the exigencies of the Union." Whether staunch states' rights advocates in Congress knew what was afoot is not clear. In any case, Congress authorized a grand convention to gather in May 1787.

Events played into Madison's hands. Soon after the Annapolis meeting, an uprising known as **Shays's Rebellion**, involving several thousand impoverished farmers, shattered the peace of western Massachusetts. No matter how hard these men worked the soil, they always found themselves in debt to eastern creditors. They complained of high taxes, of high interest rates, and, most of all, of a state government insensitive to their problems. In 1786, Daniel Shays, a veteran of the battle of Bunker Hill, and his armed neighbors closed a county courthouse where creditors were suing to foreclose farm mortgages. At one point, the rural insurgents threatened to seize the federal arsenal located at Springfield. Congress did not have funds sufficient to support an army, and the arsenal might have fallen had not a group of wealthy Bostonians raised an army of four thousand troops to put down the insurrection. The victors were in for a surprise. At the next general election, Massachusetts voters selected representatives sympathetic to Shays's demands, and a new liberal assembly reformed debtor law.

Shays's Rebellion
Armed insurrection of farmers in western Massachusetts led by Daniel Shays, a veteran of the Continental Army. Intended to prevent state courts from foreclosing on debtors unable to pay their taxes, the rebellion was put down by the state militia. Nationalists used the event to justify the calling of a constitutional convention to strengthen the national government.

Military Reports of Shays's Rebellion

SHAYS'S REBELLION This 1787 woodcut portrays Daniel Shays with one of his chief officers, Jacob Shattucks. Shays led farmers in western Massachusetts in revolt against a state government that seemed insensitive to the needs of poor debtors. Their rebellion frightened conservative leaders, who demanded a strong new federal government.

Did Daniel Shays betray or uphold the spirit of the American Revolution?

QUICK CHECK ✓

What role did Shays's Rebellion play in bringing about constitutional reform?

Nationalists throughout the United States were not so forgiving. From their perspective, Shays's Rebellion symbolized the breakdown of law and order that they had long predicted. "Great commotions are prevailing in Massachusetts," Madison wrote. "An appeal to the sword is exceedingly dreaded." The time had come for sensible people to speak up for a strong national government. The unrest in Massachusetts persuaded persons who might otherwise have ignored the Philadelphia meeting to participate in drafting a new constitution.

The Philadelphia Convention

In the spring of 1787, fifty-five men representing twelve states traveled to Philadelphia. Rhode Island refused to take part in the proceedings, a decision that Madison attributed to its "wickedness and folly." Thomas Jefferson described the convention as an "assembly of demi-Gods," but this flattering depiction is misleading. However much modern Americans revere the Constitution, they should remember that the individuals who wrote it did not possess divine insight into the nature of government. They were practical people—lawyers, merchants, and planters—many of whom had fought in the Revolution and served in the Congress of the Confederation. The majority were in their thirties or forties. The gathering included George Washington, James Madison, George Mason, Robert Morris, James Wilson, John Dickinson, Benjamin Franklin, and Alexander Hamilton, just to name some of the more prominent participants. Absent were John Adams and Thomas Jefferson, who were conducting diplomacy in Europe; Patrick Henry, a localist suspicious of strong central government, remained in Virginia, announcing he "smelled a rat."

As soon as the Constitutional Convention opened on May 25, the delegates made several procedural decisions of the utmost importance. First, they voted "that nothing spoken in the House be printed, or communicated without leave." The rule was stringently enforced. Sentries guarded the doorways to keep out uninvited visitors, windows stayed shut in the sweltering heat to prevent sound from either entering or leaving the chamber, and members were forbidden to copy the daily journal without official permission. As Madison explained, the secrecy rule saved "both the convention and the community from a thousand erroneous and perhaps mischievous reports." It also has made it extremely difficult for modern lawyers and judges to determine exactly what the delegates had in mind when they wrote the Constitution.

QUICK CHECK ✓

Why were the men who drafted the Constitution so concerned with secrecy?

In a second procedural move, the delegates decided to vote by state, but, in order to avoid the kinds of problems that had plagued the Confederation, they ruled that key proposals needed the support of only a majority instead of the nine states required under the Articles.

Inventing a Federal Republic

Even before all the delegates had arrived, Madison drew up a framework for a new federal system known as the **Virginia Plan.** The Virginia Plan envisioned a national legislature consisting of two houses, one elected *directly* by the people, the other chosen by the first house from nominations made by the state assemblies. Representation in both houses was proportional to the state's population. The

Virginia Plan also provided for an executive elected by Congress. Madison wisely persuaded Edmund Randolph, Virginia's popular governor, to present this scheme to the convention on May 29. Randolph claimed that the Virginia Plan merely revised sections of the Articles, but everyone, including Madison, knew better. "My ideas," Madison confessed, "strike… deeply at the old Confederation." He was determined to restrain the state assemblies, and in the original Virginia Plan, Madison gave the federal government power to veto state laws. Since most delegates at the Philadelphia convention sympathized with the nationalist position, Madison's blueprint for a strong federal government initially received broad support, and the Virginia Plan was referred to further study and debate. A group of men who allegedly had come together to reform the Confederation found themselves discussing the details of "a *national* Government… consisting of a *supreme* Legislature, Executive, and Judiciary."

The Virginia Plan had been pushed through the convention so fast that opponents hardly had an opportunity to present their objections. On June 15, they spoke up. William Paterson, a New Jersey lawyer, advanced the so-called New Jersey Plan, a scheme that retained the unicameral legislature in which each state possessed one vote and that at the same time gave Congress extensive new powers to tax and regulate trade. Paterson argued that these revisions, while more modest than Madison's plan, would have greater appeal for the American people. "I believe," he said, "that a little practical virtue is to be preferred to the finest theoretical principles, which cannot be carried into effect." The delegates listened politely and then soundly rejected the New Jersey Plan on June 19. Indeed, only New Jersey, New York, and Delaware voted in favor of Paterson's scheme.

Rejection of this framework did not resolve the most controversial issue before the convention. Paterson and others feared that under the Virginia Plan, small states would lose their separate identities. These delegates maintained that unless each state possessed an equal vote in Congress, the small states would find themselves at the mercy of their larger neighbors.

This argument outraged the delegates who favored a strong federal government. It awarded too much power to the states. "For whom [are we] forming a Government?" Wilson cried. "Is it for men, or for the imaginary beings called States?" It seemed absurd to claim that the 68,000 people of Rhode Island should have the same voice in Congress as Virginia's 747,000 inhabitants.

Virginia Plan
Offered by James Madison and the Virginia delegation at the Constitutional Convention, this proposal called for a new government with a strong executive office and two houses of Congress, each with representation proportional to a state's population.

James Madison, the Virginia (or Randolph) Plan (1787)

The New Jersey Plan (1787)

QUICK CHECK ✓

Did the New Jersey Plan represent a significant retreat from the main points of the Virginia Plan?

Compromise Saves the Convention

Mediation clearly offered the only way to overcome what Roger Sherman, a Connecticut delegate, called "a full stop in proceedings." On July 2, a "grand committee" of one person from each state was elected by the convention to resolve persistent differences between the large and small states. Franklin, at age 81 the oldest delegate, served as chair. The two fiercest supporters of proportional representation based on population, Madison and Wilson, were left off the grand committee, a sure sign that the small states would salvage something from the compromise.

The committee recommended that the states be equally represented in the upper house of Congress, while representation was to be proportionate in the lower house. Only the lower house could initiate money bills. Franklin's committee also decided that one member of the lower house should be selected for every thirty thousand inhabitants of a state. Southern delegates insisted that this number

three-fifths rule
Decision among committee members that, for the purpose of determining representation in the lower house, for every five slaves a Congressional district would receive credit for three free voters.

include slaves. In the so-called **three-fifths rule**, the committee agreed that for the purpose of determining representation in the lower house, slaves would be counted, but not as much as free persons. For every five slaves, a congressional district received credit for three free voters, a deal that gave the South much greater power in the new government than it would have otherwise received. As with most compromise solutions, the one negotiated by Franklin's committee fully satisfied no one. It did, however, overcome a major impasse, and after the small states gained an assured voice in the upper house, the Senate, they cooperated enthusiastically in creating a strong central government.

Despite these advances, during the final days of August, a deeply disturbing issue came before the convention. It was a harbinger of the great sectional crisis of the nineteenth century. Many northern representatives detested the slave trade and wanted it to end immediately. They despised the three-fifths ruling that seemed to award slaveholders extra power in government simply because they owned slaves. "It seemed now to be pretty well understood," Madison jotted in his private notes, "that the real difference of interest lay, not between the large and

REVOLUTION OR REFORM? THE ARTICLES OF CONFEDERATION AND THE CONSTITUTION COMPARED		
Political Challenge	**Articles of Confederation**	**Constitution**
Mode of ratification or amendment	Require confirmation by every state legislature	Requires confirmation by three-fourths of state conventions or legislatures
Number of houses in legislature	One	Two
Mode of representation	Two to seven delegates represent each state; each state holds only one vote in Congress	Two senators represent each state in upper house; each senator holds one vote. One representative to lower house represents every 30,000 people (in 1788) in a state; each representative holds one vote
Mode of election and term of office	Delegates appointed annually by state legislatures	Senators chosen by state legislatures for six-year term (direct election after 1913); representatives chosen by vote of citizens for two-year term
Executive	No separate executive: delegates annually elect one of their number as president, who possesses no veto, no power to appoint officers or to conduct policy. Administrative functions of government theoretically carried out by Committee of States, practically by various single-headed departments	Separate executive branch: president elected by electoral college to four-year term; granted veto, power to conduct policy and to appoint ambassadors, judges, and officers of executive departments established by legislation
Judiciary	Most adjudication left to state and local courts; Congress is final court of appeal in disputes between states	Separate branch consisting of Supreme Court and inferior courts established by Congress to enforce federal law
Taxation	States alone can levy taxes; Congress funds the Common Treasury by making requisitions for state contributions	Federal government granted powers of taxation
Regulation of commerce	Congress regulates foreign commerce by treaty but holds no check on conflicting state regulations	Congress regulates foreign commerce by treaty; all state regulations must obtain congressional consent

small but between the N. and Southn. States. The institution of slavery and its consequences formed a line of discrimination."

Whenever northern delegates—and on this point they were by no means united—pushed too aggressively, southerners threatened to bolt the convention, thereby destroying any hope of establishing a strong national government. Curiously, even recalcitrant southerners avoided using the word *slavery*. They seemed embarrassed to call the institution by its true name, and in the Constitution itself, slaves were described as "other persons," "such persons," "persons held to Service or Labour," in other words, as everything but slaves.

A few northern delegates such as Roger Sherman of Connecticut sought at every turn to mollify the southerners, especially the South Carolinians who spoke so passionately about preserving slavery. Gouverneur Morris, a Pennsylvania representative, would have none of it. He regularly reminded the convention that "the inhabitant of Georgia and S.C. who goes to the Coast of Africa, and in defiance of the most sacred laws of humanity tears away his fellow creatures from their dearest connections and damns them to the most cruel bondage, shall have more votes in a Government instituted for the protection of the rights of mankind, than the Citizen of Pa. or N. Jersey."

Largely ignoring Morris's stinging attacks, the delegates reached an uneasy compromise on the continuation of the slave trade. Southerners feared that the new Congress would pass commercial regulations adversely affecting the planters—taxes on the export of rice and tobacco, for example. They demanded, therefore, that no trade laws be passed without a two-thirds majority of the federal legislature. They backed down on this point, however, in exchange for guarantees that Congress would not interfere with the slave trade until 1808. The South even came away with a clause assuring the return of fugitive slaves. "We have obtained," Charles Cotesworth Pinckney told the planters of South Carolina, "a right to recover our slaves in whatever part of America they may take refuge, which is a right we had not before."

Although these deals disappointed many northerners, they conceded that establishing a strong national government was of greater immediate importance than ending the slave trade. "Great as the evil is," Madison wrote, "a dismemberment of the union would be worse."

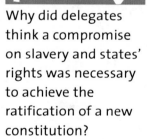

QUICK CHECK

Why did delegates think a compromise on slavery and states' rights was necessary to achieve the ratification of a new constitution?

The Last Details

On July 26, the convention formed a Committee of Detail, a group that prepared a rough draft of the Constitution. After the committee completed its work—writing a document that still, after so many hours of debate, preserved the fundamental points of the Virginia Plan—the delegates reconsidered each article. The task required the better part of a month.

During these sessions, the members of the convention concluded that the president, as they now called the executive, should be selected by an electoral college, a body of prominent men in each state chosen by local voters. The number of "electoral" votes held by each state equaled its number of representatives and senators. This awkward device guaranteed that the president would not be indebted to the Congress for his office. Whoever received the second largest number of votes in the electoral college automatically became vice president. In the event that no person received a majority of the votes, the election would be decided by the lower house—the House of Representatives—with each state casting a single vote. Delegates also armed the chief executive with veto power over legislation as well as the right to nominate judges. Both privileges, of course, would have been unthinkable a decade earlier, but the state experiments revealed the importance of having an independent executive to maintain a balanced system of republican government.

As the meeting was concluding, some delegates expressed concern about the absence in the Constitution of a bill of rights. Such declarations had been included in most state constitutions, and Virginians such as George Mason insisted that the states and their citizens needed explicit protection from possible excesses by the federal government. While many delegates sympathized with Mason's appeal, they noted that the hour was late and in any case, that the proposed Constitution provided sufficient security for individual rights. During the hard battles over ratification, the delegates to the convention may have regretted passing over the issue so lightly.

QUICK CHECK ✓

Why did the delegates to the Constitutional Convention fail to include a formal bill of rights?

We, the People

Now that many issues were settled, the delegates had to overcome the hurdle of ratifying the Constitution. They adopted an ingenious procedure. Instead of submitting the Constitution to the various state legislatures, all of which had a vested interest in maintaining the status quo and most of which had two houses, either of which could block approval, they called for the election of thirteen state conventions especially chosen to review the new federal government. Moreover, the Constitution would take effect after the assent of only nine states. There was no danger, therefore, that the proposed system would fail simply because a single state like Rhode Island withheld approval.

LIBERTY DISPLAYING THE ARTS AND SCIENCES The Library Company of Philadelphia commissioned this painting by Samuel Jennings in 1792. The broken chain at the feet of the goddess Liberty is meant to demonstrate her opposition to slavery. (*Source: The Library Company of Philadelphia.*)

How did Americans reconcile their belief in republican liberty and racial slavery?

The convention asked Gouverneur Morris of Pennsylvania, a delegate noted for his urbanity, to make final stylistic changes in the wording of the Constitution. When Morris examined the working draft, he discovered that it spoke of the collection of states forming a new government. This wording presented problems. Ratification required only nine states. No one knew whether all the states would accept the Constitution, and if not, which nine would. A strong possibility existed that several New England states would reject the document. Morris's brilliant phrase "We the People of the United States" eliminated this difficulty. The new nation was a republic of the people, not of the states.

On September 17, thirty-nine men signed the Constitution. A few members of the convention, like Mason, could not support the document. Others had already gone home. For more than three months, Madison had served as the convention's driving intellectual force. He now generously summarized the experience: "There never was an assembly of men, charged with a great and arduous trust, who were more pure in their motives, or more exclusively or anxiously devoted to the object committed to them."

QUICK CHECK

What was the "ingenious procedure for ratification" adopted by the Constitutional Convention delegates?

Whose Constitution? Struggle for Ratification

Supporters of the Constitution recognized that ratification would not be easy. After all, the convention had been authorized only to revise the Articles, but instead it produced a new plan that fundamentally altered relations between the states and the central government. The delegates dutifully dispatched copies of the Constitution to the Congress of Confederation, then meeting in New York City, and that powerless body referred the document to the separate states without any specific recommendation. The fight for ratification had begun.

WHAT

issues separated Federalists from Antifederalists during debates over ratification?

Federalists and Antifederalists

Proponents of the Constitution enjoyed great advantages over the unorganized opposition. In the contest for ratification, they took no chances. Their most astute move was the adoption of the label **Federalist**. The term cleverly suggested that they stood for a confederation of states rather than for the creation of a supreme national authority. In fact, they envisioned the creation of a strong centralized national government capable of fielding a formidable army. Critics of the Constitution, who tended to be somewhat poorer, less urban, and less well educated than their opponents, cried foul, but there was little they could do. They were stuck with the name **Antifederalist,** a misleading term that made their cause seem a rejection of the very notion of a federation of the states.

The Federalists recruited the most prominent public figures of the day. In every state convention, speakers favoring the Constitution were more polished and more fully prepared than were their opponents. In New York, the campaign to win ratification sparked publication of *The Federalist,* a brilliant series of essays written by Madison, Hamilton, and Jay during the fall and winter of 1787 and 1788. The nation's newspapers threw themselves overwhelmingly behind the new government. In fact, few journals even bothered to carry Antifederalist writings. In some states, the Federalists adopted tactics of questionable propriety in order to gain ratification.

Federalist
Supporter of the Constitution who advocated its ratification.

Antifederalist
Critic of the Constitution who expressed concern that it seemed to possess no specific provision for the protection of natural and civil rights.

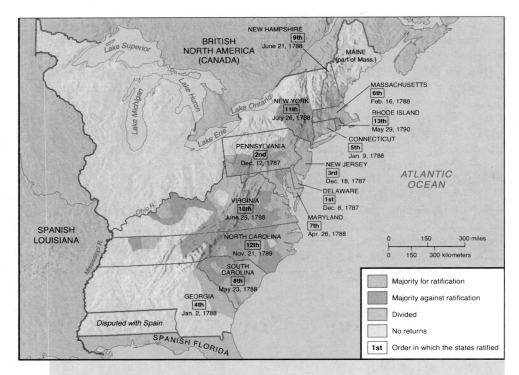

RATIFICATION OF THE CONSTITUTION   Advocates of the new Constitution called themselves Federalists, and those who opposed its ratification were known as Antifederalists.

Can you discern any regional trends in the vote for ratification?

Federalist
Paper #51
(Feb. 6, 1788)

In Pennsylvania, for example, they achieved a legal quorum for a crucial vote by dragging several opposition delegates into the meeting from the streets. In New York, Hamilton intimidated upstate Antifederalists with threats that New York City would secede from the state unless the state ratified the Constitution.

In these battles, the Antifederalists articulated a political philosophy that had broad popular appeal. Like the extreme republicans who drafted the first state constitutions, the Antifederalists were deeply suspicious of political power. During the debates over ratification, they warned that public officials, however selected, would be constantly scheming to expand their authority.

The preservation of individual liberty required constant vigilance. It seemed obvious that the larger the republic, the greater the opportunity for political corruption. Local voters could not possibly know what their representatives in a distant national capital were doing. The government outlined in the Constitution invited precisely the kinds of problems that Montesquieu had described in his famous essay, *The Spirit of the Laws.* "In so extensive a republic," one Antifederalist declared, "the great officers of government would soon become above the control of the people, and abuse their power."

Antifederalists demanded direct, personal contact with their representatives. They argued that elected officials should reflect the character of their constituents as closely as possible. It seemed unlikely that in large congressional districts, the people would be able to preserve such close ties with their representatives.

According to the Antifederalists, the Constitution favored persons wealthy enough to have forged a reputation that extended beyond a single community. Samuel Chase told the members of the Maryland ratifying convention that under the new system, "the distance between the people and their representatives will be so great that there is no probability of a farmer or planter being chosen… only the *gentry, the rich,* and the well-born will be elected."

Federalist speakers mocked their opponents' localist perspective. The Constitution deserved general support precisely because it ensured that future Americans would be represented by "natural aristocrats," individuals possessing greater insights, skills, and training than did the ordinary citizen. These talented leaders, the Federalists insisted, could discern the interests of the entire population. They were not tied to the selfish needs of local communities. "The little demagogue of a petty parish or county will find his importance annihilated [under the Constitution] and his intrigues useless," predicted Charles Cotesworth Pinckney, a South Carolina Federalist.

Historians have generally accepted the Federalist critique. It would be a mistake, however, to see the Antifederalists as "losers" or as persons who could not comprehend social and economic change. Although their rhetoric echoed an older moral view of political culture, they accepted more easily than did many Federalists a liberal marketplace in which ordinary citizens competed as equals with the rich and well-born. They believed the public good was best served by allowing individuals like themselves to pursue their own private interests. That is what they had been doing on the local level during the 1780s, and they resented the imposition of elite controls over their affairs. Although the Antifederalists lost the battle over ratification, their ideas about political economy later found many champions in the age of Andrew Jackson.

The Constitution drew support from many different types of people. In fact, historians have been unable to discover sharp correlations between wealth and occupation on the one hand and attitudes toward the proposed system of central government on the other. In general, Federalists lived in more commercialized areas than did their opponents. In the cities, artisans as well as merchants called for ratification, while those farmers who were only marginally involved in commercial agriculture frequently voted Antifederalist.

Despite passionate pleas from Patrick Henry and other Antifederalists, most state conventions quickly adopted the Constitution. Delaware acted first (December 7, 1787), and within eight months of the Philadelphia meeting, eight of the nine states required to launch the government had ratified the document. The contests in Virginia (June 1788) generated bitter debate, but they too joined the union, leaving only North Carolina and Rhode Island outside the United States. Eventually (November 21, 1789, and May 29, 1790), even these states ratified the Constitution. Still, the vote had been very close. The Constitution was ratified in New York by a tally of 30 to 27, in Massachusetts by 187 to 168, and in Virginia by 89 to 79. A swing of a few votes in several key states could have defeated the new government.

While the state conventions sparked angry rhetoric, Americans soon closed ranks behind the Constitution. An Antifederalist who represented one Massachusetts village explained that "he had opposed the adoption of this Constitution; but that he had been overruled… by a majority of wise and understanding men [and that now] he should endeavor to sow the seeds of union and peace among the people he represented."

Patrick Henry, Against Ratification of the Constitution (1788)

What were the major political issues separating Federalists from Antifederalists?

Adding the Bill of Rights

James Madison, Defense of the Bill of Rights (June 8, 1789)

The first ten amendments to the Constitution are the major legacy of the Antifederalist argument. In almost every state convention, opponents of the Constitution pointed to the need for greater protection of individual liberties, rights that people presumably had possessed in a state of nature. "It is necessary," wrote one Antifederalist, "that the sober and industrious part of the community should be defended from the rapacity and violence of the vicious and idle. A bill of rights, therefore, ought to set forth the purposes for which the compact is made, and serves to secure the minority against the usurpation and tyranny of the majority." The list of fundamental rights varied from state to state, but most Antifederalists demanded specific guarantees for jury trial and freedom of religion. They wanted prohibitions against cruel and unusual punishments. There was also considerable, though not universal, support for freedom of speech and freedom of the press.

Madison and others regarded the proposals with little enthusiasm. In *The Federalist* No. 84, Hamilton bluntly reminded the American people that "the constitution is itself... a BILL OF RIGHTS." But after the adoption of the Constitution had been assured, Madison moderated his stand. If nothing else, passage of a bill of rights would appease able men such as George Mason and Edmund Randolph, who might otherwise remain alienated from the new federal system. "We have in this way something to gain," Madison concluded, "and if we proceed with caution, nothing to lose."

The crucial consideration was caution. A number of people throughout the nation advocated calling a second constitutional convention, one that would take Antifederalist criticism into account. Madison wanted to avoid such a meeting, and he feared that some members of the first Congress might use a bill of rights as an excuse to revise the entire Constitution or to promote a second convention.

Madison carefully reviewed these recommendations as well as the various declarations of rights that had appeared in the early state constitutions, and on June 8, 1789, he placed before the House of Representatives a set of amendments designed to protect individual rights from government interference. Madison told the members of Congress that the greatest dangers to popular liberties came from "the majority [operating] against the minority." A committee compressed and revised his original ideas into ten amendments that were ratified and became known collectively as the **Bill of Rights.** For many modern Americans these amendments are the most important section of the Constitution. Madison had hoped that additions would be inserted into the text of the Constitution at the appropriate places, not tacked onto the end, but he was overruled.

Bill of Rights
The first ten amendments to the U.S. Constitution, adopted in 1791 to preserve the rights and liberties of individuals.

The Bill of Rights protected the freedoms of assembly, speech, religion, and the press; guaranteed speedy trial by an impartial jury; preserved the people's right to bear arms; and prohibited unreasonable searches. Other amendments dealt with legal procedure. Some opponents of the Constitution urged Congress to provide greater safeguards for states' rights, but Madison had no intention of backing away from a strong central government. Only the Tenth Amendment addressed the states' relation to the federal system. This crucial article, designed to calm Antifederalist fears, specified that those "powers not delegated to the United States by the Constitution, nor prohibited by it to the States, are reserved to the States respectively, or to the people."

The Bill of Rights (1789)

On September 25, 1789, the Bill of Rights passed both houses of Congress, and by December 15, 1791, the amendments had been ratified by three-fourths of the states. Madison was justly proud of his achievement. He had effectively secured individual rights without undermining the Constitution. When he asked his friend Jefferson for his opinion of the Bill of Rights, Jefferson responded with typical republican candor: "I like [it]... as far as it goes; but I should have been for going further."

QUICK CHECK ✓

Why did the men who originally drafted the Constitution not include a Bill of Rights?

Conclusion: Success Depends on the People

By 1789, one phase of American political experimentation had come to an end. During these years, the people gradually, often haltingly, learned that in a republican society, they themselves were sovereign. They could no longer blame the failure of government on inept monarchs or greedy aristocrats. They bore a great responsibility. Americans had demanded a government of the people only to discover during the 1780s that in some situations, the people could not be trusted with power, majorities could tyrannize minorities, and the best of governments could abuse individual rights.

Contemporaries had difficulty deciding just what had been accomplished. A writer in the *Pennsylvania Packet* thought the American people had preserved order. "The year 1776 is celebrated," the newspaper observed, "for a revolution in favor of liberty. The year 1787... will be celebrated with equal joy, for a revolution in favor of Government." But some aging Patriots grumbled that perhaps order had been achieved at too high a price. In 1788, Richard Henry Lee remarked, "'Tis really astonishing that the same people, who have just emerged from a long and cruel war in defense of liberty, should now agree to fix an elective despotism upon themselves and their posterity."

But most Americans probably would have accepted Franklin's optimistic assessment. As he watched the delegates to the Philadelphia convention come forward to sign the Constitution, he noted that there was a sun carved on the back of George Washington's chair. "I have," the aged philosopher noted, "... often in the course of the session... looked at [the sun] behind the President without being able to tell whether it was rising or setting; but now at length I have the happiness to know that it is a rising and not a setting sun."

For a list of additional titles related to this chapter's topics, please see www.pearsonamericanhistory.com.

MyHistoryLab

STUDY RESOURCES

KEY TERMS

republicanism

African Methodist Episcopal Church

natural rights

Articles of Confederation

Northwest Ordinance

Shays's Rebellion

Virginia Plan

three-fifths rule

Federalist

Antifederalist

Bill of Rights

CHAPTER REVIEW

WHAT were the limits of equality in the "republican" society of the new United States?

Revolutionary-era Americans proclaimed a "republican" ideology. They believed that government derived its authority from the people, not from kings. They also declared that they had created a new nation committed to civic virtue and social equality. Ordinary people rejected all forms of aristocratic privilege. When women and African Americans claimed the same rights as white men, they met resistance.

WHY did many Americans regard the Articles of Confederation as inadequate?

During the Revolution, Americans showed little interest in establishing a strong national government. Under the Articles of Confederation (1777), an underfunded Congress limped along without direction, while the states competed over western lands. Only after Virginia ceded its claims was Congress able to draft the Northwest Ordinance, which provided an orderly plan for the settlement of the Ohio Valley. The weak Congress was not even able to force the British to live up to their obligations under the Treaty of Paris of 1783.

WHY did Constitutional delegates compromise on representation and slavery?

Dissatisfied with the financial and military weakness of the national government under the Articles of Confederation, twelve states sent delegates to the Constitutional Convention in Philadelphia in 1787. James Madison's Virginia Plan provided the blueprint for a stronger national government. Delegates compromised on slavery and gave the small states equal representation with large ones in the Senate to prevent the convention from breaking up.

WHAT issues separated Federalists from Antifederalists during debates over ratification?

During the debates of 1787–88, Federalists, who favored stronger national government, defended the Constitution against Antifederalists, who opposed centralized authority. By the end of 1791, enough state conventions had endorsed the Constitution for ratification. To appease the Antifederalists, Congress in 1789 added a Bill of Rights to protect the freedoms of citizens against the power of the national government.

MAKING CONNECTIONS

1. What factors kept African Americans and women from achieving full political equality in the United States following the Revolution?
2. During the Revolution and immediately afterward, why would so many Americans have opposed the establishment of a strong national government?
3. Why did Thomas Jefferson fear that the new Constitution compromised the republican ideal of government by the people?
4. Since the Federalists and Antifederalists both believed in a republican form of government, why could they not agree on the new Constitution?

PRACTICE QUIZ

1. The brilliant U.S. astronomer and mathematician, _____, was a free African American.
   a. Benjamin Franklin   b. Benjamin Banneker
   c. Frederick Douglass   d. John Woolman

2. The African American writer _____ lived as a slave in the northern colonies.
   a. Phillis Wheatley   b. Richard Allen
   c. Benjamin Banneker   d. Abigail Adams

3. In May 1776, the _____ Congress asked the states to adopt constitutions.
   a. First Continental   b. Second Continental
   c. Third Continental   d. Fourth Continental

4. The _____ of Confederation was approved by Congress in 1777.
   a. Statutes   b. Ideas
   c. Volunteers   d. Articles

5. In 1787 the _____ provided a new government structure to the Northwest Territory.
   a. Enlightenment
   b. Second Great Awakening
   c. Industrial Revolution
   d. Northwest Ordinance

6. James Madison drew up plans for a new federal system called the
   a. New Jersey Plan   b. Virginia Plan
   c. South Carolina Plan   d. Boston Plan

7. The compromise regarding slavery that made southerners happy was the
   a. One-fifth clause.   b. Two-fifths clause.
   c. Three-fifths clause.   d. One-third clause.

8. All of the following accurately describe the debate over the slave trade in Congress *except*
   a. Southerners feared that Congress would heavily tax slave imports.
   b. Southerners remained uneasy about the Constitution's abolition of slavery after 1808.
   c. Southerners demanded that a two-thirds vote in Congress be used to pass new trade laws.
   d. Southerners retreated after Congress agreed not to interfere in the slave trade until 1808.

9. The Federalists exhibited all of the following *except*
   a. Thomas Jefferson espoused the Federalist position.
   b. They strongly supported the Constitution.
   c. They envisioned a strong government with a powerful army.
   d. They possessed more money and education than most Antifederalists.

10. Which of the following statements *does not* accurately describe the Bill of Rights?
    a. The Bill of Rights is the first ten amendments to the U.S. Constitution.
    b. The Antifederalists insisted on adding them to the Constitution.
    c. The Bill of Rights protects the individual liberties of the American people.
    d. One-fourth of the states had to ratify the amendments.

Find more practice at
www.myhistorylab.com

SAMPLE ESSAY QUESTIONS

1. Define Shays's Rebellion, and discuss how it led to U.S. constitutional reform.

2. Explain the intersection of republicanism and the rights of women and African Americans during the late 1700s.

Answers to Practice Quiz 1. b 2. a 3. b 4. d 5. d 6. b 7. c 8. b 9. a 10. d

CREDITS

Democracy and Dissent:
The Violence of Party Politics, 1788–1800

Democracy and Dissent
The Violence of Party Politics, 1788–1800

SPOTLIGHT QUESTIONS

WHY was George Washington unable to overcome division within the new government?

WHY did many Americans oppose Alexander Hamilton's blueprint for national prosperity?

HOW did foreign affairs affect domestic politics during the 1790s?

WHY was it hard for Americans to accept political dissent as a part of political activity?

WHY were some Federalists willing to sacrifice political freedoms for party advantage?

THE HERO OF TRENTON
Well-wishers spread flowers in front of George Washington as he rides through Trenton on his way from Virginia to New York for his inauguration as the first president of the United States in 1789.

What was the source of Washington's extraordinary popularity?

Force of Public Opinion

While presiding over the first meeting of the U.S. Senate in 1789, Vice President John Adams called the senators' attention to a pressing procedural question: How would they address George Washington, the newly elected president? Adams insisted that Washington deserved an impressive title, a designation lending dignity and weight to his office. The vice president warned the senators that if they called Washington simply "president of the United States," the "common people of foreign countries [as well as] the sailors and soldiers [would] despise him to all eternity." Adams recommended "His Highness, the President of the United States, and Protector of their Liberties," but some senators favored "His Elective Majesty" or "His Excellency."

Adams's initiative caught many persons, including Washington, completely by surprise. They regarded the entire debate as ridiculous. James Madison, a member of the House of Representatives, announced that pretentious European titles were

KEY EVENTS

1789   George Washington inaugurated (April)
▪ Louis XVI of France calls meeting of the Estates General (May)

1790   Congress approves Hamilton's plan for funding and assumption (July)

1791   Bank of the United States is chartered (February) ▪ Hamilton's *Report on Manufactures* rejected by Congress (December)

1793   France's revolutionary government announces a "war of all people against all kings" (February)
▪ Jefferson resigns as secretary of state (December)

1794   Whiskey Rebellion put down by U.S. Army (July–November) ▪ General Anthony Wayne defeats Indians at battle of Fallen Timbers (August)

1795   Hamilton resigns as secretary of the treasury (January) ▪ Jay's Treaty divides the nation (June)
▪ Pinckney's Treaty with Spain is a welcome surprise (October)

1796   Washington publishes Farewell Address (September) ▪ John Adams elected president (December)

1797   XYZ Affair poisons U.S. relations with France (October)

1798–1800   Quasi-War with France

1798   Congress passes the Alien and Sedition Acts (June and July) ▪ Virginia and Kentucky Resolutions protest the Alien and Sedition Acts (November and December)

1800   Convention of Mortefontaine is signed with France, ending Quasi-War (September)

1801   House of Representatives elects Thomas Jefferson president (February)

ill-suited to the "genius of the people" and "the nature of our Government." Thomas Jefferson, who was then residing in Paris, could not comprehend what motivated the vice president, and in private correspondence, he repeated Benjamin Franklin's judgment that Adams "means well for his Country, is always an honest Man, often a wise one, but sometimes, and in some things, absolutely out of his senses." When the senators learned that their efforts embarrassed Washington, they dropped the topic. The leader of the new republic would be called president of the United States. One wag, however, dubbed the portly Adams "His Rotundity."

The comic-opera quality of the debate about how to address Washington should not obscure the participants' serious concern about setting government policy. The members of the first Congress could not take the survival of republican government for granted. All of them, of course, wanted to secure the Revolution. The recently ratified Constitution transferred sovereignty from the states to the people, a bold and unprecedented decision that many Americans feared would generate chronic instability. Translating constitutional abstractions into practical legislation would have been difficult, even under the most favorable conditions. But these were especially trying times. Great Britain and France, rivals in a century of war, put nearly unbearable pressures on the leaders of the new republic and, in the process, made foreign policy a bitterly divisive issue.

Although no one welcomed them, political parties gradually took shape during this period. Neither the Jeffersonians (also called the Republicans) nor the Federalists—as the two major groups were called—doubted that the United States would one day become a great commercial power. They differed, however, on how best to manage the transition from an agrarian household economy to an international system of trade and industry. The Federalists encouraged rapid integration of the United States into a world economy, but however enthusiastic they were about capitalism, they did not trust the people or local government to do the job effectively. A modern economy, they insisted, required strong national institutions that would be directed by a social elite who understood the financial challenge and who would work in the best interests of the people.

Such claims frightened persons who came to identify themselves as Jeffersonians. Strong financial institutions, they thought, had corrupted the government of Great Britain from which they had just separated themselves. They searched for alternative ways to accommodate the needs of commerce and industry. Unlike the Federalists, the

Jeffersonians put their faith in the people, defined for the most part politically as white yeoman farmers. The Jeffersonians insisted that ordinary entrepreneurs, if they could be freed from intrusive government regulations, could be trusted to resist greed and crass materialism and to sustain the virtue of the republic.

During the 1790s, former allies were surprised to discover themselves at odds over such basic political issues. One person—Hamilton, for example—would stake out a position. Another, such as Jefferson or Madison, would respond, perhaps speaking a little more extravagantly than a specific issue demanded, goaded by the rhetorical nature of public debate. The first in turn would rebut passionately the new position. By the middle of the decade, this dialectic had almost spun out of control, taking the young republic to the brink of political violence.

Leaders of every persuasion had to learn to live with "public opinion." The revolutionary elite had invited the people to participate in government, but the gentlemen assumed that ordinary voters would automatically defer to their social betters. Instead, the Founders discovered they had created a rough-and-tumble political culture, a robust public sphere of cheap newspapers and street demonstrations. The newly empowered "public" followed the great debates of the period through articles they read in hundreds of highly partisan journals and magazines.

Principle and Pragmatism: Establishing a New Government

In 1788, George Washington enjoyed great popularity throughout the nation. The people remembered him as the selfless leader of the Continental Army, and even before the states had ratified the Constitution, everyone assumed he would be chosen president of the United States. He received the unanimous support of the electoral college, an achievement that no subsequent president has duplicated. John Adams, a respected Massachusetts lawyer who championed national independence in 1776, was selected vice president.

WHY was George Washington unable to overcome division within the new government?

Getting Started

Washington owed much of his success as the nation's first president to an instinctive feeling for the symbolic possibilities of political power. Although he possessed only modest speaking abilities and never matched the intellectual brilliance of some contemporaries, Washington sensed that he had come to embody the hopes and fears of the new republic, and thus, without ever quite articulating the attributes necessary to achieve charisma—an instinctive ability that some leaders have to merge their own personality with the abstract goals of the government—he carefully monitored his official behavior. Washington knew that if he did not convincingly demonstrate the existence of a strong republic, people who championed the sovereignty of the individual states would attempt to weaken federal authority before it was ever properly established.

As a result, the first Congress quickly established executive departments. Some congressmen wanted to prohibit presidents from dismissing cabinet-level appointees without Senate approval, but James Madison—still a voice for a strong, independent executive—led a successful fight against this restriction on presidential

167

MOUNT VERNON   A view of the west front of George Washington's Virginia mansion, Mount Vernon, here depicted by an unknown artist in the 1790s. The house was the site of the first cabinet meetings of the United States. (*Source: A view of Mount Vernon, DETAIL, 1792 or after, oil on canvas, image: .584 × .892 (23 × 35 $^1/_8$); entire fireboard: .953 × 1.095 (37 $^1/_2$ × 43 $^1/_8$). National Gallery of Art, Washington. Gift of Edgar Williams and Bernice Chrysler Garbisch. Photograph © Board of Trustees, National Gallery of Art. Washington.*)

How could Washington have reconciled his impressive mansion with his revolutionary political values?

Washington's
First Cabinet

authority. Madison recognized that the chief executive could not function unless he had personal confidence in the people with whom he worked. In 1789, Congress created the Departments of War, State, and the Treasury, and as secretaries, Washington nominated Henry Knox, Thomas Jefferson, and Alexander Hamilton, respectively. Edmund Randolph served as part-time attorney general, a position that ranked slightly lower in prestige than the head of a department.

To modern Americans accustomed to a huge federal bureaucracy, the size of Washington's government seems amazingly small. When Jefferson arrived in New York to take over the State Department, for example, he found two chief clerks, two assistants, and a part-time translator. With this tiny staff, he not only maintained contacts with the representatives of foreign governments, collected information about world affairs, and communicated with U.S. officials living overseas, but also organized the entire federal census!

Congress also provided for a federal court system. The Judiciary Act of 1789, the work primarily of Connecticut Congressman Oliver Ellsworth, created a Supreme Court staffed by a chief justice and five associate justices. In addition, the statute set up thirteen district courts authorized to review the decisions of the state courts. John Jay, a leading figure in New York politics, agreed to serve as chief justice, but since federal judges in the 1790s were expected to travel hundreds of miles over terrible roads to attend sessions of the inferior courts, few persons of outstanding talent and training joined Jay on the federal bench.

Remembering the financial insecurity of the old Confederation government, the newly elected congressmen passed the tariff of 1789, a tax of approximately 5 percent on imports. The new levy generated considerable revenue for the young republic. Even before it went into effect, however, the act sparked controversy. Southern planters, who relied heavily on European imports and the northern shippers who could control the flow of imports into the South, claimed that the tariff discriminated against southern interests in favor of those of northern merchants.

QUICK CHECK ✓

What was the structure of the federal government under President Washington?

Conflicting Visions: Jefferson and Hamilton

Washington's first cabinet included two extraordinary personalities, Alexander Hamilton and Thomas Jefferson. Both had served the country with distinction during the Revolution, were recognized by contemporaries as men of special genius as well as high ambition, and brought to public office a powerful vision of how the American people could achieve greatness.

However much these two men had in common, serious differences emerged. Washington's secretaries disagreed on precisely how the United States should fulfill its destiny. As head of the Treasury Department, Hamilton urged his fellow citizens to think in terms of bold commercial development, of farms and factories embedded within a complex financial network that would reduce the nation's reliance on foreign trade. Because Great Britain had already established an elaborate system of banking and credit, the secretary looked to that country for economic models that might be reproduced on this side of the Atlantic.

Hamilton also voiced concerns about the role of the people in shaping public policy. His view of human nature caused him to fear democratic excess. He assumed that in a republican society, the gravest threat to political stability was anarchy rather than monarchy. The best hope for the survival of the republic, Hamilton believed, lay with the country's monied classes. If the wealthiest people could be persuaded their economic self-interest could be advanced—or at least made less insecure—by the central government, then they would work to strengthen it, and by so doing, bring a greater measure of prosperity to the common people. From Hamilton's perspective, there was no conflict between private greed and public good; one was the source of the other.

On almost every detail, Jefferson challenged Hamilton's analysis. The secretary of state assumed that the strength of the American economy lay not in its industrial potential but in its agricultural productivity. The "immensity of land" represented the country's major economic resource. Contrary to the claims of some critics, Jefferson did not advocate agrarian self-sufficiency or look back nostalgically to a golden age dominated by simple yeomen. He recognized the necessity of change, and while he thought that persons who worked the soil were more responsible citizens than were those who labored in factories for wages, he encouraged the nation's farmers to participate in an expanding international market. Americans could exchange raw materials "for finer manufactures than they are able to execute themselves."

Unlike Hamilton, Jefferson expressed faith in the ability of the American people to shape policy. He instinctively trusted the people, feared that uncontrolled government power might destroy their liberties, and insisted public officials follow the letter of the Constitution, a frame of government he described as "the wisest ever presented to men." The greatest threat to the young republic, he argued, came from the corrupt activities of pseudoaristocrats, persons who placed the protection of "property" and "civil order" above the preservation of "liberty." To tie the nation's future to the selfish interests of a privileged class—bankers, manufacturers, and speculators—seemed cynical as well as dangerous. He despised speculators who encouraged "the rage of getting rich in a day," since such "gaming" activities inevitably promoted the kinds of public vice that threatened republican government. To mortgage the future of the common people by creating a large national debt struck Jefferson as particularly insane. But the responsibility for shaping the economy of the new nation fell mainly to Alexander Hamilton as the first secretary of the treasury.

QUICK CHECK ✓

Why did Alexander Hamilton and Thomas Jefferson find it so difficult to cooperate as members of Washington's cabinet?

Hamilton's Plan for Prosperity and Security

WHY

did many Americans oppose Alexander Hamilton's blueprint for national prosperity?

The unsettled state of the nation's finances presented the new government with a staggering challenge. Hamilton threw himself into the task. He read deeply in economic literature. He even developed a questionnaire designed to find out how the U.S. economy really worked and sent it to scores of commerical and political leaders throughout the country. But when Hamilton's three major reports—on public credit, on banking, and on manufacturers—were complete, they bore the unmistakable stamp of his own creative genius. The secretary synthesized a vast amount of information into an economic blueprint so complex, so innovative that even his allies were slightly baffled.

The secretary presented his *Report on the Public Credit* to Congress on January 14, 1790. His research revealed that the nation's outstanding debt stood at approximately $54 million. This sum represented various obligations that the U.S. government had incurred during the Revolutionary War. In addition to foreign loans, the figure included loan certificates the government had issued to its own citizens and soldiers. But that was not all. The states still owed creditors approximately $25 million. During the 1780s, Americans desperate for cash had been forced to sell government certificates to speculators at greatly discounted prices, and it was estimated that approximately $40 million of the nation's debt was owed to twenty thousand people, only 20 percent of whom were the original creditors.

Debt as a Source of National Strength

Hamilton's *Report on the Public Credit* contained two major recommendations covering the areas of funding and assumption. First, under his plan, the United States promised to fund its foreign and domestic obligations at full face value. Current holders of loan certificates, whoever they were and no matter how they obtained them, could exchange the old certificates for new government bonds bearing a moderate rate of interest. Second, the secretary urged the federal government to assume responsibility for paying the remaining state debts.

Hamilton reasoned that his credit system would accomplish several desirable goals. It would significantly reduce the power of the individual states in shaping national economic policy, something Hamilton regarded as essential in maintaining a strong federal government. Moreover, the creation of a fully funded national debt signaled to investors throughout the world that the United States was now solvent, that its bonds represented a good risk. Hamilton argued that investment capital, which might otherwise flow to Europe, would remain in this country, providing a source of money for commercial and industrial investment. In short, Hamilton invited the country's wealthiest citizens to invest in the future of the United States. Critics claimed that the only people who stood to profit from the scheme were Hamilton's friends—some of whom sat in Congress and who had purchased great numbers of public securities at very low prices.

To Hamilton's great surprise, Madison—his friend and collaborator in writing *The Federalist*—attacked the funding scheme in the House of Representatives. The Virginia congressman agreed that the United States should honor its debts. He worried, however, about the citizens and soldiers who, because of personal financial hardship, had been compelled to sell their certificates at prices far below face value. If the government treated the current holders of certificates less generously, Madison declared, then there might be sufficient funds to provide equitable treatment for the distressed Patriots. Whatever the moral justification for Madison's plan may have been, it proved unworkable on the national level. Far too many records had been lost since the Revolution for the Treasury Department to be able to identify all the original holders. In February 1790, Congress soundly defeated Madison's proposal.

The assumption portion of Hamilton's plan unleashed even greater criticism. Some states had already paid their revolutionary debts, and Hamilton's program seemed designed to reward certain states—Massachusetts and South Carolina, for example—simply because they had failed to put their finances in order. In addition, the secretary's opponents in Congress became suspicious that assumption was merely a ploy to increase the power and wealth of Hamilton's immediate friends.

On April 12, a rebellious House led by Madison defeated assumption. The victory was short-lived. Hamilton and congressional supporters resorted to legislative horse trading to secure passage of his program. In exchange for locating the new federal capital on the Potomac River, a move that would stimulate the depressed economy of northern Virginia, several key congressmen who shared Madison's political philosophy changed their votes on assumption. Hamilton may also have offered to give the state of Virginia more federal money than it actually deserved. Whatever the details of these negotiations may have been, in August, Washington signed assumption and funding into law. The first element of Hamilton's design was now securely in place.

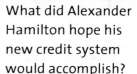

QUICK CHECK

What did Alexander Hamilton hope his new credit system would accomplish?

Interpreting the Constitution: The Bank Controversy

Hamilton submitted his second report to Congress in January 1791. He proposed that the U.S. government charter a national bank. This privately owned institution would be funded in part by the federal government. Indeed, since the **Bank of the United States** would own millions of dollars of new U.S. bonds, its financial stability would be tied directly to the strength of the federal government and, of course, to the success of Hamilton's program. The secretary of the treasury argued that a growing financial community required a central bank to facilitate increasingly complex commercial transactions. The institution not only would serve as the

Bank of the United States

National bank proposed by Secretary of Treasury Alexander Hamilton and established in 1791. It served as a central depository for the U.S. government and had the authority to issue currency.

Alexander Hamilton, "Bank" (1791)

main depository of the U.S. government but also would issue currency acceptable in payment of federal taxes. Because of that guarantee, the money would maintain its value while in circulation.

Madison and others in Congress immediately raised a howl of protest. While they were not oblivious to the many important services a national bank might provide for a growing country, they suspected that banks—especially those modeled on British institutions—might "perpetuate a large monied interest" in the United States. The Constitution said nothing specifically about chartering financial corporations, and critics warned that if Hamilton and his supporters were allowed to stretch fundamental law on this occasion, they could not be held back in the future. Popular liberties would be at the mercy of whoever happened to be in office. "To take a single step," Jefferson warned, "beyond the boundaries thus specifically drawn around the powers of Congress is to take possession of a boundless field of power, no longer susceptible to definition." On this issue, Hamilton stubbornly refused to compromise, announcing angrily, "This is the first symptom of a spirit which must either be killed or will kill the constitution of the United States."

Even though the bank bill passed Congress (February 8), Washington seriously considered vetoing the legislation on constitutional grounds. Before doing so, however, he requested written opinions from the members of his cabinet. Jefferson's rambling, wholly predictable attack on the Bank of the United States was not one of his more persuasive performances. By contrast, in only a few days, Hamilton prepared a masterful essay titled "Defense of the Constitutionality of the Bank." He assured the president that Article I, Section 8 of the Constitution— "The Congress shall have Power... To make all Laws which shall be necessary and proper for carrying into Execution the foregoing Powers"—justified issuing charters to national banks. The "foregoing Powers" on which Hamilton placed so much weight were taxation, regulation of commerce, and making war. He boldly articulated a doctrine of **implied powers**, powers which the Constitution did not explicitly grant to the federal government, but which it could be interpreted to grant. Hamilton's interpretation of the Constitution was something that neither Madison nor Jefferson had anticipated. Hamilton's "loose construction" carried the day, and on February 25, 1791, Washington signed the bank act into law.

Hamilton triumphed in Congress, but the general public looked on his actions with growing fear and hostility. When news of his proposal to fund the national debt at full face value leaked out, for example, urban speculators rushed to rural areas, where they purchased loan certificates from unsuspecting citizens at bargain prices. To backcountry farmers, making money without actually engaging in physical labor appeared immoral, unrepublican, and, certainly, un-American. When the greed of a former Treasury Department official led to several serious bankruptcies in 1792, ordinary citizens began to listen more closely to what Madison, Jefferson, and their associates were saying about growing corruption in high places.

implied powers
Powers which the Constitution did not explicitly grant the federal government, but which it could be interpreted to grant.

QUICK CHECK ✓

How did Hamilton justify the creation of the Bank of the United States?

Setback for Hamilton

In his third major report, *Report on Manufactures*, submitted to Congress in December 1791, Hamilton revealed the final details of his grand design for the economic future of the United States. This lengthy document suggested ways by which the federal government might stimulate manufacturing. If the country wanted to free itself from dependence on European imports, Hamilton observed, then it had to develop its own industry, textile mills for example. Without direct government intervention, however, the process would take decades. Americans would continue to invest in agriculture. But, according to the secretary of the treasury, protective tariffs and special industrial bounties would greatly accelerate the growth of a balanced economy, and with proper planning, the United States would soon hold its own with England and France.

In Congress, the battle lines were clearly drawn. Hamilton's opponents—not yet a disciplined party but a loose coalition of men who shared Madison's and Jefferson's misgivings about the secretary's program—ignored his economic arguments. Instead, they engaged him on moral and political grounds. Madison railed against the dangers of "consolidation," a process that threatened to concentrate all power in the federal government, leaving the states defenseless.

Jefferson attacked the *Report on Manufactures* from a different angle. He assumed—largely because he had been horrified by Europe's urban poverty—that cities breed vice. The government, Jefferson argued, should do nothing to promote their development. He believed that Hamilton's proposal guaranteed that American workers would leave the countryside and crowd into urban centers. "I think our government will remain virtuous for many centuries," Jefferson explained, "as long as they [the people] are chiefly agricultural.... When they get piled upon one another in large cities, as in Europe, they will become corrupt as in Europe." And southern congressmen saw tariffs and bounties as vehicles for enriching Hamilton's northern friends at the planters' expense. The recommendations in the *Report on Manufactures* were soundly defeated in the House of Representatives.

QUICK CHECK ✓

Why did Congress reject Hamilton's *Report on Manufactures*?

Charges of Treason: The Battle over Foreign Affairs

During Washington's second term (1793–1797), war in Europe dramatically thrust foreign affairs into the forefront of American life. The impact of this development on the conduct of domestic politics was devastating. Officials who had formerly disagreed on economic policy now began to identify their interests with either Britain or France, Europe's most powerful nations. Differences of political opinion, however trivial, were suddenly cited as evidence that one group or the other had entered into treasonous correspondence with external enemies eager to compromise the independence and prosperity of the United States.

Formal political organizations—the Federalists and Republicans—were born in this poisonous atmosphere. The clash between the groups developed over how best to preserve the new republic. The Republicans (Jeffersonians) advocated states' rights, strict interpretation of the Constitution, friendship with France, and vigilance against "the avaricious, monopolizing Spirit of Commerce and Commercial Men." The Federalists urged a strong national government, central economic planning, closer ties with Great Britain, and maintenance of public order, even if that meant calling out federal troops.

HOW did foreign affairs affect domestic politics during the 1790s?

The Peril of Neutrality

Great Britain treated the United States with arrogance. The young republic could not even compel its old adversary to comply with the Treaty of 1783, in which the British had agreed to vacate military posts in the Northwest Territory. In 1794, approximately a thousand British soldiers still occupied American land, an obstruction that Governor George Clinton of New York claimed had excluded U.S. citizens "from a very valuable trade to which their situation would naturally have invited them." Moreover, even though 75 percent of American imports came from Great Britain, that country refused to grant the United States full commercial reciprocity. Among other provocations, it barred American shipping from the lucrative West Indian trade.

France presented a very different challenge. In May 1789, Louis XVI, desperate for revenue, authorized a meeting of a representative assembly known as the Estates General. By so doing, the king unleashed explosive revolutionary forces that toppled the monarchy and cost him his life (January 1793). The men who seized power—and they came and went rapidly—were militant republicans, ideologues eager to liberate all Europe from feudal institutions. In the early years of

EXECUTION OF LOUIS XVI   The execution of the King by French revolutionaries served to deepen the growing political division in America. Although they deplored the excesses of the Reign of Terror, Jeffersonian Republicans continued to support the French people. Federalists feared that the violence and lawlessness would spread to the United States.

Why would men who had supported the American Revolution find this image disturbing?

the **French Revolution,** France drew on the American experience, and Thomas Paine and the Marquis de Lafayette enjoyed great popularity. But the French found they could not stop the violence of revolution. Constitutional reform turned into bloody purges, and one radical group, the Jacobins, guillotined thousands of people who were suspected of monarchist sympathies during the so-called Reign of Terror (October 1793–July 1794). These horrific events left Americans confused. While those who shared Jefferson's views cheered the spread of republicanism, others who sided with Hamilton condemned French expansionism and political excess.

In the face of growing international tension, neutrality seemed the most prudent course for the United States. But that policy was easier for a weak country to proclaim than to defend. In February 1793, France declared war on Great Britain—what the leaders of revolutionary France called the "war of all peoples against all kings"—and these powerful European rivals immediately challenged the official American position on shipping: "free ships make free goods," meaning that belligerents should not interfere with the shipping of neutral carriers. To make matters worse, no one was certain whether the Franco-American treaties of 1778 legally bound the United States to support its old ally against Great Britain.

Both Hamilton and Jefferson wanted to avoid war. The secretary of state, however, believed that nations desiring American goods should be forced to honor American neutrality and, therefore, that if Britain treated the United States as a colonial possession, if the Royal Navy stopped American ships on the high seas and forced seamen to serve the king—in other words, if it impressed American sailors—then the United States should award France special commercial advantages. Hamilton thought Jefferson's scheme insane. He pointed out that Britain possessed the largest navy in the world and was not likely to be coerced by American threats. The United States, he counseled, should appease the former mother country even if that meant swallowing national pride.

French Revolution
A social and political revolution in France (1789–1799) that toppled the monarchy.

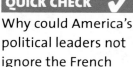

QUICK CHECK

Why could America's political leaders not ignore the French Revolution?

Jay's Treaty Sparks Domestic Unrest

Britain's refusal to abandon its forts in the Northwest Territory remained a constant source of tension. In June 1793, a new element was added. The London government blockaded French ports to neutral shipping, and in November, its navy captured several hundred American vessels trading in the French West Indies. The British had not even bothered to give the United States advance warning of a change in policy. Outraged members of Congress, especially those who identified with Jefferson and Madison, demanded retaliation, an embargo, a stoppage of debt payment, even war.

Before this rhetoric produced armed struggle, Washington made one final effort to preserve peace. In May 1794, he sent Chief Justice John Jay to London to negotiate a formidable list of grievances. Jay's main objectives were removal of the British forts on U.S. territory, payment for ships taken in the West Indies, improved commercial relations, and acceptance of the American definition of neutral rights.

Jefferson's supporters—by now openly called the Republican interest—anticipated a treaty favorable to the United States. After all, they explained, the war with France had not gone well for Great Britain, and the British people were surely desperate for American foodstuffs. Even before Jay departed, however, his mission stood little chance of success. Hamilton, anxious as ever to placate the British, had already secretly informed British officials that the United States would compromise on most issues.

Not surprisingly, when Jay reached London, he encountered polite but firm resistance. His efforts resulted in a political humiliation known simply as **Jay's Treaty.** The chief justice did persuade the British to abandon their frontier posts and to allow small American ships to trade in the British West Indies, but they rejected out of hand the U.S. position on neutral rights. The Royal Navy would continue to search American vessels on the high seas for contraband and to impress sailors suspected of being British citizens. Moreover, there would be no compensation for the ships seized in 1793 until the Americans paid British merchants for debts contracted before the Revolution. And to the particular annoyance of southerners, not a word was said about the slaves the British army had carried off at the conclusion of the war. While Jay salvaged the peace, he appeared to have betrayed the national interest.

News of Jay's Treaty produced an angry outcry in the nation's capital. Even Washington was apprehensive. He submitted the document to the Senate without recommending ratification, a sign that the president was not entirely happy with the results of Jay's mission. After an extremely bitter debate, the upper house, controlled by Federalists, accepted a revised version of the treaty (June 1795). The vote was 20 to 10, a bare two-thirds majority.

The details of the Jay agreement soon leaked to the press. The popular journals sparked a firestorm of objection. Throughout the country, people who had generally been apathetic about national politics were swept up in a wave of protest. Urban mobs condemned Jay's alleged sellout; rural settlers burned him in effigy. Jay jokingly told friends he could find his way across the country simply by following the light of those fires. Southerners announced they would not pay prerevolutionary debts to British merchants. The Virginia legislature proposed a constitutional amendment reducing the Senate's role in the treaty-making process.

In the House of Representatives, Republican congressmen, led by Madison, thought they could stop Jay's Treaty by refusing to appropriate funds for its implementation. As part of their plan, they demanded that Washington show the House state papers relating to Jay's mission. The challenge raised complex issues of constitutional law. The House, for example, was claiming a voice in treaty ratification, a power explicitly reserved to the Senate. Second, there was the question of executive secrecy in the interest of national security. Washington took the occasion to lecture the rebellious representatives that "the nature of foreign negotiations requires caution; and their success must often depend on secrecy."

The president still had a trump card to play. He raised the possibility that the House was really contemplating his impeachment. Such an action was, of course, unthinkable. Even criticizing Washington in public was politically dangerous, and as soon as he redefined the issue before Congress, petitions supporting the president flooded into the nation's capital. The Maryland legislature, for example, declared its "unabated reliance on the integrity, judgment, and patriotism of the President of the United States," a statement that clearly called into question the patriotism of certain Republican congressmen. The Federalists won a stunning tactical victory over the opposition. Had a less popular man than Washington occupied the presidency, however, they would not have fared so well. The division between the two parties was beyond repair. The Republicans labeled the Federalists

Jay's Treaty
Controversial treaty with Britain negotiated by Chief Justice John Jay in 1794 to settle American grievances and avert war. Though the British agreed to surrender forts in U.S. territory, the treaty failed to realize key diplomatic goals and provoked a storm of protest in America.

"the British party"; the Federalists believed that the Republicans were in league with the French.

By the time Jay's Treaty became law (June 14, 1795), the two giants of Washington's first cabinet had retired. Late in 1793, Jefferson returned to his Virginia plantation, Monticello, where, despite his separation from day-to-day political affairs, he remained the chief spokesman for the Republican party. His rival, Hamilton, left the Treasury in January 1795 to practice law in New York City. He maintained close ties with important Federalist officials, and even more than Jefferson, Hamilton concerned himself with the details of party organization.

QUICK CHECK ✔

Why did Jay's Treaty spark such hostility throughout the nation?

Pushing the Native Americans Aside

Before Great Britain finally withdrew its troops from the Great Lakes and Northwest Territory, its military officers encouraged local Indian groups—the Shawnee, Chippewa, and Miami—to attack settlers and traders from the United States. The Indians, who even without British encouragement fully appreciated that the newcomers intended to seize their land, won several impressive victories over federal troops in the area that would become western Ohio and Indiana. In 1790, General Josiah Harmar led his soldiers into an ambush. The following year, an army under General Arthur St. Clair suffered more than nine hundred casualties near the Wabash River. But the Indians were militarily more vulnerable than they realized, for when confronted with a major U.S. army under the command of General Anthony Wayne, they received no support from their former British allies. At the battle of Fallen Timbers (August 20, 1794), Wayne's forces crushed Indian resistance in the Northwest Territory, and the native peoples were compelled to sign the Treaty of Greenville, formally ceding to the U.S. government the land that became Ohio. In 1796, the last British soldiers departed for Canada.

The Treaty of Greenville

Shrewd negotiations mixed with pure luck helped secure the nation's southwestern frontier. For complex reasons having to do with the state of European diplomacy, Spanish officials in 1795 encouraged the U.S. representative in Madrid to discuss the navigation of the Mississippi River. Before this initiative, the Spanish government not only had closed the river to American commerce but also had incited the Indians of the region to harass settlers from the United States. Relations between the two countries probably would have deteriorated further had the United States not signed Jay's Treaty. The Spanish assumed—quite erroneously—that Great Britain and the United States had formed an alliance to strip Spain of its North American possessions.

The Treaty of San Lorenzo (Pinckney's Treaty) (1796)

To avoid this imagined disaster, officials in Madrid offered the American envoy, Thomas Pinckney, extraordinary concessions: the opening of the Mississippi, the right to deposit goods in New Orleans without paying duties, a secure southern boundary on the 31st parallel (a line roughly parallel to the northern boundary of Florida and running west to the Mississippi), and a promise to stay out of Indian affairs. An amazed Pinckney signed the Treaty of San Lorenzo (also called Pinckney's Treaty) on October 27, 1795, and in March the Senate ratified the document without a single dissenting vote. Pinckney, who came from a prominent South Carolina family, instantly became the hero of the Federalist party.

QUICK CHECK ✔

Why did "the opening of the Mississippi" figure so prominently in American politics during the 1790s?

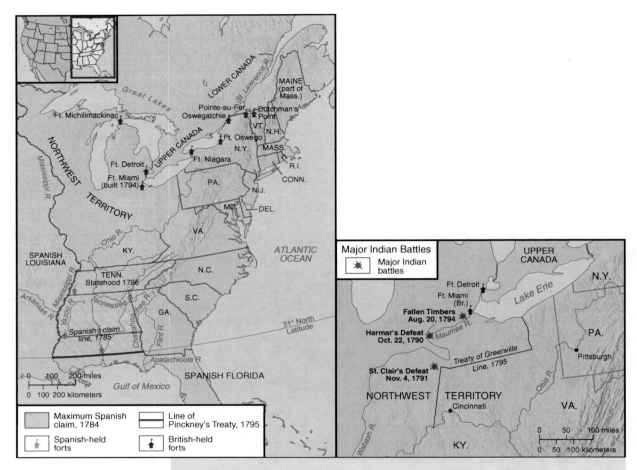

CONQUEST OF THE WEST Withdrawal of the British, defeat of Native Americans, and negotiations with Spain secured the nation's frontiers.

What role did the Mississippi River play in the economic development of the new Republic?

Popular Political Culture

WHY

was it hard for Americans to accept political dissent as a part of political activity?

More than any other event during Washington's administration, ratification of Jay's Treaty generated intense political strife. Even as members of Congress voted as Republicans or Federalists, they condemned the rising partisan spirit as a grave threat to the stability of the United States. Popular writers equated "party" with "faction" and "faction" with "conspiracy to overthrow legitimate authority." Party conflict also suggested that Americans had lost the sense of common purpose that had united them during the Revolution. Contemporaries did not appreciate the beneficial role that parties could play by presenting alternative solutions to foreign and domestic problems. Organized opposition smacked of disloyalty and therefore had to be eliminated by any means—fair or foul.

Whiskey Rebellion: Charges of Republican Conspiracy

Political tensions became explosive in 1794. The Federalists convinced themselves that the Republicans were actually prepared to employ violence against the U.S. government. Although the charge was without foundation, it took on plausibility in the context of growing party strife.

The crisis developed when a group of farmers living in western Pennsylvania protested a federal excise tax on distilled whiskey that Congress had originally passed in 1791. These men did not relish paying any taxes, but this tax struck them as particularly unfair. They made a good deal of money distilling their grain into whiskey, and the excise threatened to put them out of business.

Largely because the Republican governor of Pennsylvania refused to suppress the angry farmers, Washington and other leading Federalists assumed that the insurrection represented a direct political challenge. The president called out fifteen thousand militiamen, and, accompanied by Hamilton, he marched against the rebels. The expedition was an embarrassing fiasco. The distillers disappeared, and predictably enough, no one living in the Pittsburgh region seemed to know where the troublemakers had gone. Two supposed rebels were convicted of high crimes against the United States; one was reportedly a "simpleton" and the other insane. Washington eventually pardoned both men. As peace returned to the frontier, Republicans gained much electoral support from voters the Federalists had alienated.

In the national political forum, however, the **Whiskey Rebellion** had just begun. Spokesmen for both parties offered sinister explanations for the seemingly innocuous affair. Washington blamed the Republican clubs for promoting civil

Whiskey Rebellion Tax Protest (1794)

George Washington, Whiskey Rebellion Address to the Congress (1794)

Farewell Address (1796)

Whiskey Rebellion
Protests in 1794 by western Pennsylvania farmers resisting payment of a federal tax on whiskey. The uprising was forcibly suppressed when President George Washington called an army of 15,000 troops to the area, where they encountered almost no resistance.

THE WHISKEY REBELLION   Tarring and feathering federal officials was one way in which western Pennsylvanians protested the tax on whiskey in 1794. Washington's call for troops to put down the insurrection drew more volunteers than he had been able to raise during most of the Revolution. (*Source: Whiskey Rebellion, c. 1790s, hand-colored woodcut/North Wind Picture Archives.*)

Why did such a minor disturbance spark so dramatic a reaction?

QUICK CHECK ✓

Why did Washington and his supporters see the Whiskey Rebellion as something more sinister than just an "embarrassing fiasco"?

unrest. He apparently believed that the opposition party had dispatched French agents to western Pennsylvania to undermine the authority of the federal government. In November 1794, Washington informed Congress that these "self-created societies"—in other words, the Republican political clubs—had inspired "a spirit inimical to all order." Indeed, the Whiskey Rebellion had been "fomented by combinations of men who... have disseminated, from an ignorance or perversion of facts, suspicions, jealousies, and accusations of the whole Government."

The president's interpretation of this rural tax revolt was no less charitable than the conspiratorial explanation offered by the Republicans. Jefferson labeled the entire episode a Hamiltonian device to create an army for the purpose of intimidating Republicans.

Farewell Address
In this 1796 speech, President George Washington announced his intention not to seek a third term in office. He also stressed Federalist interests and warned the American people to avoid political factions and foreign entanglements that could sacrifice U.S. security.

Washington's Farewell

In September 1796, Washington published his famed **Farewell Address,** formally declaring his intention to retire from the presidency. In the address, which was printed in newspapers throughout the country, Washington warned against all political factions. Written in large part by Hamilton, who drew on a draft prepared several years earlier by Madison, the address served narrowly partisan ends. The product of growing political strife, it sought to advance the Federalist cause in the forthcoming election. By waiting until September to announce his retirement, Washington denied the Republicans valuable time to organize an effective campaign. There was an element of irony in this initiative. Washington had always maintained he stood above party. While he may have done so in the early years of his presidency, events such as the signing of Jay's Treaty and the suppression of the Whiskey Rebellion transformed him in the eyes of many Americans into a spokesman solely for Hamilton's Federalist party.

Washington also spoke to foreign policy matters in the address. He counseled the United States to avoid making any permanent alliances with distant nations that had no real interest in promoting American security. This statement guided foreign relations for many years and became the credo of later American isolationists, who argued that the United States should steer clear of foreign entanglements.

QUICK CHECK ✓

In what way was Washington's Farewell Address in 1796 a piece of party propaganda?

The Adams Presidency: Politics of Mistrust

WHY were some Federalists willing to sacrifice political freedoms for party advantage?

The election of 1796 took place in an atmosphere of mutual distrust. Jefferson, soon to be the vice president, informed a friend that "an Anglican and aristocratic party has sprung up, whose avowed object is to draw over us the substance, as they have already done the forms, of British government." On their part, the Federalists were convinced their Republican opponents wanted to hand the government over to French radicals.

During the campaign, the Federalists sowed the seeds of their eventual destruction. Party stalwarts agreed that John Adams should stand against the Republican candidate, Thomas Jefferson. Hamilton, however, could not leave well enough alone. From his law office in New York City, he schemed to deprive Adams of

THE ELECTION OF 1796		
Candidate	Party	Electoral Vote
J. Adams	Federalist	71
Jefferson	Republican	68
T. Pinckney	Federalist	59
Burr	Republican	30

the presidency. His motives were obscure. He apparently feared that an independent-minded Adams would be difficult to manipulate. He was correct.

Hamilton exploited an awkward feature of the electoral college. In accordance with the Constitution, each elector cast two ballots, and the person who gained the most votes became president. The runner-up, regardless of party affiliation, served as vice president. Ordinarily the Federalist electors would have cast one vote for Adams and one for Thomas Pinckney, the hero of the negotiations with Spain and the party's choice for vice president. Everyone hoped, of course, there would be no tie. Hamilton secretly urged southern Federalists to support only

PRESIDENT ADAMS John Adams in the suit and sword he wore for his 1797 inauguration. The portrait is by English artist William Winstanley, 1798.

Why would a president who preferred peace to war have chosen to appear wearing a sword in this portrait?

Pinckney, even if that meant throwing away an elector's second vote. If everything had gone according to plan, Pinckney would have received more votes than Adams, but when New Englanders loyal to Adams heard of Hamilton's maneuvering, they dropped Pinckney. When the votes were counted, Adams had 71, Jefferson 68, and Pinckney 59. Hamilton's treachery not only angered the new president but also heightened tensions within the Federalist party.

The XYZ Affair and Domestic Politics

Once he was sworn into office foreign affairs immediately occupied Adams's full attention. The French government regarded Jay's Treaty as an affront. By allowing Great Britain to define the conditions for neutrality, the United States had in effect sided with that nation against the interests of France.

Relations between the two countries had steadily deteriorated. The French refused to receive Charles Cotesworth Pinckney, the U.S. representative in Paris. Pierre Adet, the French minister in Philadelphia, openly tried to influence the 1796 election in favor of the Republicans. His meddling in domestic politics not only embarrassed Jefferson, it also offended the American people. The situation then took a violent turn. In 1797, French privateers began seizing American ships. Since neither the United States nor France officially declared war, the hostilities came to be known as the **Quasi-War.**

Quasi-War
Undeclared war between the United States and France in which French privateers began seizing U.S. ships in 1797.

Hamilton and his friends welcomed a popular outpouring of anti-French sentiment. The High Federalists—as members of Hamilton's wing of the party were called—counseled the president to prepare for all-out war, hoping that war would purge the United States of French influence. Adams was not persuaded to escalate the conflict. He dispatched a special commission in a final attempt to remove the sources of antagonism. This famous negotiating team consisted of Charles Pinckney, John Marshall, and Elbridge Gerry. They were instructed to obtain compensation for the ships seized by French privateers as well as release from the treaties of 1778. Federalists still worried that this old agreement might oblige the United States to defend French colonies in the Caribbean against British attack, something they were extremely reluctant to do. In exchange, the commission offered France the same commercial privileges granted to Great Britain in Jay's Treaty. While the diplomats negotiated for peace, Adams talked of strengthening American defenses, rhetoric that pleased the militant members of his own party.

The commission was shocked by the outrageous treatment it received in France. Instead of dealing directly with Talleyrand, the minister of foreign relations, they met with obscure intermediaries who demanded a huge bribe. The commission reported that Talleyrand would not open negotiations unless he was given $250,000. In addition, the French government expected a "loan" of millions of dollars. The Americans refused to play this insulting game. Pinckney angrily sputtered, "No, no, not a sixpence," and with Marshall he returned to the United States. When they arrived home, Marshall offered his much-quoted toast: "Millions for defense, but not one cent for tribute."

Diplomatic humiliation set off a domestic political explosion. When Adams presented the commission's official correspondence before Congress—the names of Talleyrand's lackeys were labeled X, Y, and Z—the Federalists burst out with a war cry. At last, they would be able to even old scores with the Republicans. In April 1798, a Federalist newspaper in New York City announced ominously that any American who refused to censure France "must have a soul black enough to

THE XYZ AFFAIR This cartoon, *Property Protects, à la Françoise* (1798), captures the anti-French sentiment many Americans felt after President Adams disclosed the papers of the XYZ Affair. America—depicted as a young maiden—is being plundered by five Frenchmen, who represent the five directors of the French government.

Why were so many Americans in the late 1790s hostile to their former Revolutionary allies?

XYZ Affair
A diplomatic incident in which American peace commissioners sent to France by President John Adams in 1797 were insulted with bribe demands from their French counterparts, dubbed X, Y, and Z in American newspapers. The incident heightened war fever against France.

QUICK CHECK ✓

During the XYZ Affair, why did representatives of the French government treat American diplomats with such disrespect?

be *fit for treasons, strategems,* and *spoils.*" Rumors of conspiracy, referred to as the **XYZ Affair,** spread throughout the country. Personal friendships between Republicans and Federalists were shattered. Jefferson described the tense political atmosphere in a letter to an old colleague: "You and I have formerly seen warm debates and high political passions. But gentlemen of different politics would then speak to each other, and separate the business of the Senate from that of society. It is not so now. Men who have been intimate all their lives, cross the streets to avoid meeting, and turn their heads another way, lest they should be obliged to touch their hats."

Crushing Political Dissent

In the spring of 1798, High Federalists assumed that it was just a matter of time until Adams asked Congress for a formal declaration of war. In the meantime, they pushed for a general rearmament, new fighting ships, additional harbor fortifications, and most important, a greatly expanded U.S. Army. About the need for land forces, Adams remained understandably skeptical. He saw no likelihood of French invasion.

The president missed the political point. The army the Federalists wanted was intended not to thwart French aggression but to stifle internal opposition. Indeed, militant Federalists used the XYZ Affair as the occasion to institute what Jefferson termed the "reign of witches." The threat to the Republicans was not simply a figment of the vice president's overwrought imagination. When Theodore Sedgwick, now a Federalist senator from Massachusetts, first learned of the commission's failure, he observed in words that capture the High Federalists' vindictiveness, "It will afford a glorious opportunity to destroy faction. Improve it."

During the summer of 1798, a provisional army gradually came into existence. George Washington agreed to lead the troops, but he would do so only on condition that Adams appoint Hamilton as second in command. This demand placed the president in a terrible dilemma. Several revolutionary veterans—Henry Knox, for example—outranked Hamilton. Moreover, the former secretary of the treasury had consistently undermined Adams's authority, and to give Hamilton a position of real power in the government seemed awkward at best. When Washington insisted, however, Adams was forced to support Hamilton.

The chief of the High Federalists threw himself into the task of recruiting and supplying the troops. No detail escaped his attention. He and Secretary of War McHenry made certain that in this political army, only loyal Federalists received commissions. They even denied Adams's son-in-law a post. The entire enterprise took on an air of unreality. Hamilton longed for military glory, and he may have contemplated attacking Spain's Latin American colonies. His driving obsession, however, was the restoration of political order. No doubt, he agreed with a Federalist senator from Connecticut who predicted that the Republicans "never will yield till violence is introduced; we must have a partial civil war... and the bayonet must convince some, who are beyond the reach of other arguments."

Hamilton should not have treated Adams with such open contempt. After all, the Massachusetts statesman was still the president, and without presidential cooperation, Hamilton could not fulfill his grand military ambitions. Yet whenever pressing questions concerning the army arose, Adams was nowhere to be found. He let commissions lie on his desk unsigned; he took overlong vacations to New England. He made it quite clear his first love was the navy. In May 1798, the president persuaded Congress to establish the Navy Department. For this new cabinet position, he selected Benjamin Stoddert, a person who did not take orders from Hamilton. Moreover, Adams further infuriated the High Federalists by refusing to ask Congress for a formal declaration of war. When they pressed him, Adams threatened to resign, making Jefferson president. As the weeks passed, the American people increasingly regarded the idle army as an expensive extravagance.

QUICK CHECK ✔

Why were the High Federalists willing to place party advantage over the welfare of the entire nation?

Silencing Political Opposition: The Alien and Sedition Acts

Alien and Sedition Acts Collective name given to four laws passed in 1798 designed to suppress criticism of the federal government and to curb liberties of foreigners living in the United States.

The Federalists did not rely solely on the army to crush political dissent. During the summer of 1798, the majority in Congress passed a group of bills known collectively as the **Alien and Sedition Acts**. This legislation authorized the use of federal courts and the powers of the presidency to silence the Republicans. The acts were born of fear and vindictiveness, and in their efforts to punish the followers of Jefferson, the Federalists created the nation's first major crisis over civil liberties.

Congress drew up three separate Alien Acts. The first, the Alien Enemies Law, vested the president with extraordinary wartime powers. On his own authority, he could detain or deport citizens of nations with which the United States was at war and who behaved in a manner he thought suspicious. Since Adams refused to ask

PARTY CONFLICT In the early years of the republic, political dissent sometimes escalated to physical violence. This fistfight took place on the floor of Congress, February 15, 1798. The combatants are Republican Matthew Lyon and Federalist Roger Griswold.

What political issues contributed to this dramatic breakdown in congressional procedure?

for a declaration of war, this legislation never went into effect. A second act, the Alien Law, empowered the president to expel any foreigner from the United States simply by executive decree. Congress limited the acts to two years, and while Adams did not attempt to enforce them, the mere threat of arrest caused some Frenchmen to flee the country. The third act, the Naturalization Law, was the most flagrantly political of the group. The act established a fourteen-year probationary period before foreigners could apply for full U.S. citizenship. Federalists recognized that recent immigrants, especially the Irish, tended to vote Republican. The Naturalization Law, therefore, was designed to keep "hordes of wild Irishmen" away from the polls for as long as possible.

The Sedition Law struck at the heart of free political exchange. It defined criticism of the U.S. government as criminal libel; citizens found guilty by a jury were subject to fines and imprisonment. Congress entrusted enforcement of the act to the federal courts. Republicans were justly worried that the Sedition Law undermined rights guaranteed by the First Amendment. When they protested, however, the High Federalists dismissed their complaints. The Constitution, they declared, did not condone "the most groundless and malignant lies, striking at the safety

The Alien and Sedition Acts (1798)

185

Why did leaders of the Federalist party not appreciate that the Alien and Sedition Acts undermined the Constitution of the United States?

and existence of the nation." They were determined to shut down the opposition press and were willing to give the government what seemed almost dictatorial powers to achieve that end. The Jeffersonians also expressed concern over the federal judiciary's expanded role in punishing sedition. They believed such matters were best left to state officials.

The Federalists' enforcement of the Sedition Law did not silence opposition—indeed, it sparked even greater criticism and created martyrs—the actions of the administration persuaded Republicans that the survival of free government was at stake. Time was running out. "There is no event," Jefferson warned, "... however atrocious, which may not be expected."

The Kentucky and Virginia Resolutions (1798, 1799)

Kentucky and Virginia Resolutions

Statements penned by Thomas Jefferson and James Madison to mobilize opposition to the Alien and Sedition Acts, which they argued were unconstitutional. Jefferson's statement (the Kentucky Resolutions) suggested that states should have the right to declare null and void congressional acts they deemed unconstitutional. Madison produced a more temperate resolution, but most Americans rejected such an extreme defense of states' rights.

How did the Kentucky and Virginia Resolutions propose to protect American freedoms?

Kentucky and Virginia Resolutions

By the fall of 1798, Jefferson and Madison were convinced that the Federalists envisioned the creation of a police state. According to Madison, the Sedition Law "ought to produce universal alarm." It threatened the free communication of ideas that he "deemed the only effectual guardian of every other right." Some extreme Republicans such as John Taylor of Virginia recommended secession from the Union; others advocated armed resistance. But Jefferson wisely counseled against such extreme strategies. "This is not the kind of opposition the American people will permit," he reminded his desperate supporters. The last best hope for American freedom lay in the state legislatures.

As the crisis deepened, Jefferson and Madison drafted separate protests known as the **Kentucky and Virginia Resolutions.** Both statements vigorously defended the right of individual state assemblies to interpret the constitutionality of federal law. Jefferson wrote the Kentucky Resolutions in November 1798, and in an outburst of partisan anger, he flirted with a doctrine of nullification as dangerous to the survival of the United States as anything advanced by Hamilton and his High Federalist friends.

In the Kentucky Resolutions, Jefferson described the federal union as a compact. The states transferred certain explicit powers to the national government, but, in his opinion, they retained full authority over all matters not specifically mentioned in the Constitution. Jefferson rejected Hamilton's broad interpretation of the "general welfare" clause.

When Madison drafted the Virginia Resolutions in December, he took a stand more temperate than Jefferson's. Madison urged the states to defend the rights of the American people, but he resisted the notion that a single state legislature could or should have the authority to overthrow federal law.

The Virginia and Kentucky Resolutions were not intended as statements of abstract principles and most certainly not as a justification for southern secession. They were pure political party propaganda. Jefferson and Madison dramatically reminded American voters during a period of severe domestic tension that the Republicans offered a clear alternative to Federalist rule. No other state legislatures passed the Resolutions, and even in Virginia, where the Republicans enjoyed broad support, several important figures such as John Marshall and George Washington censured the states' rights argument.

Adams's Finest Hour

In February 1799, President Adams belatedly declared his independence from the Hamiltonian wing of the Federalist party. Throughout the confrontation with France, Adams had shown little enthusiasm for war. Following the XYZ debacle, he began to receive informal reports that Talleyrand had changed his tune. The French foreign minister told Elbridge Gerry and other Americans that the bribery episode had been an unfortunate misunderstanding and that if the United States sent new representatives, he was prepared to negotiate in good faith. The High Federalists ridiculed this report. But Adams decided to throw his own waning prestige behind peace. In February, he suddenly asked the Senate to confirm William Vans Murray as U.S. representative to France.

When the new negotiators—Oliver Ellsworth and William Davie joined Murray—finally arrived in France in November 1799, they discovered that yet another group had come to power there. This government, headed by Napoleon Bonaparte, cooperated in drawing up an agreement known as the Convention of Mortefontaine. The French refused to compensate the Americans for vessels taken during the Quasi-War, but they did declare the treaties of 1778 null and void. Moreover, the convention removed annoying French restrictions on U.S. commerce. Not only had Adams avoided war, but he had also created an atmosphere of mutual trust that paved the way for the purchase of the Louisiana Territory.

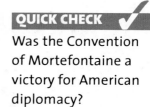

QUICK CHECK

Was the Convention of Mortefontaine a victory for American diplomacy?

The Peaceful Revolution: The Election of 1800

On the eve of the election of 1800, the Federalists were fatally divided. Adams enjoyed wide popularity among the Federalist rank and file, especially in New England, but articulate party leaders such as Hamilton vowed to punish the president for his betrayal of their militant policies. The former secretary of the treasury attempted to rig the voting in the electoral college so that the party's vice presidential candidate, Charles Cotesworth Pinckney, would receive more ballots than Adams and America would be saved from "the fangs of Jefferson." As in 1796, the conspiracy backfired. The Republicans gained 73 votes while the Federalists trailed with 65.

To everyone's surprise, however, the election was not resolved in the electoral college. When the ballots were counted, Jefferson and his running mate, Aaron Burr, had tied. This accident—a Republican elector should have thrown away his second vote—sent the selection of the next president to the House of Representatives, a lame-duck body still controlled by members of the Federalist party.

LISTEN

Jefferson and Liberty

THE ELECTION OF 1800		
Candidate	**Party**	**Electoral Vote**
Jefferson	Republican	73
Burr	Republican	73
J. Adams	Federalist	65
C. Pinckney	Federalist	64

PRESIDENT JEFFERSON   The cast of ballots by presidential electors in December 1800 resulted in a tie between Thomas Jefferson and Aaron Burr, who each received 73 votes. The election was finally decided in February 1801 when the House of Representatives, on the thirty-sixth ballot, chose Jefferson by a vote of 10 to 4. This flag commemorates Jefferson's victory in the election.

What is the significance of the 16 stars surrounding Jefferson's portrait?

As the House began its work on February 27, 1801, excitement ran high. Each state delegation cast a single vote, with nine votes needed for election. On the first ballot, Jefferson received the support of eight states, Burr six, and two states divided evenly. People predicted a quick victory for Jefferson, but after dozens of ballots, the House had still not selected a president. The drama dragged on for days. To add to the confusion, Burr unaccountably refused to withdraw. Contemporaries thought his ambition had overcome his good sense.

The logjam finally broke when leading Federalists decided that Jefferson, whatever his faults, would make a more responsible president than would the shifty Burr. Even Hamilton labeled Burr "the most dangerous man of the community." On the thirty-sixth ballot, Representative James A. Bayard of Delaware announced he no longer supported Burr. This decision, coupled with Burr's inaction, gave Jefferson the presidency, ten states to four.

The Twelfth Amendment, ratified in 1804, saved the American people from repeating this potentially dangerous turn of events. Henceforth, the electoral college cast separate ballots for president and vice president.

During the final days of his presidency, Adams appointed as many Federalists as possible to the federal bench. Jefferson protested the hasty manner in which these "midnight judges" were selected. One of them, John Marshall, became chief justice of the United States, a post he held with distinction for thirty-four years. But behind the last-minute flurry of activity lay bitterness and disappointment. Adams never forgave Hamilton. On the morning of Jefferson's inauguration, Adams slipped away from the capital—now located in Washington, D.C.—unnoticed and unappreciated.

In the address that Adams missed, Jefferson attempted to quiet partisan fears. "We are all republicans; we are all federalists," the new president declared. By this statement, he did not mean to suggest that party differences were no longer important. Jefferson reminded his audience that whatever the politicians might say, the people shared a deep commitment to a federal union based on republican ideals set forth during the American Revolution. Indeed, the president interpreted the election of 1800 as a revolutionary episode, as the fulfillment of the principles of 1776.

Recent battles, of course, colored Jefferson's judgment. The contests of the 1790s had been hard fought, the outcome often in doubt. Jefferson looked back at this period as a confrontation between the "advocates of republican and those of kingly government," and he believed that only the vigilance of his own party had saved the country from Federalist "liberticide."

The Federalists were thoroughly dispirited by the entire experience. In the end, it had not been Hamilton's foolish electoral schemes that destroyed the party's chances in 1800. Rather, the Federalists had lost touch with a majority of the American people. In office, Adams and Hamilton—whatever their own differences may have been—betrayed their doubts about popular sovereignty too often, and when it came time to marshal broad support, to mobilize public opinion in favor of the party of wealth and privilege, few responded.

DOCUMENT

Jefferson's First Inaugural Address (1801)

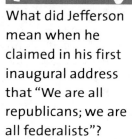

QUICK CHECK ✓

What did Jefferson mean when he claimed in his first inaugural address that "We are all republicans; we are all federalists"?

Conclusion: Danger of Political Extremism

From a broader historical perspective, the election of 1800 seems noteworthy for what did not occur. There were no riots in the streets, no attempted coup by military officers, no secession from the Union, nothing except the peaceful transfer of government from the leaders of one political party to those of the opposition.

Americans had weathered the Alien and Sedition Acts, the meddling by predatory foreign powers in domestic affairs, the shrilly partisan rhetoric of hack journalists, and now, at the start of a new century, they were impressed with their own achievement. As one woman who attended Jefferson's inauguration noted, "The changes of administration which in every government and in every age have most generally been epochs of confusion, villainy and bloodshed, in this our happy country take place without any species of distraction, or disorder." But as she well understood—indeed, as modern Americans must constantly relearn—extremism in the name of partisan political truth can easily unravel the delicate fabric of representative democracy and leave the republic at the mercy of those who would manipulate the public for private benefit.

For a list of additional titles related to this chapter's topics, please see www.pearsonamericanhistory.com.

MHL

MyHistoryLab

STUDY RESOURCES

KEY TERMS

Bank of the United States

implied powers

French Revolution

Jay's Treaty

Whiskey Rebellion

Farewell Address

Quasi-War

XYZ Affair

Alien and Sedition Acts

Kentucky and Virginia Resolutions

CHAPTER REVIEW

WHY was George Washington unable to overcome division within the new government?

George Washington was the most popular figure in the United States when he became president in 1788. Congress organized the Departments of War, State, and the Treasury. Washington nominated brilliant figures such as Thomas Jefferson and Alexander Hamilton to serve in his new cabinet. Within months, these two men began fighting over profoundly different visions for the future of the republic. Hamilton imagined an urban commercial nation with a strong central government; Jefferson championed a simple agrarian republic.

WHY did many Americans oppose Alexander Hamilton's blueprint for national prosperity?

Hamilton argued that the United States could never become strong and prosperous unless it put its finances in order. In a series of bold reports, he urged Congress to create a new system of public credit, charter a national bank, and stimulate domestic manufacturing. Jefferson and his allies criticized Hamilton's program on moral and political grounds, charging that it favored the interests of a commercial elite over those of ordinary Americans.

HOW did foreign affairs affect domestic politics during the 1790s?

The French Revolution split American opinion. Republicans cheered it; Federalists condemned it. When France declared war on Great Britain (1793), Britain began seizing American ships and impressing American sailors into the British navy. Jay's Treaty (1794) did little to address these insults. During the mid-1790s, America seized additional lands from Indians in the Northwest.

WHY was it hard for Americans to accept political dissent as a part of political activity?

In the 1790s, many Americans equated political dissent with disloyalty. During the Whiskey Rebellion (1794), both Federalists and Republicans feared the other party planned to use violence to crush political opposition. By not announcing his retirement until September 1796, President Washington denied the Republicans time to campaign for the presidency. Washington's Farewell Address warned against becoming involved in European politics.

WHY were some Federalists willing to sacrifice political freedoms for party advantage?

During the Adams presidency, French privateers waged a Quasi-War against American shipping, and French officials solicited bribes from American diplomats, causing a scandal. Many Federalists believed that the support of Jeffersonian Republicans for France had compromised American sovereignty. After the Federalist Congress passed the Alien and Sedition Acts (1798) to intimidate the Jeffersonians, James Madison and Thomas Jefferson authored the Kentucky and Virginia Resolutions asserting states' rights. In 1800, Federalist attempts at election rigging failed, handing Jefferson the presidency.

MAKING CONNECTIONS

1. How were the disagreements between Hamilton and Jefferson a reflection of popular culture in the country during the 1790s?

2. How did American foreign policy during the 1790s influence the growth of political dissent?

3. How important were popular opinion and party politics in poisoning the Adams presidency?

4. How could a constitutional republic justify the passage of highly partisan legislation such as the Alien and Sedition Acts?

PRACTICE QUIZ

1. The congressional_____ Act of 1789 created a federal court system.
   a. Legislative   **b.** Tax
   c. Judiciary   **d.** Supreme Court

2. Secretary Hamilton's *Report on the* _____ reached Congress in 1790.
   a. *Supreme Court*   **b.** *Public Credit*
   c. *Military*   **d.** *Presidency*

3. News of _____ with England produced outrage in the United States in 1794.
   a. Jefferson's Treaty   **b.** Hamilton's Treaty
   c. Franklin's Treaty   **d.** Jay's Treaty

4. In the Treaty of _____ in 1794, Indians ceded the Ohio region to the United States.
   a. Paris   **b.** Ghent
   c. Fallen Timbers   **d.** Greenville

5. At the battle of _____, General Wayne crushed Indian resistance in the Northwest.
   a. Gettysburg   **b.** Fallen Timbers
   c. Tippecanoe   **d.** Shiloh

6. Pennsylvania farmers angry over taxation in 1794 staged
   a. Bacon's Rebellion
   b. Leisler's Rebellion
   c. The Whiskey Rebellion
   d. Shay's Rebellion

7. In September 1796, President George Washington published his famous
   a. Inaugural Address
   b. Declaration of War against England
   c. Farewell Address
   d. Supreme Court nomination speech

8. Why did American leaders during the 1790s condemn the development of political parties?
   a. They raised the cost of election campaigns.
   b. They seemed to be part of a British political tradition.
   c. They revealed that Americans were no longer united on the meaning of the Revolution.
   d. They gave the states too much power in elections.

9. Which of the following *does not* accurately characterize the Kentucky and Virginia Resolutions?
   a. Jefferson and Madison drafted separate resolutions against Federalist power.
   b. Madison's stand became even more radical than Jefferson's stance.
   c. The resolutions defended the right of assemblies to interpret federal law.
   d. Jefferson became so angry that he almost wrote a doctrine of nullification.

10. All of the following statements regarding the election of 1800 are true *except*
   a. Hamilton attempted to rig the election.
   b. The House of Representatives would decide the contested election.
   c. The Twentieth Amendment was created after the election.
   d. Jefferson emerged the winner in the final House vote.

Find more practice at www.myhistorylab.com

SAMPLE ESSAY QUESTIONS

1. Describe Hamilton's vision of economic development for the early United States.

2. Trace the development of the XYZ Affair and its impact on national politics.

CREDITS

The Indians' New World: Native Americans after the European Invasion, 1585–1783

Margaret E. Newell

INTRODUCTION

As historian James Merrell points out, in the wake of the European invasion, America's native inhabitants faced a radically altered way of life—a "new world" almost as foreign to them as America was to the European colonizers. First, European diseases wrought a terrible mortality among the Indians, resulting in the destruction of entire tribes and traditions. Second, European settlers and traders, and their African slaves, introduced new goods, technologies, and agricultural methods to America, all of which affected the Indians' way of life. The new arrivals also competed with the native inhabitants for resources and military control. Native Americans in turn influenced the course of European settlement. The following readings explore relations between Europeans and Indians during the first two centuries of contact in North America, focusing on the Indians' responses.

The Indian experience was as diverse as the tribes that inhabited North America. Although the eastern coastal peoples succumbed quickly to disease and military conquest, Native Americans in the interior remained a force to be reckoned with well into the nineteenth century. Survivors migrated to escape sickness, creating diversely populated villages and new tribal alliances. Powerful groups like the six-tribe Iroquois Confederation, the Choctaws of Louisiana, and the Creeks and Cherokees of the southeast outnumbered white settlers and retained much of their land and independence for over a century.

During the colonial period, Indians and Europeans interacted in numerous ways short of war, most commonly in the related activities of trade and diplomacy. Indeed, in their early years, the small scattered European settlements depended upon the Indians for survival. Thus both groups had numerous opportunities to observe each other's culture and manners. The Indians adopted some aspects of European culture, but they also forced Europeans to adjust to the native inhabitants' presence and expectations. Some of the technology that the Dutch, French, and English introduced—guns, knives, kettles, hoes—made the Indians' agriculture, hunting, and cooking more efficient, and many tribes eagerly sought access to trade with Europeans. Indians also used English and French agents as mediators to resolve conflicts with neighboring tribes, or solicited their help in conquering their enemies. In return, the Europeans received food, furs, deerskins, information, and military aid. As the French and English battled to extend their respective empires in America, the Indians played an important role in what historian Gary Nash calls the "three-cornered fight for a continent." They took advantage of European rivalries, playing the French against the English and the colonies against each other, seeking the most advantageous trading terms and refusing to be pawns in European wars.

Relations between Indians and whites entered a new phase in 1763 after England's victory in the Seven Years' War (the French and Indian War). The elimination of the French reduced the Indians' ability to pit one enemy against another. The dramatic growth of the English colonies' population led authorities to pressure the Indians for ever-larger land cessions; with Indians and whites living side-by-side, the potential for conflict increased. In addition, the adoption of European technology had unanticipated consequences. For example, guns made war in the post-contact era a much more deadly affair for Indians, and hunters armed with muskets nearly wiped out some of the species they depended upon. Other goods, such as liquor, found wide acceptance, with devastating consequences for Indian societies. Many Native Americans grew dependent upon European cloth, guns, and ammunition, even as their ability to pay for such goods diminished. Some tribes survived by ceding their land. The Revolution left the Indians in an even more vulnerable position; after 1783, the Indians had only one partner to negotiate with—the Americans, whose land hunger outstripped that of both the English and French.

WARFARE, EXCHANGE, AND THE MEETING OF CULTURES

This section presents a discussion of the "new world" of disease, trade, subsistence, and diplomacy that Native Americans faced in the post-contact era. The authors stress the fact that the Indians were not merely part of the landscape, passive objects to be conquered and civilized along with the "wilderness." Instead, the Indians followed different strategies of adaptation, negotiation, cultural exchange, and warfare in order to preserve as much of their way of life as possible. In doing so, they affected the course of European settlement and politics in countless ways.

Indians, Europeans, and the Environment

Richard White and William Cronon are among the historians who are currently revising our understanding of the relationship among the Indians, the colonists, and the environment that both groups shared. In the following dialogue, they note that Indians and Europeans had distinct ways of extracting resources from the landscape and explore the consequences of the introduction of European technology and settlers in America. They also analyze areas of cultural interaction and exchange, stressing that influence and cultural adaptation went both ways. Excerpted from "Indians in the Land: A Conversation between William Cronon and Richard White," American Heritage 37 (August/September 1986):20–24.

William Cronon If historians thought about the environment at all up until a few years ago, they thought of it in terms of an older school of American historians who are often called "environmental determinists." People like Frederick Jackson Turner argued that Europeans came to North America, settled on the frontier, and began to be changed by the environment.

Richard White In a delayed reaction to Turner, historians in the late 1960s and early 1970s reversed this. They began to emphasize a series of horror stories when they wrote about the environment. The standard metaphor of the time was "the rape of the earth," but what they were really describing was the way Americans moving west cut down the forests, ploughed the land, destroyed the grasslands, harnessed the rivers—how they in effect transformed the whole appearance of the North American landscape.

WC Since then, I think, we've realized that both positions are true, but incomplete. The real problem is that human beings reshape the earth as they live upon it, but as they reshape it, the new form of the earth has an influence on the way those people can live. . . .

RW . . . I remember reading a Sierra Club book which claimed that Indians had moved over the face of the land and when they left you couldn't tell they'd ever been there. Actually, this idea demeans Indians. It makes them seem simply like an animal species, and thus deprives them of culture. It also demeans the environment by so simplifying it that all changes come to seem negative—as if somehow the ideal is never to have been here at all. It's a crude view of the environment, and it's a crude view of Indians.

WC Fundamentally, it's an ahistorical view. It says not only that the land never changed—"wilderness" was always in this condition—but that the people who lived upon it had no history, and existed outside of time. They were "natural."

RW That word *natural* is the key. Many of these concepts of Indians are quite old, and they all picture Indians as people without culture. Depending on your view of human nature, there are two versions. If human beings are inherently evil in a Calvinistic sense, then you see Indians as inherently violent and cruel.

They're identified with nature, but it's the nature of the howling wilderness, which is full of Indians. But if you believe in a beneficent nature, and a basically good human nature, then you see Indians as noble savages, people at one with their environment.

WC To understand how Indians really did view and use their environment, we have to move beyond these notions of "noble savages" and "Indians as the original ecologists." We have to look instead at how they actually lived. . . . There's . . . the Indians' use of "wild" animals—animals that were not domesticated, not owned in ways Europeans recognized. Virtually all North American Indians were intimately linked to the animals around them, but they had no cattle or pigs or horses.

RW . . . I'm currently writing about the Indians of the Great Lakes region. Most of them thought of animals as a species of *persons*. Until you grasp that fact, you can't really understand the way they treated animals. This is easy to romanticize—it's easy to turn it into a "my brother the buffalo" sort of thing. But it wasn't. The Indians *killed* animals. . . . [W]hen they overhunted, they did so within the context of a moral universe that both they and the animals inhabited. They conceived of animals as having, not rights—that's the wrong word—but *powers*. To kill an animal was to be involved in a social relationship with the animal. . . .

WC There's a kind of debt implied by killing animals.

RW Yes. You incur an obligation. And even more than the obligation is your sense that those animals have somehow surrendered themselves to you.

WC There's a gift relationship implied . . .

RW . . . which is also a *social* relationship. . . . Another thing that made Indians different from modern Euro-Americans was their commitment to producing for *security* rather than for maximum yield. Indians didn't try to maximize the production of any single commodity. Most tried to attain security by diversifying their diet, by following the seasonal cycles: they ate what was most abundant. What always confused Europeans was why Indians didn't simply concentrate on the most productive part of the cycle: agriculture, say. They could have grown more crops and neglected something else. But once you've done that, you lose a certain amount of security.

WC I like to think of Indian communities having a whole series of ecological nets under them. When one net failed, there was always another underneath it. If the corn died, they could always hunt deer or gather wild roots. In hard times—during an extended drought, for instance—those nets became crucial.

All of this was linked to seasonal cycles. For me, one of the best ways of understanding the great diversity of environmental practices among Indian peoples is to think about the different ways they moved across the seasons of the year. Because the seasons of North America differ markedly between, say, the Eastern forests and the Great Plains and the Southwestern deserts, Indian groups devised quite different ways of life to match different natural cycles.

New England is the region I know best. For Indians there, spring started with hunting groups drawing together to plant their crops after having been relatively dispersed for the winter. While women planted beans, squash, and corn, men hunted the migrating fish and birds. They dispersed for summer hunting and gathering while the crops matured, and then reassembled in the fall. The corn was harvested and great celebrations took place. Then, once the harvest was done and the corn stored in the ground, people broke up their villages and fanned out in small bands for the fall hunt, when deer and other animals were at their fattest. The hunt went on until winter faded and the season of agriculture began again. What they had was agriculture during one part of the year, gathering going on continuously, and hunting concentrated in special seasons. That was typical not just of the Indians of New England but of eastern Indians in general. . . .

Environmental historians have not only been reconstructing the ways Indians used and thought about the land, they've also been analyzing how those things changed when the Europeans invaded. A key discovery of the last couple of decades had been our radically changed sense of how important European disease was in changing Indian lives.

RW It was appalling. Two worlds that had been largely isolated suddenly came into contact. The Europeans brought with them diseases the Indians had never experienced. The resulting death rates are almost impossible to imagine: 90 to 95 percent in some places.

Contrary to popular images of Indians as hunters, agriculture was an important part of Native American society. (Courtesy of the Granger Collection.)

WC The ancestors of the Indians came to North America from ten to forty thousand years ago. They traveled through an Arctic environment in which many of the diseases common to temperate and tropical climates simply couldn't survive. They came in groups that were biologically too small to sustain those diseases. And they came without the domesticated animals with which we share several of our important illnesses. Those three circumstances meant that Indians shed many of the most common diseases of Europe and Asia. Measles, chicken pox, smallpox, and many of the venereal diseases vanished during migration. For over twenty thousand years, Indians lived without encountering these illnesses, and so lost the antibodies that would ordinarily have protected them.

RW Most historians would now agree that when the Europeans arrived, the Indian population of North America was between ten and twelve million (the old estimate was about one million). By the early twentieth century it had fallen to less than five hundred thousand. At the same time, Indian populations were also under stress from warfare. Their seasonal cycles were being broken up, and they were inadequately nourished as a result. All these things contributed to the tremendous mortality they suffered.

WC Part of the problem was biological; part of it was cultural. If a disease arrived in mid-summer, it had quite different effects from one that arrived in the middle of the winter, when people's nutrition levels were low and they were more susceptible to disease. A disease that arrived in spring, when crops had to be planted, could disrupt the food supply for the entire year. Nutrition levels would be down for the whole subsequent year, and new diseases would find readier victims as a result.

RW The effects extended well beyond the original epidemic— a whole series of changes occurred. If Indian peoples in fact shaped the North American landscape, this enormous drop in their population changed the way the land looked. For example, as the Indians of the Southeast died in what had once been a densely populated region with a lot of farmland, cleared areas reverted to grassy woodland. Deer and other animal populations increased in response. When whites arrived, they saw the abundance of animals as somehow natural, but it was nothing of the sort.

Disease also dramatically altered relationships among Indian peoples. . . . Those peoples living in large, populous farming villages were precisely those who suffered the greatest death rates. So the group that had once controlled the region went into decline, while another fairly marginal group rose to historical prominence.

WC That's a perfect example of biological and cultural interaction, of how complex it is. A dense population is more susceptible to disease than a less dense one: that's a biological observation true of any animal species. But which Indian communities are dense and which are not, which ones are living in clustered settlements and which ones are scattered thinly . . .—these aren't biological phenomena but *cultural* ones. . . .

. . . But there's a deeper theme underlying these things. All North American Indian peoples eventually found themselves in a relationship of dependency with the dominant Euro-American culture. At some point, in various ways, they ceased to be entirely autonomous peoples, controlling their own resources and their own political and cultural life. . . .

RW . . . Many Indians were never militarily conquered. They nonetheless became dependent on whites, partly because their subsistence economy was systematically undercut. Virtually every American Indian community eventually had to face the fact that it could no longer feed or shelter itself without outside aid. A key aspect of this was the arrival of a market economy in which certain resources came to be overexploited. The fur trade is the clearest example of this.

WC No question. The traditional picture of the fur trade is that Europeans arrive, wave a few guns and kettles and blankets in the air, and Indians come rushing forward to trade. What do they have to trade? They have beaver pelts, deerskins, bison robes. As soon as the incentive is present, as soon as those European goods are there to be had, the Indians sweep across the continent, wipe out the furbearing animals, and destroy their own subsistence. That's the classic myth of the fur trade.

RW It simply didn't happen that way. European goods often penetrated Indian communities slowly; Indian technologies held on for a long time. Indians wanted European goods, but for reasons that could be very different from why *we* think they wanted them.

WC One of my favorite examples is the kettle trade. Indians wanted kettles partly because you can put them on a fire and boil water and they won't break. That's nice. But many of those kettles didn't stay kettles for long. They got cut up and turned into arrowheads that were then used in the hunt. Or they got turned into high-status jewelry. Indians valued kettles because they were such an extraordinarily flexible resource.

RW The numbers of kettles that have turned up in Indian graves proves that their value was not simply utilitarian.

WC The basic facts of the fur trade are uncontestable. Europeans sought to acquire Indian furs, food, and land; Indians sought to acquire European textiles, alcohol, guns, and other metal goods. Indians began to hunt greater numbers of furbearing animals, until finally several species, especially the beaver, were eliminated. Those are the two end points of the fur-trade story. But understanding how to get from one to the other is very complicated. Why did Indians engage in the fur trade in the first place? That's the question.

RW We tend to assume that exchange is straightforward, that it's simply giving one thing in return for another. That is not how it appeared to Indian peoples. . . .

WC . . . [W]hen the Indian handed a beaver skin to the trader, who gave a gun in return, it wasn't simply two goods that were moving back and forth. There were *symbols* passing between them as well. The trader might not have been aware of all those symbols, but for the Indian the exchange represented a statement about their friendship. The Indian might expect to rely on the trader for military support, and to support him in return. Even promises about marriage, about linking two communities together, might be expressed as goods passed from hand to hand. It was almost as if a language was being spoken when goods were exchanged. It took a long time for the two sides to realize they weren't speaking the same language.

RW Right. But for Indians the basic meanings of exchange were clear. You gave generously to friends; you stole from enemies. Indians also recognized that not everybody could be classified simply as a friend or an enemy, and this middle ground is where trade took place.

But even in that middle ground, trade always began with an exchange of gifts. And to fail to be generous in your gifts, to push too hard on the price—Indians read that as hostility. When Europeans tried to explain the concept of a "market" to Indians, it bewildered them. The notion that demand for furs in London could affect how many blankets they would receive for a beaver skin in Canada was quite alien to them. How on earth could events taking place an ocean away have anything to do with the relationship between two people standing right here who were supposed to act as friends and brothers toward each other?

WC So one thing Indian peoples had trouble comprehending at certain stages in this dialogue was the concept of *price:* the price of a good fluctuating because of its abundance in the market. Indian notions were much closer to the medieval "just price." This much gunpowder is always worth this many beaver skins. If somebody tells me they want twice as many skins for the same gunpowder I bought last year at half the price, suddenly they're being treacherous. They're beginning to act as an enemy.

RW . . . Of course, exchange became more commercial with time. Early in the fur trade, Indians had received European goods as gifts, because they were allies against other Indians or other Europeans. But increasingly they found that the only way to receive those goods was through direct economic exchange. Gift giving became less important, and trading goods for set prices became more important. As part of these commercial dealings, traders often advanced loans to Indians before they actually had furs to trade. By that mechanism, gifts were transformed into debts. Debts could in turn be used to coerce greater and greater hunting from Indians.

WC As exchange became more commercial, the Indians' relationship to animals became more commercial as well. Hunting increased with the rise in trade, and animal populations declined in response. First the beaver, then the deer, then the bison disappeared from large stretches of North America. As that happened, Indians found themselves in the peculiar position of relying more and more on European goods but no longer having the furs they needed to acquire them. Worse, they could no longer even *make* those same goods as they once had, in the form of skin garments, wild meat, and so on. That's the trap they fell into.

RW And that becomes dependency.

Military and Diplomatic Strategies for Survival

In this selection, historian Gary Nash focuses on the Iroquois Confederation, an alliance that eventually included six tribes and controlled territory from northern New England to the Great Lakes region. Nash explores the ways in which the Iroquois maintained and even expanded their power in a century of contact with the French and English empires in America. He also assesses why the Iroquois' strategy became less effective after 1763. The following excerpt is from Gary B. Nash, Red, White, and Black: The Peoples of Early North America (Englewood Cliffs, New Jersey, 1992), 226–28, 231–33, 252–53, 257–58, 261–69.

Between 1675 and 1763 three European powers—France, Spain, and England—employed diplomacy and war in an ongoing struggle for trade and territory in the vast area between the Mississippi River and the Atlantic Ocean and in the waters of the Caribbean. Both the trade and the territory they coveted in North America required them to be in close and continual touch with the powerful tribes of interior North America. Our history books have largely forgotten what was patently obvious throughout this period—that much of the time and energy of the European governments, whether in New Spain, New France, New England, . . . was spent negotiating, trading, and fighting with and against Indians of various cultures, and filing reports, requests, and complaints to the home governments concerning the state of Indian affairs. . . .

In this three-cornered fight for a continent, it has often been imagined that Indians were merely the objects of European power, manipulated like pawns on a continental chessboard before finally being swept from the board altogether. This view is part of the myth of the overwhelming cultural superiority and military force of the European colonizers and the Indians' acquiescence when confronted with it. But the power of the Europeans has been greatly exaggerated and that of native societies greatly underestimated. It is more accurate to say that Indian societies of the interior were not only reciprocally involved in the complicated maneuvers between contending European powers but played a dynamic role in the unfolding of events. They could not turn back the clock or drive the Europeans back into the sea. But the interior tribes were far stronger than the less populous and weaker coastal tribes that had succumbed to the invaders in the seventeenth century. They were therefore able to interact with the Europeans in a much different way. Throughout the eighteenth century Indians helped to shape their own history. Pitted against each other and sometimes divided among themselves, the European powers had too few resources to overpower the inland tribes and had to rely on Indian allies to maintain themselves even in the limited areas they occupied. Understanding the Europeans' weaknesses gave Indian nations an opportunity to exercise initiative and to gain much in exchange for their support. That they were eventually the losers does not obscure the fact that the interaction was truly a two-way process. Europeans used Indians to enhance their own power, and Indians used Europeans in precisely the same way.

Iroquois Diplomacy

Only by also looking at European imperial rivalry from the Indian point of view can we understand the real nature of intercultural contact in North America. For example, while European governors and colonial bureaucrats were putting millions of words on paper, moving armies and navies across an ocean, and engaging thousands of people in the manufacture and shipment of Indian trade goods, all as a part of empire-building, the preliterate woodlands Iroquois, never numbering more than 2,500 warriors and 12,000 people, were adroitly pursuing their own self-interest and shaping events in North America. The French historian La Potherie wrote in 1722: "It is a strange thing that three or four thousand souls can make tremble a whole new world. New England is very fortunate in being able to stay in their good graces. New France is often desolated by their wars, and they are feared through a space of more than fifteen hundred leagues of the country of our allies." A generation later an Indian "expert" in New York warned the governor that "on whose ever side the [Iroquois] Indians fall, they will cast the balance."

The strategy of France, in the period after Louis XIV took the throne in 1661, was to establish an inland empire in North America that would surround the English and keep them pinned to the coast. . . . The dreams of continental hegemony that obsessed Louis XIV involved all the major European powers in a series of global wars that occupied most of his half-century reign. . . .

By the end of the seventeenth century, after years of exhausting warfare, it had become apparent to all parties involved that though the English vastly outnumbered the French, they could not defeat the Canadians because of disunity among the colonies and the unwillingness of the government at home to supply military forces. Nor could the French either destroy or forge an alliance with the Iroquois because they lacked sufficient military strength for the former and suffered a competitive disadvantage in the fur trade that prohibited the latter. The Iroquois retained the strategic geographical position in the northern part of the continent. But in spite of their successes and the expansion of their influence over tribes to the south and west of them, they paid dearly in maintaining a pivotal role in the fur trade. By the end of the seventeenth century, hard hit by French attacks, war weary, and suffering disastrous population losses, they sought a formula for maintaining their security while withdrawing from the attritional warfare that had weakened them so seriously.

The solution to their problem was sudden and bold. In the summer of 1701 the Iroquois entered negotiations with both the English and

Guerrier Iroquois.

This French depiction of an Iroquois brave represents the contemporary popular view of Native American brutality. The Iroquois, however, were shrewd diplomats and businessmen, as well as effective warriors. (Courtesy of the Library of Congress.)

the French, signing treaties almost simultaneously at Montreal and Albany. To the French they promised neutrality in any future war between England and France—a great gain for the French who had often been stung by the Iroquois military forays. To the English, who now lost a military ally, the Iroquois ceded their western hunting lands, conquered a half century before from the Hurons. By this clever piece of diplomacy, the Iroquois implied that their primary allegiance was still to the English. But it was only a symbolic land cession, for the English had no ability to occupy or control this territory; in fact the lands in question had recently been reconquered by the French and their allies, the Wyandots. To complete their compromise negotiations the Iroquois made peace with the tribes to the west of them.

For almost half a century after the 1701 treaties the Iroquois policy of playing one European power against another worked well. The Five Nations (which became the Six Nations after the addition of the Tuscaroras) disengaged from the costly beaver wars, pursued their role as fur suppliers and increased their population by absorbing remnants of coastal tribes decimated by Europeans and elements of western tribes which they had themselves conquered. Since the early seventeenth century, when they began struggling to assert themselves against other tribes of the Great Lakes region, the Iroquois had become the dominant power in the Northeast and a force to be reckoned with by both the French and the English. Though hardly more numerous than the inhabitants of the province of New York at the beginning of the eighteenth century, their will to fight, their diplomatic skill, and their strategic position athwart the fur trading routes had raised them to a position of utmost importance. The governor of Quebec respectfully took note of this when he wrote home in 1711 that war with the Iroquois was to be avoided at all costs, for "the five Iroquois villages [nations] are more to be feared than the English colonies." A decade later, after several Iroquois chiefs had visited Boston, a New Englander wrote that "they are Courted and Caressed like the potentates of the Earth." . . .

Population Increase

. . . [A] tremendous population buildup, especially in the English colonies, created a shortage of land on the coastal plain and by the 1750s was propelling thousands of land-hungry settlers toward the mountain gaps in the Appalachians in search of new territory. . . .

With capital provided by London investors, Virginia tobacco planters, and Northern merchants, land companies were formed in the 1740s and 1750s to capitalize on this demographic explosion. The Ohio Land Company, organized in 1747, laid claim to half a million acres in the Ohio Valley. The Susquehanna Land Company, organized five years later, declared rights to hundreds of thousands of acres in Pennsylvania. . . . Inexorably, the agents of English society exerted pressure on Indian leaders to cede and sell their lands in order to pave the way for new white settlements.

The farther west settlement moved, the closer it came to the western trading empire of the French and the Indian nations allied to them.

The Seven Years War

On the opposite side of the Atlantic the revival of international rivalries hastened this showdown west of the Appalachian Mountains. In 1748 France and England had composed the differences that had led them to war in 1744, but even as the ink was drying on the articles of conciliation, the way was being prepared for a renewal of hostilities. . . . [F]ighting began in the North American wilderness. By the time it was over, in the early 1760s, France would have surrendered her North Atlantic claims and thus the precious system of balancing off European powers, the key to Indian autonomy would be shattered. . . .

Indian Strategy in the Seven Years War

. . . Throughout the war the Six Nations were able to assess accurately the shifting military balance between the rival European powers and formulate their own policy accordingly. Though they wrote no field memoranda and moved no troops or supplies through the field, their communication network extended across the entire region in which the French and English were fighting. In their councils they demonstrated a keen understanding of when the strategic balance was tipping in the British direction. Most histories of the Seven Years War applaud William Johnson's skill in "winning over" the Iroquois and "persuading" them to join the English side. But the evidence indicates that the Iroquois continually reassessed their own position and calculated how their self-interest could best be served. Despite English blandishments, presents, and even the return of previously acquired territory, the Iroquois refused to join the English through the first four years of war or even to allow Anglo-American passage through their territory. But when the military superiority of the English began to show itself in 1759, the Iroquois quickly adjusted their policy of neutrality and joined in reaping the benefits of victory. If their policy of *realpolitik* failed at all, it was in not perceiving that the maintenance of French power in North America was essential to their long-range interests. . . .

For the Indian nations which had demonstrated such independence of action and impressive power during the Seven Years War, the Peace of Paris was a severe blow. Unlike the coastal tribes, whose numbers and autonomy had ebbed through contact with European colonizers, the interior tribes had grown stronger, more militarily awesome, and more technologically developed as a result of their political and economic connections with the English, French, and Spanish. Although they had become dependent on the European trade, they had been able to turn this dependency to their own advantage so long as more than one source of trade goods existed. They had mastered the European style of diplomatic intrigue, used it to serve their own self-interests, and proved their ability to evade or defeat numerically superior European forces.

. . . Control of the Atlantic by the British navy dealt a near-fatal blow to the playoff system, for the French in North America without trade goods were hardly better than no French at all. The inability to obtain French trade goods diminished Native Americans' room for maneuver and rendered futile the nascent pan-Indian movements against the English which potentially extended from Seneca country on the shores of the eastern Great Lakes to Yamasee territory in Florida and included the Miamis, Shawnees, Delawares, Cherokees, Catawbas, Creeks, Choctaws, and Chickasaws, to name only the larger tribes. A mere fraction of these peoples had driven back the Anglo-American frontier to within one hundred miles of the coast in the early stages of the Seven Years War. Had they been unified under French arms and supplies, the designs of the French imperialists to rule the continent might have materialized.

By the terms of the Peace of Paris, signed by England, France, and Spain in 1763, Canada and all of North America east of the Mississippi River was recognized as English territory. France ceded the territory west of the Mississippi to Spain. Spain ceded Florida to England. From that year onward English sway in the eastern half of North America was unchallenged in the courts of Europe. No longer could the Creeks, Cherokees, or Iroquois employ the playoff system to gain advantages in trade, since only one source of trade goods remained. Also, hostilities subsided between the colonies, which Indian groups had often exploited, for the wartime effort had unified the thirteen English provinces to an unprecedented degree. . . .

Indian-White Relations after 1763

At the conclusion of seven years of international war the English government attempted to coordinate a continental Indian policy in North America where for a century and a half each colony had been left to conduct its own Indian affairs. Stung by the fact that most of the North American tribes had given their allegiance to the French in the Seven Years War, the English government launched a new policy intended to separate Native Americans and colonizers, while guaranteeing the integrity of Indian territory. . . .

By the terms of the Proclamation of 1763, British policy makers created a racial boundary from Maine to Georgia, roughly following the crestline of the Appalachian Mountains. The various colonial governors were charged with forbidding "for the present and until our further Pleasure be known" any surveys or land grants beyond the Appalachian water shed. "All the Lands and Territories lying to the Westward of the Sources of the Rivers which fall into the Sea from the West and North West" were specifically reserved for Indian nations. All white settlers already beyond the Appalachian divide were charged to withdraw east of the line. . . .

. . . Both before and after the Proclamation Line of 1763 had been set, land poachers were staking out claims to lands to which the English, by the terms of their own treaties with Indian tribes, had no claim. . . . [None] of these treaties stopped white land speculators and settlers, who swarmed into Indian territory, secure in the knowledge that their provincial governments had neither the desire nor the power to do much about it. . . .

. . . In June 1761 the Senecas, always the most pro-French of the Six Nations, carried a red wampum belt (signifying an intention to go to war) to Detroit where the British army was garrisoned among the various tribes that had formally fought with the French—the Delawares, Shawnees, Ottawas, Hurons, Chippewas, and Potawatomies. The Senecas were taking the lead in resisting the new English Indian policy, which curtailed trade, increased British garrisons, required the Indians to bring their furs to the British forts, ended the system of annual "presents" that Indian leaders regarded as a kind of rent for land occupied by British forts, prohibited trade in rum, and in general instituted trading terms far less satisfactory to the Indians than those existing before the war. The Senecas had an additional incentive for taking to the warpath. General Amherst, the commander-in-chief of the Anglo-American forces during the Seven Years War, had seen fit to reward some of his officers with Seneca lands near Niagara in violation of a treaty between the Iroquois and the New York government. . . .

The Senecas proposed a coordinated attack by the northern tribes on all the English outposts that ranged along the Great Lakes and as far south as Pittsburgh. Acting together, the tribes would drive the English out of the Ohio Valley, out of Iroquois country, and back across the mountains to the Piedmont. . . .

Adding to the inflammatory state of affairs were the preachings of Neolin, a charismatic Delaware prophet. Just when the English were cutting off trade goods to which the Indians had become accustomed and threatening their land base, Neolin began a journey through the Delaware territories, preaching that Native Americans must return to "their original state that they were in before the white people found out their country" or face slow extinction at the hands of the settlers swarming across the mountains. Several traders described the renaissance of traditional Indian culture that the Delaware prophet preached. Neolin's vision, which he related had been conveyed to him in dreams by the Master of Life, was that the Indians' salvation lay not in adopting Christianity and European culture but in returning to ancient customs. . . .

. . . Neolin's appeal for the de-Europeanization of Delaware culture demonstrated how independently and creatively the western tribes could respond to the new situation that confronted them after the defeat of the French. His disciples carried his message throughout the western territories; large numbers of Indians, acting on his advice to boycott European trade goods, hunted only to supply their own needs. Most spectacularly, an Ottawa leader named Pontiac became a convert to Neolin's doctrine and made it the spiritual underpinning of the uprising he led against the English beginning in May 1763.

. . . But the tribes lacked vital supplies of powder, shot, and guns; in the end they were forced to sue for peace. Without the presence in North America of another European power they could not overcome their supply problems.

Though Pontiac's resistance movement collapsed, the major

interior tribes continued to preserve their political autonomy in the decade prior to the outbreak of the American Revolution. . . . But the preservation of political independence could not stem the tide of frontier land speculators and farmers. By itself this demographic pressure was enough to overcome all the efforts of the English government to fashion an Indian policy based on fair trade relations and respect for land boundaries.

. . . The main points of English Indian policy—prevention of encroachment on Indian lands and equity in the Indian trade—were reduced to a shambles in the decade before the Revolution. . . . For the interior tribes, the beneficiaries of an unenforceable English policy designed to guarantee them the land between the Appalachians and the Mississippi, the alternatives were limited after Pontiac's Revolt. They could seek other Indian allies in another attempt to forge a pan-Indian uprising, as did one faction of the Creeks led by The Mortar, who had been staunchly anti-English for decades. They could seek private revenge for white depredations and land grabbing, as did Logan, a displaced Cayuga living on the Virginia frontier, whose family had been wiped out by outlaw frontiersmen and who led a party of warriors in retaliatory raids that set off the brief but bloody Lord Dunmore's War in 1774. They could continue to seek French support in New Orleans while hoping for a renewed French presence on the continent, as did the Choctaws. Or they could bow to the white tidal wave and sell off their land, tract by tract at the best price possible, to private individuals and land companies who knew they could safely ignore both the Proclamation of 1763 and colonial statues forbidding such purchases.

Questions

1. *Compare and contrast Native American and Euro-American attitudes toward the environment. How did they differ? Were there any similarities?*
2. *What did the colonizers offer tribes like the Iroquois? How might the experience of smaller tribes have differed from that of the Iroquois?*
3. *Did contact with Europeans and their technology radically change the Indians' way of life? What was the purpose of trade for the Indians? For the Europeans?*
4. *What role did the Indians play in the French and English contests for control in North America? What factors eroded the Indians' bargaining position?*

CULTURAL EXCHANGES AND CULTURAL CLASHES

The following documents offer insight into the Indians' economic, military, and cultural relations with Europeans. These sources present several methodological problems, however; because the Indians had no indigenous written language, all the speeches, letters, petitions, and legal documents included here were written or transcribed by whites. Rather than the Indians' direct words and thoughts, the written record consists of second- and third-hand accounts of what the Indians said and did, often written long after the fact. Such sources are useful, but we must read them critically and be aware of the writers' biases, interests, and errors. Those who sympathized with the Indians sometimes glorified native oratory, while hostile government officials portrayed Indians more negatively.

First Encounters

In this selection taken from his history of the "Lost Colony" of Roanoke, Captain John Smith—promoter, soldier of fortune, and key figure in the colonization of Virginia—recounts the Algonquin Indians' response to the outbreak of disease following the English landing in North Carolina in 1585. From John Smith, "The Generall Historie of Virginia, the Somer Iles, and New England . . ." in The Complete Works of Captain John Smith *(1580–1631), ed. Philip L. Barbour, (Chapel Hill, 1986), 2:80–81.*

In addition to disease, warfare with Europeans took its toll on Native American populations, as this illustration of Captain John Smith and Opechancanough, the brother of Chief Powhatan, suggests. (Courtesy of the Library of Congress.)

One other strange Accident . . . will I mention before I end, which mooved the whole Country that either knew or heard of us, to have us in wonderfull admiration.

There was no Towne where they had practised any villany against us . . . but within a few dayes after our departure, they began to dye; in some Townes twenty, in some forty, in some sixty, and in one an hundred and twenty, which was very many in respect of their numbers. And this hapned in no place (we could learn) but where we had bin. . . . And this disease was so strange, they neither knew what it was, nor how to cure it; nor had they knowne the like time out of minde. . . . [T]hey were perswaded it was the worke of God through our meanes: and that we by him might kill and slay whom we would, without weapons, and not come neare them. . . .

This marveilous Accident in all the Country wrought so strange opinions of us, that they could not tell whether to thinke us gods or men. And the rather that all the space of their sicknesse, there was no man of ours knowne to die, or much sicke. They noted also we had no women, nor cared for any of theirs: some therefore thought we were not borne of women, and therefore not mortall. . . . Some would Prophesie there were more of our generation yet to come, to kill theirs and take their places.

Interdependence and Exchange in Colonial Louisiana

When the French began to settle the Lower Mississippi region in the late seventeenth century, they quickly sought to ally themselves with the twenty thousand member Choctaw Nation. France's settlements at New Orleans and Biloxi, which never contained more than five thousand white and four thousand black inhabitants, relied on the Choctaws for food, deerskins, and military aid against the English. This anonymous French account from the early 1700s details how the Indians sought trade contacts with the Europeans, but set the terms of exchange, demanded "presents" in the form of yearly tribute, and forced the French to use Indian ceremonies. Excerpted from John R. Swanton, "An Early Account of the Choctaw Indians," in Memoirs of the American Anthropological Association (Lancaster, Pennsylvania, 1918), 5:54–55.

The Chaquetas [Choctaws] are a hundred leagues north of Mobile. There are about four thousand bearing arms. . . . This nation is warlike against similar people. . . . The French always having needed to depend upon them in war, it has made them so insolent that they despise the French and would receive the English among them. They are much accustomed to receiving presents from the French. . . . They think that it is a right, that the French pay them for the lands which they occupy. It is this which they try to make them understand in the speeches which they make to the commandants of the posts where they go, saying:

> Formerly our ancestors occupied the place where you
> now live and came there to hunt; they have ceded it to you

as to people who wished to be their friends, in consideration for which you have promised them a certain quantity of goods, and length of time has not cancelled the continuance of the gift, and of the friendship, which, having reigned between our ancestors and the French, reigns still between you and us. You know that every time you have asked us to take vengeance on your enemies who have insulted you, we have had pity, since, being few in numbers, you were unable to go to war, and that we, regarding you as our brothers, have left our wives, children, houses, villages, harvests, and periods of hunting to attack your enemies and stain our arms with their blood; that we have often lost our people there. You know that many times on returning from war we have taken credit for the goods that you have promised us, gained at the price of our blood, because they had not yet arrived by vessel from France. You know that the English are always at our doors importuning us to make an alliance with them, and sell them our deerskins at fairer prices than you offer. We have hopes then that in consideration of all these things you will look with pity on us and will share with us as your brothers in order that we may return to our village loaded with the presents you shall have given us.

The Narragansetts Challenge Massachusetts Bay's Authority

In the 1640s, the English colony of Massachusetts Bay moved aggressively to incorporate new lands and to extend its jurisdiction over nearby Indians. The Narragansetts of Rhode Island, who earlier had fought alongside English colonists in a common war against the Pequot tribe, began to fear their former allies. When their leader, Miantonomo, was captured and executed by Mohegin Indians at Massachusetts's instigation, the Narragansetts fought back in a way that demonstrated a sophisticated grasp of English imperial politics. They submitted directly to English royal authority in 1644, which gave them equal status with the Bay Colony, and announced their intention to seek mediation in London, not Boston, in the future. The following document is taken from "The Act

*and Deed of the Voluntary and Free Submission of the Chiefe Sachem . . .
of the Nanhigansets . . . ," in* Records of the Colony of Rhode Island . . . , *ed.
John Russell Bartlett, (Providence, Rhode Island, 1856), 1:134–37.*

KNOW ALL MEN, Colonies, Peoples, and Nations, unto whom
the fame hereof shall come; that wee, the chiefe Sachems, Princes
or Governours of the Nanhigansets (in that part of America, now
called New-England), together with the joynt and unanimous
consent of all our people and subjects, inhabitants thereof, do
upon serious consideration, . . . submit, subject, and give over
ourselves, peoples, lands, rights, inheritances, and possessions
whatsoever, in ourselves and our heires successively for ever,
unto the protection, care and government of that worthy and
royal Prince, Charles, King of Great Britaine and Ireland, his
heires and successors forever, to be ruled and governed according
to the ancient and honorable lawes and customes, established in
that so renowned realme and kingdome of Old England; . . . *upon
condition of His Majesties' royal protection,* and wrighting us of what
wrong is, or may be done unto us, according to his honorable
lawes and customes, exercised amongst his subjects, in their preservation and safety, and in the defeating and overthrow of his,
and their enemies; not that we find ourselves necessitated here-
unto, . . . with any of the natives in these parts, knowing ourselves
sufficient defence and able to judge in any matter or cause in that
respect; but have just cause of jealousy and suspicion of some of
His Majesty's pretended subjects. Therefore our desire is, to have
our matters and causes heard and tried according to his just and
equall lawes, in that way an order His Highness shall please to
appoint: *Nor can we yield over ourselves unto any, that are subjects
themselves in any case;* having ourselves been the chief Sachems, or
Princes successively, of the country, time out of mind. . . .

Here followeth a copy of a letter sent to the Massachusetts, by
the Sachems of the Narrangansetts, (shortly after their subjection
to the State and Government of Old England) they being sent unto
by the Massachusetts, to make their appearance at their General
Court, then approacing [approaching].

We understand your desire is, that we should come downe into
the Massachusetts, at the time of your Courte, now approaching.
Our occasions at this same time are very great; and the more because
of the loss . . . of our late deceased brother [Miantonomo]. . . . Our
brother was willing to stir much abroad to converse with men, and
we see a sad event at the last thereupon. Take it not ill, therefore,

though we resolve to keep at home, . . . and so, at this time, do not repair unto you, according to your request. . . . [We] have subjected ourselves, our lands and possessions, with all the rights and inheritances of us and our people, either by conquest, voluntary subjection or otherwise, unto that famous and honorable government of that Royal King, Charles, and that State of Old England, . . . hereby being subjects now (and that with joint and voluntary consent), unto the same King and State yourselves are. So that if any small things of difference should fall out betwixt us, only the sending of a messenger may bring it to right again; but if any great matter should fall (which we hope and desire will not . . .), then neither yourselves, nor we are to be judges; and both of us are to have recourse, and repair unto that honorable and just Government.

Covering the Dead

The native inhabitants of America waged wars against each other long before Europeans arrived. Sometimes they fought over resources and power, but sometimes the motive was revenge for earlier killings. The Creeks, Hurons, Iroquois, and Ohio Valley tribes called this "covering the dead"; those responsible had to compensate relatives of the victims with trade goods, or with their own lives. In this selection, Sir William Johnson, the chief British Indian agent in the northern colonies from 1754 until the revolution, offered to compensate the Seneca for casualties suffered in a clash with the British. Johnson was desperately trying to gain the Iroquois' support for war against the French. (The phrase "a belt" referred to the gifts of wampum belts that Johnson presented to them during his speech.) Taken from Documents Relative to the Colonial History of the State of New-York . . . , ed. E. B. O'Callaghan, M.D., (Albany, 1856), 7:54–55.

[At a meeting of the Six Nations and their allies, 18 February 1756]

Bretheren of the Caijougas and Tedirighroonas,

By constant experience we discover that the life of Man, is as the Flower of the Field, in this transitory scene therefore Resignation becomes us under the loss of our nearest and dearest friends, comfort yourselves therefore under the losses you have sustained as becomes reasonable creatures With this Belt I cover all your dead, that they may no more offend your sight

A Belt [hands over belt].

Bretheren of the Onondagas, Oneidas, Tuskaroras, Skaniadaradighroonas, Aughquageys, and the Mohawks of both Castles.

I perform the same ceremony to you

After this ceremony six French Prisoners some of those who were taken at the late Battle near Lake George were delivered with great ceremony to the Indians in order to replace the following Indians who were killed in that Battle. . . . [T]hey received the Prisoners with the greatest mark of Gratitude and Satisfaction, every nation giving the Shout of approbation, and then carried off the Prisoners to their respective familys

Thus ended the Ceremony necessary on those occasions agreeable to their Customs

[The Answer of the Six Nations and their Allies, 19 February 1756]

Brother Warraghiyagey [Johnson]

We the Sachims and Warriours of the Seneca Nation return you our sincere [and hearty] thanks for your great affection in drying our Tears, and driving Sorrow from our Hearts, and we in return perform the same ceremony to you, with the like Hearty Affection.

A String of Wampum [presents wampum]

Brother Warraghiyagey

We are sensible of your goodness expressed to us in removing the cause of our Grief, and tenderly taking the Axe out of our Heads

A Belt

Brother Warraghiyagey

We are thankful to you for cleansing the Blood out of our sight agreeable to the antient Custom of our Forefathers

A Belt

White Indians

As historian Daniel Richter notes, aside from covering the dead with goods, the Iroquois waged "mourning wars" in which they sought captives to replace relatives who had died. High mortality from war and disease in the late 1600s and early 1700s increased this practice. Sometimes the Iroquois tortured these Indian and white captives to death before ceremonially "adopting" them, but often they incorporated captured women and children into the tribe. Mary Jemison, an Irish immigrant living in Pennsylvania, was only fifteen in 1758 when a combined force of French troops and Shawnee Indians kidnapped her family. After scalping her parents and siblings, the Shawnee handed her over to a Seneca tribe living in Ohio; she lived with the Indians for the rest of her life. Jemison's account of her experiences appeared in James E. Seaver, A Narrative of the Life of Mrs. Mary Jemison . . . *(Canandaigua, New York, 1824), 34–39.*

I was now left alone in the fort, deprived of my former companions, and of every thing that was near or dear to me but life. But it was not long before I was in some measure relieved by the appearance of two pleasant looking squaws of the Seneca tribe, who came and examined me attentively for a short time, and then went out. After a few minutes absence they returned with my former masters, who gave me to them to dispose of as they pleased.

The Indians by whom I was taken were a party of Shawanees, if I remember right, that lived, when at home, a long distance down the Ohio. . . . At night we arrived at a small Seneca Indian town. . . . Having made fast to the shore, the Squaws left me in the canoe while they went to their wigwam or house in the town, and returned with a suit of Indian clothing, all new, and very clean and nice. My clothes, though whole and good when I was taken, were now torn in pieces, so that I was almost naked. They first undressed me and threw my rags into the river; then washed me clean and dressed me in the new suit they had just brought, in complete Indian style; and then led me home and seated me in the center of their wigwam.

I had been in that situation but a few minutes, before all the Squaws in the town came in to see me. I was soon surrounded by them, and they immediately set up a most dismal howling, crying bitterly, and wringing their hands in all the agonies of grief for a deceased relative.

Their tears flowed freely, and they exhibited all the signs of real mourning. At the commencement of this scene, one of their number began, in a voice somewhat between speaking and singing, to recite some words to the following purport, and continued the recitation till the ceremony was ended . . . :

> "Oh our brother! Alas! He is dead—he has gone; he will never return! Friendless he died on the field of the slain, where his bones are yet lying unburied! Oh, who will not mourn his sad fate? . . . Oh where is his spirit? His spirit went naked, and hungry it wanders, and thirsty and wounded it groans to return! . . . Though he fell on the field of the slain, with glory he fell, and his spirit went up to the land of his fathers in war! Then why do we mourn? With transports of joy they received him, and fed him, and clothed him, and welcomed him there! Oh friends, he is happy; then dry up your tears! His spirit has seen our distress, and sent us a helper whom with pleasure we greet. Dickewamis [Mary Jemison's Indian name] has come: then let us receive her with joy! She is handsome and pleasant! Oh! she is our sister, and gladly we welcome her here. In the place of our brother she stands in our tribe. With care we will guard her from trouble; and may she be happy till her spirit shall leave us."

In the course of that ceremony, from mourning they became serene—joy sparkled in their countenances, and they seemed to rejoice over me as over a long lost child. I was made welcome amongst them as a sister to the two Squaws. . . .

I afterwards learned that the ceremony I at that time passed through, was that of adoption. The two squaws had lost a brother in Washington's war, sometime in the year before, and in consequence of his death went up to Fort Pitt, on the day on which I arrived there, in order to receive a prisoner or an enemy's scalp, to supply their loss.

It is a custom of the Indians, when one of their number is slain or taken prisoner in battle, to give to the nearest relative to the dead or absent, a prisoner, if they have chanced to take one, and if not, to give him the scalp of an enemy. On the return of the Indians from conquest, which is always announced by peculiar shoutings, demonstrations of joy, and the exhibition of some trophy of victory, the mourners come forward and make their claims. If they receive a prisoner, it is at their option either to satiate their vengeance by taking his life in the most cruel manner they can conceive of; or, to receive and adopt him into the family, in the place of him whom they have lost. All the prisoners that are taken in battle and carried to the encampment or town by the Indians, are given to the bereaved families, till their number is made good. And unless the mourners have but just received the news of their bereavement, and are under the operation of paroxysm of grief, anger and revenge; or, unless the prisoner is very old, sickly, or homely, they generally save him, and treat him kindly. But if their mental wound is fresh, their loss so great that they deem it irreparable, or if their prisoner or prisoners do not meet their approbation, no torture, let it be ever so cruel, seems sufficient to make them satisfaction. . . .

It was my happy lot to be accepted for adoption; and at the time of the ceremony I was received by the two squaws, to supply the place of their brother in the family; and I was ever considered and treated by them as a real sister, the same as though I had been born of their mother.

Sources of Conflict

The Iroquois consistently frustrated both English and French attempts to win the unqualified support of the Indian confederation in their battles for control of North America. Both sides redoubled their efforts to woo the Iroquois after the outbreak of the Seven Years' War in 1754. Peter Wraxhall, the British secretary for Indian affairs, explained the difficulty of winning over the Iroquois in a 1756 report to the newly appointed Superintendent, Sir William Johnson. Wraxhall noted that the real obstacle to alliance was the Indians' fear that victory by either side would upset the balance of power and threaten the Iroquois' control of their lands. Excerpted from Documents Relative to the Colonial History of the State of New-York . . . , *ed. E. B. O'Callaghan, M.D., (Albany, 1856), 7:14, 17–18.*

To Major Generall William Johnson His Majestys sole superintendant of the affairs of the Northern Indians &c

Sir

In consequence of your Request and upon the plan I received from you, I herewith offer you Some Thoughts on the British Indian Interest &c.

. . . [One] cause by which our Interest & Influence amongst the Indians hath been greatly injured, their esteem for and confidence in us fatally weakened, hath been from the exorbitances and Impositions of our . . . Traders [from Albany]: This not only with the six Nations but with the Western or far Indians . . .

The ill consequences to our true Interest of this reproachful and impolitic conduct, are too obvious to require my expatiating on—

. . . [O]ne of the most fatal Causes of the decrease of our Indian Interest & influence, and which hath not only weakened their good opinion and affection towards us, but has made numbers of them our enemies, sown a gloomy discontent and suspicion of our Intentions amongst the whole confederacy hath been very near loosing us their Alliance, and will in all probability wholly do it, if proper measures are not fallen on to give them satisfaction & security. This Cause is relating to their Lands

An unaccountable thirst for large Tracts of Land without the design of cultivation, hath prevailed over the inhabitants of this and the neighbouring Provinces with a singular rage Patents have been lavishly granted (to give it no worse term) upon the pretence of fair Indian purchases, some of which the Indians have alleged were never made but forged—Others bought of Indians who were no Proprietors some by making two or three Indians Drunk and giving them a trivial consideration—They say also the Surveyors have frequently run Patents vastly beyond even the pretended conditions or limits of sale

There has certainly been a great deal of unrighteous conduct in these matters Many years ago the Indians requested of our Governors, & indeed have ernestly repeated it to almost every Governor, that no Patents might be granted, but for Land sold at their General and public meetings—this hath been as often promised . . .

The vast Grant of Land to the Ohio company is . . . one of the most material articles of discontent & Jealousy to the confederate Nations and their allies, aggravated by many other Patents granted by the Governors of Virginia and Maryland

There is reason to beleive the last Pensilvania Purchase, tho' agreed to at a publick meeting, is a matter of no small Grievance to many of the six Nations, and so disgusting to the Delaware & Shawanese Indians, as hath probably occasioned those Indians now ravageing our back Settlements

That memorable and important act by which the Indians put their Patrimonial and conquered Lands under the Protection of the King of Great Britain their Father against the incroachments or Invasions of the French is not understood by them as a cession or Surrender as it seems to have been ignorantly or willfully supposed by some, they intended and look upon it as reserving the Property and Possession of the Soil to themselves and their Heirs. This Property the Six Nations are by no means willing to part with and are equally averse and jealous that any Forts or Settlements should be made thereon either by us or the French

These are their hunting Grounds, by the profits of which they are to maintain themselves and their Families, they are therefore against any settlements there because the consequence would be the driving away Game & destroying their Livelyhood and Riches. . . .

Our Six Nations and their Allies at least the Polititians amongst them look upon the present disputes betw'n the English and French in this part of the world notwithstanding our plausible pretences of rescuing their Lands, and some such pretences the French plead on their side, as a point of selfish Ambition in us both and are apprehensive that which ever Nation gains their Point will become their Masters not their deliverers—They dread the success of either and their ablest Politicians would very probably rather wish us to continue destroying each other than that either should be absolute conquerors, could the various nations of Indians form a cenfederacy equal to the Attempt there is reason to suppose they would unite and drive us and the French to a greater distance from their Hunting Grounds. . . . But the Indians suspect we have different views; that to restore their Lands to their natural state and deliver 'em over to them as Proprietors of the soil are not the ends we aim at.

Petition of the Chickasaw Headmen

Europeans also excelled at the tactics of divide and conquer, and nowhere were these tactics more successful than in the Carolinas, where, Gary Nash contends, "a white population of only about 1,500 males . . . succeeded in employing the larger tribes to enslave and shatter nearly a dozen coastal tribes." The English traders' superior goods won the allegiance of the powerful Chickasaws, but the relationship proved costly for the Indians. Disease, warfare, and the trade in Indian slaves decimated allies and enemies of the English alike, while overhunting and the loss of lands eroded their economic base. Others found themselves ever deeper in debt to the trading posts. In the spring of 1754, the Chickasaws explained their plight to Governor Glen and asked for aid. Excerpted from Colonial Records of South Carolina, Documents Relating to Indian Affairs, May 21, 1750–August 7, 1754, ed. William L. McDowell, Jr. (Columbia, South Carolina, 1958), 512–13.

To His Excellency James Glen, Esq., Governor of South Carolina, and the Honourable Council from the Head Men and Warriours of the Chickesaw Nation.

We have heard your friendly Talk . . . which together with your kind Presents confirms in us the Oppinion we have long had of your Desire that we should live and injoy our Lands against all the Attempts of our Enemies. Though your Lands and ours is far distant from each other, and that of our Enemies, the French, but a little Way from us, yet we look on you not only as our best Friends, but as our Fathers haveing always found a Readyness in you to assist us whenever we made Application to you, and although we are Red People, we can and ever will make a true Distinction between the English and ever other Nation, and shall love and esteem them all our Days.

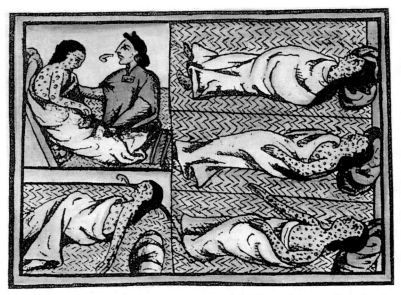

Diseases previously unknown in the New World, such as smallpox, had a catastrophic impact on Native American populations. (Courtesy of the Granger Collection.)

It's true some Years ago we did not mind how many our Enemies were, but that is not our case at Present, our Number being reduced to a Handful of Men, and thereby we are rendered uncapable of keeping our Ground without a Continuance of your friendly Assistance, we not being able to hunt nor are we free from the Hands of our Enemies even in our Towns, so that it is impossible for us to kill Dear to buy Cloathing for ourselves, our Wives, and Children, or even to purchase Amunition. This the English Traders that comes amongst us is too sencable off from the small Quantity of Skins they have carried out of this Nation these two last Years to what they used to do formerly. It's needless to trouble you with an Account of what People we have lost in a few Months. . . . Nothing but our present Necessity could oblige us at this Time to ask you for a further Suply of Guns and Ammunition, without which we must either stand and be shott, or defend the Enemies' Bullets with our Hatchets as we have nothing else at Present. Our Traders is tired out with trusting us with Ammunition and Guns, nor can we be angry with them as it has not been in our Power to pay them for it, and many other Things we had from them, so that we may now say our Lives is in your Power to save or to let the Enemy have their Desire off us. It has always been your Desire as well as our own that we should keep this Ground from the French which we have hitherto done, but now this is our very case; we must either run from it and save our Lives or die upon it, and either Ways give it up to them unless assisted by you. In former Times when we either went or sent to you we had Presents of all kinds of Cloths, Duffels, Red Coats, and a great many good Things, but now we do not desire any other then Guns and Amunition to preserve our Lives with. We still love our Lands and Liberties nor shall we chuse ever to give it up but with the Loss of our Lives.

A great many of our People has left us; a Thing we are sorry at, but young People will rather go from us to live in Peace than stay here where they are in Danger every Day. . . . If you think good to take Pity on us and send us some Ammunition and at the same Time four of your Guns that make a great Noise and will kill our Enemys at a great Distance we will either keep our Land or die along side of them Guns, and if we should be all killed the Guns would still remain on our Ground to shew the French how much the English loved us. All your old good Talks is still fresh with us, and so shall this your last Talk nor shall we ever throw them away.

Dreams of Rebellion

In 1763, the Seneca Indians abandoned neutrality and attacked English forts and settlements from Virginia to the Great Lakes. Their leader, Pontiac, was inspired by a prophet named Neolin, who claimed that the "Master of Life" had appeared to him in a dream and called on the Indians to unite in order to drive the whites out of America. Neolin's religion included elements of Christianity but emphasized the rejection of European goods and liquor and a return to the Indians' former independent life of hunting and agriculture. Pontiac's Rebellion failed, but Neolin's Dream was the first of many such "nativist" Indian movements that resurfaced in the nineteenth century. Excerpted from Anthony F. C.

Reprinted from *The Death and Rebirth of the Seneca*, by Anthony F. C. Wallace, with the assistance of Sheila C. Steen, 1970, pp. 117–118. Published by Alfred A. Knopf, New York, © 1969 by Anthony Wallace.

Wallace with the assistance of Sheila C. Steen, The Death and Rebirth of the Seneca (New York, 1970), 117–18.

I am the Master of Life, whom thou wishest to see, and to whom thou wishest to speak. Listen to that which I will tell thee for thyself and for all the Indians. I am the Maker of Heaven and earth, the trees, lakes, rivers, men, and all that thou seest or hast seen on the earth or in the heavens; and because I love you, you must do my will; you must also avoid that which I hate; I hate you to drink as you do, until you lose your reason; I wish you not to fight one another; you take two wives, or run after other people's wives; you do wrong; I hate such conduct; you should have but one wife, and keep her until death. When you go to war, . . . you sing the medicine song, thinking you speak to me; you deceive yourselves; it is to the Manito that you speak; he is a wicked spirit who induces you to evil, and, for want of knowing me, you listen to him.

The land on which you are, I have made for you, not for others: wherefore do you suffer the whites to dwell upon your lands? Can you not do without them? I know that those whom you call the children of your great Father supply your wants. But, were you not wicked as you are, you would not need them. Before those whom you call your brothers had arrived, did not your bow and arrow maintain you? You needed neither gun, powder, nor any other object. The flesh of animals was your food, their skins your raiment. But when I saw you inclined to evil, I removed the animals into the depths of the forests, that you might depend on your brothers for your necessaries, for your clothing. Again become good and do my will, and I will send animals for your sustenance. I do now, however, forbid suffering among you your Father's children; I love them, they know me, they pray to me; I supply their own wants, and give them that which they bring to you. Not so with those who are come to trouble your possessions. Drive them away; wage war against them. I love them not. They know me not. They are my enemies, they are your brothers' enemies. Send them back to the lands I have made for them. Let them remain there.

Here is a written prayer which I give thee; learn it by heart, and teach it to all the Indians and children. It must be repeated morning and evening. Do all that I have told thee, and announce it to all the Indians as coming from the Master of Life. Let them drink but one draught [of liquor], or two at most, in one day. Let them have but one wife, and discontinue running after other people's wives and daughters. Let them not fight one another. Let them not sing the medicine song, for in singing the medicine song they speak to the evil spirit. Drive from your lands those dogs in red clothing; they are only an injury to you. When you want anything, apply to me, as your brothers [i.e., the Christian whites] do, and I will give to both. Do not sell to your brothers that which I have placed on the earth as food. In short, become good, and you shall want nothing.

Questions

1. *How did the Indians react to the newcomers? What cultural differences divided Indians and Europeans in the century following contact? Who had the upper hand in relations between the two?*
2. *What strategies did the Indians use to preserve their power? Which were the most successful, and why? What did the Europeans and Indians have to offer one another?*
3. *What caused the balance of power between Native Americans and Euro-Americans to shift in favor of the latter?*

FURTHER READING

William Cronon's Changes in the Land: Indians, Colonists, and the Ecology of New England *(New York, 1983), discusses the New England Indians' interactions with their environment and describes the impact of European settlement on both the landscape and the native inhabitants. In* The Middle Ground: Indians, Empires, and Republics in the Great Lakes Region, 1650–1815 *(New York, 1991), historian Richard White stresses the cultural adjustments that both Europeans and Indians made through two centuries of contact in the upper midwest. Daniel Usner introduces a third element—the importance of black slaves—in his account of French, English, Spanish, and Indian relations in the lower Mississippi Valley,* Indians, Settlers, & Slaves in a Frontier Exchange Economy: The Lower Mississippi Valley Before 1783 *(Chapel Hill, 1992). James Merrell's* The Indians' New World: Catawbas and Their Neighbors from European Contact through the Era of Removal *(Chapel Hill, 1989) focuses on a single tribe—the Catawbas of the Carolina Piedmont—and traces their changing fortunes through the 1830s.*

What Did it Mean to Be a Puritan?

Carla Gardina Pestana

INTRODUCTION

Puritans suffer from a bad reputation. Since the early twentieth century when American social critic H. L. Mencken ridiculed the first English settlers in New England, the word "puritan" conjures up images of sexual prudery, censoriousness, and hypocrisy. Although American school children are told that the Puritans came to America to establish religious freedom, as adults we learn that they in fact repressed dissent. Not only that, they limited political participation to (adult male) church members, even though admission to the church was by no means automatic. Many college students learning anew about early New England history wonder: Why would anyone be a Puritan?

The English men and women who migrated to New England between 1630 and 1642 to settle the Massachusetts Bay Colony would probably not be surprised that they have an unflattering image. By the time they left England they were accustomed to being ridiculed. In part they departed because they were committed to a religious movement that was increasingly coming under attack. In their view, the Church of England (established by Henry VIII in 1534) ought to participate more fully in the Protestant Reformation that had converted many on the European continent. Their criticisms of religious practices and social mores had ceased to be tolerated in the years leading up to their exodus, and Archbishop William Laud was intent on suppressing their movement. Financial hardships and religious woes combined to persuade over thirteen thousand people to leave the island of their birth to travel to northern North America in the dozen years after 1629.

They carried on—in spite of the travails they experienced—because they believed that God required it of them. To understand the Puritans, we must think about that conviction and the meaning that it gave to their lives. Many women and men braved first the displeasure of the English authorities and then the dangers of colonization because of their belief that they were fulfilling God's will. Early New England residents embraced the faith that we call "Puritan" out of the sense of personal commitment to reformed Protestantism. Theologically, they generally followed the teachings of John Calvin, a leading Protestant reformer of the previous century. The Puritans' church organization has been described as "non-separating congregationalism." Congregationalists rejected the ecclesiastical hierarchy of the Church of England (with its bishops, like their old nemesis Archbishop Laud, and its system of courts); they believed that the individual congregation should be autonomous, with the power to call a minister and to admit and discipline members. They earned the appellation "non-separating" because—unlike the separatists ("Pilgrims") who settled Plymouth—they refused to renounce their affiliation with the Anglican church, claiming that they wished to work for its reformation from within. Although we may find it difficult to comprehend their beliefs and the depth of their convictions, we must understand the Puritans as people dedicated to a cause. This cause guided them to New England in the first place and led them to create a unique society once they arrived. Their commitment to their cause was their reason for being Puritans.

Religion in Early New England: From Personal Piety to Social Force

The selections that follow have been drawn from a massive literature on early New England. They attempt to convey something of the appeal that this religious faith held for the men and women who embraced it. Like all religions, Puritanism provided meaning and offered comfort, as some of these readings suggest. In addition, Puritanism shaped basic social attitudes and, hence, colonial New England society. As you read, you may conclude that a number of the accusations against the Puritans had some grounding in reality—for instance, they did police one another's behavior; but notice, too, how they thought about what they were doing. Do you consider them hypocritical and repressed after reading these selections?

Lay Puritans Form a Police Force

No scholar has done more to make the Puritans comprehensible to the modern reader than Edmund S. Morgan. In his biography of early Massachusetts governor John Winthrop (1588–1649), Morgan discusses sin and temptation as social problems for Puritans like Winthrop. This selection gives a sense of how the community viewed its obligation to monitor the activities of its members. Think about the charge of hypocrisy as you read Morgan's sympathetic account. Excerpted from Edmund S. Morgan, The Puritan Dilemma: The Story of John Winthrop, (New York, 1958), 69, 71.

John Winthrop (1588–1649) served as governor of Massachusetts for most of its first twenty years. His portrait reveals the relatively simple clothing favored by well-to-do Puritans of his era. (Courtesy of The American Antiquarian Society.)

TO PLEASE God the Puritans demanded of themselves a standard of behavior not far different from that required by most modern codes of morality. They did not think it necessary to be either prudes or prohibitionists. They did not dress in drab clothes or live in drab houses or speak in drab words. The people who appear in the pages of Winthrop's journal, the good men and women who showered him with venison and partridges and fat hogs to celebrate Margaret's arrival [i.e., Margaret Tyndal Winthrop, John's third wife], the boys and girls who skipped rope on the decks of the *Arbella*, the men who built ships and caught fish and planted corn were all human enough.

Nevertheless, the Puritans did make strong demands on human nature, for they were engaged in a mission that required great exertion. They had undertaken to establish a society where the will of God would be observed in every detail, a kingdom of God on earth. While still aboard the *Arbella*, Winthrop had explained to his fellow emigrants their solemn commitment to this task. Every nation, they all knew, existed by virtue of a covenant with God in which it promised to obey His commands. They had left England because England was failing in its promise. In high

Reprinted from *The Puritan Dilemma: The Story of John Winthrop* by Edmund S. Morgan, edited by Oscar Handlin. Published by HarperCollins Publishers, 1958. Copyright © 1958 by Edmund S. Morgan.

hope that God was guiding them and would find their efforts acceptable, they had proposed to form a new society. Now God had demonstrated His approval. He had made way for them by a "special overruling providence." By staying His wrath so long and allowing them to depart in peace, by delivering them safe across the water, He had sealed a covenant with them and given them a special responsibility to carry out the good intentions that had brought them into the wilderness. . . .

Winthrop was determined that Massachusetts should not deal falsely with God. Before arriving in New England, he and the other leaders of the exodus had thought long and hard about the articles of God's special commission, and they were confident that they knew what was required of them. They knew, in the most elementary terms, that they must punish every sin committed in Massachusetts. And punish they did, with the eager cooperation of the whole community, who knew that sin unpunished might expose them all to the wrath of God. Families became little cells of righteousness where the mother and father disciplined not only their children but also their servants and any boarders they might take in. In order that no one should escape this wholesome control, it was forbidden for anyone to live alone: unmarried men and maids were required to place themselves in some family if their own had been left behind. Parents were obliged to take care that all their children and apprentices learned to read, so that everyone would be able to see for himself in the Bible what opportunities for salvation God offered to man and what sins He forbade. The churches were thronged every Sunday with willing and unwilling worshipers—everyone was required to attend—and church members guarded each other's morals by censuring or excommunicating those who strayed from the straight path.

With virtually the whole population for a police force Winthrop found it no problem to punish sin.

Religion as a Source of Safety and Comfort

Samuel Sewall (1652–1730), a leading member of the Boston, Massachusetts community, was an educated, respectable, and pious man. His diary provides a rich source of information about his activities and attitudes. In

Samuel Sewall (1652–1730), a leading New Englander of the second generation, was a judge at the Salem witch trials. He also wrote an important condemnation of slavery. His attire, like Winthrop's, remains simple, but note the subtle changes. (Painting by John Smibert. Courtesy of the Museum of Fine Arts, Boston.)

the excerpt that follows, historian David D. Hall describes the comfort that Sewall took from various religious practices. As you will see, some of the things that Sewall did—such as driving a pin into the frame of his new house—might be classified by us as superstition. But these activities, along with those that grew more directly out of his religious faith, all drew upon supernatural forces to give Sewall a feeling of safety. Taken from David D. Hall, Worlds of Wonder, Days of Judgment: Popular Religious Belief in Early New England (Cambridge, Massachusetts, 1990), 217–19.

CRAVING SAFETY for himself, Sewall sought it earnestly for others as well. As he went about this task, he could not separate the welfare of his wife and children from the welfare of New England. Family, church, town, and country, all shared a collective destiny. He linked them together at a private fast: "Pray'd for Sister Dorothy, my family, New England, that God would fit me for his good pleasure in doing and suffering." At another fast, he begged for blessings upon his children and their kin, the governor and the General Court, Third Church and missionaries to the Indians, Connecticut and New York, "all the European Plantations in

Reprinted from *Worlds of Wonder, Days of Judgment* by David D. Hall. Copyright © 1989 by David D. Hall. Reprinted by permission of Alfred A. Knopf, Inc.

America," the Queen and "Europe." The close at hand and the distant were both deserving of his care. Yet the family always had priority. There were steps he took to safeguard his children that they alone enjoyed.

A new addition to his house was under way. Before construction began, Sewall consulted with a minister as to whether the times were propitious. While the floor was being laid he drove a pin into the frame, an act he repeated for the houses of close friends and kin, and for ships and meetinghouses. Soon after he and his family moved into their new rooms, they held a private fast asking God to bless the place where they now lived. Some years later, Sewall set up stone carvings on gateposts in front of the house, two "cherubims heads" that symbolized the presence of protecting forces.

The children born to him and Hannah were carried to the meetinghouse their first week of life to be baptized. In later life Sewall looked back fondly on those moments when he held a newborn child in his arms "upon the Sabbath Day in the Solemn Assembly of God's saints." Giving names to newborn children was no casual task, since the right choice could add protection. "I named Joseph, in hopes of the accomplishment of the Prophecy, Ezek. 37th and such like: and not out of respect to any Relation, or any other person, except the first Joseph." "I named my little daughter Sarah . . . I was struling whether to call her Sarah or Mehetabel; but when I saw Sarah's standing in the Scripture . . . I resolv'd on that side. Also Mother Sewall had a sister Sarah. . . ." For his children he also sought the benefit of "Blessing" from old men; on one occasion he transported the whole family to the bedside of a man whose word (or touch?) he deemed of special worth, and on another he presented "all my stock" to the Reverend Nehemiah Walter of Roxbury and "desired his Blessing of them; which he did."

Back within their home, father, mother, and children gathered daily for a service of devotion. The routine they practiced was that prescribed by the clergy, who envisaged every household as a "little commonwealth" exemplifying moral order. Year in and year out the Sewalls sang psalms and read Scripture at these family meetings. The prayers they offered were explicit in their reference to family problems like a son's quest for a suitable apprenticeship. Scripture-reading proceeded by a schedule that took them "in Course" from Genesis to Revelation, a sequence they resumed once the cycle was completed. Everyone within the family took his turn at reading, Joseph starting at age ten, one sister at age eight.

The psalms they sang together had particular significance. Sewall listed them by number in the diary. Here he also listed psalms he sang in Third Church, in the "closet" of his bedchamber, and in private meetings he shared with a group of laymen. This attention to the psalms was in keeping with their place in popular tradition—not the popular tradition of maypoles and Christmas, but the new vernacular tradition that emerged in post-Reformation England. For Sewall, the music that his friends and family made together was a means of imitating life as saints in heaven. "I give you this Psalm-Book," he told a relative, "in order to your perpetuating this Song; and I would have you pray that it may be an Introduction to our Singing with the Choir above." Noting the death of a Harvard classmate, he recalled that they had "sung many a Tune in Consort; hope shall sing Hallelujah together in Heaven." Together with his family he anticipated heaven as they sang the stanzas of their favorite psalms.

Puritanism's Appeal to Women

Amanda Porterfield is interested in explaining why women found Puritanism appealing. In the passage that follows, she makes an argument about how religion functioned as a source of authority for women. Although the power that pious Puritan women exercised may strike us as indirect and severely limited, a case can be made that even this degree of power represented an increase for early modern women. Porterfield contributes here to an on-going debate about the impact of the Protestant Reformation on the position of women in society. Excerpted from "Women's Attraction to Puritanism," Church History *60 (June 1991): 196–200.*

In 1566 when the Puritan ministers John Gough and John Philpot were suspended from their pulpits and banished from

"Women's Attraction to Puritanism," by Amanda Porterfield, as it appeared in *Church History*, Vol. 60, No. 2, June 1991. Copyright © 1991 by The American Society of Church History.

London for their refusal to wear the white outer robe, or surplice, marking their special holiness as priests of the church, a crowd of more than two hundred women gathered at London Bridge to cheer them on as they left the city. As Gough and Philpot crossed the bridge, the women pressed bags of food and bottles of drink on them, all the while "animating them most earnestly to stand fast in the same their doctrine." That same year, when John Bartlett was also ordered to step down from his pulpit in London for refusing to wear the surplice, sixty women assembled at the home of his bishop to protest the suspension. Such demonstrations of women's support for Puritan ministers were not isolated events. As the historian of Elizabethan Puritanism Patrick Collinson asserted, "it was the women of London who occupied the front line in defence of their preachers, and with a sense of emotional engagement hardly exceeded by the suffragettes of three and a half centuries later."

Women's support for Puritan theology, and for Puritan preachers, was no less formidable in seventeenth-century New England. By 1660 women comprised the majority of communicants in every New England church whose membership records have been preserved. Women comprised 84 percent of new communicants in the New Haven church in the 1660s, over 70 percent of new communicants in the Charlestown, Boston Third, and New London churches in the 1670s, 70 percent or more of new communicants in the Salem, Beverley, Boston First, and Hartford Second churches in the 1680s, and 76 percent and 75 percent of new communicants in the Salem and Boston Third churches during the 1690s. In 1692 Cotton Mather estimated that women made up between two-thirds and three-fourths of the membership of a church close to his home, perhaps Boston's Second Church, where he was minister, and implied that a preponderance of women church members was characteristic of all New England churches. In fact, female admissions to communion in each decade from 1660 to 1700 never dipped below 54 percent in any church in Massachusetts or Connecticut.

The seating arrangements in New England meeting houses represented the prominence of women saints in New England society as well as the relatively intimate relationship that obtained between them and their ministers. For example, during church services in seventeenth-century Dorchester, women sat on the right side of the meetinghouse, directly in front of the minister, while men sat on the left, behind the deacons. When the Dorchester congregation expanded, a new double seat "at ye righthand of ye Pulpit" was installed for women and later, a "2d Seat to ye Double Seat," also for women, was added alongside, effectively nestling the pulpit in the laps of women.

In light of such evidence of women's prominence as supporters of Puritan theology and Puritan ministers, the question of what attracted women to Puritanism arises. Which aspects of Puritan theology and Puritan culture led women to emerge as champions of Puritan ministers during Elizabeth's reign and as custodians of church membership in New England after 1660? Such questions arise with special sharpness because of the emphasis placed in recent scholarship on the patriarchal character of Puritan theology and Puritan culture. Lyle Koehler, Ben Barker-Benfield, Rosemary Skinner Keller, and Margaret Olfson Thickstun have all pointed to the laws and conventions of Puritanism that supported male dominance and discriminated against women. For example, Koehler asserts that "the need to define all women as weak and dependent was . . . deeply embedded in the character of American Puritanism." As Koehler sees it, "Puritans attempted to keep women subordinate and dependent by limiting their educational opportunities, separating the sexes whenever possible, providing no possibility of female economic security outside marriage, censuring 'old maids,' depriving women of the vote in church and commonwealth, forcing wives to relinquish control over their realty, and placing married women under the effectual supervision of their husbands." If Puritan theology and Puritan ministers represented and abetted this system of male dominance, why did women embrace Puritanism so passionately? Why did New England women outnumber men as the church members who sustained and exemplified Puritan culture?

Women were drawn to them partly because of the seductiveness of Puritan theology and Puritan ministers. Especially when delivered by an inspiring preacher, images of Christ as a ravishing Bridegroom and God as an omnipotent Father answered women's desires for powerful love objects. Thus Puritan sermons on the nature of conversion and the devotional characteristics of faith in God offered women imaginary experiences of erotic satisfaction and emotional security.

This seductive power of Puritan theology is illustrated in the conversion story of Joanna Tothill Drake (1585?–1625). In 1618 when her husband hired the forceful young preacher Thomas Hooker (1586–1647) to serve as her personal minister as well as rector of St. George's church in Esher, Surrey, Joanna Drake was distraught and angry about the sinful state of her soul. Before Hooker's arrival, she had been suicidal and violent toward others; she had swallowed pins and struck the eminent Puritan John Dod, in the midst of his prayers for her, with part of her bedstead. Under Dod's ministrations, her physical violence had subsided, but she was still terrified of hell and insistent on the hopeless state of her soul. Moreover, she had grown skillfully disputatious as a result of her arguments with the dozen ministers her husband had enlisted to cure her. With Hooker, however, Mrs. Drake was "mervellously delighted." Her spirits improved steadily under his attentions. Her arguments and debilitating sense of sinfulness disappeared and, on her deathbed, she enjoyed a prolonged and ecstatic experience of God's grace.

Hooker cured Joanna Drake by encouraging her to think about Christ as a magnificent bridegroom and about God as a strong Father. In a treatise based on his cure of Drake, Hooker identified the Christian's acceptance of Christ's suit as the means of her reunion with God; Christ's husbandly love was her "title to the promise" of union with God the Father. Moreover, Hooker exposed Drake's protestations of unworthiness as resentful claims to a better lot and urged her to relinquish her sullen displeasure with her life and rejoice in the grace she already had. Thus in the treatise that grew out of Drake's cure, Hooker likened the Christian who insisted on her unworthiness to "a sullen child that will not eat his milk because he hath it not in the golden dish." With a disarming mixture of encouragement, admonition, and titillation, Hooker encouraged Christians to "hear the best part" of themselves and not "turn the backside of our hearts to the promise." Just as a bride does not have to win her spouse's love but only accept it, so "there is nothing required on our side," wrote Hooker, "but only to receive him as a husband."

This presentation of Christ's suit must have had a very familiar ring to Joanna Drake: her own father had married her against her will to a man who seems to have wanted her love, or at least cared enough about satisfying her to enlist a dozen ministers to alleviate her unhappiness. Hooker led Joanna Drake to accept her husband's love, and her father's authority, by representing their relationships to her in the symbolic language of Puritan theology.

By picturing Christ's husbandly love and God's fatherly authority as pleasurable solutions to her soul's distress, and thereby providing her with religious symbols of sexual satisfaction and emotional security, Hooker led Joanna Drake to feel content with her life and to accept the love and authority of her husband and father. Hooker helped Drake control her anger by identifying it and making her feel guilty about it; his argument that anger was behind her preoccupation with sinfulness led her to confront that anger, and to feel that it was unworthy of a Christian. The remarkable effectiveness of inducing self-control by means of guilt resulted from the attractiveness of the images associated with that strategy; Drake was willing to take responsibility for her anger because her willingness was associated with images of God and Christ that elicited imaginary experiences of erotic satisfaction and emotional pleasure. In effect, the process of embracing Christ advocated by Hooker entailed accepting symbols of emotional gratification for the price of emotional restraint.

Puritan theology and Puritan preachers attracted women not only because they offered women symbols of emotional gratification, but also because Puritan theology and Puritan culture enabled women to exercise an indirect, often public and deliberate authority. These two sources of women's attraction to Puritanism were not unrelated; women's ability to exercise influence over their preachers was part of the same interpersonal, cultural system as their emotional vulnerability to symbols of espousal to Christ, and to erotically charged relationships with the preachers who represented themselves as Christ's ambassadors. Joanna Drake exerted considerable influence in Thomas Hooker's life through her responsiveness to his guidance. His reputation grew out of her acceptance and support; she indirectly shaped Hooker's career as the subject of his first published work, *The Poor Doubting Christian Drawn Unto Christ*, which established his reputation as a pastoral theologian. As was the case with many Puritan preachers, Hooker's success derived in part from his ability to please women.

Puritan Attitudes Toward Sex

One of the charges most frequently leveled against the Puritans is that of sexual prudery, so much so that the popular connotation of the term "Puritan" suggests repressed sexuality. This view comes largely from such early twentieth-century critics of Puritanism as H. L. Mencken, who attacked the mores of late nineteenth century American society by derisively labelling them "Puritan." In one of his earliest publications on early New England history, Edmund S. Morgan defended the Puritans against the charge of prudery. Morgan's definition of what constitutes a "healthy attitude" toward sex may seem somewhat dated now, however. Abridged from Edmund S. Morgan, "The Puritans and Sex," New England Quarterly 15 (December 1942):591–94.

[The nineteenth-century historian] Henry Adams once observed that Americans have "ostentatiously ignored" sex. He could think of only two American writers who touched upon the subject with any degree of boldness—Walt Whitman and Bret Harte. Since the time when Adams made his penetrating observation, American writers have been making up for lost time in a way that would make Bret Harte, if not Whitman, blush. And yet there is still more truth than falsehood in Adams's statement. Americans, by comparison with Europeans or Asiatics, are squeamish when confronted with the facts of life. My purpose is not to account for this squeamishness, but simply to point out that the Puritans, those bogeymen of the modern intellectual, are not responsible for it.

At the outset, consider the Puritans' attitude toward marriage and the role of sex in marriage. The popular assumption might be that the Puritans frowned on marriage and tried to hush up the physical aspect of it as much as possible, but listen to what they themselves had to say. Samuel Willard, minister of the Old South Church in the latter part of the seventeenth century and author of the most complete textbook of Puritan divinity, more than once expressed his horror at "that Popish conceit of the Excellency of Virginity." Another minister, John Cotton, wrote that

Women are Creatures without which there is no comfortable Living for man: it is true of them what is wont to be said of Governments, *That bad ones are better than none:* They are a sort of Blasphemers then who dispise and decry them, and call them *a necessary Evil,* for they are *a necessary Good.*

These sentiments did not arise from an interpretation of marriage as a spiritual partnership, in which sexual intercourse was a minor or incidental matter. Cotton gave his opinion of "Platonic love" when he recalled the case of

one who immediately upon marriage, without ever approaching the *Nuptial Bed,* indented with the *Bride,* that by mutual consent they might both live such a life, and according did sequestring themselves according to the custom of those times, from the rest of mankind, and afterwards from one another too, in their retired Cells, giving themselves up to a Contemplative life; and this is recorded as an instance of no little or ordinary Vertue; but I must be pardoned in it, if I can account it no other than an effort of blind zeal, for they are the dictates of a blind mind they follow therein, and not of that Holy Spirit, which saith *It is not good that man should be alone.*

Here is as healthy an attitude as one could hope to find anywhere. Cotton certainly cannot be accused of ignoring human nature. Nor was he an isolated example among the Puritans. Another minister stated plainly that "the Use of the Marriage Bed" is "founded in mans Nature," and that consequently any withdrawal from sexual intercourse upon the part of husband or wife "Denies all reliefe in Wedlock vnto Human necessity: and sends it for supply vnto Beastiality when God gives not the gift of Continency." In other words, sexual intercourse was a human necessity and marriage the only proper supply for it. These were the views of the New England clergy, the acknowledged leaders of the community, the most Puritanical of the Puritans. As proof that their congregations concurred with them, one may cite the case in which the members of the First Church of Boston expelled James Mattock because, among other offenses, "he denied Coniugall fellowship vnto his wife for the space of 2 years together vpon pretense of taking Revenge upon himself for his abusing of her before marryage." So strongly did the Puritans

insist upon the sexual character of marriage that one New Englander considered himself slandered when it was reported, "that
he Brock his deceased wife's hart with Greife, that he wold be
absent from her 3 weeks together when he was at home, and wold
never come nere her, and such Like."

There was just one limitation which the Puritans placed upon
sexual relations in marriage: sex must not interfere with religion.
Man's chief end was to glorify God, and all earthly delights must
promote that end, not hinder it. Love for a wife was carried too far
when it led a man to neglect his God:

> . . . sometimes a man hath a good affection to Religion, but
> the love of his wife carries him away, a man may bee so
> transported to his wife, that hee dare not bee forward in
> Religion, lest hee displease his wife, and so the wife, lest
> shee displease her husband, and this is an inordinate
> love, when it exceeds measure.

Sexual pleasures, in this respect, were treated like other kinds of
pleasure. On a day of fast, when all comforts were supposed to be
foregone in behalf of religious contemplation, not only were tasty
food and drink to be abandoned but sexual intercourse, too. On
other occasions, when food, drink, and recreation were allowable,
sexual intercourse was allowable too, though of course only between persons who were married to each other. The Puritans
were not ascetics; they never wished to prevent the enjoyment of
earthly delights. They merely demanded that the pleasures of the
flesh be subordinated to the greater glory of God: husband and
wife must not become "so transported with affection, that they
look at no higher end than marriage it self." "Let such as have
wives," said the ministers, "look at them not for their own ends,
but to be fitted for Gods service, and bring them nearer to God."

Toward sexual intercourse outside marriage the Puritans
were as frankly hostile as they were favorable to it in marriage.
They passed laws to punish adultery with death, and fornication
with whipping. Yet they had no misconceptions as to the capacity
of human beings to obey such laws. Although the laws were
commands of God, it was only natural—since the fall of Adam—
for human beings to break them. Breaches must be punished lest
the community suffer the wrath of God, but no offense, sexual or
otherwise, could be occasion for surprise or for hushed tones of
voice.

Puritanism as a Source of Social Stability

In an important essay on the social stability that characterized early New England society, Timothy H. Breen and Stephen Foster suggest that Puritanism played an important role in creating that stability. If most New Englanders approved of the society that Breen and Foster describe, they would have appreciated their faith all the more for the kind of community that it helped them to erect. Abridged from "The Puritans' Greatest Achievement: A Study of Social Cohesion in Seventeenth-Century Massachusetts," Journal of American History *60 (June 1973): 10–13.*

Left to themselves, however, the Massachusetts colonists found Congregationalism a source of stability. Flexible enough to accommodate moderate differences of opinion, the orthodox faith still served as a useful test for detecting and expelling extremists, thereby precluding any prolonged clash over religious fundamentals. Irreconcilables quickly discovered the charms of Rhode Island and left the Bay Colony in relative peace. Nathaniel Ward, the colony's most exuberant propagandist, explained this phenomenon in his *Simple Cobler of Aggawam:* "True Religion is *Ignis probationis* [a testing fire] which doth *congregare homogenea & segregare heterogenia* [bring together the alike and drive away the different]."

Ward was correct to emphasize the homogenizing effect of "true religion," any true religion, providing it could be widely and exclusively inculcated as in Massachusetts. The Bay Colony fortunately possessed an official priestly caste supported at public expense and periodically replenished by the graduates of Harvard College. Unhampered by anything but the most futile and sporadic opposition, the authorized interpreters of the exclusive faith provided the citizens of the Bay Colony with meaning for their present, a mission for their future, and, what was more, and perhaps most of all, a synthetic but compelling past. . . .

Puritanism gave to Massachusetts the same kind of provincial identity that was supplied by local tradition in the counties of seventeenth-century England. Indeed, in its physical situation no less than in its mental set the Bay Colony would have made a typical county community. The colony was small in extent, its popu-

1653 cartoon depicts "Father Christmas" (center) being turned away by a Puritan while another man welcomes him. The image was intended to lampoon Puritan hostility to Christmas which they regarded as a pagan holiday. Which of the two men flanking Father Christmas is wealthier? Why did the artist choose to distinguish the two in that way? (Courtesy of The Library of Congress.)

lation was about the right size and relatively compact in distribution, it possessed a coherent intellectual and gentry class, and it was ready to offer fierce resistance to central power emanating from London. . . .

By contributing a common ideology to the Bay Colony, Puritanism did much to create in America the kind of community capable of maintaining order within its borders. If anything, the artificiality of Massachusetts "countyness" assisted its function. Conflicting loyalties to patrons, family, or guilds, which could tear apart even the most traditional European community, were all comparatively weak or absent in New England. In this sense the social utility of Puritanism lay in its position as the monopoly faith rather than in its particular tenets. Hinduism might have served equally well if Harvard could have turned out genuine Brahmins trained in the learned exposition of the *Bhagavad-gita* and the printing press, pulpit, and schools been adapted to the inculcation of the Word in Sanskrit. But the specific preachings of the Puritan Word also had a contribution to make.

From the very first the leaders of New England spoke of love as the foundation of their society. While still aboard the *Arbella*, John Winthrop set the tone for life in the Bay Colony, urging the settlers to be "knitt together in this worke as one man" and warning that their failure to do so would make them "a story and a by-word through the world." Winthrop and the other Puritans who moved to Massachusetts assumed that the Lord had made a covenant with them as He had once done for the people of England. This initial "national Covenant" was followed by a proliferation of other covenants on every level of life in New England. The Massachusetts Puritans organized churches, towns, indeed, the entire commonwealth upon the contractual model. The essential ingredient in this contract was free will: the individual voluntarily promised to obey civil and scriptural law, for the seventeenth-century Puritans believed that meaningful obedience could only grow out of voluntary consent, never out of coercion. With this principle in mind, Thomas Hooker insisted that the man who desired to enter a social convenant had to "*willingly* binde and ingage himself to each member of that society . . . or else a member actually he is not." The strong sense of communal responsibility that developed out of this voluntary commitment influenced the character of conflict within the Bay Colony. It was incumbent upon all men to work out their disputes as peacefully as possible, thinking always of their greater obligation to the commonwealth as a whole and ultimately to God himself. Thus, when the future townsmen of Dedham drew up their covenant, they pledged to practice "everlasting love," and should that bond ever be strained by local differences "then, such party or parties shall presently refer all such differences unto some one, two or three others of our said society to be fully accorded and determined without any further delay."

The logic of the covenant determined that the towns and churches of New England would be homogeneous units. Puritan villagers excluded anyone from their midst whom they believed endangered their way of life, and unwanted strangers were frequently "warned out" when they failed to meet the community's standards. In Winthrop's time the concern for social purity was so great that colonial authorities sometimes asked newcomers to present evidence of good character before allowing them to settle.

Such conscious self-selection strengthened social cohesion within Massachusetts by forcing potential troublemakers to find homes in other parts of America. Historians have often criticized the leaders of the Bay Colony for their intolerance of other men's opinions, but when one considers Catholics fighting Protestants in colonial Maryland or the Dutch quarreling with the English in New York, one begins to understand why the Puritan fathers acted as they did.

Questions

1. *Both Hall and Porterfield discuss the appeal of Puritanism for the individual believer, but the issues they emphasize differ. Compare and contrast the two discussions, then think about ways in which their points of view might be integrated.*

2. *Edmund S. Morgan directly addresses the older criticisms of Puritanism with regard to the questions of "community watchfulness" and sexuality. What does he assert in an effort to force us to reconsider our view of the Puritans? How persuasive do you find his arguments?*

3. *Why would any of the people described in these selections have wanted to be a Puritan? What was appealing about the society that they created? What do you find unappealing?*

Puritan Faith:
The Personal and the Political

Since the popular negative image of Puritanism is a fairly recent develop-ment, the Puritans themselves did not respond systematically to the various charges that have been levelled against them. Thus, the written records they left—a sampling of which is reprinted below—do not neces-sarily address our issues. For the Puritans, the compelling question—Am I saved or damned?—was unanswerable in this life. Unable to know their fates, each wondered how can I handle not knowing my fate, and how does God require me to live my life? As they struggled with these issues, they produced a wide variety of documents that can suggest to us why they made the choice to join the Puritan movement and what that decision meant for the society that they created in New England.

God's Judgment as a Lesson

Increase Mather (1639–1723), an influential Boston minister, wrote a best-selling book that recounted examples of "God's Providence"—that is, God's direct intercession in people's lives. Mather collected stories from all over New England to illustrate that God did take an active role in daily life. In the preface to his book, he related the following incident from an earlier English manuscript that made his point quite well; Mather criticizes then-prevailing religious practices (such as church discipline) even as he approvingly relates the tale of poor Mr. Juxon. From the unpaginated preface to An Essay for the Recording of Illustrious Providences . . . *(Boston, 1684).*

This M. *SS.* [manuscript] doth also mention some most *Remarkable Judgments* of God upon Sinners, as worthy to be Recorded for Posterity to take notice of. It is there said, that when Mr. *Richard Juxon* was a Fellow of *Kings Colledge* in *Cambridge*, he led a most vicious life: and whereas such of the Students as were serious in matters of Religion, did endeavour by solemn Fasting and Prayer to prepare themselves for the Communion which was then (this was about the year 1636) on *Easter-Day*. This *Juxon* spent all the time of preparation in Drunken wild Meetings, and was up late and Drunk on . . . Saturday night. Nevertheless, on the Lords day, he came with others to the Communion, and sat next to the Relator [storyteller], who knowing his Disorder the night before, was much troubled: but had no remedy; Church-Discipline not being then so practiced as ought to have been. The Communion being ended, such of the Scholars as had the fear of God in their hearts, repaired to their Closets [or small rooms]. But this *Juxon* went immediately to a Drunken-meeting, and there to a Cock-fight, where he fell to his accustomed madness, and pouring out a volley of Oaths and Curses; while these were between his Lips, God smote him dead in the twinkle of an eye. And though *Juxon* were but young, and of a comely person, his Carcase was immediately so corrupted as that the stench of it was insufferable, insomuch that no house would receive it; and his Friends were forced to hire some base Fellows to watch the Carcase till night; and then with Pitch and such like Gums covered him in a Coffin, and so made a shift to endure his Interment. There stood by a Scholar, whose name was *George Hall*, and who acted his part with *Juxon* in his prophaneness: but he was so astonished with this amazing Providence of God, as that he fell down upon his knees, begging pardoning mercy from Heaven, and vowing a Reformation; which vow the Lord enabled him to keep, so as that afterwards he became an able and famous Minister of the Gospel.

Preface to "An Essay for the Recording of Illustrious Providences," by Increase Mather, published by Samuel Green for Joseph Browning, Boston, 1684.

John Dane Grapples with His Sinfulness

Every Puritan thought about his (or her) spiritual state, confronting the sinful inclinations inherent in human nature and praying for God's help in overcoming temptation. Shortly before his death in 1683, John Dane (born in 1612) composed an autobiography intended to edify his children and grandchildren, from which the following excerpt is extracted. His narrative gives some insight into the attitudes of lay people. Taken from "A Declaration of Remarkabell Prouedenses in the Corse of My Lyfe," in New England Historical Genealogical Register, *(Boston 1854) 8:149–51) [In the following selection, the Latin "u" is often substituted for the English "v".]*

Consarning my self; when I was but a lettell boy, being edicated under godly parents, my Conshans [conscience] was ueary apt to tell me of euells that I should not doe. Being now about aight yers ould, I was giuen mutch to play and to run out without my fathers Consent and againe his comand. One a time, I haueing gone out most parte of the day, when my father saw me cum home, he toke me and basted [beat] me. I then cept [kept] home, and folowed my busenes two or thre dase. My father and mother Comended me, and tould me that god would bles me if I obeyed my parents, and what the contrary would ishew [issue] in. I then thout in my harte, o that my fatther would beat me more when I did amis. I fard [feared], if he did not, I should not be good. . . .

I did think myself in a good condishon. I was conuinsed that I should pray and durst doe no other, and Red and here sarmons and durst doe no other; yet I was giuen to pastime and to dansing, and that I thout lawfull. Now uppone a time, when I was groune 18 yers of age or thare abouts, I went to a dansing scoll to larne to dans. My father hering of it, when I cam home tould me, if I went agayne, he would bast me. I tould him, if he did he should neuer bast me againe. With that, my father toke a stick and basted me. I toke it patiently, and said nothing for a day or [two], but on morning betimes I Res and toke 2 shurts on my back and the best sute I had, and a bybell in my pocet, and set the dores open and went to my fathers chamber dore and said, god by father, god by mother. Why, whether are you going? To seke my fortin, I

255

answared. Then said my mother, *goe whare you will, god he will find you out*. This word, the point of it, stuck in my breast, and afterwards god struck it home to its head.

Allthough I thout my fatther was two Strict, I thout Soloman said, be not holy ouer mutch, and daued [David] was a man after gods oun harte, and he was a danser [dancer]: but yet I went my Journey, and was from him half a yere before he hard whare I was. I first settled in barcumsted, and thare Rought on a shobord that had bene improud that waie. On a nyte [night], when most folke was a bead, a mayd cam into the shopbord and sat with me, and we Jested togetther; but at the last she cared it so, and put huself in sutch a poster, as that I made as If I had sum speshall ocashon abrod and went out; for I fared, If I had not, I should haue cumitted foley with hur. But I ofen thout that it was the prayers of my parents that preuaild with god to kepe me. I then gaue my self mutch to dansing and staying out and heatting myself and lying in haymowes, the pepell being a bed whare I abod that I lost my culler and neuer Recuferd it a gaine. . . .

I now being at harford, M'[ister] Goodin preacht thare, and he preacht consarning prayer. But on saboth day, not being in that trim that i would haue bene in [i.e., not being able to dress as he would like], . . . I would not goe to metting but walkt in the filds close by a meadow sid. Thare was, whetther fly, wasp or hornet, I cannot tell, but it struck my finger, and watter and blod cam out of it and paind me mutch. I went up to a hous and shoud it, but thay knew not what a sting I had at my harte. Now I thout of my mothers words, that god would find me out. I hastend home to the Chamber I lay in, at my masters house; and when i cam thare I toke my bybell and lokt ouer sum instructions my father had Ret, and I weapt sorly. The payne and swelling increast & sweld up to my shoulder. I prayd ernistly to god that he would pardon my sinn and heall my arme. I went to a surgin and askt him what it was. He said it was *the take*. I askt him what he meant. He said it was taken by the prouedens [providence] of god. This knoct home on my hart what my mother said, *god will find you out*. Now I made great promises that if god would here me this time I would Reforme.

An Artist Contemplates the Struggle to Overcome Sin

The Puritan poet Anne Bradstreet (1612?–1672) approaches the struggle over sin that engaged John Dane and indeed all Puritans from a more philosophical perspective in the poem reprinted below. In "The Flesh and The Spirit" the natural (or sinful) side of the Christian believer debates with the spiritual side. Note that the spirit derides worldly pleasures, contrasting these with spiritual pleasures to come. Reprinted from The Complete Works of Anne Bradstreet, *ed. Joseph R. McElrath, Jr., and Allan P. Robb (Boston, 1981), 175–77.*

The Flesh and the Spirit.

In secret place where once I stood
Close by the Banks of *Lacrim* flood
I heard two sisters reason on
Things that are past, and things to come;
One flesh was call'd, who had her eye
On worldly wealth and vanity;
The other Spirit, who did rear
Her thoughts unto a higher sphere:
Sister, quoth Flesh, what liv'st thou on
Nothing but Meditation?
Doth Contemplation feed thee so
Regardlesly to let earth goe?
Can Speculation satisfy
Notion without Reality?
Dost dream of things beyond the Moon
And dost thou hope to dwell there soon?
Hast treasures there laid up in store
That all in th' world thou count'st but poor?
Art fancy sick, or turn'd a Sot
To catch at shadowes which are not?
Come, come, Ile shew unto thy sence,

What Did It Mean To Be a Puritan?

Industry hath its recompence.
What canst desire, but thou maist see
True substance in variety?
Dost honour like? acquire the same,
As some to their immortal fame:
And trophyes to thy name erect
Which wearing time shall ne're deject.
For riches dost thou long full sore?
Behold enough of precious store.
Earth hath more silver, pearls and gold,
Then eyes can see, or hands can hold.
Affect's thou pleasure? take thy fill,
Earth hath enough of what you will.
Then let not goe, what thou maist find,
For things unknown, only in mind.
Spir. Be still thou unregenerate part,
Disturb no more my setled heart,
For I have vow'd (and so will doe)
Thee as a foe, still to pursue.
And combate with thee will and must,
Untill I see thee laid in th' dust.
Sisters we are, yea twins we be,
Yet deadly feud 'twixt thee and me;
For from one father are we not,
Thou by old Adam wast begot,
But my arise is from above,
Whence my dear father I do love.
Thou speak'st me fair, but hat'st me sore,
Thy flatt'ring shews Ile trust no more.
How oft thy slave, hast thou me made,
When I believ'd, what thou hast said,
And never had more cause of woe
Then when I did what thou bad'st doe.
Ile stop mine ears at these thy charms,
And count them for my deadly harms.
Thy sinfull pleasures I doe hate,
Thy riches are to me no bait,
Thine honours doe, nor will I love;
For my ambition lyes above.
My greatest honour it shall be
When I am victor over thee,

WHAT DID IT MEAN TO BE A PURITAN?

And triumph shall, with laurel head,
When thou my Captive shalt be led,
How I do live, thou need'st not scoff,
For I have meat thou know'st not off;
The hidden Manna I doe eat,
The word of life it is my meat.
My thoughts do yield me more content
Then can thy hours in pleasure spent.
Nor are they shadows which I catch,
Nor fancies vain at which I snatch,
But reach at things that are so high,
Beyond thy dull Capacity;
Eternal substance I do see,
With which inriched I would be:
Mine Eye doth pierce the heavens, and see
What is Invisible to thee.
My garments are not silk nor gold,
Nor such like trash which Earth doth hold,
But Royal Robes I shall have on,
More glorious then the glistring Sun;
My Crown not Diamonds, Pearls, and gold,
But such as Angels heads infold.
The City where I hope to dwell,
There's none on Earth can parallel;
The stately Walls both high and strong,
Are made of pretious *Jasper* stone;
The Gates of Pearl, both rich and clear,
And Angels are for Porters there;
The Streets thereof transparent gold,
Such as no Eye did e're behold,
A Chrystal River there doth run,
Which doth proceed from the Lambs Throne:
Of Life, there are the waters sure,
Which shall remain for ever pure,
Nor Sun, nor Moon, they have no need,
For glory doth from God proceed:
No Candle there, nor yet Torch light,
For there shall be no darksome night.
From sickness and infirmity,
For evermore they shall be free,
Nor withering age shall e're come there,

But beauty shall be bright and clear;
This City pure is not for thee,
For things unclean there shall not be:
If I of Heaven may have my fill,
Take thou the world, and all that will.

Drawing Upon Faith in the Face of Affliction

Although Puritans—like religious peoples in many other faith tradi-tions—feared divine judgment, they also found solace in their religious faith. When dealing with the death of a loved one, Puritans often sought comfort in their religious beliefs. Anne Bradstreet wrote the following poem while struggling to come to terms with the death of her grand-daughter. From The Complete Works of Anne Bradstreet, *ed. Joseph R. McElrath, Jr., and Allan P. Robb (Boston, 1981), 187.*

> *In memory of my dear grand-child . . .*
> *Who deceased* June 20. 1669. *being three years and*
> *seven Moneths old.*
> With troubled heart & trembling hand I write,
> The Heavens have chang'd to sorrow my delight.
> How oft with disappointment have I met,
> When I on fading things my hopes have set?
> Experience might 'fore this have made me wise,
> To value things according to their price:
> Was ever stable joy yet found below?
> Or perfect bliss without mixture of woe.
> I knew she was but as a withering flour,
> That's here to day, perhaps gone in an hour;
> Like as a bubble, or the brittle glass,
> Or like a shadow turning as it was.
> More fool then I to look on that was lent,

As if mine own, when thus impermanent.
Farewel dear child, thou ne're shall come to me,
But yet a while, and I shall go to thee;
Mean time my throbbing heart's chear'd up with this
Thou with thy Saviour art in endless bliss.

"To Walke Together":
The Role of the Puritan Congregation

The preceding selections from Mather, Dane, and Bradstreet dealt with religion on a personal level, but Puritans believed that their spirituality ought to have a public component as well. One way in which they expressed their commitment publicly was by joining a church. In seventeenth-century Massachusetts and Connecticut, only those who seemed to their peers to be saved—that is, to have undergone a legitimate conversion experience—could become church members. Once accepted into a congregation, new members entered into a church covenant. In many churches, such as the one founded in Salem, Massachusetts in 1629, a written covenant was publicly endorsed by all members. The text of the Salem covenant explains why the Puritans thought it necessary to organize churches. Taken from The Records of the First Church in Salem Massachusetts, 1629–1736, *ed. Richard D. Pierce (Salem, Massachusetts, 1974), 3–5.*

Wee whose names are here under written, members of the present Church of Christ in Salem, haveing found by sad experience how dangerous it is to sitt loose to the Covenant wee make with our God: and how apt wee are to wander into by pathes, even to the looseing of our first aimes in entring into Church fellowship: Doe therefore, solemnly in the presence of the Eternall God both for our owne comforts and those which shall or maye be joyned unto us renewe that Church covenant we find this Church bound unto at theire first begining. vizt: That we Covenant with the Lord and one with an other, and doe bynd our selves in the presence of God, to walke together in all his waies, according as he is pleased to reveale him selfe unto us in his Blessed word of truth. And doe more explicitely in the name and feare of God, profess and protest to walke as followeth through the power and grace of our Lord Jesus.

1. first wee avowe the Lord to be our God, and our selves his people in the truth and simplicitie of our Spirits

2. Wee give our selves to the Lord Jesus Christ, and the word of his grace, fore the teaching, ruleing and sanctifyeing of us in matters of worship, and conversation resolveing to cleave to him alone for life and glorie; and oppose all contrarie wayes, cannons and constitutions of men in his worship.

3. Wee promise to walk with our brethren and sisters in the Congregation with all watchfullness, and tendernis avoyding all jelousies, suspitions, backbyteings, conjurings, provoakings, secrete riseings of spirit against them, but in all offences to follow the rule of the Lord Jesus, and to beare and forbeare, give and forgive as he hath taught us.

4. In publick or private, we will willingly doe nothing to the ofence of the Church but will be willing to take advise for ourselves and ours as ocasion shall be presented.

5. Wee will not in the Congregation be forward eyther to show our owne gifts or parts in speaking or scrupuling [2] or there discover the fayling of our brethren or sisters butt attend an orderly cale there unto; knowing how much the Lord may be dishonoured, and his Gospell in the profession of it, sleighted by our distempers, and weaknesses in publyck.

6. Wee bynd ourselves to studdy the advancment of the Gospell in all truth and peace, both in regard of those that are within, or without, noe waye sleighting our sister Churches, but useing theire Counsell as need shalbe; nor laying a stumbling block, before any, noe not the Indians, whose good we desire to promote, and soe to converse, as wee may avoyd the verrye appearance of evill,

7. Wee hereby promise to carrye ourselves in all lawfull obedience, to those that are over us in Church or Common weale, knowing how well pleasing it wilbe to the Lord, that they should have incouragement in theire places, by our not greiveing theyre spirites through our iregulareties.

8. Wee resolve to prove our selves to the Lord in our particular calings, shunning ydlenes as the bane of any state, nor will wee

deale hardly, or opressingly with Any, wherein wee are the Lords stewards: alsoe

9. promyseing to our best abilitie to teach our children and servants, the knowledge of God and his will, that they may serve him alsoe and all this, not by any strength of our owne, but by the Lord Christ, whose bloud we desire may sprinckle this our Covenant made in his name.

A Puritan Justifies Intolerance

The New England Puritans were criticized for more than leaving England at a time of intense struggle; they were also attacked as religious bigots. In the following selection, Puritan legal scholar Nathaniel Ward (1570–1653) attempts to justify intolerance. Although he and his co-religionists were criticized for these attitudes in their own day, we must bear in mind that principled opposition to religious diversity was fairly common among their contemporaries. This passage is taken from The Simple Cobler of Aggawam in America, *5th ed. (Boston, 1713), 5–6. Aggawam was an early name for the town of Ipswich, Massachusetts.*

My heart hath natura'ly detested four things: The standing of the Apocrypha in the Bible; Forainers dwelling in my Country, to crowd out Native Subjects into the corners of the Earth; Alchymized Coines; Tolerations of divers Religions, or of one Religion in segregant shapes: He that willingly assents to the last, if he examines his heart by day-light, his Conscience will tell him, he is either an Atheist, or an Heretick, or an Hypocrite, or at best a captive to some Lust: Poly-piety is the greatest impiety in the World. True Religion is *Ignis probation is* which doth *congregare homogenea & segregare heterogenea [True Religion is a Testing Fire which doth Bring Together the alike and drive away the different or heterodox].*

Excerpted from *The Simple Cobler of Aggawam in America*, Fifth Edition, by Nathaniel Ward a.k.a. Theodore de la Guard, printed by J.D. & R.I. Reprinted for Daniel Henchman at his shop in King Street, Boston, Massachusetts, 1713.

Not to tolerate things meerly indifferent to weak Consciences, argues a Conscience too strong: pressed uniformity in these, causes much disunity: To tolerate more than indifferents, is not to deal indifferently with God: He that doth it, takes his Scepter out of his hand, and bids him stand by. Who hath to do to institute Religion but God. The power of all Religion and Ordinances, lies in their Purity: their Purity in their Simplicity: then are mixtures pernicious. I lived in a City, where a Papist Preached in one Church, a Lutheran in another, a Calvinist in a third; a Lutheran one part of the day, a Calvinist the other, in the same Pulpit: the Religion of that Place was but motly and meagre, their affections Leopard-like.

If the whole Creature should conspire to do the Creator a mischief, or offer him an insolency, it would be in nothing more, than in erecting untruths against his Truth, or by sophisticating his Truths with humane medleyes: the removing of some one iota in Scripture, may draw out all the life, and traverse all the Truth of the whole Bible: but to authorize an untruth, by a Toleration of State, is to build a Sconce against the walls of Heaven, to batter God out of his Chair: To tell a practical lye, is a great Sin, but yet transient; but to set up a Theorical untruth, is to warrant every lye that lyes from its root to the top of every branch it hath, which are not a few.

Edward Johnson Exhorts
All People to Follow Christ

In this final excerpt, lay author Edward Johnson interrupts his history of early New England to call all nations to Christ. Because he sees New England as the fulfillment of God's plan for humanity, this call seems to him not an interruption, but an integral part of the history he is relating. The language he uses in this passage is inspired by the Bible. Taken from Edward Johnson, A History of New-England *[better known as* Wonder-working Providence] *(London, 1654), 32–33.*

An Exhortation to all People, Nations and Languages, to indeavour the advancing of the Kingdome of Christ in the purity of his Ordinances, seeing he hath done such admirable Acts for these poore shrubs.

AND now all you whose affections are taken with wonderfull matters (Attend) and you that thinke Christ hath forgotten his poore despised people (Behold) and all you that hopefully long for Christs appearing to confound *Antichrist* (Consider) and rejoyce all yee his Churches the World throughout, for the Lambe is preparing his Bride, and oh! yee the antient Beloved of Christ, whom he of old led by the hand from *Egypt* to *Canaan*, through that great and terrible Wildernesse, looke here, behold him whom you have peirced, preparing to peirce your hearts with his *Wonder-working Providence,* and to provoke you by this little handfull of his people to looke on him, and mourne. Yet let no man think these few weake Wormes would restraine the wonderfull Workes of Christ, as onely to themselves, but the quite contrary, these but the Porch of his glorious building in hand, and if hee have shewed such admirable acts of his providence toward these, what will he doe when the whole Nation of *English* shall set upon like Reformation according to the direct Rule of his Word? Assured confidence there is also for all Nations, from the undoubted promise of Christ himselfe.

The Winter is past, the Raine is changed and gone, come out of the holes of the secret places, feare not because your number is but small, gather into Churches, and let Christ be your King, yee *Presbytery,* Lord it not over them or any Churches, but feed every one, that one flock over which Christ hath made you overseers, and yee people of Christ give your *Presbytery* double honours, that they with you may keepe the watch of the Lord over his Churches. Yee *Dutch* come out of your hods-podge, the great mingle mangle of Religion among you hath caused the Churches of Christ to increase so little with you, standing at a stay like Corne among Weeds, Oh, yee *French*! feare not the great swarmes of *Locusts,* nor the croking *Frogs* in your Land, Christ is reaching out the hand to you, look what hee hath done for these *English,* and sure hee is no Respecter of Persons, &c. yee *Germanes* that have had such a bloudy bickering, Christ is now comming to your aide, then cast off your loose, and carelesse kinde of Reformation, gather into Churches, and keepe them pure, that Christ may delight to dwell among you: oh *Italy!* The Seat and Center of the Beast, Christ will

Excerpted from *A History of New England,* better known as *Wonder-working Providence,* printed for Nath. Brooke at the *Angel* in Corn Hill, 1654.

now pick out a People from among you for himselfe, see here what wonders hee workes in little time. Oh! yee *Spaniards* and *Portugalls*, Christ will shew you the abominations of that beastly Whore, who hath made your Nations drunke with the Wine of her Fornication. Dread not that cruell murtherous Inquisition, for Christ is now making Inquisition for them, and behold, here how hee hath rewarded them, who dealt cruelly with these his people.

Finally, oh all yee Nations of the World, behold great is the worke the glorious King of Heaven and Earth hath in hand; beware of neglecting the call of Christ: and you the Seed of *Israel* both lesse and more, the ratling of your dead bones together is at hand, Sinewes, Flesh and Life.

Questions

1. *Some of the passages above suggested that these religious beliefs caused people to feel fearful, other passages suggested that these religious beliefs that they served as a source of comfort. Which aspect of the experience seems comprehensible to you? Can the fear and comfort be integrated somehow? How did the Puritans integrate them?*

2. *What obligations did the Puritans' faith place upon them, in terms of their personal behavior, their churches, and their society?*

3. *What impact do you think Puritanism as a social or religious force had on the history of New England?*

4. *Why would a seventeenth-century English man or woman have found the Puritan message and movement appealing? Why would some people have been outraged by the very existence of such a movement?*

FURTHER READING

Edmund Morgan's biography of John Winthrop, The Puritan Dilemma: The Story of John Winthrop *(Boston, 1958), offers a good starting place on the early history of Puritanism in Massachusetts.* Worlds of Wonder, Days of Judgment: Popular Religious Belief in Early New England *(New York, 1989) by David D. Hall treats popular religion in New England. A fairly basic general account of the experiences of the first migrants to Puritan New England can be found in Virginia DeJohn Anderson,* New England's Generation: The Great Migration and the Formation of Society and Culture in the Seventeenth Century *(New York, 1991). John Demos's* A Little Commonwealth: Family Life in Plymouth Colony *(New York, 1970), addresses the social history of an early New England settlement.*

The Salem
Witchcraft Scare

Carla Gardina Pestana

INTRODUCTION

English colonists brought with them beliefs about witches and, once in America, occasionally suspected some residents of practicing witchcraft. According to contemporary wisdom, witches entered into a pact with Satan and thereby acquired supernatural powers. They used these powers to harm their neighbors, in acts of witchcraft known as maleficum. Individuals were suspected of witchcraft in many English colonies in the seventeenth century, including Connecticut, Maryland, Massachusetts, the Somers Island (or Bermuda), and Virginia. Nowhere in Anglo-America, however, were more witches accused than in Massachusetts, the most populous and powerful of the "Puritan" colonies of New England. The bulk of the accusations and trials there occurred in 1692 in the northeastern part of the colony, in a witchcraft scare that has come to be associated with the town of Salem, where the outbreak began.

In 1692, some residents of the coastal town of Salem became convinced that many of their neighbors had become witches. The scare began with a group of adolescent girls and young women who were dabbling in occult practices in an effort to learn about the future. When a number of them fell into strange fits, a physician diagnosed these as the work of a witch. The afflicted then made a series of accusations, adult community members supported their charges and fingered others, and the "witch hunt" was on.

At the time of the outbreak the colony had only a provisional government, while it awaited a new royal charter and the arrival of a governor. (This state of uncertainty had developed since the revocation of the charter in 1686. At that time, the colony had been subsumed under a new "Dominion of New England," but it later rose in revolt hoping to get support from King William and Queen Mary for a return to its old charter. This support had not materialized, so the colony rather nervously awaited a new charter and a new governor in 1692.) With no legitimate claim to govern, the colony's leaders were loath to try capital crimes such as witchcraft. So, as the number of accused witches soared to over a hundred, the authorities simply jailed the suspects while awaiting word from England. By the time the new governor, Sir William Phipps, arrived, the jails were overflowing. Many colonists were certain that witches were conspiring to take over the colony. The governor appointed an emergency court with broad powers to try the cases and it ordered nineteen people hanged in the months that followed.

The crisis came to a close that autumn for a number of reasons. Popular support for the trials waned as more individuals with good reputations (some of them drawn from the ranks of the elites) were accused. The populace may also have felt revulsion at the violence of the many executions. When a group of ministers led by the influential Increase Mather publicly questioned some of the evidence the judges were accepting, the authority of the court was seriously undermined. In October the governor replaced the first court with a new one that had more limited powers; his instructions to the second court indicated a need for greater restraint. He reprieved the few witches that it did convict and then granted a general pardon, emptying the jails of the remaining suspects.

Participants in the trials and scholars subsequently have struggled to make sense of one of the most dramatic and disturbing episodes in colonial history. After 1692, colonists gave up the practice of witch hunting, and no major outbreak followed the one that has made Salem infamous. But colonists were slower to give up their belief that the devil played an active role in their lives. Indeed, the first attempts to explain what had gone wrong at Salem attributed the debacle to a "delusion of Satan" that caused the community to see a witch conspiracy where none existed. Since that time, many interpretations have been offered to explain the witchcraft crisis. Modern Americans, inclined to believe that *the religious bigotry of the Puritans can explain anything distressing in their history, find it surprising that the ministers helped to halt the trials. Other aspects of the witch scare may surprise you as well.*

WHO WAS ACCUSED OF WITCHCRAFT AND WHY: SCHOLARS' EXPLANATIONS

The selections below, taken from recent histories of the witchcraft scare, all grapple with the question: What motivated the accusations? All four historians identify specific groups in the society liable to be the objects of witchcraft charges. And they all suggest that late-seventeenth-century Massachusetts was gripped by social tensions of one sort or another, tensions that led to the fears that sparked the charges against members of these suspect groups.

Whichever argument you find most appealing, it is important to recall that everyone in seventeenth-century New England believed in the existence of witches with the power to do harm. What is at issue here is whom among their neighbors did they identify as members of that frightening group.

Economic and Political Causes

The first excerpt outlines economic and political divisions in the community. Abridged from Paul Boyer and Stephen Nissenbaum, "Salem Possessed: The Social Origins of Witchcraft," in Colonial America: Essays in Politics and Social Development, *ed. Stanley N. Katz and John M. Murrin, 3d ed. (New York, 1983), 346–53, 358–59, 361, 363–65.*

The first three women to be accused can be seen as "deviants" or "outcasts" in their community—the kinds of people who anthropologists have suggested are particularly susceptible to such accusations. Tituba was a West Indian slave; Sarah Good was a pauper who went around the Village begging aggressively for food and lodging; "Gammer" Osborne, while somewhat better off, was a bedridden old woman.

In March, however, a new pattern began to emerge. Two of the three witches accused in that month—the third was little Dorcas Good—were church members (a sign of real respectability in the seventeenth century) and the wives of prosperous freeholders. This pattern continued and even intensified for the duration of the outbreak. The twenty-two persons accused in April included the wealthiest shipowner in Salem (Phillip English) and a minister of the gospel who was a Harvard graduate with a considerable estate in England (George Burroughs). By mid-May warrants had been issued against two of the seven selectmen of Salem Town; and by the end of the summer some of the most prominent people in Massachusetts and their close kin had been accused if not officially charged. As the attorney who prepared the cases against the accused wrote at the end of May, "The afflicted spare no person of what quality so ever."

True, except for Burroughs, none of these persons of quality was ever brought to trial, much less executed. Some escaped from jail or house arrest, others were simply never arraigned. Nevertheless, the overall direction of the accusations remains clear: up the social ladder, fitfully but perceptibly, to its very top. Whatever else they may have been, the Salem witch trials cannot be written off as a communal effort to purge the poor, the deviant, or the outcast.

Just as the accusations thrust steadily upward through the social strata of provincial society, so, too, they pressed outward across geographic boundaries. Beginning within Salem Village itself, the accusations moved steadily into an increasingly wide orbit. The first twelve witches were either residents of the Village or persons who lived just beyond its borders. But of all the indictments which followed this initial dozen, only fifteen were directed against people in the immediate vicinity of Salem Village. The other victims came from virtually every town in Essex

County, including the five which surrounded the Village. (In the town of Andover alone, there were more arrests than in Salem Village itself.)

While almost all these arrests were made on the basis of testimony given by the ten or so afflicted girls of Salem Village (although in some cases they merely confirmed the validity of others' accusations), it is clear that the girls themselves did not actually know most of the people they named. Accusers and accused were in many if not most cases personally unacquainted. Whatever was troubling the girls and those who encouraged them, it was something deeper than the kind of chronic, petty squabbles between near neighbors which seem to have been at the root of earlier and far less severe witchcraft episodes in New England.

But if the outbreak's geographic pattern tends to belie certain traditional explanations, it raises other, more intriguing, interpretive possibilities. As Map 1 shows, there were fourteen accused witches who lived within the bounds of Salem Village. Twelve of these fourteen lived in the eastern section of the Village.

There were thirty-two adult Villagers who testified against these accused witches. Only two of these lived in that eastern section. The other thirty lived on the western side. In other words, the alleged witches and those who accused them resided on opposite sides of the Village.

There were twenty-nine villagers who publicly showed their skepticism about the trials or came to the defense of one or more of the accused witches. Twenty-four of these lived in the eastern part of the Village—the same side on which the witches lived—and only two of them in the west. Those who defended the witches were generally their neighbors, often their immediate neighbors. Those who accused them were not.

. . . Even before 1692 Salem Village had hardly been a haven of tranquility. For years its 600-odd residents had been divided into two bitterly antagonistic factions. The source of their troubles lay in the very circumstances under which the Village had first come into existence. Originally the settlement (which is now the city of Danvers, and not to be confused with Salem proper) had simply been a part of the town of Salem, and when it was granted a limited and partial legal existence as "Salem Village" in 1672, it still remained in many ways a mere appendage of its larger and more prosperous neighbor. Some people in the Village were quite

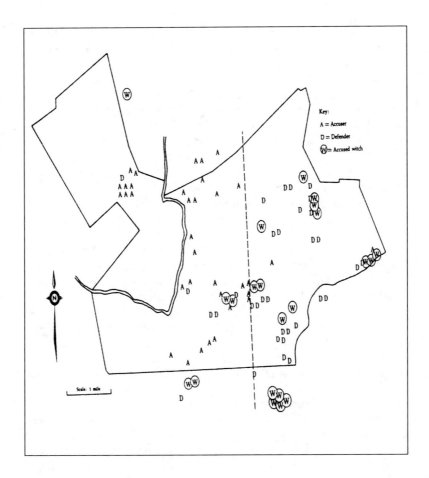

Map 1 The Geography of Witchcraft: Salem Village, 1692

Sources: Residential map of Salem Village in 1692 included as a frontispiece to volume one of Charles W. Upham, *Salem Witch-craft,* 22 vols. (Boston, 1867); W. Elliot Woodward, *Records of Salem Witchcraft Copied from the Original Documents,* 2 vols. (Roxbury, Mass., Privately printed, 1864; reissued in one volume, New York, Da Capo Press, 1969).

content with this satellite status, but others resented it and pressed for complete independence. The latter group, led by a numerous and powerful local family named Putnam, focused its efforts on an attempt to establish a separate church—the central pillar of any Puritan town. . . .

At last in 1689, however, the independence-minded group in Salem Village managed to get its way, and a church was formed under the ministry of Samuel Parris, a thirty-six-year-old former merchant. But this victory was purchased at a heavy price, for the new minister, and the church he headed, represented only a single group in the community—a group led by the Putnams. (Fully half of the original twenty-six church members bore the Putnam name!) The formation of the church, in short, did not serve to unify Salem Village, but only to intensify its inner divisions.

. . . Those Villagers who had all along opposed establishment of the church, and who now refused to join it—a group that included some of the community's wealthiest residents—determined to drive Parris out of his position. They refused to worship in the Village meetinghouse, pointedly attending elsewhere, and withheld payment of their local taxes (which went for the minister's salary and firewood). But their most deadly stroke came at the annual Village election in October 1691 when they swept out of office the existing five-man Village Committee (the local equivalent of a board of selectmen), dominated by Parris' friends, and elected a new Committee made up, to a man, of his known opponents.

The new anti-Parris Committee went quickly to work: it refused even to assess taxes for the payment of Parris' 1692 salary, and it challenged the legality of his "fraudulent" acquisition of the ministry-house and lands in 1689. Parris, now wholly dependent on the voluntary contributions of his supporters for money to purchase the necessities of life—and even for firewood to heat his house—was in desperately serious trouble at the beginning of 1692, and his Putnam supporters knew it.

Thus we begin to see the significance of the fact that of the first four "afflicted girls" in Salem Village, two lived in the household of Samuel Parris himself, and a third, Ann Putnam, was the twelve-year-old daughter of Parris' most dogged supporter, Thomas Putnam Jr. (In the coming weeks, the Thomas Putnam household would produce two more afflicted girls: Mercy Lewis, a servant girl, and Mary Walcott, a young relative.)

Samuel Parris (1653–1720) served as minister in Salem Village in 1692. The Witchcraft scare began in his home, with various women of his household, including his slave Tituba, involved. Historians have placed some of the blame for the unprecedented number of executions at his door. (Courtesy of Massachusetts Historical Society.)

While these girls themselves may well have been unacquainted with the details of factional politics in the Village, they could hardly have remained untouched by the bitterness and resentment that pervaded their own households. It may be no accident that their physical torments set in after they had attempted, with scary results, to predict the future—a future that loomed as highly uncertain not only for the girls themselves but for the adults they knew best. . . .

. . . [T]he richest men in the Village opposed Parris by a margin of better than two-to-one, while the poorest supported him in almost precisely the same proportion. . . . [Those] who lived nearest Salem Town (or, in a few cases, just over the Village line in the Town) opposed Parris by a ratio of six-to-one. Those whose houses were in the northwestern half of the Village, most remote from the Town, *supported* Parris by a ratio of better than four to one. . . . [N]ot every Villager had reason to feel alienated from the Town. Indeed, the economic and social transformation of the Town in these years affected different Villagers in quite different ways. The very developments which threatened many of them gave others reason to take heart. It was this fact, above all, that produced the factional lines which from the beginning divided the Village.

From the 1670's on, proximity to the Town, and even a direct involvement in its economic life, repeatedly emerged as a determining factor in the divisions which plagued the Village. These divisions pitted people who continued to identify with Salem

Town against others for whom the Village, and what they saw as its distinctive interests, were paramount. . . .

. . . In at least two important respects—quality of land and access to market—those farmers on the eastern (or Town) side of the Village had a significant advantage. Modern topographical maps show what any Salem Village farmer knew from first-hand experience: the best lands in the Village were the broad, flat meadows of the eastern part, nearest the coast, while the western part was increasingly broken up by sharp little hills and marshy depressions. The eastern side of the Village, too, was significantly closer to the network of roads and waterways which gave access to Salem Town and her markets. (The additional two or three miles may seem negligible today, but for the farmer who had to convey his goods by ox cart over rutted, muddy, and often flooded paths before reaching the better-maintained Ipswich Road, they certainly loomed large.) In both these respects, then, the farmers on this side of the Village had a crucial edge in supplying the needs of Salem Town. . . .

More than any other inhabitants of the community, the Villagers who lived along the Ipswich Road were exposed to the Town and its concerns. . . . It is not surprising that a number of the men living on or very near the Ipswich Road were engaged in occupations which brought them into regular contact with a wide range of individuals: occupations such as potter, physician, carpenter, innkeeper, sawmill operator, shoemaker, miller, sawyer (that is, wood finisher), and "dishturner." Particularly important, in terms of the Townward orientation of this part of Salem Village, were the four taverns which stood along a short stretch of the Ipswich Road as it passed through Salem Village. Three of these actually lay within the Village: the licensed taverns of Joshua Rea, Jr. and Walter Phillips, and the unlicensed—but well known and well patronized—tavern of Edward and Bridget Bishop. The other, operated by John Proctor, stood about a mile south of the Village boundary. . . .

The pro-Parris faction thus emerges as a coalition whose shared fears united it in support of Parris: a core group of Villagers of middling wealth who were also church members, supplemented by another group, approximately twice as large, of poorer Villagers who were not church members but who identified with the Village church and its minister. The church members provided the institutional structure and the political impetus, the others supplied the votes and the signatures.

Since the pro-Parris faction also played a leading role in the witchcraft prosecutions, it has typically been portrayed as a powerful and domineering clique. From the evidence, however, this group emerges as by far the more vulnerable of the two: less wealthy than its opposition, owning less land, quite literally hedged in by more flourishing anti-Parris neighbors and less able to benefit from the commercial developments centered in Salem Town.

If the Ipswich Road helped shape and define the anti-Parris faction, it also provided an objective focus for the amorphous fears of the pro-Parris group, for whom it would have seemed not so much the line which separated the Village from the Town, but the very channel through which the Town penetrated the Village. The road stood as a perpetual affront to those who felt the integrity of the Village to be menaced from just this quarter. Its residents, with their more commercial outlook and occupations, had in many cases already succumbed to the lure which menaced the Village as a whole. . . .

A revealing glimpse into the social circumstances surrounding the establishment of one of these taverns emerges from John Proctor's request to the Salem selectmen in 1666 for a license to operate a tavern in his house on the Ipswich Road near the Salem Village line. His residence, he said, was "in the common roadway, which occasioneth several travelers to call in for some refreshment as they pass along." Since the free entertaining of these wayfarers was proving to be expensive, Proctor added: "I do therefore earnestly request that you would be pleased to grant me liberty to set up a house of entertainment to sell beer, cider [and] liquors." The court granted Proctor's petition, with the stipulation that he sell exclusively to strangers. Thus, from the Salem Village perspective, the Proctor house became a rendezvous point for outsiders—and *only* for outsiders.

For the pro-Parris Salem Villagers, with their particular anxieties, this generalized concern over taverns must have been especially intense. Given such a background, it is not surprising to find that three of the four Ipswich Road tavern keepers figured prominently in the climatic Village events of the 1690's—and two of these three as victims of those events. Joshua Rea, Jr., publicly expressed his opposition to the witchcraft trials in 1692 by signing a petition seeking to save Rebecca Nurse from the gallows. In 1695 Rea's name appears on the anti-Parris petition. Two of the other tavern keepers, Bridget Bishop and John Proctor, were unable to take a stand for or against Parris in 1695: they had been hanged three years before for committing witchcraft.

Gender Tensions

The following selection examines the gender issues at play in the witch-craft scare at Salem and in other accusations made in colonial New England. Taken fron Carol Karlsen, The Devil in the Shape of a Woman: Witchcraft in Colonial New England *(New York, 1987), 47–48, 50–52, 101–2, 104, 107–8, 115–16.*

The single most salient characteristic of witches was their sex. At least 344 persons were accused of witchcraft in New England between 1620 and 1725. Of the 342 who can be identified by sex, 267 (78 percent) were female. Roughly half of the seventy-five males accused (thirty-six), as the historian John Demos has pointed out, were "suspect by association": they were the hus-bands, sons, other kin, or public supporters of female witches. . . .

The idea that witches were women seems to have been more strongly held by local authorities, magistrates, and juries—men who had the power to decide the fates of the accused—than it was by accusers as a whole. This bias is most noticeable in non-out-break witchcraft cases: although women made up a sizeable 83 percent of the accused in these cases, and although local officials sent roughly the same proportion of female and male suspects to the colony-wide courts for trial, fifteen of the sixteen *convicted* witches (94 percent) were women. . . . The only man to be found guilty was Wethersfield carpenter John Carrington, who was hanged with his wife Joan in 1651. Though he was married to a reputed witch and was one of the poorest men in his community, it remains unclear why, leaving outbreaks aside, he was the only man to receive a punishment normally reserved for women. . . .

Statistics can establish the extent to which New Englanders considered witchcraft the special province of women, but they

Sex of Witches, Salem, 1692

	Female	Male	Total
Accused	141	44	185
Tried	52	7	59
Convicted	26	5	31
Executed	14	5	19

Adapted from a table in Karlsen, *The Devil in the Shape of a Woman.*

cannot convey the vindictiveness that characterized the treatment of female suspects. This sexual double standard is perhaps most vividly seen in the different punishments meted out to confessed witches outside of the Salem outbreak.

Deeming voluntary confession one of the best "proofes sufficient for Conviccion," ministers and magistrates put considerable pressure on women to admit they had covenanted with the Devil. No comparable coercion was used with men. When Wethersfield's Mary Johnson succumbed to this insistence in 1648, admitting that she and the Devil provided many services for one another, she was convicted of familiarity with Satan and hanged. After Rebecca Greensmith described the nature of her covenant with Satan in Hartford in 1662, she too was executed. Similarly, confession doomed the widow Glover in Boston in 1688. Except during the Salem events, when the magistrates decided to put off the executions of people who admitted their guilt until all local witches were discovered, women who incriminated themselves were almost all punished in accordance with the biblical injunction, "Thou shall not suffer a witch to live."

Men who incriminated themselves were treated quite differently. When John Bradstreet of Rowley confessed in 1652 to having familiarity with Satan, the Essex County court ordered him whipped or fined "for telling a lie." In 1674, Christopher Brown was also released by Essex County magistrates, on the grounds that *his* confession seemed "inconsistent with the truth," despite his admission that he had been "discoursing with . . . the devil." Though Hugh Crosia of Stratford confessed in 1692 that he had "signed to the devells book and then seald it with his blood" five years earlier, and that ever since he had "been practising Eivel against Every man," the Connecticut Court of Assistants refused to try him, discharging him upon payment of his jail fees and the costs of bringing him to Hartford. Men who confessed to witch-craft outside of the Salem outbreak were punished, to be sure—but whereas most confessing women were taken at their word and executed, confessing men were almost all rebuked as liars.

Even when the courts took charges against individual men more seriously, their responses to these men were noticeably less severe than were their responses to the women whose cases they acted upon. As the following accounts illustrate, the repercus-sions of an accusation were likely to be far graver and longer lasting for a woman than for a man, even when their personal circumstances and the evidence were strikingly similar. . . .

[Karlsen then provides a detailed account of six women's experiences.]

. . . The six women featured in these histories were either (1) daughters of parents who had no sons (or whose sons had died), (2) women in marriages which brought forth only daughters (or in which the sons had died), or (3) women in marriages with no children at all. These patterns had significant economic implica-tions. Because there were no legitimate male heirs in their imme-diate families, each of these six women stood to inherit, did in-herit, or were denied their apparent right to inherit substantially larger portions of their fathers' or husbands' accumulated estates than women in families with male heirs. Whatever actually hap-pened to the property in question—and in some cases we simply do not know—these women were aberrations in a society with an inheritance system designed to keep property in the hands of men.

These six cases also illustrate fertility and mortality patterns widely shared among the families of accused witches. A substan-tial majority of New England's accused females were women without brothers, women with daughters but no sons, or women in marriages with no children at all. . . . Of the 267 accused females, enough is known about 158 to identify them as either having or not having brothers or sons to inherit: only sixty-two of the 158 (39 percent) did, whereas ninety-six (61 percent) did not. More striking, *once accused*, women without brothers or sons were even more likely than women with brothers or sons to be tried, convicted, and executed: women from families without male heirs made up 64 percent of the females prosecuted, 76 percent of those who were found guilty, and 89 percent of those who were executed. . . .

Numbers alone, however, do not tell the whole story. More remains to be said about what happened to these inheriting or potentially inheriting women, both before and after they were accused of witchcraft.

It was not unusual for women in families without male heirs to be accused of witchcraft shortly after the deaths of fathers, husbands, brothers, or sons. . . . Not all witches from families without male heirs were accused of conspiring with the Devil *after* they had come into their inheritances. On the contrary, some were accused prior to the death of the crucial male relative, many times before it was clear who would inherit. Eunice Cole was one of these women. Another was Martha Corey of Salem, who was accused of witchcraft in 1692 while her husband was still alive. Giles Corey had been married twice before and had several daughters by the time he married the widow Martha Rich, probably in the 1680s. With no sons to inherit, Giles's substantial land holdings would, his neighbors might have assumed, be passed on to his wife and daughters. Alice Parker, who may have been Giles's daughter from a former marriage, also came before the magistrates as a witch in 1692, as did Giles himself. Martha Corey and Alice Parker maintained their innocence and were hanged. Giles Corey, in an apparently futile attempt to preserve his whole estate for his heirs, refused to respond to the indictment. To force him to enter a plea, he was tortured: successively heavier weights were placed on his body until he was pressed to death.

What seems especially significant here is that most accused witches whose husbands were still alive were, like their counterparts who were widows and spinsters, over forty years of age—and therefore unlikely if not unable to produce male heirs. Indeed, the fact that witchcraft accusations were rarely taken seriously by the community until the accused stopped bearing children takes on a special meaning when it is juxtaposed with the anomolous position of inheriting women or potentially inheriting women in New England's social structure.

Witches in families without male heirs sometimes had been dispossessed of part or all of their inheritances before—sometimes long before—they were formally charged with witchcraft. Few of these women, however, accepted disinheritance with equanimity. Rather, like Susanna Martin, they took their battles to court, casting themselves in the role of public challengers to the system of male inheritance. In most instances, the authorities sided with their antagonists. . . .

Looking back over the lives of these many women—most particularly those who did not have brothers or sons to inherit—we begin to understand the complexity of the economic dimension of New England witchcraft. Only rarely does the actual trial testimony indicate that economic power was even at issue. Nevertheless it is there, recurring with a telling persistence once we look beyond what was explicitly said about these women as witches. Inheritance disputes surface frequently enough in witchcraft cases, cropping up as part of the general context even when no direct link between the dispute and the charge is discernible, to suggest the fears that underlay most accusations. No matter how deeply entrenched the principle of male inheritance, no matter how carefully written the laws that protected it, it was impossible to insure that all families had male offspring. The women who stood to benefit from these demographic "accidents" account for most of New England's female witches. . . .

. . . If daughters, husbands, and sons of witches were more vulnerable to danger in 1692 than they had been previously, they were mostly the daughters, husbands, and sons of inheriting or potentially inheriting women. As the outbreak spread, it drew into its orbit increasing numbers of women, "unlikely" witches in that they were married to well-off and influential men, but familiar figures to some of their neighbors nonetheless. What the impoverished Sarah Good had in common with Mary Phips, wife of Massachusetts's governor, was what Eunice Cole had in common with Katherine Harrison, and what Mehitabel Downing had in common with Ann Hibbens. However varied their backgrounds and economic positions, as women without brothers or women without sons, they stood in the way of the orderly transmission of property from one generation of males to another.

Character Traits

John Demos, after suggesting that the witch prosecutions cannot be described as simply a war of the sexes, offers an explanation that relies largely on individual personality traits. Like Karlsen, Demos looks at evidence from other witchcraft cases rather than just from Salem. Abridged from John Putnam Demos, Entertaining Satan: Witchcraft and the Culture of Early New England *(New York, 1982)*, 63–64, 86, 89, 91–94.

An easy hypothesis—perhaps too easy—would make of witchcraft a single plank in a platform of "sexist" oppression. Presumably, the threat of being charged as a witch might serve to constrain the behavior of women. Those who asserted themselves too openly or forcibly could expect a summons to court, and risked incurring the ultimate sanction of death itself. Hence the dominance of *men* would be underscored in both symbolic and practical terms. Male dominance was, of course, an assumed principle in traditional society—including the society of early New England. Men controlled political life; they alone could vote and hold public office. Men were also leaders in religion, as pastors and elders of local congregations. Men owned the bulk of personal property (though women had some rights and protections). Furthermore, the values of the culture affirmed the "headship" of men in marital and family relations and their greater "wisdom" in everyday affairs. Certainly, then, the uneven distribution of witchcraft accusations and their special bearing on the lives of women were consistent with sex-roles generally.

But was there *more* to this than simple consistency? Did the larger matrix of social relations enclose some dynamic principle that would energize actual "witch-hunting" so as to hold women down? On this the evidence—at least from early New England—seems doubtful. There is little sign of generalized (or "structural") conflict between the sexes. Male dominance of public affairs was scarcely an issue, and in private life there was considerable scope for female initiative. Considered overall, the relations of men and women were less constrained by differences of role and status than would be the case for most later generations of Americans. It is true that many of the suspects displayed qualities of assertiveness and aggressiveness beyond what the culture deemed proper. But these displays were not directed at men as such; often enough the targets were other women. Moreover, no single line in the extant materials raises the issue of sex-defined patterns of authority. Thus, if witches were at some level protesters against male oppression, they themselves seem to have been

T.H. Matteson's 1855 painting Examination of a Witch dramatized an imagined scene from the witch trials. By the middle of the nineteenth century, New Englanders were intrigued by the trials, and painters depicted the events based on a fairly crude understanding of what occured. In reality, a suspected witch's body would be examined for telltale signs by a delegation of women that would then report to the court. (Courtesy of Peabody Essex Museum.)

unconscious of the fact. As much could be said of the accusers, in the (putative) impulse to dominate. . . .

And one final point in this connection: a large portion of witchcraft charges were brought against women *by* other women. Thus, if the fear of witchcraft expressed a deep strain of misogyny, it was something in which both sexes shared. . . .

With the witches' sex, age, personal background, family life, propensity to crime, occupations, and social position all accounted for (as best we can manage), there yet remains one category which may be the most important of all. What were these people like—as people? What range of motive, of style, and of behavior would they typically exhibit? Can the scattered artifacts of their separate careers be made to yield a composite portrait, a model, so to speak, of witch-character? . . .

. . . Witchcraft was *defined* in reference to conflict; and most charges of witchcraft grew out of specific episodes of conflict.

Hence it should not be surprising that the suspects, as individuals, were notably active that way. . . .

To be sure, most of the evidence on the motives and behavior of witches comes by way of their accusers; what, then, of its relation to "objective" reality? Perhaps such evidence should be viewed as inherently prejudiced, indeed as a reflection of the accusers' *own* character and inner preoccupations. This difficulty can be countered, if not entirely resolved, in several ways. For one thing, at least some of the pertinent testimony derives from situations which had nothing to do with witchcraft. . . . There are also various comments made in court *by* the suspects—in short, self-reports—to much the same effect. (Mary Johnson declared that general "discontent" had tempted her to invoke the Devil. Katherine Harrison apologized for slandering her neighbors with "hasty, unadvised, and passionate expressions." Hugh Parsons admitted that "in his anger he is impatient, and doth speak what he should not.") Finally, there is the simple probability that so much opinion, of such a broadly convergent sort, cannot entirely misrepresent actual experience—the proverbial "fire" burning unseen but rightly inferred behind a cloud of all-too-evident "smoke." Hostile characterization usually finds some truth on which to fasten, even where it also expresses a deeply subjective concern. . . .

However disagreeable they seemed to their peers, the suspects were tough, resilient, purposive. John Godfrey was not merely a frequent litigant; he was also a determined and successful one. Anne Hibbens would bend, but never break, in the face of unanimous censure by her brethren in the Boston church. Katherine Harrison countered the animus of her Wethersfield neighbors by way of formal actions at court and informal (personally given) rebuke. Indeed it was this configuration of qualities that made the individuals involved seem not only suspect but genuinely fearsome. Had they been "crazed," "distracted," or "impotent . . . in understanding," their words and deeds would not have counted for very much. In reality, they seemed anything

---

but "impotent." Their general ill will, their presumed envies and resentments, their explicit threats to do harm would all be treated with the utmost seriousness precisely because, in a certain sense, they were *strong*. . . .

From this long and somewhat tortuous exercise in prosopography a rough composite finally emerges. To recapitulate, the typical witch:

1. was female.
2. was of middle age (i.e. between forty and sixty years old).
3. was of English (and "Puritan") background.
4. was married, but was more likely (than the general population) to have few children—or none at all.
5. was frequently involved in trouble and conflict with other family members.
6. had been accused, on some previous occasion, of committing crimes—most especially theft, slander, or other forms of assaultive speech.
7. was more likely (than the general population) to have professed and practiced a medical vocation, i.e. "doctoring" on a local, quite informal basis.
8. was of relatively low social position.
9. was abrasive in style, contentious in character—and stubbornly resilient in the face of adversity.

Religious Tensions

Finally, Christine Heyrman puts forth the only thesis considered here that places religion at the center of the controversy: she asserts that associates of the small community of Quaker dissenters were especially likely to be targeted. Excerpted from Christine Heyrman, "Specters of Subversion, Societies of Friends: Dissent and the Devil in Provincial Essex County, Massachusetts," in Saints and Revolutionaries: Essays on Early American History, *ed. David D. Hall, John M. Murrin, and Thad W. Tate (New York, 1984), 47–48, 51–53, 55.*

Even before her alleged bewitchment in the fall of 1692, Mary Stevens had probably become an object of local concern because of

289

her courtship by Francis Norwood, Jr., the Quaker grandson of Clement Coldom. The marriage of Mary to Francis would not have been the first merging of orthodox and dissenting families in Gloucester, but it was a union of tremendous social significance. For Mary was not a servant maid or the daughter of an ordinary local farmer up in Goose Cove, but the child of Deacon James Stevens of the First Church, one of Gloucester's most prominent citizens; and Francis was not the stepson of an obscure Quaker farmer, but an avowed Friend from a fairly affluent family. Francis's suit of Mary Stevens thus marked the first movement of the Friends in Gloucester out of their position on the periphery of local society and the neighborhood of the remote northern Cape and into the mainstream. Their betrothal persuaded Lt. William Stevens, Mary's older brother and a major local merchant, that only demonic influences could have prevailed upon his sister to accept the attentions of a Quaker. As alarmed by the discovery of dissenting affinities among his own kin as Clement Coldom had been earlier, William Stevens acted to defend his family's integrity and to dissuade his sister from a disastrous alliance by declaring that she was bewitched. Stevens also sent for four of Salem Village's "afflicted girls," the instigators of the witchcraft trials held earlier in 1692, who claimed to have the power to discern who troubled the victims of malefic magic. But when William Stevens sought assistance from Salem Village, he and his neighbors already suspected who had bewitched his sister—her prospective father-in-law, Francis Norwood, Sr., whom everyone in Gloucester had long believed to be a wizard. . . .

What endows the story of Mary Stevens with some importance for understanding the history of heterodoxy in Massachusetts is that this case was not singular. In fact, the same fears of heresy's infecting orthodox families through intermarriage or other ties to dissenters that stirred William Stevens underlay many of the other witchcraft prosecutions in Essex County during 1692. The center of the hysteria that had peaked earlier in that year was Salem, the town with the largest concentration of Quakers in the county. As in Gloucester, the connection in Salem between actual prosecutions for witchcraft and religious heterodoxy was indirect: few Quakers, and none of Essex County's most prominent Friends, were accused of the crime. The situation in Salem differed from the Stevens possession in Gloucester in only one way: here it was the "witches" rather than the bewitched who had ties of blood, marriage, affection, or friendship to the Quakers. But many of the Salem trials, like the Stevens case, reflect the same anxieties over the merging of the orthodox and dissenting communities.

A substantial number of the witches accused by Salem Village's "afflicted girls" came from families or households that included Quaker members. A case in point is the apparently puzzling prosecution of Rebecca Nurse. The pattern of indictments in Salem conformed to that of Andover and Gloucester insofar as those initially accused were all social outcasts in some sense—poor or shrewish women prone to violent or unseemly behavior, and usually reputed to have practiced malefic magic against their neighbors. The sole exception was Rebecca Nurse, a paragon of matronly piety, a pillar of respectability, a church member, and the wife of a substantial Salem Village farmer, Francis. There was only one reason that her neighbors had for disliking Rebecca Nurse: namely, that in 1677 the young Samuel Southwick, the orphaned son of a local Quaker farmer, John Southwick, chose the Nurses as his guardians and that they took the boy into their home. Rebecca and Francis were not Quakers, but their ward was.

Among those accused of witchcraft later in the trial proceedings were a large number of people who shared with Rebecca Nurse the same kind of indirect Quaker affinities, connections of kinship, and friendship with religious dissidents. There was the Proctor family, for example, of which five members—John, his wife, Elizabeth, and three of their children—were charged with witchcraft. What made the Proctors suspect in the eyes of their neighbors was less that John ran a tavern on the Ipswich Road than that his wife's family, the Bassets of Lynn, included a large number of Quakers. . . .

Along with the bonds of blood and marriage, geographic propinquity to the Quaker community characterized many of the accused witches of Salem Village. Since most of these accused witches lived in Salem Village's more prosperous eastern part, situated adjacent to Salem Town, and since the majority of the accusers came from the more remote and economically stagnant western side, it has been suggested that western farmers both envied and resented the east's exposure to the affluent, cosmopolitan town. But more prominent in the thinking of the western Villagers than the greater proximity of their eastern neighbors to commercial Salem Town may have been the even shorter physical distance separating the residences of the accused from Salem's Quaker enclave. . . .

. . . [T]ypically the accused witches were not themselves members of dissenting sects, and their connections with heterodoxy consisted in more tangential ties to dissenters among blood relatives, in-laws, household members, or neighbors and friends. Even in the case of Abigail Somes, accusations passed over Samuel Gaskill, for decades a central figure in the Salem Meeting, and focused instead on his ward, the child of an orthodox father and a heretical mother. Her background and that of many other accused witches suggest that the focus of anxiety was less on dissenters themselves than on those individuals who because of their relations or residences fell under suspicion of harboring if not heterodox sympathies then at least sympathy for the heterodox. The very ambiguity of their affinities and the division of their religious loyalties by the ties of family and friendship made such figures even more threatening to the maintenance of orthodoxy than known dissenters.

Questions

1. *What explanation offered by these scholars do you find the most convincing?*
2. *Demos, writing prior to Karlsen, criticizes a simplistic explanation that relies on sex roles; do you believe that Karlsen has answered his objections in her analysis of the role of gender?*
3. *The excerpts by Boyer and Nissenbaum and Heyrman both refer to residential patterns in the accusations; whose interpretation do you find most convincing?*
4. *Can you think of any way to tie these various theories about who would be accused together: Is there, for instance, an underlying theme to unite them all?*

CONTEMPORARY IDEAS ABOUT WITCHES AND THE EVENTS AT SALEM

The documents that follow examine Salem witchcraft from a number of different perspectives. The case against Bridget Bishop includes depositions taken largely from lay people who came forward to accuse this woman of witchcraft. The statement by a group of ministers lays out the somewhat belated clerical opposition to the trials, which played a key role in ending them. The documents authored by Increase and Cotton Mather present some of their views, penned either while the trials were still going on or ten years after they had ended. Together, these documents provide a glimpse of attitudes toward the supernatural in late-seventeenth-century New England.

The Case Against Bridget Bishop

One of nineteen people executed as a witch in 1692, Bridget Bishop had some of the classic attributes her New England neighbors were inclined to associate with a witch. For one thing, she was alienated from the religious faith of the community, having never attended worship services. In addition, she ran a tavern, where excessive drinking and game playing were common. She seems to have been seen as embodying relaxed sexual attitudes; deponents elsewhere mention her red bodice and a number of men may have had illicit thoughts about her, as they recount nocturnal visits to their beds by her specter (or ethereal image).

The excerpts below from the depositions taken against her offer typical examples of behavior attributed to alleged witches: she caused illness or death to people and animals, her image could appear as a specter, and she could change herself into other shapes. On one count, however, Bridget Bishop was unique. Only she was accused of keeping puppets (or "popites") to use in tormenting her victims. This evidence, contained in a deposition given below, caused one modern student of Salem witchcraft to conclude that Bishop was a witch, intent on using magical powers to harm her neighbors. Bishop was the wife of Edward Bishop at the time of her trial and execution, but she had previously been married to a man named Oliver, and the trial records refer to her by both names. These documents are taken from The Salem Witchcraft Papers: Verbatim Transcripts of the Legal Documents of the Salem Witchcraft Outbreak of 1692, *ed. Paul Boyer and Stephen Nissenbaum, (New York, 1977), 1:94–101, 103. Punctuation has been added and abbreviations expanded to clarify meaning.*

Deposition 1: Samuel Gray, May 30, 1692

Samuell Gray of Salem Aged aboute 42 yeares Testifieth and sayth that about fourteen years agoe he goeing to bed well one Lords Day at night, and after he had beene asleep some time, he awakened & looking up, saw the house light as if a candle or candles were lighted in it and the dore locked & that little fire there, was Raked up. He did then see a woman standing between the Cradle in the Roome and the Bed side and seemed to look upon him. Soe he did Rise up in his bed and it vanished or disappeared. Then he went to the dore and found it locked. And unlocking and Opening the dore, he went to the Entry dore and looked out, and then againe did see the same Woman he had a little before seene in the Rome [room], and in the same garbe she was in before. Then he said to her "in the name of God what doe you come for?" Then she vanished away. Soe he Locked the dore againe & went to bed. And between sleepeing & wakeing he felt some thing Come to his mouth or lipes cold, & thereupon started & looked up & againe did see the same woman with some thing betweene both her hands holding before [it] his mouth. Upon which she moved. And the Child in the Cradle gave a great screech out as if it was greatly

---

"Depositions," excerpted from *The Salem Witchcraft Papers: Verbatim Transcripts of the Legal Documents of the Salem Witchcraft Outbreak of 1692*, Paul Boyer and Stephen Nissenbaum, editors, Harvard University Press, 1977.

hurt. And she [the specter] disappeared. And [he] takeing the child up could not quiett it in some howres. From which tyme, the child that before was a very likely thriveing Child did pine away and was never well, althow it Lived some moneths after, yet in a sad Condition and soe dyed. . . .

Deposition 2: The Reverend John Hale, May 20, 1692

The said Bishop did entertaine people in her house at unseasonable houres in the night, to keep drinking and playing at shovelboard, whereby discord did arise in other families & young people were in danger to bee corrupted &. . . . The said [Christian, wife of John Trask, a neighbor] Trask knew these things & had once gon into the house; & fynding some at shovel-board had taken the peices thay played with & thrown them into the fyre & had reprooved the said Bishop for promoting such disorders, But received no satisfaction from her about it. . . .

But as to Christian Trask, the next news I heard of her was that she was distracted; & asking her husband [John] Trask when she was so taken [he told] mee shee was taken distracted that night after shee [came from] my house when shee complained against Goody Bishop.

She continueing some time Distracted, wee sought the Lord by fasting & prayer & the Lord was pleased to restore the said [Trask] to the use of her reason agen [again]. I was with her often in [her] distraction (& took it then to bee only distraction, yet fearing sometimes somewhat worse). But since I have seen the fitts of those bewitched at Salem Village I call to mind some of hers to be much like some of theirs. . . .

Her distraction (or bewitching) continued about a month and in those intervalls wherein shee was better shee earnestly desired prayers. & the Sabboth before she dyed I received a note for prayers on her behalf which her husband said was written by her selfe; & I judge was her owne hand writing, beeing well acquainted with her hand.

As to the wounds she dyed of, I observed 3 deadly ones; apeice of her wind pipe cutt out. & another wound above that threww the windpipe & Gullet & the veine they call jugular. So that I then judge & still doe apprehend it impossible for her with so short a pair of cissars [scissors] to mangle her selfe so, without some extraordinary work of the devill or witchcraft.

Deposition 3: Samuel Shattock, June 2, 1692

Sundry other tymes she came in a Smooth flattering maner in very Slighty Errants [errands]; we have thought Since [that she did this] on purpos to work mischief. At or very near this tyme our Eldest Child, who promised as much health & understanding both by Countenance and actions as any other Children of his years, was taken in a very drooping Condition. And as She Came oftener to the hous he grew wors & wors. As he would be standing at the door, [he] would fall out & bruis his face upon a great Step Stone, as if he had been thrust out bye an invisible hand, often tymes falling & hitting his face in a very miserable maner. . . .

. . . [H]e grew wors in his fits; and [when he was] out of them, would be allmost allways crying, [so] that for many months he would be crying till nature's strenght was spent & then would fall a sleep and then awake & fall to crying & moaning: that his very Countenance did bespeak Compassion. And at length wee perceived his understanding decayed, Soe that wee feared (as it has Since proved) that he would be quite bereaft of his witts; for Ever Since he has bin Stupified and voide of reason, his fitts still following of him. . . .

Deposition 4: John Louder, June 2, 1692

John Louder of Salem Aged aboute thurtey two Yeares Testifieth and sayth that aboute seaven or Eight years since [ago], I then Liveing with Mr John Gedney in Salem and haveing had some Controversy with Bridgett Bushop the wife of Edward Bushop of Salem, Sawyer [wood finisher], aboate her fowles that used to Come into our orchard or garden. Some little tyme after which, I goeing well to bed, aboute the dead of the night [I] felt a great weight upon my Breast. And awakening [I] looked and, it being bright moonlight, did clearly see said Bridget Bushop or her likeness sitting upon my stomake. . . . [I put] my Armes of[f] of the bed to free myselfe from that great oppression, [but] she presently layd hold of my throat and allmost Choked mee. And I had noe strenth or power in my hands to resist or help my selfe. And in this Condition she held mee to [until] almost day. Some tyme after this, my Mistress Susannah Gedney was in our orchard and I was then with her. And said Bridget Bushop, being then in her Orchard which was next adjoyneing to ours, my Mistress told said Bridget that I said or afirmed that she came one night & satt upon my brest as aforesaid, which she denyed and I afirmed to her face to be true and that I did plainely see her. Upon which discourse with her, she Threatened mee. And some tyme after that I being not very well stayed at home on a Lords day. And on the afternoon of said day, the dores being shutt, I did see a black pig in the Roome Coming towards mee; soe I went towards itt to kick it and it vanished away.

Immediately after I satt down in an Narrow Bar and [I] did see a black thing Jump into the window; and [it] came & stood Just before my face, upon the bar. The body of itt looked like a Munky only the feete ware like a Cocks feete with Claws and the face somewhat more like a mans than a Munkiey. And I being greatly affrighted, not being able to speake or help my selfe by Reason of fear, I suppose; soe the thing spake to mee and said 'I am a Messenger sent to you, for I understand you are trobled in mind, and if you will be Ruled by mee, you shall want for Nothing in this world.' Upon which I endeavered to clap my hands upon itt, and sayd 'You devill I will Kill you.' But I could feale noe substance. . . .

I Againe did see that or the like creture that I before did see within dores, in such a posture as it seemed to be agoeing to fly at mee. Upon which I cryed out: 'the whole armor of god be between mee and you.' Soe itt sprang back and flew over the apple tree, flinging the dust with its feet against my stomake. Upon which I was struck dumb, and soe Continued for aboute three days tyme. And also shook many of the apples of[f] from the tree which it flu over.

Deposition 5: John Bly, Sr., and William Bly, June 2, 1692

Jno Blye Senior aged about 57 years & William Blye aged about 15 years both of Salem Testifieth and sayth that, being Imployed by Bridgitt Bushup Alies Oliver of Salem to help take downe the Cellar wall of The owld house she formerly Lived in, wee the said Deponants, in holes of the said owld wall Belonging to the said sellar, found Severall popitts made up of Raggs And hoggs Brusells with headles pins in Them, with the points out ward & this was about Seaven years Last past.

Deposition 6: John Bly, Sr., and Rebecca Bly, no date

Jno Bly Bought a Sow of Edward Bushop of Salem . . . and Bridgett, the wife of Said Edward Bushop, because she could not have the mony or vallue agreed for, payd unto her, she [came] to the house of the deponents in Salem and Quarrelled with them aboute it. Soon after which the sow haveing piged, she was taken with strange fitts, Jumping up and knocking hir head against the fence and seemed blind and deafe and would not Eat neither Lett her pigs suck, but foamed at the mouth . . . wee did then Apprehend or Judge & doe still that said Bishop had bewitched said sow.

Bringing the Witch Trials to an End

Increase Mather, the leading minister in the colony in 1692, returned from London, where he had been negotiating a new charter for the Massachusetts government, and confronted the witch scare. After observing the proceedings for a time, he joined with other ministers to produce the statement reprinted below. The effect of their declaration was to bring the trials to a halt, since in it the ministers questioned the judges' use of evidence. Whereas the judges were willing to believe that the appearance of one's specter proved that one was a witch, the ministers suggested that the devil might cause an innocent person's likeness to appear as a way to bring charges down on the godly. Because ministers were experts on the theological questions raised by witchcraft prosecutions, their opinions mattered to the governor and his council, to whom this statement was addressed. This document was printed in Increase Mather's Cases of Conscience *(Boston, 1693), unpaginated appendix.*

The Return of several Ministers consulted by his Excellency, and the Honourable Council, upon the present Witchcrafts in *Salem* Village.

Boston, June 15. 1692

I. The afflicted State of our poor Neighbours, that are now suffering by Molestations from the Invisible World, we apprehend so deplorable, that we think their Condition calls for the utmost help of all Persons in their several Capacities.

II. We cannot but with all Thankfulness acknowledge, the Success which the merciful God has given unto the sedu-

298

lous and assiduous Endeavors of our honourable Rulers, to detect the abominable Witchcrafts which have been committed in the Country; humbly *praying that the discovery of these mysterious and mischievous Wickednesses, may be perfected.*

III.   We judge that in the prosecution of these, and all such Witchcrafts, there is need of a very critical and exquisite Caution, left by too much Credulity for things received only upon the Devil's Authority, there be a Door opened for a long Train of miserable Consequences, and Satan get an Advantage over us, for we should not be ignorant of his Devices.

IV.   . . .'tis necessary that all Proceedings thereabout be managed with an exceeding tenderness toward those that may be complained of; especially if they have been Persons formerly of an unblemished Reputation.

V.   When the first Enquiry is made into the Circumstances of such as may lie under any just Suspicion of Witchcrafts, we could wish that there may be admitted as little as is possible, of such Noise, Company, and Openness, as may too hastily expose them that are examined; and that there may nothing be used as a Test, for the Trial of the suspected, the Lawfulness whereof may be doubted among the People of God; but that the Directions given by such Judicious Writers as Perkins and Bernard, be consulted in such a Case.

At the close of his pamphlet opposing the witch trials, Increase Mather added a postscript protesting that he did not want to be misunderstood. In particular, Mather feared that readers might think he did not believe in witches or that he intended to criticize the trial judges. These excerpts from his postscript reveal how uncomfortable New England elites felt about publishing their differences; in addition they suggest that Mather did not want to be seen as contributing to irreligion by denying again the existence of the supernatural.

The Design of the preceding *Dissertation,* is not to plead for Witchcrafts, or to appear as an Advocate for Witches: I have therefore written another Discourse proving that there are such horrid Creatures as Witches in the World; and that they are to be extirpated and cut off from amongst the People of God, which I have Thoughts and Inclinations in due time to publish; and I am abundantly satisfied that there have been, and are still most cursed Witches in the Land. More then one or two of those now in

Prison, have freely and credibly acknowledged their Communion and Familiarity with the Spirits of Darkness; and have also declared unto me the Time and Occasion, with the particular Circumstances of their Hellish Obligations and Abominations.

Nor is there designed any Reflection on those worthy Persons who have been concerned in the late Proceedings at *Salam:* They are wise and good Men, and have acted with all Fidelity according to their Light, and have out of tenderness declined the doing of some things, which in our own Judgments they were satisfied about: Having therefore so arduous a Case before them, Pitty and Prayers rather than Censures are their due; on which account I am glad that there is published to the World (by my Son) a *Breviate of the Tryals* of some who were lately executed, whereby I hope the thinking part of Mankind will be satisfied, that there was more than that which is called *Spectre Evidence* for the Conviction of the Persons condemned.

Cotton Mather Assesses the Witch Trials

In the following passage, Cotton Mather—also a Boston minister like his father, Increase Mather—addresses three questions. First, what had been the principle evidence in the witch trials; second, what led him to conclude that the trials went too far; and, third, what were the most serious mistakes made at Salem? Note that Mather, like his father, continued to believe that Satan works evil in the world through witches, even as he suggests that witches may not have been the source of the problem in this particular case. The following is taken from Mather's monumental history of early New England, Magnalia Christi Americana *(1702); this excerpt was taken from the 1820 edition, 2:413–14.*

By these things you may see how this matter was carry'd on, *viz.* chiefly by the complaints and accusations of the afflicted (bewitch'd ones, as it was suppos'd) and then by the confessions of the *accus'd* condemning themselves and others. Yet experience shew'd, that the more there were apprehended, the more were still afflicted by satan; and the number of confessors increasing, did but increase the number of the *accused;* and the executing of

Cotton Mather (1663–1728) was a clergyman in one of the Boston churches in 1692. Because he had previously assisted with the case of a girl who was apparently bewitched, he was considered something of an expert on the supernatural. In this, he followed in the footsteps of his powerful and important father, Increase Mather who—along with Cotton and other ministers—helped to bring the trials to an end (Courtesy of the New York Public Library.)

some, made way for the apprehending of others: For still the afflicted complain'd of being tormented by new objects, as the former were remov'd. So that those that were concern'd, grew amaz'd at the number and quality of the persons accus'd, and feared that satan by his wiles had enwrapped innocent persons under the imputation of that crime. And at last, it was evidently seen, that there must be a stop put, or the generation of the children of God, would fall under that condemnation. Henceforth therefore the juries generally acquitted such as were tried, fearing they had gone too far before. And Sir *William Phips* the Governour, repriev'd all that were condemn'd, even the confessors as well as others. And the confessors generally fell off from their confession, some saying, *They remembred nothing of what they had said;* others said, *They had belied themselves and others.* Some broke prison and ran away, and were not strictly searched after. Some acquitted, some dismissed, and one way or other, all that had been accused, were set or left at liberty. . . .

It may be queried, How doth it appear that there was a going too far in this *affair?*

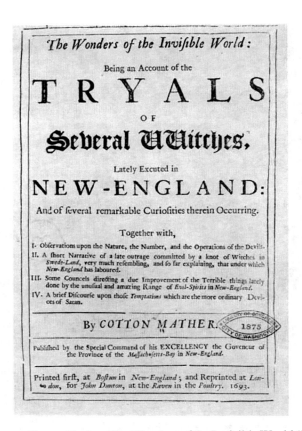

Title page to Cotton Mather, The Wonders of the Invisible World *(London, 1693). Mather, who had grave reservations about the work of the court that tried the witchcraft cases in 1692, nonetheless felt compelled to defend it against critics. His account, contained in this pamphlet, reveals his conflicted attitudes. The title of his pamphlet refers back to an early work by his father, Increase Mather, that argued in favor of "an invisible world" against skeptics. (Courtesy of the Library of Congress.)*

By the numbers of the persons accus'd, which at length increas'd to about an hundred; and it cannot be imagin'd that in a place of so much knowledge, so many in so small a compass of land, should so abominably leap into the devil's lap all at once.

The quality of several of the accus'd was such, as did bespeak *better things, and things that accompany salvation;* Persons, whose blameless and holy lives before did testifie for them; Persons that had taken great pains to bring up their children in the nurture and admonition of the Lord; such as we had charity for, as for our own souls: And charity is a christian duty commended to us.

The number of the afflicted daily increased until about fifty persons were thus vex'd by the devil. This gave just ground to suspect some mistake, which gave advantage to the *accuser of the brethren* to make a breach upon us.

It was considerable, that *nineteen* were executed, and all denied the crime to the death, and some of them were knowing persons, and had before this been accounted blameless *livers*. . . .

When this prosecution ceas'd, the Lord so *chain'd up satan,* that the afflicted grew presently well: The accused are generally quiet; and for five years since, we have no such molestation by them.

It sways much with me, which I have since heard and read, of the like mistakes in other places. As in Suffolk in England, about the year 1645 was such a prosecution, until they saw, that unless they put a stop, it would bring all into blood and confusion. The like hath been in France, until nine hundred were put to death. And in some other places the like So that New-England is not the only place circumvented by the *wiles of the wicked and wily serpent in this kind*. . . .

As to our case at *Salem,* I conceive it proceeded from some mistaken principles: As, that satan cannot assume the shape of an innocent person, and in that shape do mischief to the bodies and estates of mankind: and that the devil, when he doth harm to persons in their body or estate, it is (at least, most commonly, generally and frequently) by the help of our neighbour, some witch in covenant with the devil; and that when the party suspected looks on the parties suppos'd to be bewitch'd, and they are thereupon struck down into a fit, as if struck with a cudgel, it is a proof of such a covenant.

Questions

1. *If they continued to believe in the existence of witchcraft, how did various leading colonists come to oppose the trials?*
2. *What do the depositions reveal about popular attitudes regarding witches?*
3. *Can you see any differences between lay and clerical thinking when you compare the depositions and the ministers' statements?*

FURTHER READING

The most popular book on Salem witchcraft among undergraduates remains Salem Possessed: The Social Origins of Witchcraft, *by Paul Boyer and Stephen Nissenbaum (Cambridge, Massachusetts, 1974). John Putnam Demos's* Entertaining Satan: Witchcraft and the Culture of Early New England *(New York, 1982) and Carol Karlsen's* The Devil in the Shape of a Woman: Witchcraft in Colonial New England *(New York, 1987) examine the Salem accusations in the context of the long history of witch fears in colonial New England. The* Devil's Dominion: Magic and Religion in Early New England *(New York, 1992), by Richard Godbeer, includes two chapters on Salem. Trial transcripts are available in* The Salem Witchcraft Papers: Verbatim Transcripts of the Legal Documents of the Salem Witchcraft Outbreak of 1692, *ed. Paul Boyer and Stephen Nissenbaum, 3 vols. (New York, 1977); other original documents can be found in* Witch-hunting in Seventeenth-Century New England: A Documentary History, 1638–1692, *ed. David D. Hall (Boston, 1991).*

Marriage in Colonial America

Randolph A. Roth

INTRODUCTION

Historians once viewed the eighteenth century as a simple time, when men and women married for practical reasons and expected less of each other emotionally. They have since discovered, however, that many eighteenth-century marriages were emotionally intense and that many couples did not think much about the future before they married and conceived children. Historians are no longer certain such marriages were less prevalent then than they are today.

Marriage worked best when husbands and wives agreed on how authority and responsibility would be divided. Nowhere in eighteenth-century America were women the complete equals of their spouses. But a few marriages, particularly among the Quakers, were relatively egalitarian. In many marriages, especially in Puritan New England, husbands and wives worked together on most economic and family tasks as partners.

Likewise, marriage worked best when husbands and wives had the same goals. Most people married someone of the same age, class, religion, and ethnicity, so couples often began married life with a good deal of common ground. But even compatible couples argued, and spouses could find themselves suddenly incompatible. One spouse might join a dissenting church, for example, or begin drinking too much or take up with new friends.

Finally, marriage worked best if husbands and wives handled their chores effectively. Couples had many more domestic responsibilities than they do today. They had to settle disputes, supervise laborers, educate children, house relatives, nurse the sick, and keep the family farm or business running. Because of this range of responsibilities it is likely that earlier historians were correct in their evaluation that people in the eighteenth century picked spouses for more practical reasons than romantic ones.

MARRIAGE IN NEW ENGLAND AND THE CHESAPEAKE

Historians have long debated the roles of married men and women in colonial society. Some historians claim that men subordinated women and restricted their activities to the domestic sphere, while others insist that women were often engaged in public life and were more independent than some historians have made them out to have been. Laurel Thatcher Ulrich, David Hackett Fischer, and Jack P. Greene separately arrive at a third conclusion: that marriages were unequal partnerships in which the roles of women and men overlapped and lines of authority were blurred. Greene argues that marriages in the Chesapeake were much like the marriages Ulrich finds in New England, although women's roles grew more circumscribed over time. Fischer argues that Chesapeake marriages were more patriarchal and less loving than New England marriages.

Women as Deputy Husbands

The following selection looks at the roles of wives in New England households. Abridged from Laurel Thatcher Ulrich, Good Wives: Image and Reality in the Lives of Women in Northern New England, 1650–1750 *(New York, 1982), 36–40, 42–43, 50.*

There is a revealing little anecdote in a deposition recorded in Essex County in 1672. Jacob Barney of Salem had gone to Phillip

Cromwell's house to negotiate a marriage. Although both Cromwell and his wife were present, Barney had turned to the husband, expecting, as he said, "to have their minds from him." But because Cromwell had a severe cold which had impaired his hearing, he simply pointed to his wife and said that whatever she agreed upon, "he would make it good." This incident dramatizes three assumptions basic to family government in the traditional world:

1. The husband was supreme in the external affairs of the family. As its titular head, he had both the right and the responsibility to represent it in its dealings with the outside world.

2. A husband's decisions would, however, incorporate his wife's opinions and interest. (Barney expected to hear their minds from him.)

3. Should fate or circumstance prevent the husband from fulfilling his role, the wife could appropriately stand in his place. As one seventeenth-century Englishman explained it, a woman "in her husband's absence, is wife and deputy-husband, which makes her double the files of her diligence. At his return he finds all things so well he wonders to see himself at home when he was abroad."

. . . As deputy husbands a few women, like Mistress Cromwell, might emerge from anonymity; most women did not. . . . To talk about the independence of colonial wives is not only an anachronism but a contradiction in logic. A woman became a wife by virtue of her dependence, her solemnly vowed commitment to her husband. . . .

One can be dependent, however, without being either servile or helpless. To use an imperfect but nonetheless suggestive analogy, colonial wives were dependent upon patriarchal families in somewhat the same way seventeenth-century ministers were dependent upon their congregations or twentieth-century engineers are dependent upon their companies. That is, they owned neither their place of employment nor even the tools of their trade. No matter how diligently they worked, they did not expect to inherit the land upon which they lived any more than a minister expected to inherit his meetinghouse or an engineer his factory. Skilled service was their major contribution, secure support their primary compensation. Unlike professionals in either century, they could

This woodcut illustrates the various tasks that colonial women performed as productive workers in the family. (Courtesy of Corbis-Bettmann.)

not resign their position, but then neither could they be fired. Upon the death of a husband they were entitled to maintenance for life—or until they transferred their allegiance (symbolized by their name) from one domestic establishment to another.

The skilled service of a wife included . . . specialized house-keeping skills . . . , but it also embraced the responsibilities of a deputy husband. Since most productive work was based within the family, there were many opportunities for a wife to "double the files of her diligence." A weaver's wife, like Beatrice Plummer, might wind quills. A merchant's wife, like Hannah Grafton, might keep shop. A farmer's wife, like Magdalen Wear, might plant corn. . . .

. . . Almost any task was suitable for a woman as long as it furthered the good of her family and was acceptable to her husband. . . . Under the right conditions any wife not only *could* double as a husband, she had the responsibility to do so. . . .

To explain fully the contradictions in such a system, we must return to the day-to-day behavior of individual husbands and wives, first examining the factors which enhanced the role of deputy husband and then exploring conditions which muted its significance for colonial women.

. . . [T]here was as much variation in seventeenth- and eighteenth-century families as there is today. Some wives were servile, some were shrews, others were respected companions who shared the authority of their spouses in the management of family affairs. Important conditions, however, separated the colonial world from our own. The most basic of these was spatial. . . . Male and female space intersected and overlapped. Nor was there the sharp division between home and work that later generations experienced. Because servants and apprentices lived within the household, a family occasion—mealtime or nightly prayer— could become a business occasion as well.

In June of 1661 a young maid named Naomi Hull described a discussion which took place in the parlor of the Samuel Symonds' home in Ipswich, Massachusetts, early in that year. The case concerned the length of indenture of two Irish servants. According to the maid, all of the family had gathered for prayer when one of the Irishmen asked if a neighbor's son was coming the next day to plow. *Mistress* Symonds said she thought so. One of the men asked who would plow with him. *Mistress* Symonds said, "One of you." When the two men announced that their indenture was up and that they would work no longer, both the master and the mistress questioned the servants. At one point Mistress Symonds interrupted her husband. "Let them alone," she said. "Now they are speaking let them speak their own minds." Because the involvement of Mistress Symonds was not at issue, this casual description of her participation is all the more impressive. Such an anecdote shows the way in which boundaries between male and female domains might blur in a common household setting.

Ambitious men in early America were often involved in many things at once—farming and running a gristmill, for example, or cutting timber and fishing. Because wives remained close to the house, they were often at the communications center of these diverse operations, given responsibility for conveying directions, pacifying creditors, and perhaps even making some decisions about the disposition of labor. On a day-to-day basis this might be a rather simple matter: remembering to send a servant to repair a breach in the dam after he finished in the field, for example, or knowing when to relinquish an ox to a neighbor. But during a prolonged absence of her husband a woman might become involved in more weighty matters.

Sometime in the 1670s Moses Gilman of Exeter, New Hampshire, wrote to his wife from Boston:

> Loving wife Elisabeth Gillman these are to desire you to speake to John Gillman & James Perkins and so order the matter thatt Mr. Tho. Woodbridge may have Twelve thousand fott [feet] of merchantable boards Rafted [logs tied in two large rafts and floated down river to the mills] by thirsday night or sooner if poseble they Can for I have Absolutly sould [sold] them to him & if John Clough sen [Senior] or any other doe deliver bords to make up the sum Give Receits of whatt you Receive of him or any other man and lett no bote [body] bee prest [for payment] or other ways disposed of untill I Returne[.] being from Him who is yos till death
>
> Moses Gilman

If Gilman had doubted his wife's ability to "order the matter," he could have written a number of separate letters—to John Gilman, James Perkins, John Clough, and perhaps others. But securing a shipment of twelve thousand feet of merchantable boards entirely by letter would have been complicated and time-consuming. Instead, Gilman relied on the good sense of his wife, who would be respected as his surrogate, and who probably had acquired some expertise in making out receipts for forest products and in conveying instructions to lumbering and shipping crews. A "loving wife" who considered herself his "till Death" was more trustworthy than a hired servant or business associate. As a true consort, she would know that by furthering her husband's interest she furthered her own.

Thus, a wife with talent for business might become a kind of double for her husband, greatly extending his ability to handle affairs. . . . But two cautions are in order. First, the biases of the twentieth century may tempt historians to give undue significance to what were really rather peripheral enterprises. Acting as attorney to one's husband is not equivalent to practicing law. To colonial women, it may even have been less desirable than keeping house. This leads to the second point. The value of any activity is determined by its meaning to the participant, not to the observer. In early America position was always more important than task. Colonial women might appear to be independent, even aggressive, by modern standards, yet still have derived their status primarily from their relationship to their husbands.

This is well illustrated in a New Hampshire court record of 1671. A carpenter named John Barsham testified about an argument he had heard between Henry Sherburne and his second wife, Sarah, who was the widow of Walter Abbott. Barsham had come to the house to get some nails he needed for repairing a dwelling he had rented from them. According to Barsham, Sarah became so angry at her husband's opposition that she "rose off from the seat where she was setting & came up to him with her arms akimbo saying we should have nayles & he had nothing to [do] in it." As if to add the final authority to her demand, she asked him "why he trode upon Walter Abbotts floor & bid him get out of doors, & said that he had nothing to do there." Sarah Sherburne was an experienced and assertive woman. She had kept tavern "with two husbands and none." The house in which she and Sherburne lived had been part of her inheritance from her first husband. But in the heat of the argument she did not say, "Get out of *my* house" or "Get out of the house *I* provided." She said, "Get out of Walter Abbott's house." Her identity was not as property owner, but as wife. To assert her authority over her husband, she invoked the memory of his predecessor. . . .

The role of deputy husband reinforced a certain elasticity in premodern notions of gender. No mystique of feminine behavior prevented a woman from driving a hard bargain . . . and under ideal conditions day-to-day experience in assisting with a husband's work might prepare her to function competently in a male world—should she lose her husband, should she find herself without a grown son, should she choose not to remarry or find it impossible to do so. But in the immediate world such activities could have a far different meaning. The chores assigned might be menial, even onerous, and, whatever their nature, they competed for attention with the specialized housekeeping responsibilities which every woman shared.

Marriage and Gender in the Chesapeake

David Hackett Fischer draws a sharp contrast between marriages in New England and the Chesapeake. Excerpted from David Hackett Fischer, Albion's Seed: Four British Folkways in America (New York, 1989), 281, 283–87, 291–93, 295–97.

Virginia and New England were alike in their ideas of universal marriage; both rejected the ideal of celibacy which was so strong in Catholic countries. But these two Protestant cultures of British America also differed in many ways as to their ideas of marriage, and their matrimonial institutions. In Massachusetts, . . . marriage was thought to be a covenant which could be terminated when its terms were not fulfilled. In Virginia, matrimony was regarded as an indissoluble union—a sacred knot that could never be untied by mortal hands. Divorce in the modern sense did not exist. Only permanent separation and maintenance could be obtained, and even that release was rarely granted. . . .

Children were rarely made to marry against their will, but neither were they left to decide the question for themselves. Parents and guardians entered into complex negotiations to settle the size of the marriage portion or "dot" which a couple needed to make its way in the world. . . . In both England and Virginia, many of these unions were cousin-marriages that had been arranged by elders. . . . The marriage of first cousins was condemned by New England Puritans as violating the law of consanguinity. But many an Anglican lady "changed her condition but not her name." [That is, married a close relative.] The same custom was common in Virginia, and fundamentally important to the cohesion of the tidewater elite. The culture of New England created a different set of matrimonial priorities.

One consequence of these customs appeared in the pattern of age at marriage. Male Virginians married at nearly the same age as in New England, twenty-five or twenty-six on the average. But brides in the Chesapeake colonies were much younger than in

---

Puritan Massachusetts. Before 1700, most Virginia girls found a husband by the age of seventeen. Mean age at marriage was a little higher—eighteen to twenty—but below the Massachusetts average. . . .

Other inequalities appeared in the proportion of Virginians who married at all. Though the ideal was universal marriage, the reality was very different in seventeenth-century Virginia, because so few immigrants were females. Nearly all women were able to marry, but for men the pattern was very different. One study of estate-inventories in southern Maryland from 1658 to 1708 finds that one-quarter of men died without ever marrying. A man's chances of finding a wife were a function of his social rank. Here was yet another system of inequality in this hierarchical society.

The Virginia pattern developed within a culture where marriage was regarded as something to be arranged between families, something that did not require love as a precondition, something that could never be dissolved, and something that joined husband and wife in an organic and patriarchal hierarchy. Given such an idea of matrimony, it seemed right and fitting in this culture that a typical Virginia marriage in the seventeenth century should join a man of maturity to a miss in her teens. These Virginia customs were very different from the marriage ways of Massachusetts. . . .

. . . In every culture there are happy marriages and unhappy ones. But historians of the family have remarked upon the extent of marital discord among the gentry of Virginia. . . . The trouble commonly arose from deep contradictions in the gender ways of Virginia. Perhaps the most common cause of trouble was money. Men were taught to believe that they were masters of their households. But women often possessed property of their own, and wished to make economic decisions independent of their husbands. An example was the disastrous marriage of Colonel John Custis of Arlington, one of the most powerful men in Virginia, and Frances Parke Custis. . . . The strife in this union seems to have arisen mainly from disputes over property. Mrs. Custis was a woman of wealth, which her husband had the right to manage as he wished. But he also had the duty to pass her property intact to her children. An elaborate marriage contract existed, but it became an invitation to struggle between husband and wife. So bitter was this strife that Col. Custis ordered that a record of his domestic misery should be carved upon his gravestone.

For years, this unhappy couple refused to speak to one another, communicating only through their slaves. Long silences were punctuated by outbursts of rage so wild and violent as to border upon madness. After one such tempest, Col. Custis surprised his lady by inviting her to go driving with him. They rode in sullen silence through the Virginia countryside, until suddenly the colonel turned his carriage out of the road, and drove straight into Chesapeake Bay.

"Where are you going, Mr. Custis?" the lady asked, as the horses began to swim.

"To hell, Madam," he replied.

"Drive on," said she, "any place is better than Arlington.". . .

Another cause of domestic conflict rose from the politics of family life. . . . A wife was bound by her marriage vows to obey her husband. An apparently male essayist in the Virginia *Gazette* laid down rules of "matrimonial felicity" for the instruction of wives: "Never dispute with him . . . if any altercation or jars happen, don't separate the bed, whereby the animosity will increase . . . read often the matrimonial service, and overlook not the important word OBEY."

But the unwritten customs of the culture encouraged women to demand more freedom and respect. In 1687, for example, a

In this eighteenth-century portrait, the mother is the prominent figure among the family. (Courtesy of Children's Television Workshop.)

spirited lady named Sarah Harrison married Dr. James Blair, the future founder of William and Mary College. When the minister recited the marriage vows, she startled the congregation by responding, "No OBEY!" Three times the vows were repeated. Three times Sarah Harrison answered with increasing firmness "No Obey," until Dr. Blair finally agreed to take his chances and the wedding went forward without any promise of obedience. Their married life together proved to be deeply unhappy. Some years later, William Byrd noted in his diary:

> Went to the Commissary's, where . . . I was very much surprised to find Mrs. Blair drunk, which is growing pretty common with her, and her relations disguise it under the name of consolation.

Few women were as outspoken as Sarah Harrison. But many resisted by other means. Yet most were compelled to obey their husbands, often much against their will, in matters which they cared deeply about. Thus William Byrd compelled his wife to send her sick baby Otway to her mother-in-law, who lived at a plantation which was thought to be more healthy. The wife replied,

> I am very sorry you have limited Poor, sweet Otway, so that he has but a short time to stay with me. Poor dear babe . . . But Sir, your Orders must be obeyed whatever reluctance I find thereby.

Here was a fertile source of domestic strife.

A particular cause of trouble was the use of physical violence and verbal abuse by husbands against wives, and sometimes by wives against husbands as well. Here again the customs of the country were inconsistent. Men were expected to exercise authority over their wives, and were encouraged by custom to use moderate "chastisement" from time to time. But wife-beating was thought to be dishonorable and was punished in both England and America. . . .

Yet another tension in gender roles developed from ideas about love. Husbands and wives were expected to love one another—but not overmuch. Landon Carter complained of a Virginia lady who was "more fond of her husband perhaps than the politeness of the day allows for." Even in happy marriages, the love that men felt for their wives was not a love between equals, and sometimes it seemed to be less a love for a person than for a valuable piece of property. One gentleman wrote when his wife died:

> All grief will allow me to say of her is, that she was known to be a humble pious, virtuous, discreet woman, an ornament to her sex, and a crown to her husband. But woe is me the crown has fallen from my head.

A further source of conflict arose from a confusion of roles for women in Virginia. They were expected to be feminine, refined, delicate, gracious, modest, virtuous. At the same time, all but the most privileged of women were also expected to do farm work and even field labor as well as housewifery. Women of every estate were required to be resourceful but self-effacing. . . .

There were even theological disputes in Virginia on questions of gender. Some members of this culture shared a deeper sense of spiritual inequality between men and women than commonly existed in Massachusetts. At a rich planter's table as late as 1773, the northern tutor Philip Fithian was startled to hear an argument on the question of whether women had souls. That ancient conundrum had long since been laid to rest among the Puritans. But it still remained a topic of debate in Virginia.

All of these conflicts had a common denominator. In this society of English-speaking people, the rights which Christian Englishmen claimed for themselves were a standing reproach to the status of women in their society. A free-born English gentleman was in many ways the unfittest of all males to argue his wife into a condition of dependency. By an early date in the eighteenth century some of the ladies of Virginia were thinking of themselves as "She-Britons," and demanding a share of the rights that their husbands enjoyed. As early as 1736, the Virginia *Gazette* published an angry poem called "The Lady's Complaint," which captured the deepest contradiction in the genderways of Virginia:

> They plainly can their Thoughts disclose,
>   Whilst ours must burn within:
> We have got Tongues, and Eyes, in vain,
>   And Truth from us is sin. . . .
> Then Equal Laws let Custom find,
>   And neither Sex oppress;
> More Freedom give to Womankind,
>   Or give to Mankind less.

A Different View of Marriage

Unlike David Hackett Fischer, Jack P. Greene concludes that marriages in the Chesapeake were much like those in Britain's other colonies, although they had changed over time. Excerpted from Jack P. Greene, Pursuits of Happiness: The Social Development of Early Modern British Colonies and the Formation of American Culture *(Chapel Hill, 1988), 82, 94–95.*

[After 1680] improved life expectancy, a more equal sex ratio, and earlier marriages among creoles [native-born colonists] raised the birthrate, net reproduction nearly equaling deaths by the 1670s and exceeding them by the 1690s. In combination, these developments contributed by the end of the century to a total white population of nearly ninety thousand, a majority of whom were native-born. The same developments also led to a more settled and typically European nuclear family structure, more extended kinship networks, and considerably more compact settlements in all but the most newly occupied areas. . . .

In the private world of the family, quite as much as in the public world of politics and religion, the Chesapeake became far more settled—and far more like metropolitan Britain—during the eighteenth century. Despite improving demographic conditions, the genealogical depth of families remained shallow and the range of kinship connections relatively narrow during the early decades of the century. As in the previous century, this shallowness encouraged a broad conception of the family. Households tended to be open and associations with non-kin both intimate and extensive. With continuing increases in life expectancy through the middle decades of the century, however, the Chesapeake family became more susceptible to traditional definition. Parents began to live longer, typically into their mid-fifties and to have an average of four to five children who survived into adulthood. Grandparenthood, relatively rare in the previous century, became widespread and kinship networks much more extensive and intensive.

These developments may have turned Chesapeake families inward and made them more private, child-centered, nurturant, and affectionate and thereby brought them into close conformity with trends that were evident throughout the contemporary North Atlantic world. Much more important, they seem to have altered power relationships within the family. Just as an enlarging pool of older men lent strength to political and religious institutions at the local and provincial levels, so longer-lived fathers helped to bolster paternal authority within families. In the seventeenth century, higher survival rates for women had turned the Chesapeake into what one scholar has termed a "widowarchy" in which women, despite their disproportionately small numbers, enjoyed a role in family and economic life far more extensive than was usual among their counterparts in England. As disparities in survival rates among women and men dropped in the eighteenth century, however, husbands and fathers sought to transform the family into the well-ordered patriarchal units that had long been the ideal, if not necessarily always the norm, in metropolitan Britain. In consequence of these efforts, women found themselves more and more restricted to a domestic and ornamental role, and the Chesapeake, like Britain, became an even more male-dominated society.

Yet if Chesapeake fathers liked to think of themselves as patriarchs who presided firmly over deferential wives and children, the patriarchy they actually succeeded in establishing seems to have been a highly permissive one. They may have preached obedience to parents and encouraged passivity in daughters, but few of them, recent studies suggest, appeared to have tried to use their control over family land and other resources to establish a tight family discipline. Indeed, to enable their sons to function effectively in the fluid and competitive world of the Chesapeake, parents seem rather to have tried to inculcate in their offspring not obedience and deference but independence, self-assertiveness, self-confidence, and a reliance upon self-control. Not restraint but indulgence seems to have characterized parents' relations with their children, who enjoyed wide latitude in their behavior and were subjected to a minimum of parental interference in their lives.

Questions

1. *What tasks were reserved for women? men? What tasks were shared by men and women? What determined whether a task was "male" or "female"?*

2. *Are there signs that the marriages Ulrich describes were distinctively "Puritan"? that the marriages Fischer describes were distinctively "Anglican"? Did religious beliefs affect relationships between men and women?*

3. *How do contemporary marriages differ from those of colonial America? In what ways do they remain similiar? What broad forces that shaped marriage in the eighteenth century do not operate today? What new forces are at work shaping the nature of love and marriage?*

FRACTIOUS COURTSHIPS
AND MARRIAGES

The stories of Samuel Sewall and Elizabeth Ashbridge show that couples in eighteenth-century America had as much trouble resolving their differences as couples do now. Men held the upper hand in courtship and marriage, legally and economically. But women asserted themselves. The result was a struggle to define the terms on which marriage would be based. The struggle led sometimes to violence, sometimes to love and friendship, sometimes to peaceful coexistence.

Samuel Sewall (1652–1730)

Samuel Sewall was a prominent Boston merchant who entered politics and rose to chief justice of Massachusett's highest court. From 1673 until his death, Sewall kept a diary, an extraordinary record of his thoughts, feelings, and spiritual progress. The passages below begin with the death of Sewall's second wife, Abigail, in May 1720. Sewall mourned for several months, but by October he had set aside his grief and begun his search for a new wife. Taken from The Diary of Samuel Sewall, 1674–1729, *ed. M. Halsey Thomas, (New York, 1973), 2:950–51, 955, 957–67, 988–90, 993.*

[29 May 1720]

God having in his holy Sovereignty put my Wife out of the Fore-Seat [his second wife, Abigail, had died on May 26], I appre-

Excerpt from *The Diary of Samuel Sewall*, M. Halsey Thomas, ed., published by Farrar, Straus & Giroux, 1973, from the original manuscript at the Massachusetts Historical Society.

hended I had Cause to be ashamed of my Sin, and to loath my self for it; and retired into my Pue. . . . I put up a Note to this purpose; Samuel Sewall, depriv'd of his dear Wife by a very sudden and awfull Stroke, desires Prayers that GOD would sanctify the same to himself, and Children, and family. Writ and sent three; to the South, Old, and Mr. Colman's [churches]. . . .

[Tuesday, 31 May 1720]

Buried my dear Wife. . . . [H]ad a Comfortable day; though threatened with Rain. *Laus Deo.* I went into the Tomb: The good Lord prepare for me a House not made with Hands, eternal in the Heavens, and the Consideration of that will make the Grave a Lightsom place. My Son prays in his Sister's Chamber very pertinently, affectionatly. . . .

[5 September 1720]

Going to Son Sewall's I there meet with Madam Winthrop, told her I was glad to meet her there, had not seen her a great while; gave her Mr. Homes's Sermon. . . .

[Saturday, 1 October 1720]

I went to Madam Winthrop's just at 3. Spake to her, saying, my loving wife died so soon and suddenly, 'twas hardly convenient for me to think of Marrying again; however I came to this Resolution, that I would not make my Court to any person without first Consulting with her. Had a pleasant discourse about 7 Single persons . . . viz. Mad'm Rebekah Dudley, Catharine Winthrop, Bridget Usher, Deliverance Legg, Rebekah Loyd, Lydia Colman, Elizabeth Bellingham. She propounded one and another for me; but none would do. . . .

[3 October 1720]

Waited on Madam Winthrop again; 'twas a little while before she came in. Her daughter Noyes being there alone with me, I said, I hoped my Waiting on her Mother would not be disagreeable to her. She answer'd she should not be against that that might be for her Comfort. . . . By and by in came Mr. Airs, Chaplain of the Castle, and hang'd up his Hat, which I was a little startled at, it seeming as if he was to lodge there. At last Madam Winthrop came in. After a considerable time, I went up to her and said, if it might not be inconvenient I desired to speak with her. She assented, and spake of going into another Room; but Mr. Airs and Mrs. Noyes presently rose up, and went out, leaving us there alone. . . . I pray'd that Katharine *[Mrs. Winthrop]* might be the person assign'd for me. She instantly took it up in way of Denyal [denial], as if she had catch'd at an Opportunity to do it . . . could not leave her Children. I express'd my Sorrow . . . , pray'd her Consideration, and ask'd her when I should wait on her agen. She setting no time, I mention'd that day Sennight [one week hence]. Gave her Mr. Willard's Fountain open'd with the little print and verses; saying, I hop'd if we did well read that book, we should meet together hereafter, if we did not now. . . .

[6 October 1720]

A little after 6. p. m. I went to Madam Winthrop's. She was not within. I gave Sarah Chickering the Maid 2s. [shillings], Juno [Mrs. Winthrop's African American servant], who brought in wood, 1s. Afterward the nurse came in, I gave her 18d. [pence], having no other small Bill. After awhile Dr. Noyes came in with his Mother; and quickly after his wife came in: They sat talking, I think, till eight a-clock. I said I fear'd I might be some Interruption to their Business: Dr. Noyes reply'd pleasantly: He fear'd they might be an Interruption to me, and went away. Madam seem'd to harp upon the same string. Must take care of her Children; could not leave that House and Neighbourhood where she had dwelt so long. I told her she might doe her children as much or more good by bestowing what she laid out in Hous-keeping, upon them. Said her Son would be of Age the 7th of August. I said it might be inconvenient for her to dwell with her Daughter-in-Law, who must be Mistress of the House. I gave her a piece of Mr. Belcher's Cake and Ginger-Bread wrapped up in a clean sheet of Paper; told her of her Father's kindness to me when Treasurer, and I Constable. My Daughter Judith was gon from me and I was more lonesom—might help to forward one another in our Journey to Canaan. . . . I took leave about 9 aclock. I told [her] I came now to refresh her Memory as to Monday-night; said she had not forgot it. In discourse with her, I ask'd leave to speak with her Sister; I meant to gain Mad'm Mico's favour to persuade her Sister. She seem'd surpris'd and displeas'd, and said she was in the same condition! . . .

[10 October 1720]

In the Evening I visited Madam Winthrop, who treated me with a great deal of Curtesy; Wine, Marmalade. I gave her the News-Letter about the Thanksgiving; Proposals, for sake of the verses for David Jeffries. She tells me Dr. Increase Mather visited her this day, in Mr. Hutchinson's Coach. . . .

[11 October 1720]

I writ a few Lines to Madam Winthrop to this purpose: "Madam, These wait on you with Mr. Mayhew's Sermon, and Account of the state of the Indians on Martha's Vinyard. I thank you for your Unmerited Favours of yesterday; and hope to have the Happiness of Waiting on you to-morrow before Eight a-clock after Noon. . . .

[12 October 1720]

Mrs. Anne Cotton came to door (twas before 8.) said Madam Winthrop was within, directed me into the little Room, where she was full of work behind a Stand; Mrs. Cotton came in and stood. Madam Winthrop pointed to her to set me a Chair. Madam Winthrop's Countenance was much changed from what 'twas on Monday, look'd dark and lowering. At last, the work, (black stuff or Silk) was taken away, I got my Chair in place, had some Converse, but very Cold and indifferent to what 'twas before. Ask'd her to acquit me of Rudeness if I drew off her Glove [in order to hold her hand]. Enquiring the reason, I told her twas great odds between handling a dead Goat, and a living Lady. Got it off. I told her I had one Petition to ask of her, that was, that she would take off the Negative she laid on me the third of October; She readily answer'd she could not, and enlarg'd upon it; She told me of it so soon as she could; could not leave her house, children, neighbours, business. I told her she might do som Good to help and support me. Mentioning Mrs. Gookin, Nath, the widow Weld was spoken of; said I had visited Mrs. Denison. I told her Yes! Afterward I said, If after a first and second Vagary she would Accept of me returning, Her Victorious Kindness and Good Will would be very Obliging. She thank'd me for my Book (Mr. Mayhew's Sermon), But said not a word of the Letter. When she insisted on the Negative, I pray'd there might be no more Thunder and Lightening, I should not sleep all night. I gave her Dr. Preston, The Church's Marriage and the Church's Carriage, which cost me

6s. at the Sale. The door standing open, Mr. Airs came in, hung up his Hat, and sat down. After awhile, Madam Winthrop moving, he went out. John Eyre look'd in, I said How do ye, or, your servant Mr. Eyre: but heard no word from him. Sarah fill'd a Glass of Wine, she drank to me, I to her, She sent Juno home with me with a good Lantern, I gave her 6d. and bid her thank her Mistress. In some of our Discourse, I told her I had rather go to the Stone-House adjoining to her, than to come to her against her mind. Told her the reason why I came every other night was lest I should drink too deep draughts of Pleasure. She had talk'd of Canary [wine from the Canary Islands], her Kisses were to me better than the best Canary. . . .

[Monday, 17 October 1720]

In the Evening I visited Madam Winthrop, who Treated me Courteously, but not in Clean Linen as somtimes. She said, she did not know whether I would come again, or no. I ask'd her how she could so impute inconstancy to me. (I had not visited her since Wednesday night being unable to get over the Indisposition received by the Treatment received that night, and I *must* in it seem'd to sound like a made piece of Formality.) Gave her this day's Gazett. . . . Dr. Noyes and his wife came in, and sat a Considerable time; had been visiting Son and dâter [daughter] Cooper. Juno came home with me.

[18 October 1720]

Visited Madam Mico, who came to me in a splendid Dress. I said, It may be you have heard of my Visiting Madam Winthrop, her Sister. She answered, Her Sister had told her of it. I ask'd her good Will in the Affair. She answer'd, If her Sister were for it, she should not hinder it. I gave her Mr. Homes's Sermon. She gave me a Glass of Canary, entertain'd me with good Discourse, and a Respectfull Remembrance of my first Wife. I took Leave.

[19 October 1720]

Midweek, Visited Madam Winthrop; Sarah told me she was at Mr. Walley's, would not come home till late. I gave her Hannah's 3 oranges with her Duty, not knowing whether I should find her or no. . . . I went and found her there, with Mr. Walley and his wife in the little Room below. At 7 a-clock I mentioned going home; at 8. I put on my Coat, and quickly waited on her home. She found occasion to speak loud to the servant, as if she had a mind to be known. Was Courteous to me; but took occasion to speak pretty earnestly about my keeping a Coach: I said 'twould cost £100 per annum: she said twould cost but £40. . . . Came away somewhat late.

[20 October 1720]

. . . Madam Winthrop not being at Lecture, I went thither first; found her very Serene with her dâter Noyes, Mrs. Dering, and the widow Shipreev, sitting at a little Table, she in her arm'd Chair. She drank to me, and I to Mrs. Noyes. After awhile pray'd the favour to speak with her. She took one of the Candles, and went into the best Room, clos'd the shutters, sat down upon the Couch. She told me Madam Usher had been there, and said the Coach must be set on Wheels, and not by Rusting. She spake somthing of my needing a Wigg. Ask'd me what her Sister said to me. I told her, She said, If her Sister were for it, She would not hinder it. But I told her, she did not say she would be glad to have me for her Brother. Said, I shall keep you in the Cold, and ask her if she would be within to morrow night, for we had had but a running Feast. She said she could not tell whether she should, or no. I took Leave. As were drinking at the Governour's, he said: In England the Ladies minded little more than that they might have Money, and Coaches to ride in. I said, And New-England brooks its Name. At which Mr. Dudley smiled. Gov'r said they were not quite so bad here.

[Friday, 21 October 1720]

My Son, the Minister, came to me p. m. by appointment and we pray one for another in the Old Chamber; more especially respecting my Courtship. About 6. a-clock I go to Madam Winthrop's; Sarah told me her Mistress was gon out, but did not tell me whither she went. She presently order'd me a Fire; so I went in, having Dr. Sibb's Bowels with me to read. I read the two first Sermons, still no body came in: At last about 9. a-clock Mr. John Eyre came in; I took the opportunity to say to him as I had done to Mrs. Noyes before, that I hoped my Visiting his Mother would not be disagreeable to him; He answered me with much Respect. When twas after 9. a-clock He of himself said he would go and call her, she was but at one of his Brothers: A while after I heard Madam Winthrop's voice, enquiring somthing about John.

After a good while and Clapping the Garden door twice or thrice, she came in. I mention'd somthing of the lateness; she banter'd me, and said I was later. She receiv'd me Courteously. I ask'd when our proceedings should be made publick: She said They were like to be no more publick than they were already. Offer'd me no Wine that I remember. I rose up at 11 a-clock to come away, saying I would put on my Coat, She offer'd not to help me. I pray'd her that Juno might light me home, she open'd the Shutter, and said twas pretty light abroad; Juno was weary and gon to bed. So I came hôm by Star-light as well as I could. . . .

[22 October 1720]

Dâter Cooper visited me before my going out of Town. . . . Coming back, near Leg's Corner, Little David Jeffries saw me, and looking upon me very lovingly, ask'd me if I was going to see his Grandmother? I said, Not to-night. Gave him a peny, and bid him present my Service to his Grandmother.

[24 October 1720]

. . . [S]top't at Madam Winthrop's. . . . I told her, being encourag'd by David Jeffries loving eyes, and sweet Words, I was come to enquire whether she could find in her heart to leave that House and Neighbourhood, and go and dwell with me at the South-end; I think she said softly, Not yet. I told her It did not ly in my lands to keep a Coach. If I should, I should be in danger to be brought to keep company with her Neighbour Brooker, (he was a little before sent to prison for Debt). Told her I had an Antipathy against those who would pretend to give themselves; but nothing of their Estate. I would a proportion of my Estate with my self. And I suppos'd she would do so. As to a Perriwig [a type of wig], My best and greatest Friend, I could not possibly have a greater, began to find me with Hair before I was born, and had continued to do so ever since; and I could not find in my heart to go to another. She commended the book I gave her, Dr. Preston, the Church's Marriage; quoted him saying 'twas inconvenient keeping out of a Fashion commonly used. I said the Time and Tide did circumscribe my Visit. She gave me a Dram of Black-Cherry Brandy, and gave me a lump of the Sugar that was in it. She wish'd me a good Journy. I pray'd God to keep her, and came away. . . .

Samuel Sewall, a prominent judge in colonial Massachusetts, recorded both the grief he experienced over the death of his wife, as well as his careful search for another, in his diary. (Painting by John Smibert, 1729. Courtesy of the Museum of Fine Arts, Boston. Bequest of William L. Barnard [by exchange] and the Emily L. Ainsley Fund.)

[2 November 1720]
. . . [W]ent again, and found Mrs. Alden there, who quickly went out. Gave her about 1/2 pound of Sugar Almonds, cost 3s. per £. Carried them on Monday. She seem'd pleas'd with them, ask'd what they cost. Spake of giving her a Hundred pounds per annum if I dy'd before her. Ask'd her what sum she would give me, if she should dy first? Said I would give her time to Consider of it. She said she heard as if I had given all to my Children by Deeds of Gift. I told her 'twas a mistake, Point-Judith was mine &c. That in England, I own'd, my Father's desire was that it should go to my eldest Son; 'twas 20£ per annum; she thought 'twas forty. I think when I seem'd to excuse pressing this, she seem'd to think twas best to speak of it; a long winter was coming on. Gave me a Glass or two of Canary.

[Friday, 4 November 1720]
. . . I ask'd Madam what fashioned Neck-lace I should present her with, she said, None at all. I ask'd her Whereabout we left off last time; mention'd what I had offer'd to give her; Ask'd her what She would give me; She said she could not Change her Condition: She had said so from the beginning; could not be so far from her Children, the Lecture. Quoted the Apostle Paul affirming that a single Life was better than a Married. I answer'd That was for the present Distress. Said she had not pleasure in things of that nature as formerly: I said, you are the fitter to make me a Wife. If she held in that mind, I must go home and bewail my Rashness in making

more haste than good Speed. However, considering the Supper, I desired her to be within next Monday night, if we liv'd so long. Assented. She charg'd me with saying, that she must put away Juno [let him go from her service], if she came to me: I utterly deny'd it, it never came in my heart; yet she insisted upon it; saying it came in upon discourse about the Indian woman that obtained her Freedom this Court. About 10. I said I would not disturb the good orders of her House, and came away. . . .

[Monday, 7 November 1720]

. . . I went to Mad. Winthrop; found her rocking her little Katee in the Cradle. I excus'd my Coming so late (near Eight). She set me an arm'd Chair and Cusheon; and so the Cradle was between her arm'd Chair and mine. Gave her the remnant of my Almonds; she did not eat of them as before; but laid them away; I said I came to enquire whether she had alter'd her mind since Friday, or remained of the same mind still. She said, Thereabouts. I told her I loved her, and was so fond as to think that she loved me: She said had a great respect for me. I told her, I had made her an offer, without asking any advice; she had so many to advise with, that twas a hindrance. The Fire was come to one short Brand besides the Block, which Brand was set up in end; at last it fell to pieces, and no Recruit was made: She gave me a Glass of Wine. I think I repeated again that I would go home and bewail my Rashness in making more haste than good Speed. I would endeavour to contain myself, and not go on to sollicit her to do that which she could not Consent to. Took leave of her. As came down the steps she bid me have a Care. Treated me Courteously. Told her she had enter'd the 4th year of her Widowhood. I had given her the News-Letter before: I did not bid her draw off her Glove as sometime I had done. Her Dress was not so clean as sometime it had been. Jehovah jireh! ['The Lord will provide!' With this exclamation, Sewall gave up his courtship.]

[9 November 1720]

. . . Dine at Bro'r Stoddard's: were so kind as to enquire of me if they should invite M'm Winthrop; I answer'd No. . . .

[Soon after Sewall gave up his effort to court Mrs. Winthrop, he turned his attentions to Mrs. Mary Gibbs, a widow who lived in

Newton, Massachusetts.]

[Copy of a Letter to Mrs. Mary Gibbs, Widow, at Newtown,
January 12th, 1721/22]
Madam, your Removal out of Town, and the Severity of the
Winter, are the reason of my making you this Epistolary Visit. In
times past (as I remember) you were minded that I should marry
you, by giving you to your desirable Bridegroom. Some sense of
this intended Respect abides with me still; and puts me upon
enquiring whether you be willing that I should Marry you now,
by becoming your Husband; Aged, and feeble, and exhausted as I
am, your favourable Answer to this Enquiry, in a few Lines, the
Candor of it will much oblige, Madam, your humble Serv't. . . .

S.S.

[Friday, 26 January 1721/22]
I rode to Newtown in the Coach, and visited Mrs. Gibbs.
Spake of the proposals I had intimated per Mr. H. Gibbs; for her
Sons to be bound to save me harmless as to her Administration;
and to pay me £100. provided their Mother died before me: I to
pay her £50. per annum during her Life, if I left her a Widow. She
said 'twas hard, she knew not how to have her children bound to
pay that Sum; she might dye in a little time. Mr. Cotton, whom she
call'd, spake to the same purpose, spake of a Joynture. I said I was
peremptory as to the indemnifying Bond; Offer'd to take up with
that alone, and allow her £40. per annum; Scolly's Tenement yielded
but £33., and then I made no question but that there must be a
Deduction for Repairs. She said she would consider of it: I said, I
would also Consider. Afterward she excus'd her speaking to me. I
suppose she meant the word Hard. Carried her a pound of Glaz'd
Almonds, and a Duz. Meers Cakes; Two bottles of Canary. Visited
Mrs. Cotton, wish'd her Joy of her young daughter Elizabeth. Gave
little Mary 2s. Had a very good Legg of Pork, and a Turkey for
Dinner. Mrs. Gibbs help'd me on with my Coat at Coming away;
and stood in the Front door till the Coach mov'd, then I pull'd off my
Hat, and she Curtesied. I had moved to be published next Thorsday;
to carry in our names to Col. Checkley. . . .

[29 March 1721/22]
Samuel Sewall, and Mrs. Mary Gibbs were joined together in
Marriage by the Rev'd Mr. William Cooper.

Elizabeth Ashbridge (1713–1755)

Elizabeth Ashbridge was an indentured servant when she married Mr. Sullivan, a teacher who loved singing and dancing. As it turned out, he was an alcoholic and had trouble holding onto a job. Ashbridge grew depressed as they moved from town to town along the mid-Atlantic coast. Lonely and miserable, she took a trip to Pennsylvania to visit relatives who happened to be members of the Society of Friends (Quakers). She was impressed by their kindness and devotion and gradually overcame her earlier prejudice against the Friends, who were generally despised for their pacifism, enthusiasm, and strange customs (which included silent meetings, simple dress, and preaching by both men and women). Her conversion angered her husband, who demanded that she abandon her newly pious ways; but Ashbridge, steeled by her faith, demanded that he be the one to change. Excerpted from Elizabeth Ashbridge, Some Account of the Early Part of the Life of Elizabeth Ashbridge . . . *(Concord, New Hampshire, 1810), 21–35.*

I now hired to keep a school, and hearing of a place for my husband, I wrote, and desired him to come. . . . Before he reached me, he heard I was turned Quaker; at which he stamped, [unreadable] said, "I had rather have heard she was dead, well as I love her; for, if it be so, all my comfort is gone.["] He then came to me; it was after an absence of four months; I got up and said to him, "My dear, I am glad to see thee." At this, he flew into a great rage, exclaiming, 'The devil thee, thee, thee, don't thee me.' I endeavored, by every mild means, to pacify him; and, at length, got him fit to speak to my relations. As soon after this as we were alone, he said to me, "And so I see your Quaker relations have made you one;". . . . He said he would not stay amongst them; and having found a place to his mind, hired, and came directly back to fetch me, walking, in one afternoon, thirty miles to keep me from meeting the next day, which was first day. He took me, after resting this day, to the place where he had hired, and to lodgings he had engaged at the house of a churchwarden. This man was a bitter enemy of Friends, and did all he could to irritate my husband against them.

. . . When my husband and he used to be making their diversions and reviling, I sat in silence, though now and then an involuntary sigh broke from me; at which he would say, 'There, did not I tell you your wife was a Quaker, and she will become a preacher.' On such an occasion as this, my husband once came up to me, in a great rage, and shaking his hand over me, said, "You had better be hanged in that day." I was seized with horror, and again plunged into despair, which continued nearly three months. I was afraid that, by denying the Lord, the heavens would be shut against me. I walked much alone in the woods, and there, where no eye saw, nor ear heard me, lamented my miserable condition. . . .

. . . At length, when he and his friend thought themselves too weak to overset me, he went to the priest at Chester, to inquire what he could do with me. This man knew I was a member of the [Anglican] Church, for I had shown him my certificate. His advice was, to take me out of Pennsylvania, and settle in some place where there were no Quakers. My husband replied, he did not care where we went, if he could but restore me to my natural liveliness of temper. As for me, I had no resolution to oppose their proposals, nor much cared where I went. I seemed to have nothing to hope for. I daily expected to be made a victim of divine wrath, and was possessed with the idea that this would be by thunder.

When the time of removal came, I was not permitted to bid my relations farewell; and, as my husband was poor, and kept no horse, I was obliged to travel on foot. We came to Wilmington, 15 miles, and from thence to Philadelphia by water. Here we stopt at a tavern, where I became the spectacle and discourse of the company. My husband told them his wife had become a Quaker, and he designed if possible to find out a place where there were none. . . . [H]e told them that I had been a good dancer, but now he could get me neither to dance or sing. One of the company then started up, and said, "I'll fetch a fiddle, and we'll have a good dance;" a proposal with which my husband was pleased. When the fiddle was brought my husband came and said to me, "My dear, shake off that gloom, and let us have a civil dance; you would, now and then, when you were a good churchwoman, and that's better than a stiff Quaker." I had taken up the resolution not to comply with his request, whatever might be the consequence; this I let him know, though I durst say little, for fear of his choleric temper. He pulled me round the room, till the tears fell from my eyes, at the sight of which the musician stopt, and said, "I'll play no more; let your wife alone." There was a person in company that came from Freehold, in East Jersey, who said, "I see your wife's a Quaker, but if you'll take my advice you need not go so far as you intend; come and live with us; we'll soon cure her of her Quakerism, and we want a schoolmaster and schoolmistress too." He consented, and a happy turn it was for me, as will shortly be seen. . . .

In our way to Freehold, as we came to Stony Brook, my husband turned towards me, and tauntingly said, "Here's one of Satan's synagogues, don't you long to be in it; I hope to see you cured of your new religion." . . . After walking nearly a mile, we came to a house, which proved to be a sort of tavern. My husband called for some spirituous liquors, and I got some weakened cider mulled, which rendered me extremely sick; so that, after we were a little past the house, being too faint to proceed, I fell down.—"What's the matter now?" said my husband, "what, are you drunk? Where's your religion now?" He knew I was not drunk, and, at that time, I believ he pitied me, although he spoke in this manner. After I was a little recovered, we went on, and came to another tavern, where we lodged. The next day, . . . we met a man riding full speed, who, stopping, said to my husband, "Sir, are you a schoolmaster?" He answered, "Yes." "I am come," replied the stranger, "to tell you of two new schoolhouses, two miles apart, each of which wants a master." How this person came to hear of us, who arrived but the night before, I never knew. I was glad he was not called a Quaker, lest it should have been thought a plot by my husband, to whom I turned and said, "My dear, look on me with pity, if thou hast any affection left for me, which I hope thou hast, for I am not conscious of having done any thing to alienate it. Here is an opportunity to settle us both, and I am willing to do all in my power, towards getting an honest livelihood." After a short pause, he consented to go with the young man. . . .

. . . We took a room, in a friend's house, one mile from each school, and eight from the meetinghouse. I now deemed it proper to let my husband see I was determined to join with Friends. When first day came, I directed myself to him in this manner: "My dear, art thou willing to let me go to meeting?" He flew into a rage, and replied, "No you sha'n't." Speaking firmly, I told him, 'That, as a dutiful wife, I was ready to obey all his lawful commands; but, when they imposed upon my conscience, I could not obey him. I had already wronged myself, in having done it too long;

and though he was near to me, and, as a wife ought, I loved him; yet God, who was nearer than all the world to me, had made me sensible that this was the way in which I ought to go. I added, that this was no small cross to my own will; but I had given up my heart, and I trusted that He who called for it would enable me, for the remainder of my life, to keep it steadily devoted to his service; and I hoped I should not, on this account, make the worse wife.' I spoke, however, to no purpose; he continued inflexible.

I had now put my hand to the plough, and resolved not to draw back; I therefore went without leave. I expected he would immediately follow and force me back, but he did not. I called at the house of one of the neighbors, and, getting a girl to show me the way, I went on rejoicing, and praising God in my heart.

Thus, for some time, I had to go eight miles on foot to meeting, which I never thought hard. My husband had a horse, but he would not suffer me to ride on it; nor, when my shoes were worn out, would he let me have a new pair; but, though he hoped, on this account, to keep me from meeting, it did not hinder me:—I have tied them round with strings to keep them on.

Finding that all the means he had yet used could not alter my resolutions, he several times struck me with severe blows. I endeavored to bear all with patience, believing that the time would come when he would see I was in the right. Once he came up to me, took out his penknife, and said, "If you offer to go to meeting to-morrow, with this knife I'll cripple you, for you shall not be a Quaker." I made him no answer. In the morning I set out as usual; he did not attempt to harm me. Having despaired of recovering me himself, he fled for help to the priest, whom he told that I had been a very religious woman, in the way of the Church of England, of which I was a member, and had a good certificate from Long Island; that I was now bewitched, and had turned Quaker, which almost broke his heart. . . .

. . . [He] got the horse and set off to fetch me, arriving just as the meeting broke up. I got on horseback as quickly as possible, lest he should hear I had been speaking; he did hear of it nevertheless, and, as soon as we were in the woods, began with saying, "Why do you mean thus to make my life unhappy? What, could you not be a Quaker, without turning fool in this manner?" I answered in tears, "My dear, look on me with pity, if thou hast any; canst thou think that I, in the bloom of my days, would bear all that thou knowest of, and much that thou knowest not of, if I did not feel it my duty?" These words touched him, and he said, "Well, I'll e'en give you up; I see it wont avail to strive; if it be of God I cannot overthrow it; and, if of yourself, it will soon fall." I saw the tears stand in his eyes, at which I was overcome with joy, and began already to reap the fruits of my obedience. But my trials were not yet over. . . .

. . . I joined the society. My husband still went to no place of worship. One day he said to me, "I would go to meeting only I'm afraid I shall hear your clack, which I cannot bear." I used no persuasions. When meeting-time came, he got the horse, took me behind him, and went. For several months, if he saw me offer to rise, he went out; till one day I rose before he was aware, and then, as he afterwards owned, he was ashamed to do it.

From this time, he left off the practice, and never hindered me from going to meeting. Though he did not take up the cross, yet his judgment was convinced; and, sometimes, melting into tears, he would say to me, "My dear, I have seen the beauty there is in the truth, and that thou hast followed the right way, in which I pray God to preserve thee." I told him, that I hoped He who had given me strength would also favor him, "O," said he, "I cannot bear the reproach thou dost, to be called turn-coat, and become a laughing-stock to the world; but I'll no longer hinder thee." This I considered a favor, and a little hope remained that my prayers, on his account, would he heard.

We lived in a small house by ourselves, which, though mean, and though we had little to put in it, our bed being no better than chaff, I was truly content. The only desires I had were for my own preservation, and to be blessed with the reformation of my husband. He was connected with a set of men whom he feared would make game of him, which indeed they already did; asking him when he designed to commence preacher, for they saw he intended to turn Quaker, and seemed to love his wife better since she became one, than before. They used to come to our house, and provoked him to sit up and drink with them, sometimes till near day, while I have been sorrowing in a stable. Once, as I sat in this condition, I heard him say to his company, "I can't bear any longer to afflict my poor wife in this manner; for, whatever you may think of her, I do believe she's a good woman." He then came to me and said: . . . 'Come in, my dear, God has given thee a deal of patience: I'll put an end to this practice.' This was the last time they sat up late at night.

My husband now thought that if he was in any place where it was not known he had been so bitter against friends, he could do better. I objected to this, fearing it would not be for his benefit. Frequently, in a broken and affectionate manner, he condemned his ill usage of me. I answered, that I hoped it had been for my good, and therefore desired he would not be afflicted on that account. . . . My advice was for him to stay where he was, I was afraid he would grow weaker in his good resolutions, if he removed.

All I could say would not avail. Hearing of a place at Bordentown, he went thither, but was not suited. He next removed to Mount Holly, where he settled. We had each of us a good school; we soon got our house pretty well furnished, and might have done very well. Nothing seemed wanting to complete my happiness, except the reformation of my husband, which I had much reason to doubt I should not see soon. It fell out according to my fears. He addicted himself much to drinking, and grew worse than before. . . . I murmured not; nor do I recollect that I ever uttered any harsh expressions except on one occasion. My husband coming home a little intoxicated, (a state in which he was very fractious) and finding me at work by a candle, he put it out, fetching me, at the same time, a box on the ear, and saying, 'You don't earn your light.' At this unkind usage, which I had not been used to for the last two years, I was somewhat angry, and said . . . 'Thou art a vile man.' He struck me again; but my anger had cooled, and I received the blow without so much as a word in return. This also displeased him and he went on in a distracted-like manner, uttering such expressions of despair as, he believed he was predestined to damnation, and he did not care how soon God struck him dead. I said very little, till, at length, in the bitterness of my soul, I broke out into these expressions, 'Lord, look down on my afflictions, and deliver me by some means or other.' My prayer was granted, but in such a manner that I thought it would have killed me. He went to Burlington, where he got drunk, and enlisted to go as a common soldier to Cuba, in the year 1740. I had drunk many bitter cups, but this seemed the bitterest of them all. A thousand times I blamed myself for making such a request, which I was afraid had displeased God, who had, in displeasure, granted it for my punishment.

I have since had cause to believe that he was benefitted by his rash act, as, in the army, he did what he could not at home; he suffered for the testimony of truth. When they came to prepare for an engagement, he refused to fight; he was whipt, and brought before the general, who asked him, why he enlisted if he would not fight. 'I did it,' said he, 'in a drunken frolic, when the devil had the better of me; but now my judgment is convinced I ought not to fight, neither will I, whatever I suffer. I have but one life, and you may take that if you please, for I'll never take up arms.' He adhered to his resolution. By their cruel usage of him in consequence, he was so much disabled that the General sent him to Chelsea Hospital, near London. In nine months afterwards he died at this place, and I hope made a good end.

Questions

1. *What ambitions did Sewall and Ashbridge bring to courtship and marriage? Did their spouses or potential spouses understand their ambitions? share them?*
2. *Did Puritanism make Katherine Winthrop blunt, or did age and experience? Did Quakerism turn Elizabeth Ashbridge against her husband, or Was it discontent with a migratory life? Did religion shape marriage more than personality and circumstance?*
3. *Judging by the stories, what role did romantic love play in courtship and marriage?*

Further Reading

Most histories of marriage in eighteenth-century America cover marriages of a specific faith or region. See Edmund S. Morgan, The Puritan Family: Religion and Domestic Relations in Seventeenth-Century New England, rev. ed. *(Westport, Connecticut 1966); John Demos,* A Little Commonwealth: Family Life in Plymouth Colony *(New York, 1970); Daniel Blake Smith,* Inside the Great House: Planter Family Life in Eighteenth-Century Chesapeake Society *(Ithaca, 1980); Joan M. Jensen,* Loosening the Bonds: Mid-Atlantic Farm Women, 1750–1850 *(New Haven, 1986); and Barry Levy,* Quakers and the American Family: British Settlement in the Delaware Valley *(New York, 1988). An exception is Marylynn Salmon,* Women and the Law of Property in Early America *(Chapel Hill, 1986).*

Colonial American Political Culture: Deference or Democracy?

Margaret E. Newell

INTRODUCTION

A number of tensions shaped colonial political culture in the century before the Revolution. On the one hand, economic, cultural, and political ties with England grew stronger in the 1700s. Many Americans gloried in the privileges and "rights of Englishmen" that they enjoyed as members of the British empire. They also praised the British Constitution as the best form of government. Rather than a single document or frame of government, the British Constitution referred to the three estates of English society—the king, the aristocracy, and the people. English men and women regarded a proper tension and balance between these groups as essential to the stability of their nation. They believed that the king and the English Parliament—which included the House of Lords and the House of Commons—gave each group proper representation in government and prevented any one group from dominating the rest. Americans believed that they replicated this perfect system in their colonial assemblies, where the royal governor took the place of the king, an upper house or council took the place of the Lords, and the lower house or assembly represented all the people. Yet despite their approving rhetoric, the colonists' actions challenged English notions of balance and power. During the eighteenth century, the lower houses of the colonial assemblies regularly challenged the royal governors' authority; most colonies also lacked a hereditary aristocracy capable of turning colonial councils into another House of Lords. This meant that the elective colonial assemblies exerted far more influence than was proper under the British Constitution, which worried many imperial authorities.

The distribution of political power within the colonies them-selves generated another set of tensions. Both religious teachings and social custom instructed people to obey political authorities. England, including its colonies, was a monarchy, and the king occupied the top position in a hierarchical social structure. Few Americans questioned the justice of this inequality in the colonial period; indeed, most believed that inequality and the deference of inferiors to superiors were crucial to the maintenance of political and social order. Members of the colonial elite—merchants in northern port cities, slaveholding planters in the South—domi-nated political office in the colonies. Women, blacks, and those white men without property were prevented from voting. Yet because of the availability of land and economic opportunity, many colonists (as many as 50 to 90 percent of white males over twenty-one in some areas) were able to meet the property require-ments for voting. Far more Americans could participate in politi-cal life and influence elections than in contemporary England, where, by the mid-eighteenth century, a man needed the equiva-lent of $80,000 to vote. But did the right to participate translate into democracy? Or did customs of deference and hierarchy con-tinue to influence voters? Did the growing power of the assemblies translate into a fairer, more democratic government for all?

THE ONE, THE FEW, THE MANY: DEMOCRACY AND DEFERENCE IN COLONIAL POLITICS

The following secondary works reflect an ongoing debate among early American historians over whether colonial America was a democratic society. They examine the extent of suffrage, but also attempt to explore how and whether the colonists exercised their political rights and who held the power in the relationship between elite officeholders and common voters. In addition, the readings help place the colonists' actions within a framework of beliefs about the proper nature of society and government—beliefs derived from English notions of the importance of balance and hierarchy—that shaped people's political behavior and choices.

Democracy

Robert Brown provides the most forceful assertion of the existence of colonial democracy. Examining the economic background to colonial society, Brown argues that in an era when political participation was tied to property ownership, the ease with which Americans acquired land made for a relatively democratic society. The following is abridged from Robert E. Brown, Middle-Class Democracy and the Revolution in Massachusetts, *1691–1780 (New York, 1968), 1–6, 9–10, 16–20.*

In colonial days, . . . there was a close connection between political democracy and what, for want of a better term, we might call "economic democracy," that is, the opportunity which the average man had to acquire property and to get ahead in society. This connection was close because there were property qualifications for voting, which meant that if a man could not acquire property he would never be entitled to political rights.

Therefore, any understanding of colonial democracy must of necessity be prefaced by a discussion of some of the economic aspects of Massachusetts society. Since the right to vote depended on the possession of worldly goods, we would want to know how much property was required, what part of the population possessed property, how much property men had, and what opportunity existed for the acquisition of property by those who did not have it. Was there a political aristocracy which rested on the existence of an economic aristocracy, or was there much economic opportunity, that is, economic democracy, so that the average man could acquire property? Was the "common man" excluded from political life because he lacked the opportunity to acquire sufficient property, or could he easily become a property holder and therefore a voter? . . .

. . . [O]ne thing on which both foreign observers and contemporary Americans concurred was the vast difference between European and American societies. There was little doubt in their minds that the people who came here from Europe had not simply transplanted their old-country class structure to the New World. In fact, observers agreed that a unique social order had developed in the American colonies.

One of the best known of the European observers, and one who was particularly struck by the contrast between Europe and America, was the French immigrant, Michel-Guillaume Jean de Crèvecoeur. Unlike Europe, said Crèvecoeur, America did not have a few great lords who possessed everything and a herd of people who had nothing. There were no aristocratical families, no courts, no kings, no bishops, no great manufacturers employing thousands of workers, and no great refinements of luxury. There was not the wide gulf between the rich and the poor that existed in Europe. . . .

. . . America, said Crèvecoeur, was the most perfect society then in existence, where men were as free as they ought to be—a predominantly middle-class, equalitarian society.

The reason for this, continued Crèvecoeur, was the abundance of economic opportunity. Immigrants received ample compensation for their labor, and this in turn enabled them to procure land. Their labor was founded on self-interest, the fruits of which were not claimed by despotic princes, rich abbots, or mighty lords. Their land gave them the rank of independent freeholders, which in turn conferred all the political honors in the society. . . .

Another observer who had firsthand knowledge of the differences between European and American societies was Benjamin Franklin. Franklin pointed out that . . . [i]n Europe, all the land was occupied, forcing some men to work for others; labor was plentiful, which meant low wages; and the result was a slow increase in population. But conditions in America were just the opposite. Land was plentiful and so cheap that a laboring man could soon save enough money to buy a farm, raise a family, and be assured that cheap land would provide economic opportunity for his children. . . . Labor would never be cheap in America, for no man continued to work for others very long; either he acquired a farm or, if he were an artisan, went out to a new settlement to set up for himself. . . . In short, America was what Franklin called "the land of labour," a land in which an "almost general mediocrity of fortune" prevailed among the people. . . .

As for Massachusetts, there is ample evidence that the social order there was also relatively equalitarian rather than sharply divided into classes. . . . John Adams spoke of the "equality of knowledge, wealth, and power" which prevailed, maintaining that this equality was fostered by a colonial law for the distribution of intestate estates which resulted in frequent divisions of landed property and prevented monopolies of land. On another occasion he declared that the land was divided among the common people in every state so that nineteen-twentieths of the property was in their hands. The Boston merchant-politician Andrew Oliver also explained to an English friend that land did not descend to the eldest son or heir as in England, but that the law provided for an equal distribution of all property, real and personal, among all the children except for a double portion for the eldest son. And Thomas Hutchinson, merchant, legislator, judge, historian, and colonial governor, wrote as follows: "Property is more equally distributed in the colonies, especially those to the northward of Maryland than in any nation in Europe. In some towns you see scarce a man destitute of a competency to make him easy." . . .

Almost any Massachusetts town would demonstrate the generalizations made thus far, but the available records make Northampton a particularly good example. The tax lists show that almost all the people were property owners, that the spread in the amount of property owned was not wide, and that the vast majority of men were farmers. Furthermore, a comparison of tax lists for different years shows that practically all men increased their holdings over a period of years. A list of shops in Northampton in 1773 reveals that workers other than farmers were not day laborers who worked for wages, but skilled artisans who worked for themselves—blacksmiths, goldsmiths, joiners, tanners, weavers, tailors, clothiers, traders, shoemakers, barbers, sadlers, coopers, and hatters. Furthermore, the fact that most of them owned substantial amounts of real estate indicates that they were both farmers and artisans. In fact, the wealthiest man in town, Seth Pomeroy, was listed as a blacksmith. Most of these artisans were town proprietors, that is, men who owned a share in the common lands, and many were town officials, including some who were not proprietors. . . .

I am not contending that the people of Massachusetts were all equal economically, but only that there was relative equality compared, for example, with Europe at that time or America today. The probate records show that a few men had little property when they died, particularly sailors and fishermen in towns such as Boston, Salem, and Marblehead, but these were few compared with those who were property owners. At the other extreme there were a few well-to-do. Thomas Hutchinson estimated the Apthorp estate between £20,000 and £30,000 sterling, which he called "a large property." Andrew Oliver's estate was valued at £9,121, and Thomas Gerry, father of Elbridge Gerry, had property worth £7,919. But between these extremes was the vast majority of the population, men of middling property, farmers whose farms were not only their homes but also their capital stock. These farms generally averaged from 75 to 150 acres, with a value of from £300 to £1,200. . . . The Adams' homestead in Braintree (Quincy), consisting of buildings and 53 acres of land, would have been considered a small farm in colonial times, yet the land and buildings alone were worth £440. So while there was a spread of ten or fifteen to one between the estates of Andrew Oliver or Thomas Gerry and that of an average farmer, this difference is small indeed compared with the difference in the estates of men in similar circumstances today. . . .

When we interpret the society of Massachusetts . . . we need to remember that, economically speaking, it was a relatively equalitarian, middle-class society in which there was a great deal of economic opportunity. Land was cheap and easy to acquire, and most men acquired some; wages were high, so that a worker could save money to buy land; apprentices could easily become masters and owners of their own small business in some new community; few men could be called day laborers, or if they were, few remained day laborers for long; most "workers" were self-employed artisans, not day laborers. Even men who were designated "laborers" were nevertheless owners of considerable land. More than 90 per cent of the people were farmers, most of whom owned their own farms. In fact, a vastly greater part of the population owned property then than now, and there was a much smaller gap between the wealthy and the ordinary people. These are some of the factors we need to keep in mind when we consider the problem of political democracy.

Aristocracy

The following study discusses the ways in which Virginia's gentry dominated the colony's political offices and decision making. Charles Sydnor also notes that the gentry made certain concessions to voters' power. Abridged from Charles S. Sydnor, American Revolutionaries in the Making: Political Practices in Washington's Virginia *(New York, 1965), 60–64, 66–68, 70–73.*

The readiness with which the eighteenth-century Virginian came to elections, the efforts of the candidates to win his support, and his assumption that they owed him plentiful quantities of rum punch suggest that the freeholders had a large measure of political power which they freely exercised. Political power truly rested in the people; democracy was a real and active force. At the

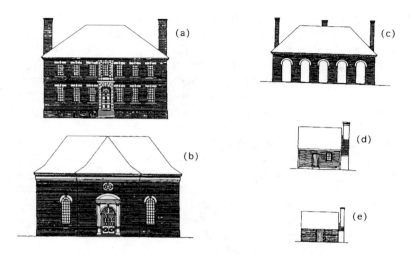

Colonial architecture reflected the hierarchical relationships in American society, as demonstrated in these images of a great house, a church, a courthouse, a planter's house, and a slave cabin, respectively. (Reproduced from *The Transfiguration of Virginia, 1740-1790* by Rhys Issac, (1982), published for the Omohundro Institute of Early American History and Culture, courtesy of the Universityof North Carolina Press.

same time a large measure of political power was vested in the few; aristocracy was also a strong and positive force in politics. Eighteenth-century Virginia did not regard democracy and aristocracy as contradictory kinds of government. It employed both of these qualities in its political system, and it was the interplay of these two forces, democratic and aristocratic, that gave to the government of colonial Virginia much of that distinctive quality which made for the selection of those men who ruled Virginia during the era of the American Revolution.

Colonial Virginians, with their British background of a class society and with obvious differences in wealth and social position on every hand in Virginia, accepted the inequality of man as a fact. The Reverend James Maury . . . once put the matter very bluntly by contrasting "gentlemen" on the one hand with the members of "the vulgar herd" on the other. Although Maury's distinction was too sharp and his language too harsh for some of his contemporaries, most of them would have agreed that society was composed of several levels which were "separated by no marked lines, but shading off imperceptibly from the top to bottom." At the top were the "aristocrats, composed of the great landholders who had seated themselves below tide water on the main rivers, and lived in a style of luxury and extravagance, insupportable by the other inhabitants, and which, indeed, ended, in several instances, in the ruin of their own fortunes." Next were "the younger sons and daughters of the aristocrats, who inherited the pride of their ancestors, without their wealth. Then came the pretenders, men who from vanity, or the impulse of growing wealth, or from that enterprize which is natural to talents, sought to detach themselves from the plebeian ranks, to which they properly belonged, and imitated, at some distance, the manners and habits of the great. Next to these, were a solid and independent yeomanry, looking askance at those above, yet not venturing to jostle them."

The term "gentry" was usually applied to the upper segment of society, and the individual men of the class were spoken of as "gentlemen." The eighteenth-century Virginian could recognize a gentleman by his name, his manners, and his dress, by the wig that he wore and the carriage that he provided for his family. In religion he was likely to be an Episcopalian; often he was a vestryman. His house was large, his lands extensive, and his slaves numerous. Shunning solitude, he sought pleasure in the chase and horse-racing, gaming and heavy drinking. He was "open-handed and open-hearted; fond of society, indulging in all its pleasures, and practising all its courtesies. But these social virtues also occasionally ran into the kindred vices of love of show, haughtiness, sensuality."

Although many of the gentry were educated, few had the scholarly instincts and thoughtfulness of Madison and Jefferson. But learning was respected by many of those who wanted no part of it for themselves. Philip Fithian, after spending a year as tutor in Virginia, came to the conclusion that Virginians rated men largely in terms of wealth, "excepting always the value they put upon posts of honour, & mental acquirements." To illustrate his point he observed that a Princeton graduate "would be rated, without any more questions asked, either about your family, your Estate, your business, or your intention, at 10,000£; and you might come, & go, & converse, & keep company, according to this value; and you would be dispised & slighted if yo[u] rated yourself a farthing cheaper.". . .

A Virginia gentleman could also be recognized by the offices that he held, for office, except such lowly posts as constable, was a prerogative of men of property and family. The law required no more property of the officeholder than it did of the voter, but custom and public opinion were more demanding. Jefferson once objected to the office of county lieutenant being given to a man "not possessing an inch of property in the county or other means of obtaining influence over the people, and of a temper so ungovernable that instead of reconciling he will by his manner of executing revolt the minds of the people against the calls of government." Governor Dinwiddie sent a scathing letter to an official who had bestowed a colonelcy on a man who "has no Estate in the County, and keeps an Ordinary," and a captaincy on "a Person insolvent and not able to pay his Levy. . . . This Conduct is prostituting my Commissions entrusted with You, and pray what Gentlemen of Character will role with such Persons that have neither Land nor Negroes, at same time of very bad Characters, having no just Cal[l]ing to maintain themselves, and in Course makes great Distractions in the County? Your Family and Property engaged Me to confide in You, but I am sorry that I am obliged to say Your Conduct is much contrary to my Expectations, and, indeed, to that of a Gentleman of Your Family and Estate." . . .

Membership in a prominent family and the possession of a considerable estate did not, of course, necessarily place a man in office. But those in office so generally had these qualifications that lists of local and provincial officials constitute a convenient index to the names of the families that composed the gentry.

At the peak of the official hierarchy were the members of the council, who were chosen from the top families of the planter aristocracy. They held important and lucrative offices such as auditor general, receiver general, and secretary of the colony, and they were in a favorable position, which they did not hesitate to use, to secure large grants of land. Good family helped to put a man in the council; in turn, membership in the council enabled a man to improve the fortunes of his family. The advantages of this office were enjoyed by a rather small number of families interrelated by blood and marriage. One kind of relationship is indicated by the fact that only fifty-seven family names appear in a list of the ninety-one men appointed to the council from 1680 to the Revolution. Nine family names account for almost a third of the councilors during this century; and fourteen other names for almost another third. Five councilors bore the name of Page; three each the names of Burwell, Byrd, Carter, Custis, Harrison, Lee, Ludwell, and Wormley.

The most numerous and widespread of the officeholders were the justices of the peace. . . . [J]ustices of the peace were generally members of the gentry. They were also men of much power in local affairs, for all of the justices were members of the county court, the governing body of the county.

In the last twenty years before the American Revolution some 1600 men were justices of the peace in Virginia. Four hundred and twenty of the 1600 belonged to one or another of fifty-five families, using the word family in its ample Virginia sense. No more than three or four hundred families supplied at least three fourths of the justices during the last twenty years of the colonial period. These three or four hundred families—some of which like the Randolphs were clans spread widely over the colony—made up a large part of that segment of society known as the gentry. . . .

These men of wealth, social position, and great power in county government also had much influence in burgess elections and therefore in provincial government. . . .

Several legal devices enabled the man of wealth and social position to make his political influence felt. One device was the practice of oral voting. When [eminent leaders like] Lord Fairfax, Colonel James Wood, and Colonel John Carlyle voted for a candidate at the beginning of the election, they turned to that candidate the votes of lesser men who respected their judgment or who were obligated to them. If a young man wished to rise in politics, society, or wealth, it was well for him to vote for those who had the power to aid him in winning his goal. A tavernkeeper, a blacksmith, or a cobbler would be tempted to vote as his wealthier patrons voted. The man in straitened circumstances would be inclined to support those to whom he was beholden or who might give him aid.

The political influence of the wealthy man was enhanced by the provision allowing him to vote in every county in which he could meet the freehold requirement. The wealthy man was eligible to vote in more counties than a yeoman farmer, and he could more readily spare the time to go from county court to county court when elections were being held.

The man with extensive landholdings could also weigh his

chances in the various counties in which he owned land and stand a poll in the one which offered the brightest prospects. . . .

As members of the county court, the important men of the county wielded something of a corporate influence at election time. If an election turned into a sharp division between gentry and small farmers, the justices could muster a considerable block of votes from among themselves, their families, and the various officials of the court; and they could count on the votes of cautious freeholders who, remembering the great powers of the court, would hesitate to vote for a candidate who was clearly disapproved of by the justices. . . .

Some of the customs and attitudes of the times also operated to the advantage of the gentry in elections. The practice of treating the voters excluded a poor man from candidacy for the simple reason that he could not afford to buy meat and drink for the voters in the large quantities that were expected. Samuel Overton of Hanover County estimated that his expenses for two elections amounted to £75. George Washington spent about £25 on each of two elections, over £39 on another, and approximately £50 on a fourth. These were large amounts for that day—several times more than enough to buy the house and land of the voter who barely met the minimum franchise requirements. The custom of giving expensive treats also implied that candidates were wealthy and that they lived with the open-handed, lavish generosity of gentlemen. If a poor man scraped up enough money to stand an election and attempted to treat the voters like a gentleman, his performance was more likely to excite ridicule or pity than respect.

Like the custom of treating, the convention that candidates must not solicit votes for themselves operated in favor of the privileged class. Gentlemen could profit by the existence of the rule even though they did not always follow it. By frowning on house-to-house canvassing and other forms of personal solicitation of votes, they were, in effect frowning on candidates who lacked the self-respect, the dignity, and some of the political advantages of the gentry. Gentlemen, let it plainly be said, wanted office despite their hostility to aggressive electioneering. But gentlemen knew how to seek support with such delicacy of phrase as to avoid the appearance of doing so, as did Colonel Richard Bland in the following note to Theoderick Bland, Sr.:

"Our election is to be on Thursday, the 27, of this month, which is this day week. I shall be glad to see you at it, . . . I hope I have given no occasion to the county, to refuse me at this time, and I shall always act to the utmost of my capacity, for the good of my electors, whose interest and my own, in great measure, are inseparable."

The gentleman-candidate, knowing the leading men of the countryside, could ask their advice about standing for office and in the course of the conversation learn what support or "interests" he could count on. Asking for a man's support was more respectable than asking for a man's vote; and it was more rewarding. Thus the convention against personal canvassing among the voters worked to the advantage of gentlemen. So long as it could be maintained against the tendency of anxious candidates to breach it, Virginia was likely to fill its elective offices with members of the gentry. . . . The gentry had great influence in burgess elections, but they did not have absolute and unchallenged power to choose the county's representatives. Always they had to remember that freeholders were numerous enough to turn an election against an unpopular candidate even though he was supported by all the political weapons in the gentry's arsenal. In a Fairfax election of 1755 the gentry carried the day by the narrowest of margins. William Ellzey with the support of only one justice polled 220 votes, only two below George William Fairfax for whom eleven justices voted and twelve below John West who was supported by ten justices. There is at least a hint that the gentry was discomfited when James Littlepage defeated Nathaniel West Dandridge in Hanover County in 1764. . . .

The justices ran much risk in supporting candidates who were not generally popular; democracy was strong enough to moderate autocratic tendencies in the gentry. In most elections, however, there is no evidence of tension between the justices and an opposition faction; the votes of the justices were usually divided among all of the candidates. The result in general was the election of burgesses who were more or less acceptable both to the leaders and to the rank and file of the voters.

Whether supported by the justices or not, the candidates for the House of Burgesses were almost without exception members of the gentry. Even Ellzey, who was opposed by nearly all of the justices of Fairfax County in 1755, was a ranking member of the county court just as West and Fairfax were. . . .

The truth of the matter is that the roster of eighteenth-century gentlemen served almost like a permanent list of nominees for political office. The function of the gentry was to provide candidates and often a measure of guidance as to which of these candidates to elect. The function of the rank and file of the freeholders was to decide which of the several gentlemen to send to the House of Burgesses and in the process to act as a check on any autocratic tendencies in the gentry. It was the interplay of these two forces, aristocratic and democratic, that produced the political leadership of revolutionary Virginia.

Monarchy

In this selection Richard Bushman assesses the significance of the colonists' participation in the rituals of the English empire. Although Bushman argues that "monarchy rested . . . lightly on Massachusetts Bay," he stresses the importance of the hierarchical social order that the king anchored and its implications for politics in the colonies. Abridged from Richard Bushman, King and People in Provincial Massachusetts *(Chapel Hill, 1985), 13-20, 25.*

[I]n 1776 the colonists declared their independence from monarchy as well as from Great Britain. . . . It is difficult now to understand what the colonists abandoned when they repudiated the king. Monarchy rested so lightly on Massachusetts Bay in the seventeenth century as to seem weightless. In the provincial period the king's presence was little felt amidst the clamor of everyday politics. The king was a ceremonial personage, entering into rhetoric and political ritual. . . .

We begin to grasp the meaning of monarchy when we view the incessant round of ceremonies exalting the king and listen to the ceaseless flow of monarchical rhetoric. . . . On a Saturday in late December 1760, news of the death of George II reached Boston. The royal governor, Francis Bernard, at once issued an order that the old king's grandson, Prince George, was to be proclaimed the new king, to reign as George III. The town readied itself for two days and then on Tuesday morning, December 30, began the solemn ritual which was occurring at many places in the empire at this season. The governor, lieutenant governor, the Council, the House of Representatives, and a number of principal gentlemen left the old statehouse under military escort and proceeded to the Council chambers. There assembled were a regiment of militia and "a vast Concourse of People of all Ranks." From the balcony of the courthouse the proclamation was read in a loud voice.

> We . . . do now, with full Voice and Consent of Tongue and Heart, Publish and Proclaim, That the High and Mighty Prince GEORGE, Prince of Wales; is now . . . become our only Lawful and Rightful Liege Lord GEORGE the Third. . . . To Whom we acknowledge all Faith and constant Obedience, with all hearty and humble Affection: Beseeching GOD . . . to bless the Royal King GEORGE the Third, with long and happy Years to Reign over us.

After the concluding "God save the king!" three huzzahs rang out from the throng, and the militia fired three volleys. At a signal, sixty-three cannon were discharged at Castle William in the harbor, echoed immediately by batteries on the Boston and Charlestown shores. In the evening candles illuminated the town, and a handsome entertainment was provided in Faneuil Hall, "where the Health of his Majesty King George the Third, the Royal Family, and many other loyal Healths were drank." Two days later the town mourned the passing of George II. Bells tolled from early morning until late in the day, soldiers discharged seventy-seven minute guns, one for each year of the dead king's life, and the General Court with the governor listened to sermons morning and afternoon.

The display of affection for His Britannic Majesty was not new to Boston, nor did it soon disappear from the town's public life. Boston celebrated the king's birthday and the anniversary of his coronation annually until the eve of the tea party in 1773. Cannons, toasts, and huzzahs echoed through the century before the Revolution, leaving a long record of monarchical celebrations. . . .

The meaning of the coronations, royal birthdays, anniversaries of coronations, and all the other declarations of loyalty and allegiance can be glimpsed through the eyes of Thomas Prince, the young Harvard graduate who stood among the throngs watching the coronation procession of George I in 1714. Thirteen years later in a sermon in Boston at the accession of George II, Prince recalled his reactions:

I shall never forget the Joy that swell'd my Heart; when in the Splendid Procession at his *Coronation*, preceeded by all the Nobles of the Kingdom, and then his Son and Heir apparent, our other Hope, with their Ermine Robes and Coronets—That *Royal Face* at length appear'd, which Heaven had in that Moment sent to Save these Great Nations from the Brink of Ruin. Nor do I speak it as my case alone, but as what appear'd to be the equal Transport of the Multitudes round about me. The Tears of Joy seem'd to rise and swim in every Eye: And we were hardly able to give a Shout, thro' the labouring Passions that were swelling in us.

. . . Much of the culture of monarchy was implicit in the scene Prince viewed in 1714. Processions were designed for the very purpose of educating onlookers. Tradition had carefully crafted the coronation to display the social order in all its splendor and to evoke awe and respect in the multitude. . . .

. . . The impact of the king's appearance lay not in his splendor alone but in the fact that he stood at the peak of a pyramid. . . .

He was head of state, commander in chief, head of the church, wealthiest of the wealthy, largest landowner, the leader of society, and the fountain of honor. Might that is divided in pluralistic societies came to a single focus in the monarch. . . .

The word that summarized the entire relationship was "dependence." "Dependence" implied a hierarchy of power, with great ones above exercising their power on behalf of lesser ones below, and the lesser ones returning obedience out of gratitude, affection, duty, and interest. "Dependence" described the archetypical relationships of king and people, of father and family, and could be extended to include virtually every other relationship of superior and inferior. Exemplified and justified by the king's tender care of his people, "dependence" was the fundamental module of monarchical culture and the wellspring of the emotion that flowed through the multitude in 1714 when Thomas Prince watched the coronation procession move toward Westminster.

Questions

1. *Which was a more powerful impulse in colonial society, deference or democracy? How did the colonists define democracy? What information would you need in order to determine how democratic early America was?*

2. *Can a hierarchical society be democratic? Was America an egalitarian society or an unequal society? Who held the power in early America? Did the king play a significant role in colonial politics?*

3. *How did American society and political culture differ from England's? In what way were they similar? Did politics function in the same way in both Virginia and Massachusetts?*

4. *What is the relationship between economic opportunity and political opportunity? Why did voters permit members of the gentry to dominate political office? What sorts of influence did the gentry exert?*

STATE AND SOCIETY: THEORY AND PRACTICE

The following documents either offer insight into the political theories of the seventeenth and eighteenth centuries or explore the relationship between economic and political equality in colonial America. In sermons, diaries, public speeches, and pamphlets, civil and religious leaders discussed the duty of citizens to obey and of rulers to guard the people's well-being; they defined patriotism and public service in exalted terms as an unselfish desire to advance the common good. These first five selections represent an ideal, not necessarily a reality; nonetheless, they reveal important concepts that shaped the colonists' political understanding.

The Rulers and the Ruled: John Winthrop's Definition of Liberty

One of the original planners of the Massachusetts Bay Colony, John Winthrop (1588–1649) served as governor or deputy governor almost every year from 1630 until his death. He delivered the following speech after his acquittal in a trial in which he was accused of exceeding his authority. Excerpted from The History of New England from 1630 to 1649, *ed. James Savage (Boston, 1826), 2:228–30.*

The great questions that have troubled the country, are about the authority of the magistrates [officeholders] and the liberty of the people. It is yourselves who have called us to this office, and being called by you, we have our authority from God, in way of an ordinance, such as hath the image of God eminently stamped

John Winthrop was one of the original planners of the Massachusetts Bay Colony and also one of its chief political figures for two decades. (Courtesy of the American Antiquarian Society.)

upon it, the contempt and violation whereof hath been vindicated with examples of divine vengeance. I entreat you to consider, that when you choose magistrates, you take them from among yourselves, men subject to like passions as you are. Therefore when you see infirmities in us, you should reflect upon your own, and that would make you bear the more with us, and not be severe censurers of the failings of your magistrates. . . .

For the other point concerning liberty, I observe a great mistake in the country about that. There is a twofold liberty, natural (I mean as our nature is now corrupt) and civil or federal. The first is common to man with beasts and other creatures. By this, man, as he stands in relation to man simply, hath liberty to do what he lists [likes]; it is a liberty to evil as well as to good. This liberty is incompatible and inconsistent with authority, and cannot endure the least restraint of the most just authority. The exercise and maintaining of this liberty makes men grow more evil, and in time to be worse than brute beasts. . . . This is that great enemy of truth and peace, that wild beast, which all the ordinances of God are bent against, to restrain and subdue it. The other kind of liberty I call civil or federal, it may also be termed moral, in reference to the covenant between God and man, in the moral law, and the politic covenants and constitutions, amongst men themselves. This liberty is the proper end and object of authority, and cannot subsist without it; and it is a liberty to that only which is good, just and honest. This liberty you are to stand for, with the hazard (not only of your goods, but) of your lives, if need be. Whatsoever crosseth this, is not authority, but a distemper thereof. This liberty is maintained and exercised in a way of subjection to authority; it is of the same kind of liberty wherewith Christ hath made us free. The woman's own choice makes such a man her husband; yet being so chosen, he is her lord, and she is to be subject to him, yet in a way of liberty, not of bondage; and a true wife accounts her subjection her honour and freedom, and would not think her condition safe and free, but in her subjection to her husband's authority. Such is the liberty of the church under the authority of Christ, her king and husband; his yoke is so easy and sweet to her as a bride's ornaments; and if through frowardness or wantonness &c. she shake it off, at any time, she is at no rest in her spirit, until she take it up again; and whether her lord smiles upon her, and embraceth her in his arms, or whether he frowns, or rebukes, or smites her, she apprehends the sweetness of his love in all, and is refreshed, supported and instructed by every such dispensation of his authority over her. On the other side, ye know who they are that complain of this yoke and say, let us break their bands &c. we will not have this man to rule over us. Even so, brethren, it will be between you and your magistrates. If you stand for your natural corrupt liberties, and will do what is good in your own eyes, you will not endure the least weight of authority, but will murmur, and oppose, and be always striving to shake off that yoke; but if you will be satisfied to enjoy such civil and lawful liberties, such as Christ allows you, then will you quietly and cheerfully submit unto that authority which is set over you, in all the administrations of it, for your good. Wherein, if we fail at any time, we hope we shall be willing (by God's assistance) to hearken to good advice from any of you, or in any other way of God; so shall your liberties be preserved, in upholding the honour and power of authority amongst you.

Jonathan Mayhew on the Limits of Obedience

Jonathan Mayhew, Congregationalist minister of Boston's West Church, offered another perspective on the relationship between magistrates and the populace in this 1750 sermon. Starting from a New Testament text, St. Paul's Letter to the Romans, Mayhew rebuts the notion that the Bible called for unlimited obedience and outlines the conditions under which the people might remove a leader who violated the public trust. Taken from Jonathan Mayhew, A Discourse Concerning Unlimited Submission and Non-Resistance to the Higher Powers . . . *(Boston, 1750), 12, 28–30.*

There is one very important and interesting point which remains to be inquired into; namely, the *extent* of that subjection *to the higher powers,* which is here enjoined as a duty upon all christians. . . .

. . . [St. Paul's] arguments to enforce submission, are of such a nature, as to conclude only in favour of submission *to such rulers as he himself describes;* i.e. such as rule for the good of society, which is the only end of their institution. Common tyrants, and public oppressors, are not intitled to obedience from their subjects, by virtue of any thing here laid down by the inspired apostle.

I now add, farther, that the apostle's argument is so far from proving it to be the duty of people to obey, and submit to, such rulers as act in contradiction to the public good, and so to the design of their office, that it proves *the direct contrary.* For, please to observe, that if the end of all civil government, be the good of society; . . . it follows, that when no such good end can be answered by submission, there remains no argument or motive to enforce it; if instead of this good end's being brought about by submission, a *contrary end* is brought about, and the ruin and misery of society effected by it, here is a plain and positive reason against submission in all such cases, should they ever happen. And therefore, in such cases, a regard to the public welfare, ought to make us with-hold from our rulers, that obedience and subjection which it would, otherwise, be our duty to render to them. If it be our duty, for example, to obey our king, merely for this reason, that he rules for the public welfare, (which is the only argument the apostle makes use of) it follows, by a parity of reason, that when he turns tyrant, and makes his subjects his prey to devour and to destroy, instead of his charge to defend and cherish, we are bound to throw off our allegiance to him, and to resist. . . . Let me make use of this easy and familiar *similitude* to illustrate the point in hand—Suppose God requires a family of children, to obey their father and not to resist him; . . . Suppose this parent at length runs distracted, and attempts, in his mad fit, to cut all his children's throats: Now, in this case, is not the reason before assigned, why there children should obey their parent while he continued of a sound mind, namely, *their common good*, a reason equally conclusive for disobeying and resisting him, since he is become delirious, and attempts their ruin?

William Livingston on Patriotism and the Duty of Public Service

---

New York lawyer and politician William Livingston (1723–1790) published a series of essays on politics in a periodical called The Independent Reflector. *In this essay, Livingston defined patriotism as a willingness to suppress selfish interest in favor of the common good. Because of his stress on unity, Livingston viewed political parties as illegitimate, since they represented special interest groups and created political conflict. Taken from William Livingston, "Of Patriotism,"* The Independent Reflector, *3 May 1753, 93–94.*

He is a Patriot who prefers the Happiness of the Whole, to his own private Advantage; who, when properly called upon, is ready to rise up in its Defence, and with a manly Fortitude, shield it from Danger. He is a Patriot, the ruling Object of whose Ambition, is the public Welfare: Whose Zeal, chastised by Reflection, is calm, steady and undaunted: He whom lucrative Views cannot warp from his Duty: Whom no partial Ties can prevail on to act traitorously to the Community, and sacrifice the Interest of the *Whole* to that of a *Part*: He whom Flattery cannot seduce, nor Frowns dismay, from supporting the public Interest when it is in his Power: Who mourns for their Vices, and exerts his Abilities to work a Reformation: Who compassionates their Ignorance, and endeavours to improve their Understandings: He who aims to cultivate Urbanity and social Harmony. To conclude, he is a true Patriot whose Love for the Public is not extinguished, either by their Insensibility or Ingratitude; but goes on with unwearied Benevolence in every public-spirited Attempt. . . .

The noisy intemperate Froth of a political Enthusiast, is as far removed from a steady Principle of Patriotism, as the Dignity of solid Understanding from the Fumes of poetical Madness.—

Party-Faction and personal Resentment, have often imposed themselves upon Mankind for the divine Operations of public Spirit. We shall find Hypocrites of this sort, more frequently inveighing against Men, than reasoning upon Facts: Ridicule is their favourite Engine—to mislead the Judgment by warming the Imagination, is their peculiar Art.

The superstitious Zealot, and the religious Bigot, have not so much as an Idea of a Public: When they presume to act the Part of Patriots, there is something so unnatural and absurd in their Manner, that they can scarcely deceive any but their own Herd.

When these Characters lay Claim to Patriotism, we may be sure they are Imposters, and we should treat them as Hypocrites.

Landon Carter Defines Representation

Representation in the eighteenth century Anglo-American world meant something very different from representation today. Rather than representing the particular interest of local constituents, English Members of Parliament believed that they represented all the people, and therefore

Reprinted from *The Diary of Colonel Landon Carter of Sabine Hall, 1752–1778*, Vol. I, edited by Jack P. Greene, published by The University Press of Virginia, 1965. Copyright © 1965 by The Virginia Historical Society.

were free to make their own decisions regarding which measures were in the common interest. In the following selection, Virginia planter-politician Landon Carter (1710–1778) describes a debate in the Virginia House of Burgesses between defenders of this English conception of representation and others who were moving towards a more "popular" constituent-responsive definition of representation. Abridged from The Diary of Colonel Landon Carter of Sabine Hall, 1752–1778, *ed. Jack P. Greene (Charlottesville, Virginia, 1965), 1:116–17.*

[T]he question was Whether a Representative was obliged to follow the directions of his Constituents against his own Reason and Conscience or to be Governed by his Conscience. The Arguments for implicit obedience [to his constituents' wishes] were that the first institution of a Representative was for the avoiding the Confusion of a Multitude in assembly. He, therefore, was to Collect the sentiments of his Constituents and whatever that Majority willed ought to be the rule of his Vote. Thus argued the favourers of Popularity, who were all headed by the Speaker, for these were nearly his own words. The Admirers of Reason and Liberty of Conscience distinguished upon it and said, where the matter related particularly to the interest of the Constituents alone, there implicit obedience ought to Govern, but, where it was to affect the whole Community, Reason and Good Conscience should direct, for it must be absurd to Suppose one part of the Community could be apprized of the good of the whole without Consulting the whole. For that Part, therefore, to order an implicit vote must be absurd and the Representative acting accordingly could only augment the Absurdity because he must suppose his people so perverse as not to be moved by Reasons ever so good that might be advanced by other parts of the Community. Many other Arguments do so naturally arise to support this last and best Opinion that I need not insert them.

The Practice of Politics: How to Get Elected— An Eighteenth-Century Guide

In 1770, Robert Munford, a colonel in the Virginia militia and office-holder at many levels of local government, wrote a play about electioneering in his home colony. Although satirical and comic, The Candidates contains some realistic accounts of political practices in pre-revolutionary Virginia. The main character, Mr. Wou'dbe (i.e. "would be"), wishes to run for the House of Burgesses. As a gentleman, Wou'dbe scorns campaigning and expresses mixed feelings about serving in public office. He believes that voters should recognize the quality of gentlemen candidates and automatically elect them to office. But in order to defeat his opponents—Sir John Toddy, Mr. Strutabout, and Mr. Smallhopes—Wou'dbe adopts a number of not-so-idealistic strategies. Munford describes the practice of "treating" voters with rum, barbecues, and breakfasts before elections and recounts conversations in which candidates make various promises to the freeholder constituents. Taken from "Robert Munford's The Candidates," ed. Jay B. Hubbell and Douglass Adair The William and Mary Quarterly 5 (April 1948): 231, 237–44.

Act I. Scene I. *Mr. Wou'dbe's house. Enter Wou'dbe with a newspaper in his hand.*

. . . Well, our little world will soon be up, and very busy towards our next election. Must I again be subject to the humours of a fickle croud? Must I again resign my reason, and be nought but what each voter pleases? Must I cajole, fawn, and wheedle, for a place that brings so little profit? . . .

[In the next scene, Wou'dbe discusses the proper qualifications for serving in the House of Burgesses with a freeholder (voter), Guzzle.]

Wou'dbe. I'm sorry Mr. Guzzle, you are so ignorant of the necessary qualifications of a member of the house of burgesses. . . . I'll make it a point of duty to dispatch the business, and my study to promote the good of my county.

Guzzle. Yes, damn it, you all promise mighty fair, but the devil a bit do you perform; there's Strutabout, now, he'll promise to move mountains. He'll make the rivers navigable, and bring the tide over the tops of the hills, for a vote.

Strutabout. You may depend, Mr. Guzzle, I'll perform whatever I promise.

Guzzle. I don't believe it, damn me if I like you. . . .

Wou'dbe. Don't be angry, John, let our actions hereafter be the test of our inclinations to serve you. . . . who are you for?

Guzzle. For the first man that fills my bottle: so Mr. Wou'dbe, your servant.

Wou'dbe. Ralpho, go after him, and fill his bottle. . . .

Wou'dbe. (pulling out his watch.) 'Tis now the time a friend of mine has appointed for me to meet the freeholders at a barbecue; well, I find, in order to secure a seat in our august senate, 'tis necessary a man should either be a slave or a fool; a slave to the people, for the privilege of serving them, and a fool himself, for thus begging a troublesome and expensive employment.

To sigh, while toddy-toping sots rejoice,
To see you paying for their empty voice,
From morn to night your humble head decline,
To gain an honour that is justly thine,
Intreat a fool, who's your's at this day's treat,
And next another's, if another's meat,
Is all the bliss a candidate acquires,
In all his wishes, or his vain desires. . . .

[The next scene takes place at a barbecue Wou'dbe has sponsored in order to woo the voters. Freeholders Twist, Stern, Prize, and their wives discuss the candidates. Sir John Toddy arrives with his aide, Guzzle, and proceeds to "glad-hand" the voters. Note that Guzzle has to whisper their names to Sir John, who pretends that he knows his constituents. Finally, Twist presses Mr. Wou'dbe about what he specifically would do for the voters once in office.]

Stern. Pray, gentlemen, what plausible objection have you against Mr. Wou'dbe? he's a clever civil gentleman as any, and as far as my poor weak capacity can go, he's a man of as good learning, and knows the punctilios of behaving himself, with the best of them. . . .

Lucy. If the wives were to vote, I believe they would make a better choice than their husbands.

Twist. You'd be for the funnyest—wou'dn't you?

Lucy. Yes, faith; and the wittiest, and prettiest, and the wisest, and the best too; you are all for ugly except when you choose me.

Catharine. Well done, Lucy, you are right, girl. If we were all to speak to our old men as freely as you do, there would be better doings.

Stern. Perhaps not, Kate. . . .

Catharine. Husband, you know Mr. Wou'dbe is a clever gentleman; he has been a good friend to us.

Stern. I agree to it, and can vote for him without your clash.

Sarah. I'll be bound when it comes to the pinch, they'll all vote for him. . . .

Enter Sir John Toddy.

Sir John. Gentlemen and ladies, your servant, hah! my old friend Prize, how goes it? how does your wife and children do?

Sarah. At your service, sir. *(making a low courtsey.)*

Prize. How the devil come he to know me so well, and never spoke to me before in his life? *(aside.)*

Guzzle. *(whispering [to] Sir John)* Dick Stern.

Sir John. Hah! Mr. Stern, I'm proud to see you; I hope your family are well; how many children? does the good woman keep to the old stroke?

Catharine. Yes, an't please your honour, I hope my lady's well, with your honour.

Sir John. At your service, madam.

Guzzle. *(whispering [to] Sir John)* Roger Twist.

Sir John. Hah! Mr. Roger Twist! your servant, sir. I hope your wife and children are well.

Twist. There's my wife. I have no children, at your service. . . .

Twist. [to Mr. Wou'dbe] . . . I've heard a 'sponsible man say, he could prove you were the cause of these new taxes.

Wou'dbe. Do you believe that too? or can you believe that it's in the power of any individual member to make a law himself? If a law is enacted that is displeasing to the people, it has the concurrence of the whole legislative body, and my vote for, or against it, is of little consequence.

Guzzle. And what the devil good do you do then?

Wou'dbe. As much as I have abilities to do.

Guzzle. Suppose, Mr. Wou'dbe, we were to want you to get the price of rum lower'd—wou'd you do it?

Wou'dbe. I cou'd not.

Guzzle. Huzza for Sir John! he has promised to do it, huzza for Sir John!

Twist. Suppose, Mr. Wou'dbe, we should want this tax taken off—cou'd you do it?

Wou'dbe. I could not.

Twist. Huzza for Mr. Strutabout! he's damn'd, if he don't. Huzza for Mr. Strutabout!

Stern. Suppose, Mr. Wou'dbe, we that live over the river, should want to come to church on this side, is it not very hard we should pay ferryage; when we pay as much to the church as you do?

Wou'dbe. Very hard.

Stern. Suppose we were to petition the assembly could you get us clear of that expence?

Wou'dbe. I believe it to be just; and make no doubt but it would pass into a law.

Stern. Will you do it?

Wou'dbe. I will endeavour to do it.

Stern. Huzza for Mr. Wou'dbe! Wou'dbe forever!

Prize. Why don't you burgesses, do something with the damn'd pickers [*tobacco inspectors*]? If we have a hogshead of tobacco refused, away it goes to them; and after they have twisted up the best of it for their own use, and taken as much as will pay them for their trouble, the poor planter has little for his share.

Wou'dbe. There are great complaints against them; and I believe the assembly will take them under consideration.

Prize. Will you vote against them?

Wou'dbe. I will, if they deserve it.

Prize. Huzza for Mr. Wou'dbe! you shall go, old fellow; don't be afraid; I'll warrant it.

Equality and Opportunity in Eighteenth-Century America

Since the colonies required a minimum property holding of those white males who wished to qualify for suffrage, the extent to which Americans had access to land and economic opportunity affected political participation. In this selection, J. Hector St. John (1735–1813), a French immigrant who settled in New York in 1765, compares American and European society, stressing the relatively egalitarian nature of the colonies. Crèvecoeur's essay, first published in 1782, focuses on the political and economic consequences of the lack of social hierarchy. Excerpted from J. Hector St. John, Letters From An American Farmer . . . *(Philadelphia, 1793), 42–46.*

I wish I could be acquainted with the feelings and thoughts which must agitate the heart and present themselves to the mind of an enlightened Englishman, when he first lands on this continent. . . . He is arrived on a new continent; a modern society offers itself to his contemplation, different from what he had hitherto seen. It is not composed, as in Europe, of great lords who possess every thing, and of a herd of people who have nothing. Here are no aristocratical families, no courts, no kings, no bishops, no ecclesiastical dominion, no invisible power giving to a few a very visible one; no great manufacturers employing thousands, no great refinements of luxury. The rich and the poor are not so far removed from each other as they are in Europe.

Some few towns excepted, we are all tillers of the earth, from Nova Scotia to West Florida. We are a people of cultivators, scattered over an immense territory, communicating with each other by means of good roads and navigable rivers, united by the silken bands of mild government, all respecting the laws without dreading their power, because they are equitable. We are all animated with the spirit of industry, which is unfettered and unrestrained, because each person works for himself. If he travels through our rural districts, he views not the hostile castle, and the haughty mansion, contrasted with the clay-built hut and miserable cabbin, where cattle and men help to keep each other warm, and dwell in meanness, smoke, and indigence. A pleasing uniformity of decent competence appears throughout our habitations. The meanest of our log-houses is a dry and comfortable habitation. Lawyer or merchant are the fairest titles our towns afford; that of a farmer is the only appellation of the rural inhabitants of our country. It must take some time ere he can reconcile himself to our dictionary, which is but short in words of dignity, and names of honour. There, on a Sunday, he sees a congregation of respectable farmers and their wives, all clad in neat homespun, well mounted, or riding in their own humble waggons. There is not among them an esquire, saving the unlettered magistrate. There he sees a parson as simple as his flock, a farmer who does not riot on the labour of others. We have no princes, for whom we toil, starve, and bleed: we are the most perfect society now existing in the world. Here man is free as he ought to be; nor is this pleasing equality so transitory as many others are. . . .

. . . Every thing has tended to regenerate them; new laws, a new mode of living, a new social system; here they are become men: in Europe they were as so many useless plants, wanting vegetative mould, and refreshing showers; they withered, and were mowed down by want, hunger, and war: but now, by the power of transplantation, like all other plants they have taken root and flourished! Formerly they were not numbered in any civil list of their country, except in those of the poor; here they rank as citizens. By what invisible power has this surprizing metamorphosis been performed? By that of the laws and that of their industry. The laws, the indulgent laws, protect them as they arrive, stamping on them the symbol of adoption; they receive ample rewards for their labours; these accumulated rewards procure them lands; those lands confer on them the title of freemen; and to that title every benefit is affixed which men can possibly require. This is the great operation daily performed by our laws. From whence proceed these laws? From our government. Whence that government? It is derived from the original genius and strong desire of the people, ratified and confirmed by government. This is the great chain which links us all.

A Vertical Society:
Hierarchy in Colonial Virginia

In this fragment from his 1806 autobiography, Devereux Jarratt (1732–1801), an Episcopalian minister from Virginia, remembers—and expresses nostalgia for—the yawning social and material gulf that separated freeholders from elites in early America. Note that when Jarratt began to ascend the social ladder in taking a position as schoolmaster, he did so only with the help of a wealthy patron and that he sought out a wig, the sign of a gentleman, symbolic of his new station in life. Abridged from Devereux Jarratt, The Life of the Reverend Devereux Jarratt *. . . (Baltimore, 1806), 12–16, 25–26.*

I was born in *New Kent,* a county in Virginia, about 25 miles below Richmond, on January 6th, 1732–3, O. S. [Old Style dating].

I was the youngest child of *Robert Jarratt* and *Sarah* his wife. My grand-father was an Englishman, born, I believe, in the city of *London.* . . . My grand-mother, as I was told, was a native of *Ireland.* Both she and my grand-father died before I was born, and I have had no account of them, except that they were poor people, but industrious, and rather rough in their manners. They acquired a pretty good tract of land, of near 1200 acres, but they had no slaves—probably they were prejudiced against that kind of property. . . .

My father was brought up to the trade of a carpenter, at which he wrought till the very day before he died. He was a mild, inoffensive man, and much respected among his neighbors. My mother was the daughter of Joseph Bradley, of *Charles City,* a county bordering on *New Kent.* None of my ancestors, on either side, were either rich or great, but had the character of honesty and industry, by which they lived in credit among their neighbors, free from real want, and above the frowns of the world. This was also the habit, in which my parents were. They always had plenty of plain food and raiment, wholesome and good, suitable to their humble station, and the times in which they lived. Our food was altogether the produce of the farm, or plantation, except a little sugar, which was rarely used; and our raiment was altogether my mother's manufacture, except our hats and *shoes,* the *latter* of which we never put on, but in the winter season. We made no use of *tea* or *coffee* for breakfast, or at any other time; nor did I know a single family that made any use of them. Meat, bread and milk was the ordinary food of all my acquaintance. I suppose the *richer sort* might make use of *those* and other luxuries, but to such people I had no access. We were accustomed to look upon, what were called *gentle folks,* as beings of a superior order. For my part, I was quite shy of *them,* and kept off at a humble distance. A *periwig,* in those days, was a distinguishing badge of *gentle folk*— and when I saw a man riding the road, near our house, with a wig on, it would so alarm my fears, and give me such a disagreeable feeling, that, I dare say, I would run off, as for my life. Such ideas of the difference between *gentle* and *simple,* were, I believe, universal among all of my rank and age. But I have lived to see, a vast alteration, in this respect, and the contrary extreme prevail. In our high *republican times,* there is more *levelling* than ought to be, consistent with good government. I have as little notion of oppression and tyranny as any man, but a due subordination is essentially requisite in every government. . . .

My parents neither sought nor expected any titles, honors, or great things, either for themselves or children. Their highest ambition was to teach their children to read, write, and understand the fundamental rules of arithmetic. I remember also, they taught us short prayers, and made us very perfect in repeating the *Church Catechism*. They wished us all to be brought up in some honest calling, that we might earn our bread, by the sweat of our brow, as they did. . . .

One of the most remote means, as I consider it, which led me to the station, which I now fill, was my being called from the *ax* to the *quill*. . . . One *Jacob Moon*, living in Albemarle county, . . . sent me word, that he should be glad to employ me as a schoolmaster . . . I readily embraced the proposal, and soon packed up my *all*, which consisted in such things, as made no great baggage, for I think I carried the whole on my back, except one shirt. . . . My whole dress and apparel consisted in a pair of coarse breeches, one or two oznaburgs shirts, a pair of shoes and stockings, an old felt hat, a bear skin *coat*, which, by the by, was the first coat I ever had made for me, since my childhood. And that I might appear something more than common, in a strange place, and be counted somebody, I got me an old wig, which, perhaps being cast off by the master, had became [become] the property of his slave, and from the slave it was conveyed to me.

Who Could Vote and for Whom Did They Vote? The Statistics from Massachusetts

The following tables provide information regarding the distribution of wealth, eligibility for suffrage and patterns of voting in Massachusetts. Table 1 offers estimates of the percentage of adult males who could vote in several Massachusetts towns. In Table 2, Gary Nash notes change over time in the proportion of "polls"—people with enough property to be taxed who formed the pool from which voters were selected—in the overall population of Boston. In Table 3, Robert Gross examines the socio-economic background of the men who served as selectman—a town government office—in Concord, Massachusetts; in Table 4 Gross calculates who controlled the wealth and resources in Concord. Table 1 is taken from Robert E. Brown, Middle-Class Democracy and the

Table 1

Estimated Percentage of Voters in the Adult Male Population

Town	County	No. of reps.	Least no. of voters	No. of polls	Est. polls 16 to 21	Est. No. adult males	Est. % of adult male voters
Roxbury	Suff.	3	220	356	89	267	82.4
Watertown	Mid.	2	120	185	46	139	86.3
Northampton	Hamp.	4	320	451	113	338	94.6 (1777)
Worcester	Worc.	4	320	438	109	329	97.2
Charlton	Worc.	3	220	308	77	231	95.2
Boston	Suff.	12	1120	2664	666	1998	56.0
Salem	Essex	7	620	1193	298	895	69.2
Ipswich	Essex	5	420	1016	254	762	55.1
Marblehead	Essex	5	420	1047	262	785	53.5
Gloucester	Essex	5	420	939	235	704	59.6
Newbury	Essex	5	420	704	176	528	79.5
Medford	Mid.	2	120	190	47	143	83.9
Monson	Hamp.	2	120	197	49	148	81.0 (1777)
Bridgewater	Ply.	6	520	1130	282	848	61.3
Leicester	Worc.	2	120	212	53	159	75.4 (1777)
New Braintree	Worc.	2	120	185	46	139	86.3 (1777)
Sheffield	Berk.	3	220	338	84	254	86.6 (1777)

Revolution in Massachusetts, 1691–1780 *(New York, 1955), 50. Table 2 is from Gary Nash, "Urban Wealth and Poverty in Pre-Revolutionary America,"* The Journal of Interdisciplinary History 6 *(Spring 1976): 465. Tables 3 and 4 are from Robert A. Gross,* The Minutemen and Their World *(New York, 1976), 196, 212.*

Table 2
Rateable Polls in Boston, 1728–1771

Year	Population	Polls
1728	12,650	c3,000
1733	15,100	c3,500
1735	16,000	3,637
1738	16,700	3,395
1740	16,800	3,043
1741	16,750	2,972
1745	16,250	2,660
1750	15,800	c2,400
1752	15,700	2,789
1756	15,650	c2,500
1771	15,500	2,588

Table 3
Percentage Distribution of the Selectmen in Quintiles Over Time

	Top 20%	UM20%	Mid 20%	Bottom 20%	N
1745–54	81	12	6	0	16
175[5]–64	71	8	12	0	17
1765–74	69	31	0	0	13

[Key: Top 20%=wealthiest 20% of white males eligible for office; UM 20%=next wealthiest 20%; Mid 20%=next wealthiest 20%; N=size of sample, i.e. number of selectmen that Gross studied in each period.]

Table 4
Percentage of Wealth Held in Each Category

Year	Top 10%	Top 20%	Mid 40%	Bottom 40%	N
1746	22.8	38.4	41.6	20.1	346
1757	23.2	38.8	40.9	20.2	289
1770	26.7	42.7	39.2	18.0	292

[Key: Gross is estimating who owned the wealth in Concord. For example, "Top 10%"=amount of wealth and resources owned by wealthiest 10%. N=size of sample, or number of individuals included in the survey.]

Questions

1. *What was the relationship between ideals and practice in colonial politics? Did Munford's candidates live up to the standards of patriotism, integrity, and unselfishness that William Livingston and Landon Carter outlined?*

2. *What changed between John Winthrop's discussion of the relationship between authority and liberty in 1645 and Jonathan Mayhew's sermon on the same subject in 1750? Both used the metaphor of a father's authority within the family to describe the relationship between the rulers and the ruled; how did they apply the metaphor differently?*

3. *How democratic was colonial American society? Who voted? Who served in office? Did this change over time? Did the freeholders in The Candidates influence policy in Virginia?*

4. *Does the right to vote translate automatically to democracy? What would Devereux Jarratt think?*

5. *Do the statistics on wealth and officeholding confirm or contradict Crèvecoeur's view of America?*

FURTHER READING

Bernard Bailyn's The Origins of American Politics *(New York, 1968) describes the relationship between royal officials and the colonial assemblies and discusses the extent and limits of elite political power. Gordon S. Wood's* The Creation of the American Republic, 1776–1787 *(Chapel Hill, 1969) offers an excellent analysis of the meaning of the British Constitution and describes the "whig science of politics"— Anglo-American theories of the relationship between power and liberty, balance and stability. For popular and urban politics see Gary Nash's study of Philadelphia, New York, and Boston in the eighteenth century,* The Urban Crucible: Social Change, Political Consciousness, and the Origins of the American Revolution *(Cambridge, Massachusetts, 1979). Patricia Bonomi's* A Factious People: Politics and Society in Colonial New York *(New York, 1971) explores the distinct political culture of New York.*